Heritage in the Modern World: Historical Preservation in Global Perspective

Edited by Paul Betts and Corey Ross

OXFORD
UNIVERSITY PRESS

OXFORD
UNIVERSITY PRESS

1 Great Clarendon Street, Oxford OX2 6DP

Oxford University Press is a department of the University of Oxford.
It furthers the University's objective of excellence in research, scholarship,
and education by publishing worldwide in

Oxford New York

Athens Auckland Bangkok Bogotá Buenos Aires Cape Town
Chennai Dar es Salaam Delhi Florence Hong Kong Istanbul Karachi
Kolkata Kuala Lumpur Madrid Melbourne Mexico City Mumbai Nairobi
Paris São Paulo Shanghai Singapore Taipei Tokyo Toronto Warsaw

with associated companies in Berlin Ibadan

Oxford is a registered trade mark of Oxford University Press
in the UK and in certain other countries

Published in the United Kingdom
by Oxford University Press Inc., New York

A catalogue for this book is available from the British Library

Library of Congress Cataloging in Publication
Data (data available)

ISBN 0-00-000000-0
ISBN 978-0-19-873358-4

Subscription information for Past & Present is available
from:jnls.cust.serv@oup.com

Typeset by Cenveo Publisher Services, Bangalore, India
Printed by Bell and Bain Ltd, Glasgow, UK

Past and Present Supplements

Supplement 10, 2015

Heritage in the Modern World:
Historical Preservation in Global Perspective
Edited by Paul Betts and Corey Ross

Submissions should be made via the online submission system: http://mc.manuscriptcentral.com/past. Intending contributors should request a copy of 'Notes for Contributors'. Other communications, editorial correspondence, etc., should be addressed to The Editors, *Past and Present*, 103 Walton Street, Oxford OX2 6EB, UK. Tel: +44 (0)1865 511147; E-mail: editors@pastandpresent.org.uk.

Heritage in the Modern World: Historical Preservation in Global Perspective

CONTENTS

List of Illustrations

Modern Historical Preservation—Towards a Global Perspective

Paul Betts and Corey Ross

This volume is devoted to reconsidering the history of historical preservation from an international perspective.[1] Even though the origins of modern preservationism are often traced back to early eighteenth-century Europe, the aim is to address the broader factors behind the global spread of this changing historical sensibility toward ancestral pasts in the nineteenth and twentieth centuries. How, why, and in what form these diverse conservation practices developed in various international settings is the departure point of enquiry.

The modern 'hunger for heritage' is commonly understood as a cultural by-product of the French Revolution and the Industrial Revolution, which fundamentally altered the perceived relationship between past and present, first in Europe and then in the wider world. While the European roots of this modern political interest in heritage arguably originated with the Swedish Royal Proclamation of 1666, which declared all objects from antiquity to be the property of the Crown, and the 1717 creation of England's Society of Antiquaries some fifty years later, it was really the 'dual revolution' that generated these broader transformations of historical consciousness and claims of political stewardship toward pasts deemed worth preserving.[2] After all, it was during the French Revolution that vast numbers of royal, aristocratic, and ecclesiastical buildings came under new state ownership, sparking wide discussion about the making of a new 'national' French past; and it was the Industrial Revolution that inspired the romance of ruins that shaped much of nineteenth-century cultural life, as evidenced in the creation of national museums, cathedral restoration projects, and national park movements, as well as the Victorian cult of antiquities and ancient civilizations. As industrialization spread to other parts of the European continent

---

[1] The collection presented here is the outcome of a conference held at the University of Sussex, 8-9 June 2012, generously supported by the Past & Present Society together with the Universities of Sussex and Birmingham.

[2] The concept of 'dual revolution' derives from Eric Hobsbawm, *The Age of Revolution 1789-1848* (London, 1962).

and North America, so too did the urge to protect relics of the past from the ravages of modernization.

The period since 1914 is often portrayed as a devastating Age of Extremes characterized by war, revolutions, mass death and destruction; yet it was also an age that saw sustained efforts to protect cherished cultures, objects, and landscapes under threat from military conflict and violent social engineering projects of all stripes. Across much of the world, the legacy of war and devastation spurred new movements that were dedicated to preserving all types of cultural and physical heritage, often for the sake of nationalism, religious identity, and/or civilization itself. Such shifting attitudes could be seen throughout the period: for instance, in the condemnation of the German shelling of Rheims Cathedral and the Louvain Library in World War I as war crimes, in the creation of UNESCO as an international organization devoted to the conservation of a newly designated 'world heritage', as well as in the blossoming of green activist groups in the 1970s, such as Greenpeace, which were—and are—intent on reversing the environmental effects of industrialization. How the past became politicized (and visualized in print media, photography, and film) could also be noted in the manner in which the Soviet Union, Maoist China, and post-1945 Japan used archaeology to broadcast new links between ancient history and national identity in a Cold War setting. The rise of the heritage industries across the West in the 1980s— to say nothing of the nostalgic reinvention of the communist past in various Eastern European museums in the 1990s—is a further important example of this contest over the 'spoils of history'. With this in mind, this volume endeavours to explore a general theme that is usually given short shrift in conventional accounts of the supposedly hyper-modernizing thrust of twentieth-century global politics, namely the reinvention and mobilization of tradition itself.

Quite obviously, it would be impossible to consider all of the dimensions of 'heritage in the modern world' in a single volume. The collection therefore features case studies from around the world that consciously seek to draw links with one another in order to discern wider patterns and to follow ideas and practices as they circulated. Contributions revolve around a number of overarching questions. What was the relationship between war, revolution, imperialism, and the growing interest in heritage? Why was there such a powerful perceived need, even among avowedly revolutionary societies, to integrate elements of the distant past, including ancient ruins, into contemporary life? What was the role of the state in the rise of heritage preservation, and how did this relate to claims of political legitimacy or a 'civilizing mission' broadly conceived? Who claimed to speak on behalf of heritage, who were their critics and how did this map on to questions of sovereignty and power? What was the role of law, custom, and notions of the sacred in shaping heritage management? And finally, how did the changing means of 'packaging' heritage—for example, with the rise of mass tourism—influence what was or was not preserved and venerated? Though hardly an exhaustive list of questions, they nonetheless serve to highlight many of the principal developments in the transnational history of modern heritage preservation.

Although the focus of the volume is on the period since 1850, it is important to recognize that the modern fascination with heritage had deep historical roots. In many societies around the world, the importance of safeguarding certain relics of ancestral pasts was in itself nothing new. In Europe, for example, preservation arose in part as a reaction to religious-inspired iconoclasm and destruction. In 1560 Queen Elizabeth issued a proclamation forbidding the 'defacing of monuments of antiquity, being set up in the churches or other public places for memory, and not for superstition'. This was done in response to the post-Reformation desecration of churches and other buildings and a new worry about the delicate religious sensibilities of her subjects.[3] Safeguarding the heritage of the past was in this context the result of political strife and violence, and twentieth-century international law (as we shall see) responded in kind to war and military destruction around the world. No less important was the legacy of the French Revolution for heritage preservation, for it was during this period that the business of preservation became a matter of large-scale secular state intervention. Here, as in various other historical contexts, the effort to separate church and state bore clear consequences for historical preservation, in particular whenever the process was framed as a 'clash of civilizations'. The disestablishment of the Church in Ireland in 1869, for example, meant that ruins belonging to the former Irish Church were now transferred to the Irish Board of Works. Such struggles between a secular state and organized religion over the preservation of cultural property persisted throughout much of the modern period, as noted in the contributions by Indra Sengupta on colonial India as well as Stephen Smith's piece on the Soviet Union and Maoist China.

By the early nineteenth century this urge to preserve was not only bolstered by the expansion of the modern secular state, but was also closely linked to the development of Romanticism and the desire to retain crumbling pasts. This nostalgic sensibility was not completely new to the post-Napoleonic period: it

---

[3] John Delafons, *Politics and Preservation: A Policy History of the Built Heritage, 1882–1996* (London, 1997), 9. For a full discussion, see Alexandra Walsham, 'Skeletons in the Cupboard: Relics after the English Reformation', in Alexandra Walsham (ed.), *Relics and Remains* (Past & Present Supplement 5) (Oxford, 2010), 121–43; and more generally, David Freedberg, *Iconoclasts and Their Motives* (The Hague, 1989).

was, after all, the encounter with Roman ruins that inspired Edward Gibbon to write his *Decline and Fall of the Roman Empire*. Nonetheless, such sentiments were rife in the 1820s, as evidenced in Walter Scott's adventure novels as well as the first volume of John Britton's *The Architectural Antiquities of Great Britain* (1805). The religious revival in the 1820s, which was a sort of reaction to the excesses of French violent radicalism, sparked new Romantic interest in Gothic architecture, leading to the formation of national societies dedicated to preserving the Gothic inheritance. In fact, churches remained the primary subjects and targets for restorationists across Europe in the early nineteenth century.[4] While France is generally credited with taking the lead in listing buildings, similar legislative activity took place in Denmark (1807) and Greece (1834) during this period, and by the end of the century, virtually every European state had legislated its own Monuments Act to ensure effective national preservation provisions.[5] This impulse was hardly confined to Europe. As Astrid Swenson discusses in her piece, the Gothic heritage was a principal focus of preservationist efforts throughout much of the Levant as well.

But whereas the protection of monuments and heritage in the early nineteenth century was often seen as a defence of traditional values against radicalism, over the following decades it was increasingly viewed as a defence against industrial modernization. By the end of the century, this trend was increasingly manifested in specific national legislation. Britain passed its first Ancient Monuments Act in 1882, whilst the National Trust was founded in 1895.[6] Although these were modest beginnings,[7] they nonetheless laid the basis for future preservation initiatives internationally. Japan was among the first to recognize the value of patrimony as a matter of political prestige in the international arena. In 1871—only three years after the Meiji restoration— the Japanese government decreed the survey and preservation of antiquities, and in 1897 Japanese national preservation policy was extended to buildings with the Law for the Protection of Temples and Shrines. Concurrent efforts to generate a new national consciousness around designated heritage sites and

---

[4] Michael Thompson, *Ruins Reused: Changing Attitudes to Ruins since the late 18th Century* (London, 2006), 4–5. A good example is F. A. Baley, *The Church Restorers: A Tale Treating of Ancient and Modern Architecture and Church Decorations* (London, 1844).

[5] Delafons, *Politics and Preservation*, 27.

[6] C. Chippendale, 'The Making of the First Ancient Monuments Act, 1882, and its Administration under General Pitt-Rivers', *Journal of the British Archaeological Association*, 136 (1983), 1–55.

[7] The 1882 Act listed only 29 monuments in England and Wales, along with 21 in Scotland, and 18 in Ireland. Delafons, *Politics and Preservation*, 1.

objects was also present in much of Latin America (as seen in the contributions by Patience Schell and Alan Knight), along with later attempts by anti-colonial nationalist groups to mobilize popular sentiments against their European overlords. This fascination with the beauty of ruins became a leitmotif of twentieth-century cultural politics, even surfacing in regimes supposedly dedicated to radical modernization and social engineering. Nowhere was this more evident than in Albert Speer's 'ruin theory of value', in which Hitler's architect was keen to create buildings designed to be fetching ruins for onlookers in a thousand years' time.[8] Such contending attitudes toward the built environment not only underscore the complexities behind this 'hunger for heritage', they also demonstrate the broad impulse to conserve newly minted cultural heritage as a kind of common denominator of nation-building, even if there were sharp differences about what counted as a preserved ruin.

In this respect, imperialism played a signal role in shaping the modern heritage industry. Recent literature has placed empire at the centre of the history of preservation by focusing not only on the interactions between British metropolitan and dependent heritages, but also by placing these relations within the wider context of European imperial expansion.[9] This volume seeks to internationalize the story still further in significant ways. In her contribution, Astrid Swenson addresses the nexus of national, imperial, and international forces which shaped the history of heritage by focusing on the reclaiming of sites built by the European Crusaders (or their successors) in Palestine, Syria, Cyprus, Rhodes, and Malta between 1798 and 1940. Caroline Ford then explores how and why the French came to claim Algeria's Roman past as an expression of North Africa's Western and Mediterranean heritage and how from the period of conquest (1830) they increasingly transformed the vestiges of that heritage into a French *patrimoine*. Indra Sengupta provides a different story, examining the development of such state-regulated practices of monument-making in colonial India. As she shows, guardianship of India's ancient past and its relics, and the attempt to create a broader

---

[8] Julia Hell, 'Imperial Ruin Gazers, or Why did Scipio Weep?', in J. Hell and A. Schoenle (eds), *Ruins of Modernity* (Durham, 2012), 169–92.

[9] Astrid Swenson and Peter Mandler (eds), *From Plunder to Preservation: Britain and the Heritage of Empire, c.1800–1940* (Cambridge, 2013). See also Charlotte Trümpler (ed.), *Das grosse Spiel: Archäologie und Politik zur Zeit des Kolonialismus, 1860–1940* (Cologne, 2010); Gábor Klaniczay, Michael Werner, and Ottó Geiser, *Multiple Modernities: Ancient Histories in Nineteenth Century European Culture* (Frankfurt am Main, 2011); and on collecting, Maya Jasanoff, *Edge of Empire: Lives, Culture, and Conquest in the East, 1750–1850* (New York, 2006).

awareness of the aesthetic and emotional appeal of monuments as well as an appreciation of their historical-pedagogical importance, were an essential feature of the notion of custodianship that India's colonial rulers had always used to justify their authority. The regulation of India's ancient past and its built heritage became a key locus of exchange between the imperial state, colonial administration, and local residents in specific Indian settings.[10]

The battle over heritage was also a manifestation of imperial rivalry. Preservation was seen not only as a marker of civilization against perceived inferiors, but also as a means of distinguishing the Great Powers from one another. To be sure, this competitive impulse originated somewhat earlier. During the French Revolution, for example, Abbé Grégoire posited an elective affinity between preservation and civilization in his famous phrase that 'only Barbarians and slaves destroy works of art and science. Free men love and preserve them'.[11] It was Grégoire who coined the neologism *vandalisme* to condemn the excesses of the Revolution, suggesting that iconoclasm was itself anti-revolutionary; over the course of the next century and beyond, the language of vandalism was appropriated by leading conservators, restorers, and preservationists, first in Europe and then around the world.[12] Nineteenth-century Germans, French, and British vied with each other over heritage preservation, even as they commonly cited it as a marker of European cultural superiority in the Age of Expansion.[13] Preservation was thus a showcased civilizational credential, a crucial badge of fitness to rule as an imperial power. If nothing else, this meant that accusations of being behind a rival power in the protection of cherished monuments or artefacts

---

[10] Upinder Singh, *The Discovery of Ancient India: Early Archaeologists and the Beginning of Archaeology* (Chicago/New Delhi, 2004), and more generally, C. A. Bayly, *Empire and Information: Intelligence Gathering and Social Communication in India, 1780–1870* (Cambridge, 1996).

[11] Abbé Grégoire, *Patrimoine et Cité*, ed. D. Auderie (Bordeaux, 1999).

[12] Astrid Swenson, *The Rise of Heritage: Preserving the Past in France, Germany and England, 1789–1914* (Cambridge, 2013), 33-5 and A. Vidler, 'The Paradoxes of Vandalism: Henri Grégoire and the Thermidorian Discourse on Historical Monuments', in J. D. Popkin and R. H. Popkin, *The Abbé Grégoire and His World* (London, 2000), 129–56.

[13] H. Hoock, 'The British State and the Anglo-French Wars over Antiquities', *Historical Journal*, 50 (2007), 49–72; Suzanne Marchand, *German Orientalism in the Age of Empire: Religion, Race and Scholarship* (Cambridge, 2009); Stefan Altekamp, 'Italian Colonial Archaeology in Libya, 1912–1941', in M. L. Galaty and C. Watkinson (eds), *Archaeology under Dictatorship* (New York, 2004), 55–72 and Mia Fuller, *Moderns Abroad: Architecture, Cities and Italian Imperialism* (London, 2007).

became a powerful weapon in the hands of the heritage lobby.[14] Such a view was in many respects a corollary of the imperial doctrine of *terra nullius*, which regarded most non-European territories as devoid of civilization and accordingly cast their inhabitants as 'people without history'. In this context, the 'civilizing achievement was redefined as a European ability to preserve'.[15]

Ironically, however, the enlistment of archaeology and heritage preservation for the purpose of defining imperial or national difference was more a matter of convergence than divergence. The distinctions and divisions it sought to construct were very much an international phenomenon that looked increasingly similar across the very boundaries it was trying to reinforce.[16] The following essays explore how these new discrete 'heritage industries' were linked to empire and international developments. England's Ancient Monuments Protection Act of 1882, for example, was followed by the Indian Ancient Monuments Preservation Act of 1904, with similar heritage laws passed in Africa and Asia in the interwar years. Even beyond the bounds of empire, the multi-faceted 'invention of tradition' was a common feature across the Americas, Asia, and the Middle East by the middle of the twentieth century.[17] To what extent this international remaking of ancestral legacies reflected shared new attitudes toward the vulnerability and power of the past is one of the central questions explored in the pages that follow. Significantly, such activity was not only a product of empire-building, national constuction, or 'seeing like a state'. The heritage industry was also championed by a range of civic organizations, NGOs and/or powerful benefactors that sought to nudge states into action through lobbying and publicity, as noted in the contributions of Indra Sengupta, David Gange, Alan Knight, Paul Betts, and Erika Hanna. In different ways they all draw attention to the presence and power of middle managers and indigenous interlocutors in various preservation campaigns across the world.

[14] Lord Curzon, 'Address to the Bengal Asiatic Society', 6 February 1900, reprinted in Dilip K. Chakrabarti, *A History of Indian Archaeology from the Beginning to 1947* (New Delhi, 1988), 229–30, quoted in Astrid Swenson, 'The Heritage of Empire', in Swenson and Mandler (eds), *From Plunder to Preservation*, 14.

[15] Swenson, 'The Heritage of Empire', 11; Eric R. Wolf, *Europe and the People without History* (Berkeley, 1982).

[16] Chris Bayly, *The Birth of the Modern World, 1780–1914: Global Connections and Comparisons* (Oxford, 2004); Claire Lyons and John K. Papadopoulos, *The Archaeology of Colonialism* (Los Angeles, 2002).

[17] Nicolas Thomas, *Entangled Objects: Exchange, Material Culture and Colonialism in the Pacific* (Cambridge, MA, 1991); Annie Coombes, *Reinventing Africa: Museums, Material Culture and Popular Culture in Victorian and Edwardian England* (New Haven, 1994).

That heritage was central to the imperial project may at first seem odd to some, given that colonies were often seen as key laboratories of modernity.[18] But the preservation of civilizations past was equally as prominent among imperial scientists and cultural elites. In many respects, the notion of a colonial 'laboratory of modernity' captures these impulses to preserve cherished patrimony quite well. The imperial conservation drive epitomized by the likes of Lord Curzon and others was quintessentially 'modern' in two senses—not only in its effort to build links to the past as a salve against the ravages of time and modernization, but also because this preservation drive was conducted through modern means. This volume accordingly takes as its starting point the idea that these entangled histories of heritage were much more than wistful responses to the threat of modernization, but rather are better understood as central aspects of the modernization process itself. Whilst many early efforts were steeped in Romanticism and often carried a strong whiff of conservative cultural pessimism, they were not merely a matter of turning history into escapist nostalgia. Instead, they were also part of the wider attempt to overlay or even subsume local particularisms within new, 'modern' forms of identity. In many ways the obsession with heritage reflected the need to engineer a new form of historical consciousness geared toward a modern world of rationality and technology and to circumscribe an appropriate place for it. On this score it is no coincidence that the establishment of conservation groups coincided with the emergence of a number of photographic record societies, for instance the Scottish Photographic Survey in 1890 and its English equivalent in 1897.[19]

For all of its transnational linkages, however, this preservation drive was of course closely linked to nationalism.[20] It became a formative part of nineteenth-century nation-building and its attendant invented traditions as cultural ballast and political legitimacy—a trend that went worldwide over the

---

[18] Paul Rabinow, *French Modern: Norms and Forms of the Social Environment* (Cambridge, MA, 1989); Gwendolyn Wright, *The Politics of Design in French Colonial Urbanism* (Chicago, 1991); Omnia El Shakry, *The Great Social Laboratory: Subjects of Knowledge in Colonial and Postcolonial Egypt* (Stanford, 2007).

[19] Kevin Walsh, *The Representation of the Past: Museums and Heritage in the Post-Modern World* (London, 1992), 71. See too Elizabeth Edwards, 'Commemorating a National Past: The National Photographic Record Association, 1897–1910', *Journal of Victorian Culture*, 10:1 (2005), 123–31.

[20] Philip L. Kohl and Clare Fawcett (eds), *Nationalism, Politics and the Practice of Archaeology* (Cambridge, 1995); David Lowenthal, *The Past is a Foreign Country* (Cambridge, 1985), 389, 393.

course of the twentieth century.[21] In his contribution, Jordan Sand looks at a key Japanese case study that illustrates how the meaning of heritage shifted over the decades: namely Ise Shrine, the high church of imperial Shinto, which was entirely rebuilt every twenty years. His article traces how the interpretation of this iconic site transformed the conception of ancestral legacies from romantic orientalism into the robust essence of national tradition as the notion of periodic reconstruction became a model of Japanese heritage. In her contribution, Patience Schell analyses the 1838 founding of Chile's 'national' museum in Santiago, and explores the uncertainty about how to depict the two main ingredients of national history and heritage: the Spanish colonial period and the indigenous legacy. By contrast, David Gange shows how the period between 1880 and 1914 saw the formation of Egyptian archaeology as a European university discipline with preservation concerns written through its didactic literature. What he reveals is the seamy side of the heritage industry, one in which intense inter-personal conflicts, political jealousies and the 'cheapness and tractability' of local labour created unique circumstances that pointed up the vast gap between the rhetoric and reality of preservation. Alan Knight then turns toward revolutionary Mexico for a different perspective. Even as the Mexican Revolution raged between 1910 and 1920, revolutionary intellectuals and policy-makers were devising a project of 'forging a fatherland' based on an ambitious project of 'cultural nationalism' and applied anthropology, one which involved the excavation, preservation, and celebration of major pre-Columbian sites to justify its nationalist and *indigenista* mission.[22]

Nowhere was this nationalization of heritage more evident than with the birth of modern archaeology. While archaeology as a field is generally seen as a product of the Renaissance, its modern incarnation was largely the product of nineteenth-century nationalism.[23] In fact, the plain identification of ruins for national identity started in Spain in the 1830s, where a series of provincial

---

[21] Elazar Barkan and Ronald Bush (eds), *Claiming the Stones, Naming the Bones: Cultural Property and the Negotiation of National and Ethnic Identity* (Los Angeles, 2003).

[22] Relatedly, Paul Gillingham, *Cuauhtémoc's Bones: Forging National Identity in Modern Mexico* (Albuquerque, 2011); Christina Bueno, 'Forjando Patrimonio: The Making of Archaeological Patrimony in Porfirian Mexico', *Hispanic American Historical Review*, 90:2 (May 2010), 215–45.

[23] Neil Asher Silberman, 'Promised Lands and Chosen Peoples: The Politics and Poetics of Archaeological Narrative', in Kohl and Fawcett (eds), 249–61; Neil Asher Silberman, *Between Past and Present: Archaeology, Ideology, and Nationalism in the Modern Middle East* (New York, 1989); Peter Gathercole and David Lowenthal (eds), *The Politics of the Past* (London, 1989).

museums was founded—along with a national museum in 1840—paving the way for the birth of archaeology as a new field of study. (Spain's National Archaeological Museum was opened in 1867). Such attitudes found common expression across the world; the link between archaeology and nationalism even occurred in countries with no ancient past, like the United States. Egyptian nationalism, perhaps unsurprisingly, was in part predicated on re-claiming its ruins as national patrimony.[24] The birth of Chinese archaeology was also linked to a new sense of nationalism born of the 1919 May 4th Movement. After half a century of Western looting of Chinese antiquities, China looked to archaeology as a scientific means to underpin a new national agenda after World War I. China's first archaeological excavations took place in 1921.[25] This trend to nationalize ancient ruins continued through the 1930s, particularly among fascist regimes. Efforts to construct a new Spanish identity around material heritage were intensified under Franco, as he worked to overcome the regional dissonances of Catalan and Basque na-tionalism and coordinate them into an overarching national framework. Parallel developments also took place under Salazar's Portugal.[26] For their part, the Nazis used archaeology to justify racist and territorial goals;[27] even the Soviet Union's post-war archaeological interest in its Slavic roots is often construed as a kind of reaction to Nazism's search for 'ethno-genetic' expansion.[28]

National heritage was closely related to the birth of modern tourism. The nineteenth century witnessed the 'democratization' of the old aristocratic Grand Tour, as thousands of people across the West now set out to discover and enjoy the sites of the ancient world. As part of the late nineteenth-century 'Egyptomania' that swept across Europe, Karl Baedeker, Thomas Cook, and John Murray enlisted specialists to draft large sections of their commercial guidebooks that tourists brought with them on popular excursions up the

---

[24] David Malcolm Reid, *Whose Pharaohs? Archaeology, Museums and Egyptian National Identity from Napoleon to World War I* (Berkeley, 2003).

[25] Enzheng Tong, 'Thirty Years of Chinese Archaeology (1949–1979)', in Kohl and Fawcett (eds), 184.

[26] Margarita Diaz-Andreu, 'Archaeology and Nationalism in Spain', in Kohl and Fawcett (eds), 39–46; Katina T. Lillios, 'Nationalism and Copper Age Research in Portugal during the Salazar Regime (1932-1974)', in Kohl and Fawcett (eds), 57–68.

[27] Bettina Arnold, 'The Past as Propaganda: Totalitarian Archaeology in Nazi Germany', *Antiquity*, 64 (1990), 464–78.

[28] Victor A. Shnirelman, 'From Internationalism to Nationalism: Forgotten Pages of Soviet Archaeology in the 1930s and 1940s', in Kohl and Fawcett (eds), 134.

Nile.[29] With time a new genre of sightseeing emerged that was tightly linked to the burgeoning preservation industry: battlefield tourism. While the first tours of battlefields were organized in the mid-nineteenth century—the 1854 British tour to Waterloo is considered the first modern instance[30]—the transformation of battlefields as tourist destinations first emerged with the American Civil War and Boer War, and became a widespread phenomenon after the Great War.[31] For some countries, such as Canada and Australia, the heritage industry associated with the war became the very crucible of national identity.[32]

However, these preserving impulses were by no means solely secular. The late nineteenth century saw remarkable expressions of religious revival in Western Europe, including the well-publicized visions of the Virgin Mary, be it at Lourdes, Pontmain, and La Salette in France, Marpingen in Germany, Knock in Ireland, or Pompeii in Italy. The Catholic Church certainly capitalized on the possibilities of mass travel in developing the sites of Marian apparitions for mass pilgrimages—over a million people travelled to Lourdes annually by 1908.[33] By 1900 the British travel company Thomas Cook was organizing numerous tours for some 12,000 people to visit the Holy Land.[34] And in terms of preservation, Christian missionaries were major suppliers of ethnographic objects from the New World, the Pacific, and Australia to the museums of Europe. The Vatican Ethnological Museum in Rome houses over 60,000 objects from outside Europe; in 1925 Pope Pius XI organized an exhibit celebrating missionary work across the non-Western world, eventually returning only about half of the more than 100,000 objects that had been sent to the show.[35] Stephen Smith takes up this battle over heritage between state and church, but does so by looking at two unusual case studies: the Communist regimes of the Soviet Union and People's Republic of

---

[29] Reid, *Whose Pharaohs?*, 12, and Piers Brendon, *Thomas Cook: 150 Years of Popular Tourism* (London, 1991).

[30] Edmund Swinglehurst, *The Romantic Journey: The Story of Thomas Cook and Victorian Travel* (London, 1974), 174.

[31] George Mosse, *Fallen Soldiers: Reshaping the Memory of the World Wars* (New York, 1990), esp. 34–50; David W. Lloyd, *Battlefield Tourism: Pilgrimage and the Commemoration of the Great War in Britain, Australia and Canada, 1919-1939* (Oxford, 1998), 1–48.

[32] Lloyd, *Battlefield Tourism*, esp. 181-216.

[33] David Blackbourn, *The Marpingen Visions: Rationalism, Religion and the Rise of Modern Germany* (London, 1993), 54–6 and Ruth Harris, *Lourdes: Body and Soul in a Secular Age* (London, 1999).

[34] J. G. Davies, *Pilgrimage Yesterday and Today* (London, 1988), 148–51.

[35] Jeanette Greenfield, *The Return of Cultural Treasures* (Cambridge, 2007), 99–100.

China. Both states conducted a policy towards religious heritage that wavered between outright suppression and 'museification', wherein the monuments, artefacts, and cultural practices of the past were made accessible to the public, but with a strong concern to demonstrate the superiority and historic necessity of socialism. While the Bolsheviks were inheritors of a European tradition of conservation and broadly saw themselves as engaged in a policy of making available the finest examples of elite and folk art to the public, the Chinese tradition of preserving the material culture of the past had always been comparatively weak. As seen here and elsewhere, religious heritage preservation played a central if underestimated role in this larger heritage story, especially in the face of what was seen as the encroachments of hostile secular state-building.[36]

Nor was the preservation drive confined to the products of human hands, as the frenzy to create national parks, nature reserves and wildlife sanctuaries clearly attests. The establishment of Yellowstone National Park in 1872 was quite literally an important landmark in this respect, and served as a global model of natural heritage conservation over the following decades.[37] Around the turn of the century the protection of cherished landscapes and 'wilderness' as an antidote to the increasing rationalization of the countryside had spawned a range of new organizations—the Sierra Club (1892), the Société pour la protection des paysages de France (1901), the Bund Heimatschutz (1904), the Dutch Vereiniging tot Behoud van Natuurmonumenten (1904)—whose common aim, in the words of one conservationist, was to ensure that 'the treasures of free nature will in future receive a similar level of care as has long been successfully practiced on the monuments of earlier art'.[38]

Here, too, some of the most far-reaching efforts were linked to imperialism. In his contribution, Corey Ross explores the relationship between heritage, empire, and nature by focusing on how the concept of 'nature as global patrimoine' emerged in the early decades of the twentieth century out of the interaction between long-standing images of tropical Edens, the rise of international conservation networks and the opportunities afforded above all by Europe's colonial expansion. Irrespective of the intentions behind it, the

---

[36] On this theme, Nina Tumarkin, *Lenin Lives! The Lenin Cult in Soviet Russia* (Cambridge, MA, 1997); S. A. Smith, 'Bones of Contention: Bolsheviks and the Struggle against Relics, 1918-1930', *Past & Present*, 204 (2009), 155–94.

[37] Bernhard Gißibl, Sabine Höhler, and Patrick Kupper (eds), *Civilizing Nature: National Parks in Global Perspective* (London and New York, 2012); Dan Hicks et al., *Envisioning Landscape: Situations and Standpoints in Archaeology and Heritage* (Walnut Creek, 2007).

[38] Hugo Conwentz, *Die Gefährdung der Naturdenkmäler und Vorschläge zu ihrer Erhaltung* (Berlin, 1911), 206.

framing of supposedly unspoiled nature as a 'global trust' bore all the hallmarks of colonial asymmetries of power, and moreover furnished a powerful validation for conservationist intervention long after the demise of colonialism. In their joint contribution, Paul Basu and Vinita Damodaran extend this discussion to consider the internationalization of 'heritage law' in the context of colonialism. In particular they are interested in exploring the flows and circulations of heritage legislation within the British Empire, drawing on the history of 'natural heritage' in South Asia and that of 'cultural heritage' in West Africa, and considering the legacy of these legislative migrations in the shaping of postcolonial national heritages, including India, Sri Lanka, Pakistan, Nigeria, Ghana, and Sierra Leone. In so doing they affirm the significant role that the colonies played in the formation of Britain's own national heritage. Peter Coates shifts attention to natural landscapes and especially animals. Focusing mainly on the twentieth century, his article explores how and why certain animals have entered the pantheon of national identity, and become objects of a nationalistic preservationist concern (among them England's red squirrel, the USA's buffalo, and South Africa's lion).

But even if these expanding heritage industries were often closely tied to national rivalry or nation-building, they were by no means entirely coterminous with it. When viewed in a global context, another key aspect of heritage preservation was its remarkable centrality in the creation of a body of international law, often in response to war. Between 1790 and 1815 French armies looted whatever they could carry from the conquered territories stretching from Flanders to Egypt. Soon thereafter, a raft of new international treaties sought to outlaw such looting of art in the future.[39] In fact, Hugo Grotius may be seen as the father of preservation in that he suggested moral rules for military commanders in the handling of cultural property such as buildings and monuments.[40] Another key instance of the legal protection of cultural property in wartime can arguably be traced back to the famed Lieber Codes published in the United States during the American Civil War (1863), which instructed Union soldiers on how to treat enemy combatants and civilians as well as the cultural property of the American South.[41] Even so,

---

[39] Swenson, 'The Heritage of Empire', 22-5.

[40] Leon Friedman, *The Law of War*, vol. 1 (New York, 1972); Jan Kolasa, *International Intellectual Cooperation: The League Experience and the Beginnings of UNESCO* (Warsaw, 1962).

[41] Neeru Chadha, 'Protection of Cultural Property during Armed Conflict: Recent Developments', *ISIL Year Book on International Humanitarian and Refugee Law*, 12 (2001), 219-29.

the major milestones in the history of international preservation were the Hague Conventions for Protection of Cultural Heritage in 1899 and 1907, respectively. Much attention has been given to how these conventions set out the rules of wartime conduct and treatment of enemy combatants, but they also concerned the preservation of material artefacts in war zones. In a rapidly globalizing world, a perceived need to devise an international framework greatly intensified.[42]

Such links between preservation and war are among the most important yet remarkably under-appreciated dimensions of the modern enthralment with heritage. As the string of laws above attests, the establishment of international standards in the treatment of sacred artefacts and of enemy civilians and combatants often progressed in tandem. The common denominator was the reaction to man-made mass destruction; the establishment of rules of civility to minimize it; and the desire to create a protective membrane around things of high intrinsic value, whether human life or cherished relics from the past. In the First World War, for example, the German shelling of the world-famous medieval library of Louvain became a source of popular outrage across Europe, and was considered a 'crime against humanity' by both the court of international public opinion and by the Allied peacemakers gathered outside Paris after the war.[43] In this sense, the response to Louvain was not just a manifestation of the general urge for international cooperation amid the wreckage of national rivalries, but was also part of a broader impulse to reaffirm values of 'civilization' against the backdrop of the terrifying destructive capacity of modernity itself.

But it was the years following the Great War that saw the most vigorous international attention toward preservation. Indeed, the League of Nations' International Museums Office (IMO) and International Commission on Historical Monuments endeavoured to create new legal instruments to conserve cultural heritage, often in the name of a progressive cultural diplomacy. In fact, the League's first attempt to set up a cultural heritage conservation initiative came in 1923 in the wake of the worldwide coverage and popular

---

[42] R. O'Keefe, *The Protection of Cultural Property in Armed Conflict* (Cambridge, 2006) and W. Treue, *Art Plunder: The Fate of Works of Art in War, Revolution and Peace* (London, 1960).

[43] Alan Kramer, *Dynamic of Destruction: Culture and Mass Killing in the First World War* (Oxford, 2007), 6-30. More generally, Nicholas J. Saunders (ed.), *Matters of Conflict: Material Culture, Memory and the First World War* (London, 2004); and N. Lambourne, *War Damage in Western Europe: The Destruction of Historical Monuments during the Second World War* (Edinburgh, 2001), 12-39; and R. Bevan, *The Destruction of Memory: Architecture at War* (London, 2006).

excitement about the discovery of King Tutankhamun's tomb the year before. The hope was to use this international interest in antiquities to press for more cooperation. The League's IMO was founded in 1926 to carry on the mission, and it organized large expositions in Rome (1931) and Madrid (1934) dedicated to the preservation of art, whilst a 1931 Athens conference was devoted to the preservation of the archaeological heritage of 'mankind'. In 1933 the Draft International Convention on the 'Repatriation of Objects of Artistic, Historical or Scientific Interest, Which Have been Lost, Stolen or Unlawfully Alienated or Exported' was conceived, and in 1935 the League went on to found the International Commission on Historical Monuments in order to protect and preserve historical monuments. A follow-up 'Manual on the Technique of Archaeological Excavations' was even drafted in 1940.[44]

After the even greater destruction of World War II there was a concerted move to make good on this interwar legacy. While the League may never have progressed beyond drafts, it did provide a new internationalist lexicon for historical preservation. In fact, the draft text of the 1939 'Draft Declaration Concerning the Protection of Historical Buildings and Works of Art in Time of War' was used by UNESCO in its founding documents, and spurred the conception of the 1954 Hague Convention on the preservation of world heritage. It was designed to build on articles (in particular Articles 22, 27, and 29) of the Universal Declaration of Human Rights, in which cultural heritage matters were linked to human rights. This was a clear response to the widespread destruction wrought by the Second World War, including the full-scale destruction of whole cities (Dresden, Rotterdam, Warsaw, and Hiroshima), which prompted a determination to safeguard what was seen as a common heritage of mankind. In 1964 UNESCO took the lead in helping draft an International Charter for the Conservation and Restoration of Monuments and Sites, often known as the Venice Charter.[45] Significantly, the first historical monuments meeting in 1931 (Athens) included only Europeans; Tunisia, Mexico, and Peru joined the UNESCO Convention in 1964; and by 1979, some 80 nations together drafted the World Heritage Convention.[46] By the late 1960s, the new idea of World Heritage Sites was

---

[44] Sarah M. Titchen, 'On the Construction of Outstanding Universal Value: Unesco's World Heritage Convention (Convention Concerning the Protection of the World Cultural and Natural Heritage, 1972) and the Identification and Assessment of Cultural Places for Inclusion in the World Heritage List', PhD Thesis, Australian National University, April 1995, 15-35.

[45] Titchen, 'On the Construction of Outstanding Universal Value', 50-2.

[46] Françoise Choay, *L'Allegorie du patrimoine* (Paris, 1992), 10-12.

taking root.[47] In his contribution, Paul Betts looks at UNESCO's highly publicized twenty-year preservation project to broadcast its role as guardian of what was called at the time 'world civilization'—the restoration of the Nubian Monuments in Egypt and the Sudan—as a revealing case study of budding Cold War internationalism in the world of material culture.

Yet alongside this internationalization of heritage management, the link between preservation and national identity became ever more pronounced after 1945. It was a key factor in shaping new post-1945 cultural identities, as the heritage industry became a booming business after World War II. In fact, 95% of all existing museums post-date the Second World War.[48] This was certainly the case in a Europe decimated by war, where a concerted effort in many European cities to reconstruct a pre-war urban heritage was a source of ongoing controversy about which past to resuscitate and why, and how (especially in the German case) these pasts related to attitudes toward war guilt.[49] In Japan, archaeology was explicitly used to counter emperor worship and extreme nationalism.[50] That such heritage could thus be used both to fuel or temper nationalist sentiment underscores its status as a crucial field for contestation over social identity, community, and belonging. In her essay, Erika Hanna focuses on the controversy over the fate of Dublin's Fitzwilliam Street, Europe's longest intact eighteenth-century street. Her piece examines how the 'heritage' of Fitzwilliam Street was discussed in the architectural and national press, with particular attention to the tension between an international language of modernism and a postcolonial discourse of modern Irish identity.

To be sure, the urge towards a preservationist universalism often sat uneasily with post-war anti-colonial nationalism. The Algerian head of the country's UNESCO committee stated that the 'restitution and return of cultural property [is] one of the key problems of the Third World'.[51] The debate about the return of cultural property has been a long-running theme, beginning with the controversy over the British acquisition of the Elgin Marbles in the early nineteenth century.[52] Yet such rancour greatly intensified with

---

[47] Henry Cleere, *Approaches to the Archaeological Heritage* (Cambridge, 1984); Henry Cleere (ed.), *Archaeological Heritage Management in the Modern World* (London, 1989).

[48] David Lowenthal, *The Heritage Crusade and the Spoils of History* (Cambridge, 1998), 3.

[49] Jeffrey Diefendorf (ed.), *Rebuilding Europe's Bombed Cities* (London, 1990).

[50] Clare Fawcett, 'Nationalism and Postwar Japanese Archaeology', in Kohl and Fawcett (eds), 232-46.

[51] David Lowenthal, 'Identity, Heritage and History', in John R. Gillis (ed.), *Commemorations: The Politics of National Identity* (Princeton, 1994), 41-57, here 45.

[52] J. H. Merryman, 'Whither the Elgin Marbles?', in J. H. Merryman (ed.), *Imperialism, Art and Restitution* (Cambridge, 2006), 98-113 and Reid, *Whose Pharoahs?*

decolonization, as newly independent Nigeria led the African campaign for the return of its treasures as part of the anti-colonial struggle.[53] The shared assumption was that these countries would be bereft of tradition and identity without these newly valued heritage artefacts. This did not mean that the imperial heritage was evaluated negatively in every instance. For example, Pandit Nehru once remarked that 'After every other Viceroy has been forgotten Curzon will be remembered because he restored all that was beautiful in India'.[54] But the imperial material legacy has often been a target of postcolonial anger, and even the universalism undergirding the World Heritage Convention has been a perennial source of friction within many former colonies.[55] Sometimes these heritage issues exploded into fully fledged international controversies, as was the case in 1974 when it was claimed that Israel had damaged the cultural heritage of Jerusalem after the 1967 War. Critics asserted that Israeli archaeology was directed toward the 'rediscovery' of early Jewish history (disengaging the Wailing Wall and uncovering the Temple of Solomon), which necessitated the clearance and disturbance of Arab dwellings and the adjacent urban environment. UNESCO's General Assembly passed a resolution the next year condemning the Israeli excavation, which set off a torrent of international indignation.[56] Occasionally these heritage issues even served as unlikely lightning rods of political revolution. At the Tallinn Song Festival in 1988, two years after the Estonian Heritage Society was founded, the leader of the Heritage Society sent shockwaves across the Soviet Union when he openly called for the restoration of Estonian independence.[57]

As this example suggests, the enthusiasm for heritage has been at the centre of the construction of Cold War and post-Cold War identities in Europe. A conspicuous example was the conversion of key Cold War emblems into

[53] Greenfield, *Return of Cultural Treasures*, 122.

[54] Thompson, *Ruins Reused*, 52.

[55] Henry Cleere, 'The World Heritage Convention in the Third World', in Francis P. McManamon (ed.), *Cultural Resource Management in Contemporary Society: Perspectives on Managing and Presenting the Past* (London, 2000), 99-106. The Nara Convention drafted in Japan in 1994 explicitly pleaded for a more plural idea of the authenticity of cultural heritage, insofar as the Western conception of physical material gave way to how other cultures place value on the site, its attending rituals and the periodic renewal of its fabric, as Jordan Sand explains.

[56] Richard Hoggart, *An Idea and its Servants: Unesco from Within* (New York, 1978), 75-9. See, more controversially, Nadia Abu El Haj, *Facts on the Ground: Archaeological Practice and Territorial Self-Fashioning in Israeli Society* (Chicago, 2001).

[57] Norman Davies, *Vanished Kingdoms: The History of Half-Forgotten Europe* (London, 2011), 722-3.

tourist attractions in Berlin, such as the Luftbrücke Memorial, Checkpoint Charlie Museum and the remnants of the Wall itself, as German (and Berliner) identities were being redrawn in the 1990s. This was also the case with the remaking of identities (and tourist sites) throughout much of ex-communist Eastern Europe, including the commercialization of symbols of the Soviet past.[58] Questions of heritage in divided countries—such as in the post-Velvet Revolution Czech Republic—have witnessed acrimonious debates about issues of urban identity,[59] and bitter contests over heritage were very much present in the former Yugoslavia through the 1990s and beyond.[60] Heritage issues were also instrumental in fashioning a more integrated post-Cold War European identity. For example, the Second Summit of the Council of Europe (Strasbourg) in 1997 affirmed its dedication 'to the protection of our European cultural and natural heritage and to the promotion of awareness of this heritage', building on the 1975 European Charter of Architectural Heritage that introduced the idea of an 'integrated heritage conservation' across the Cold War divide. The European Union also set up a Task Force for International Cooperation on Holocaust Education in Stockholm in 2000, as delegates from EU member states (13 at the time) decided that from 2003 onwards European countries should commemorate the anniversary of the liberation of the Auschwitz concentration camp on January 27 each year. This was a new declaration of heritage in which, as Henry Rousso put it, 'Europe was being refounded on the basis of one of the most terrible acts ever committed and the worst events ever known in recent European history'.[61]

The battle over cultural property—and the ethics of collecting it—is an on-going matter of great international controversy.[62] Illicit traffic in antiquities

[58] Duncan Light, 'An Unwanted Past: Contemporary Tourism and the Heritage of Communism in Romania', *International Journal of Heritage Studies*, 6:2 (2000), 145-60; James Mark, 'What Remains? Anti-Communism, Forensic Archaeology, and the Retelling of the National Past in Lithuania and Romania', in Walsham (ed.), *Relics and Remains*, 276-300.

[59] R. Hammesley and T. Westlake, 'Urban Heritage in the Czech Republic', in G. J. Ashworth and P. J. Larkham (eds), *Building a New Heritage: Tourism, Culture and Identity in the New Europe* (London, 1994), 178-200.

[60] K. S. Brown, 'Contests of Heritage and the Politics of Preservation in the Former Yugoslav Republic of Macedonia', in Lynn Meskell (ed.), *Archaeology under Fire* (London, 1998), 68-86.

[61] Henry Rousso, 'History of Memory, Policies of the Past: What For?', in Konrad Jarausch and Thomas Lindenberger (eds), *Conflicted Memories: Europeanizing Contemporary History* (Oxford and New York, 2007), 33.

[62] Phyllis Mauch Messenger (ed.), *The Ethics of Collecting Cultural Property: Whose Culture? Whose Property?* (Albuquerque, 1989).

around the world remains a flourishing trade.[63] It is estimated that out of 80 million icons in Russia, around one quarter have been removed from Russia since 1980.[64] The frustration about these stolen goods has at times even led to a veneration of what others would consider theft. In 1982 a Mexican journalist stole an Aztec codex from the Bibliotheque Nationale in Paris and then gave it to the Mexican state, whereafter his 'patriotic' theft was 'widely hailed' as the rightful return of 'Mexican heritage' by illicit means.[65] The problem of 'plundering' and illegal trade is one in which the links between war and heritage are particularly apparent. Atrocities in the Balkan and Gulf Wars leave no doubt that the Hague Conventions on the safeguarding of cultural property were hardly respected during the conflicts. In 1992, as conflict flared between Hindus and Muslims in India over religious sites claimed by both sides, a particular source of tension was the Babri Mosque in Ayodhya, built in 1528 by Babur. The burning of this mosque by militant Hindus who claimed that it occupied the birthplace of Lord Rama incited rioting on a national scale, claiming some two thousand lives and destabilizing the secular government.[66] Perhaps the most notorious instance came in 2001 in Afghanistan when the Taliban detonated the Bamiyan Buddhas in a flagrant act of cultural iconoclasm designed to erase all traces of a non-Muslim past and to convey the violence of the new order through the deliberate destruction of cultural heritage.[67] It was after this destruction that the neologism 'cultural terrorism' came to international prominence.[68]

Yet against this backdrop of demolition and conflict it is important to recognize that there have also been moves in the other direction, as heritage and its 'management of the past' have increasingly been identified as tools for reconciliation in conflict-ridden ancestral zones stretching from Canada and Southern Africa to Australasia.[69] Prime examples include the successful efforts to return objects to their rightful owners, as bones and objects have increasingly been repatriated in response to growing criticism around the

---

[63] Neil Brodie, Jennifer Doole, and Colin Renfrew (eds), *Trade in Illicit Antiquities: The Destruction of the World's Archaeological Heritage* (Cambridge, 2001).

[64] Greenfield, *Return of Cultural Treasures*, 183.

[65] Lowenthal, *Heritage Crusade*, 237.

[66] B. B. Lal, 'A Note on the Excavation of Ayodhya with Reference to the Mandir-Masjid Issue', in Robert Layton, Peter G. Stone, Julian Thomas (eds), *Destruction and Conservation of Cultural Property* (London, 2001), 117-26.

[67] Finbarr Barry Flood, 'Between Cult and Culture: Bamiyan, Islamic Iconoclasm, and the Museum', *The Art Bulletin*, 84:4 (2002), 641-59.

[68] Greenfield, *Return of Cultural Treasures*, 352.

[69] J. E. Tunbridge and G. J. Ashworth, *Dissonant Heritage: The Management of the Past as a Resource in Conflict* (London, 1995).

world.[70] The Museum of Medical History in Berlin, for instance, has recently returned dozens of skulls to tribes in Australia, Papua New Guinea and the Torres Strait Islands, in this case following the lead of the Smithsonian Institute in Washington, which has been returning the bones of Native Americans since the 1980s and 1990s.[71] If nothing else, such actions underline the point that heritage today is hardly escapist nostalgia, but a fundamental element of identity politics globally.

In many respects the current volume marks an attempt to contextualize these attitudes and activities. While it deliberately builds on the recent work on imperial heritages, it ventures beyond the colonial context to consider how the impulses of modern preservation both transcended and outlived the broader edifice of European empire. For the first time, this collection brings together scholars working not only on Europe and its colonial territories but also on Latin America, China, Japan, the Soviet Union, and North America to consider the extent to which the various attempts to define, protect, and mobilize ancestral pasts were part and parcel of an increasingly global and interconnected approach to heritage and its preservation in the nineteenth and twentieth centuries. Its purpose is not to dispute the importance of the 'nationalization' of heritage, which continues to be a conspicuous feature of historical consciousness in today's world. Rather, the aim is to reconsider its increasing 'internationalization' and the ways in which the different layers of heritage preservation between the local and the universal overlapped and interacted. The volume thus seeks to do more than simply chronicle how preservation evolved from an elitist pastime into a populist movement. It also moves beyond the argument that in a 'world beset with poverty and hunger', 'we seek comfort in past bequests partly to allay these griefs'.[72] The yearning for rooted legacies and ancestral worship has been fundamental to the construction of modern identities in a variety of ways, and hopefully this volume goes some way towards showing its global importance in doing so.

[70] Andrew Guilford, 'Bones of Contention: The Repatriation of Native American Human Remains', *The Public Historian*, 18 (1996), 119-43.

[71] Doreen Carvajal, 'Skeletons Get Ticket Home', *New York Times*, International Weekly, 2 June 2013, 1, 4. On the broader issue, see Tiffany Jenkins, *Contesting Human Remains in Museum Collections: The Crisis of Cultural Authority* (London, 2011).

[72] Lowenthal, *Heritage Crusade*, xiii.

Crusader Heritages and Imperial Preservation[1]

Astrid Swenson

Re-entangling histories

Visitors keen to see French heritage in a nutshell need not stray far from the Eiffel Tower. At the Museum of French Monuments, reopened in 2007 as part of the National City of Architecture and Heritage, one can experience the history of French architecture, sculpture, and wall painting in three dimensions. A 'point of reference for all audiences, permitting them to understand the historic roots of the most contemporary aims in architectural creation and urban policies', the museum's own development is less visible.[2] Founded in 1879 as a cast collection for the training of architects and the education of the public, the displays always consisted of models and copies. In contrast to originals, these copies could be ordered on demand, allowing the curators to create an ideal museum, easily adaptable to changing understandings of heritage. Its history is therefore a microcosm for observing broader transformations in the heritage canon. For a long time, this canon was not limited to the art of the Hexagon. The institution was in fact founded as the Museum of Comparative Sculpture, juxtaposing French medieval to ancient and foreign works of art. It was only in the 1930s that it was rebranded as the Museum of French Monuments. Yet despite the new title, the display was not confined to works originating in metropolitan France, but rather explicitly included material that demonstrated the spread of French influence beyond national borders. A particular highlight was a new room on the art of the Crusades. Filled with casts from the Levant, at its centre stood a model of what T. E. Lawrence called 'perhaps the best preserved and most wholly admirable castle

[1] I am grateful to Paul Betts, Corey Ross, Rana Mitter, and the participants of the 'Heritage in the Modern World' conference, and to Peter Mandler, Simon Goldhill, Richard Evans, David Motadel, Tamson Pietsch, Alison Carrol, Tamara van Kessel, Krishan Kumar, and Samuel Aylett as well as to the anonymous readers for their comments on the paper, and to the Leverhulme Trust and the British Academy for supporting the research.

[2] Ministère de la Culture et de la Communication, Cité de l'Architecture et du Patrimoine, http://www.citechaillot.fr/fr/cite/trois_departements/departement_patrimoine/ [accessed 25 February 2013].

in the world', the Crac des Chevaliers in Syria.[3] France had acquired the Crac in 1934 and restored it extensively. A publicity campaign through the Colonial Exhibition in 1931, at the Museum of French Monuments and the Museum of the Colonies at Vincennes, accompanied the restoration and acquisition.[4] For a domestic audience, the exhibitions tried to interweave national and colonial consciousness by creating a narrative in which the Crusades became the first chapter of France's empire.[5] To international visitors they signalled France's primacy in producing and preserving Crusader architecture, as the sites were not only symbols of colonial expansion for France, but also served as proxies for broader imperial claims by other rival powers that were likewise trying to get their hands on medieval remains across the Mediterranean.

After the end of the Empire, the exhibitions disappeared silently. The model of the Crac des Chevaliers is now in storage, hidden and largely forgotten. At the former Museum of the Colonies, which now houses the National City for Immigration, only the names of Crusaders inscribed on the building's sidewall, behind some shrubs, offer a semi-visible reminder of the centrality the Crusades once had to national colonial ideas.[6] With decolonization, the expansionist view of the nation was no longer opportune for a former colonial power. Former colonies, for their part, also erased this history as they claimed the Crusader sites for themselves. The process of dissociation was further reinforced by the dispersal of the related archives across multiple countries.

This erasure of earlier entanglements by a double process of re-nationalization is representative of broader trends in the historiography of heritage, which has largely been written about within the framework of national or area studies. More recently, the 'transnational turn' engendered a growing sense for the importance of former interactions, and we have been

---

[3] T. E. Lawrence, *Crusader Castles* (London, 1936); Paul Deschamps, 'Project d'amenagement du Musée des monuments français', 5 April 1935, Archives des Musées nationaux, Paris (hereafter AMN), U1 Trocadéro. In the sources of the period both 'Crac' and 'Krak des Chevaliers' were used to refer to the fortress known in Arabic as 'Hisn al Akrad'.

[4] Maureen Murphy, *Un Palais pour une Cité: Du Musée des colonies à la Cité nationale de l'histoire de l'immigration* (Paris, 2007), 42.

[5] Exposition coloniale internationale de Paris 1931. Commissariat général. Section rétrospective française, *Les Colonies et la vie française pendant huit siècles* (Paris, 1933).

[6] With the exception of Léon Pressouyre, 'Un Grand Musée en quête de sens' in Léon Pressouyre (ed.), *Le Musée des Monuments français* (Paris, 2007), 36–40, the publications that accompanied the museum's reopening say little on the international and colonial aspects of its history.

gaining a better understanding of exchanges within Europe, across the Atlantic, and between metropole and colonies in individual empires.[7] Yet we are only really beginning to map the processes of entanglement.

As a result, many chapters of colonial preservation are still unwritten, and the intra-imperial relations that framed them remain largely unexplored. Approaches to heritage in different empires have hardly been compared, nor do we know much about how imperial and trans-imperial networks relate to the more general internationalization of preservation that took place over the last two centuries. In order to think about similarities and differences in colonial preservation, and to better conceptualize some of the entanglements that operated across national and imperial borders, this article will follow the trail of the Crusader Room in the Museum of French Monuments and investigate the preservation of 'Crusader sites' in the Mediterranean from the Napoleonic wars to the interwar period, through four interconnected case studies on Malta, Cyprus, Syria, and Palestine.

These 'Crusader heritages' are an informative case study for comparative imperial histories, as they were not only a significant chapter in French heritage history but were also representative of a broader European interest in the Crusades, which manifested itself in explorations, restorations, and acquisitions by individuals and government and a thriving presence in popular culture. This interest emerged when the territories once conquered by Crusaders and their successors 'again' came under the rule of the expanding European powers during the modern colonization of the Mediterranean. The French conquered Malta in 1798, followed by British rule over the island after 1814. A second chapter began in 1878 with the British purchase of Cyprus and the Italian colonization of Rhodes in 1912, before the heartland of the Crusades came under European domination at the end of the First World War with the British Mandate in Palestine and the French Mandate in Syria and Lebanon.

The rich literature on the reception of the Crusades, which has drawn attention to the relationship between historiography and national and colonial

---

[7] For a broader analysis of historiographic developments see Melanie Hall (ed.) *Towards World Heritage: International Origins of the Preservation Movement* (Aldershot, 2011); Astrid Swenson, *The Rise of Heritage: Preserving the Past in France, Germany and England, 1789-1914* (Cambridge, 2013); Astrid Swenson and Peter Mandler (eds), *From Plunder to Preservation: Britain and the Heritage of Empire, c.1800-1940* (Proceedings of the British Academy clxxxvii, Oxford, 2013); Michael Falser, Monica Juneja (eds), *Kulturerbe und Denkmalpflege transkulturell. Grenzgänge zwischen Theorie und Praxis* (Bielefeld, 2013).

projects, is relatively silent with regard to the treatment of sites and artefacts.[8] Yet in a region of competing imperial claims, sites connected to the history of the Crusades attracted the attention of all the major European powers. While the French, British, and Italians established formal empires in the Mediterranean, other European (especially German) interest in these sites was also strong. For each nation, interventions for restoration or acquisition were not limited to territories under their own rule, but extended into Ottoman territories, post-independence Greece, as well as the other European empires. These cross-cutting linkages allow us to use the Crusader sites as a prism for comparing formal and informal preservation policies and for tracing the inter-dependencies between them. Imperial actors were of course not the only ones interested in these sites. Maltese, Greek, Turkish, Arab, and Hebrew nationalists had their own agendas for their preservation or destruction, as had trans-national bodies, especially the various successor organizations to the Knights of St John.

My focus here will be on British and French colonial preservation policies, but by inscribing these within broader interactions in the Mediterranean, I hope to raise more general questions about transnational and trans-imperial entwinements. Highlighting these interactions helps us understand the creation of the very category of 'Crusader art', which encompassed artefacts produced over a huge span of time and space. At the same time, consideration of the local contexts in Malta, Cyprus, Syria, and Palestine will also underscore the substantial variation in approaches due to differing relations with local populations.

Finally, the Crusader vestiges are also a particularly intriguing case for reflecting on the construction of heritage across borders given that, for all the participants concerned, they represented a unique category between a heritage of the self and a heritage of the other. Sites of conflict and of encounter in the past as well as the present, and altered by various conquerors over the centuries, they could alternatively be seen as a European, Christian, national, or colonial legacy. When viewed in relation to other monuments in the metropoles and colonies, they reveal in a pertinent way which notions of lineage informed ideas about a 'common' heritage in Europe.

---

[8] See, e.g., Elizabeth Siberry, 'Images of the Crusades in the Nineteenth and Twentieth Centuries' in Jonathan Riley-Smith (ed.), *The Oxford Illustrated History of the Crusades* (Oxford, 1995); Peter Lock, *The Routledge Companion to the Crusades* (London, 2006), 255–72; Adam Knobler, 'Holy Wars, Empires, and the Portability of the Past: The Modern Uses of Medieval Crusades', *Comparative Studies in Society and History*, xlviii (2006) 293-325; Ronnie Ellenblum, *Crusader Castles and Modern Histories* (Cambridge, 2007).

Malta: the legacy of the Knights

In 1935 the British were troubled by the thought that in Egypt, 'Latin', 'and in particular French cultural ascendancy, dates back to the Crusades'. Worse still, it had 'continued constantly until the British occupation of Egypt in 1882'.[9] As much as contemporary French propaganda would have revelled in this tale of uninterrupted presence, the supposed links between the Crusades and modern French imperialism were only slowly established in the wake of Napoleon's Egyptian campaign. In the seventeenth century Gottfried Wilhelm Leibnitz, in the employment of the Elector of Mainz, had tried in vain to find ways to divert Louis XIV's aggression from France's eastern border to more distant eastern lands by mobilizing the idea of completing the Crusades. His memorandum was forgotten and, as it happened, Napoleon only read an abridged version *after* his return from Egypt.[10] Modern engagement with the tangible heritage of the Crusades also started not so much with reclaiming but rather demolishing the last outpost of the Crusades. Seizing Malta en route to Egypt in 1798, the French portrayed themselves as liberators of the Maltese from the tyranny of the Order of the Knights of St John, who had ruled the island since their expulsion from Rhodes in the sixteenth century. To obliterate their memory, streets and places were renamed (the Palace of the Grand Masters, for instance, became Palais National), many religious houses and churches were closed and monuments were destroyed. As the French Knight Louis de Boisgelin remembered:

> Everything in the public buildings, which bore the stamp of nobility, or recalled to mind the celebrated exploits performed by illustrious chiefs, was broken and destroyed. These new Goths and Vandals likewise threw down with impious hand the bust of those heroes who had graced the annals of chivalry . . . such an outrage as this, was not even committed by the Musulmen [sic] at Rhodes; where honourable marks still remain of the residence of the knights of St John of Jerusalem in that island.[11]

---

[9] Sir Percy Loraine's dispatch on Egypt, sent with a letter from Charles Bridge to Rex Leeper, 5 March 1935, The National Archives (hereafter TNA), BW 29/3 British Council Archives. My thanks to Tamara von Kessel for drawing my attention to this reference.

[10] Ellenblum, *Crusader Castles*, 11.

[11] Louis de Boisgelin, *Ancient and Modern Malta* (London 1804), III, 98-9, quoted in Dennis Castillo, ' "The Knights cannot be admitted": Maltese Nationalism, the Knights of St John, and the French Occupation of 1798–1800', *The Catholic Historical Review*, lxxix (1993), 445–6.

De Boisgelin's condemnation of Goths and Vandals resonated with Abbé Grégoire's speeches against revolutionary 'vandalism' made three years before the conquest of Malta. During the end of the Terror, Grégoire managed to stop iconoclasm in France by redefining works of art as embodiments of the national and hence revolutionary spirit, inventing the word 'vandalism' to brandish iconoclasts as barbarians.[12] The idea of the sanctity of the past did not, however, travel with the soldiers to Malta, nor did the arriving army see the heritage of the Knights as their own.

While the Maltese welcomed the end of the rule of the Knights, the French committed a mistake by treating the memory of the Knights and that of the Catholic Church as one. Following three months of French rule, the Maltese revolted. Aggrieved by French looting, the decision to strip the ecclesiastical establishments of Mdina for minting provided the trigger for massacring the French garrison.[13] The Treaty of Amiens in 1802 planned to restore the island to the Knights of St John, but the Maltese objected and opted instead for British rule, which was formally established by the Treaty of Paris in 1814.[14]

Given the recent expulsion of the Knights, what was then to happen to their legacy? Intuitively, it would seem unsurprising if neither the Maltese nor the British colonial administration immediately valued the Knights' 'heritage' as their own. Yet British travellers who stopped in Malta on their way to Egypt, the Holy Land, or India romanticized it. Even half a century later, 'very few of the numerous Englishmen who visit Malta seem to have any idea of the archaeological treasures of the Phoenicians',[15] and 'very many of [the island's] treasures have escaped notice, and some of priceless value have been neglected and ultimately lost'.[16] By contrast, 'all the world' seemed to 'know Malta' and its 'noble palaces, formerly inhabited by the famous knights'.[17] While it was now the Governor of the island (and for one winter in 1838 the Queen Dowager) who resided in the palace of the Grand Masters,[18] in the visitors' imagination it was 'the Grand-Master and all his knights' who 'still possessed the island' (see Figure 1).[19] Preservationists

---

[12] Henri Grégoire, *Patrimoine et Cité*, ed. Dominique Audrerie (Bordeaux, 1999).

[13] Carmel Casser, *A Concise History of Malta* (Malta, 2002), 141-3; Carmel Testa, *The French in Malta, 1798-1800* (Malta, 1997).

[14] Castillo, ' "The Knights" '.

[15] A. H. Sayce, 'The Antiquities of Malta', *The Times* (5 February 1883), 12.

[16] Count Bologna Strickland, 'The Antiquities of Malta', *The Times* (13 February 1883), 8.

[17] *Half Hours in the Holy Land. Travels in Egypt, Palestine, Syria* (London, 1898), 12–14.

[18] Despatch of 7 Dec 1838, Centre des Archives Diplomatiques, Nantes (hereafter CADN), 166PO/D45/2 Constantinople, Correspondence avec les Echelles, Serie D Malte.

[19] *Half Hours in the Holy Land*, 12–14.

Figure 1. Street in Malta from *Half Hours in the Holy Land. Travels in Egypt, Palestine, Syria* (London, 1898), 14.

across the British Empire complained that the authorities did too little to protect this heritage—or any heritage—on the island, which mirrored the attitude towards ancient monuments prevalent in Britain and the colonies more broadly. As Major Keith, Archaeological Surveyor for Central India, pointed out in 1888 in a report comparing India and Malta for the Society for the Protection of Ancient Buildings in London: 'Neither in India nor in other dependencies has our Government hit on a systematised plan to check destruction or repress vandalism'.[20]

[20] Society for the Protection of Ancient Buildings (SPAB), *Annual Report* (1888), 57-8; SPAB Archives, London, Committee Minute Book, 26 July 1888.

Letters to *The Times* in London often pointed out that the government lagged behind private initiatives in matters of preservation. A Roman villa was excavated and placed under the guardianship of a custodian at the public expense at Civita Vecchia (Mdina), and the Maltese antiquarian and librarian Dr Caruana drew up a report on the antiquities of Malta at the suggestion of the Government.[21] In addition, 'many treasures of the latter period of the Knights of Malta' were preserved by individual Maltese. But despite the foundation of a learned society inventorying monuments,[22] a proposal by Caruana for the foundation of a national museum, as well as public calls in the London press in the early 1880s that 'a Government official should be responsible for at least preserving a record of existing and future archaeological discoveries' in Malta as 'a subject of general interest', no institution was founded.[23] In 1888, Major Keith tried to alert Sir Lintorn Simmons, Governor of Malta:

> I invited his attention to the fact that, owing to the want of conservative measures, a dependency which had a varied history extending back to 1400 BC, including the dominion of the Phoenicians, Greeks and Romans, Saracens, and Maurs, to say nothing of the chivalrous mediaeval Knights of Malta, had been for years systematically plundered and depleted of its valuables. His Excellency [...] listened with much attention, and I hope my representations may lead to the forming of a national museum. Had such a museum been formed at the time the Island was ceded to England, Malta would have possessed a collection of antiquities second to none in Europe.[24]

In a climate where the preservation of heritage was increasingly proclaimed to be 'a yardstick for a people's cultural attainment', such indifference could undermine British criticisms of the treatment of heritage by indigenous populations in India or Egypt, and harmed the argument that British guardianship was needed until indigenous populations would mature to take responsibility.[25] Given the 'neglect of antiquities of Malta' and the

---

[21] A. H. Sayce, 'The Antiquities of Malta', *The Times* (5 February 1883), 12. More broadly see Nicholas C. Vella and Oliver Gilkes, 'The Lure of the Antique: Nationalism, Politics and Archaeology in British Malta (1880-1964)', *Papers of the British School at Rome*, 69 (2001), 353-84.

[22] National Library of Malta, Ms. 588, *Archaeological and Geological Society of Malta*.

[23] Strickland, 'The Antiquities of Malta', 8.

[24] SPAB, *Annual Report* (1888), 60.

[25] See Astrid Swenson, 'The Heritage of Empire', in Swenson and Mandler (eds), *From Plunder to Preservation*.

'shortcoming of our own in the countries subject to us', it was unsurprising, an editorial in *The Times* concluded, 'If, then, the Egyptians are indifferent to the past, they may certainly plead Western example in their defence. It is in fact, Western example, which directly or indirectly is the root of all the mischief.'[26]

In many ways, this story of neglect is much exaggerated. If we turn from the metropolitan perspective to Maltese records, it becomes apparent that although no particular institution for preservation was founded and no Antiquities Law or Monument Act was passed before the early twentieth century, there was nevertheless a strong sense of the importance of preservation within the colonial administration. Malta was singular among our case studies in that the Crown inherited all the buildings of the Knights, making it the owner not only of the fortresses but also of the Palace of the Grand Masters and of various Catholic churches, including St John's Co-Cathedral in Valetta. Already in 1801 Downing Street gave the Civil Commissioner for the affairs of Malta detailed instruction to familiarize himself with laws and customs put in place by the Knights. Mindful of what the vandalism of churches had cost the French in Malta, subsequent British governors stressed in their dispatches to London the importance of preserving St John's Cathedral, as neglect might provoke the ire of the Maltese. Several careful repairs and restorations were executed throughout the century and preservation was conducted as a collaborative project between members of the Maltese and colonial elites.[27]

But without a special bureaucracy in charge of monuments, not much was publicized about these conservation policies. It is significant for the broader story here that the history of neglect only really became a cause of public concern in the 1930s as preservation became a matter of imperial competition at 'a time of emerging nationalist political activism and local political flirtation with fascist Italy'.[28] The restoration of the city of Rhodes, which followed Italian conquest, created fears that the Italians might also use the Knights'

---

[26]   *The Times* (5 Feb 1883), 9 (Leader).

[27]   Lord Hobart to Charles Cameron, London, 14 May 1801. National Archives of Malta (hereafter NAM) GOV 1/2/1; Sir Thomas Maitland to Earl Barthurst, Malta, 27 January 1814, NAM, GOV 1/2/1; Bouverie to Lord John Russell, Malta, 7 July 1840, NAM, GOV 1/2/19, fols 190-201; More O'Ferrall to Earl Grey, Malta, 5 October 1848, NAM, GOV 1/2/23, fols 647; Marchant to Bulwer Lytton, Malta, 27 November 1858, NAM, GOV 1/3/9 27, fols 377-8.

[28]   Paul Sant Cassia, 'Tradition, Tourism and Memory in Malta', *The Journal of the Royal Anthropological Institute*, v (1999), 248.

heritage to claim the 'return' of Malta into Italian hands.[29] As a result, the Lieutenant Governor of Malta, Sir Harry Luke, initiated a widely publicized restoration campaign, including an embellishment of the city of Mdina in sicolo-norman style.[30] This awakening to the cultural-political importance of public acts of preservation becomes even more apparent when we turn our attention from Malta to Cyprus.

Cyprus: the heritage of kings

There are many similarities between the treatment of monuments in Malta and Cyprus, but as Cyprus was integrated into the Empire much later and with a different status, there were also significant differences. The link to the Crusades was at one level more distant (in terms of time elapsed) and at another level more proximate (in terms of possibilities to construe national links). Richard Lionheart's conquest of the island and his marriage in a hilltop castle made it (as noted repeatedly by Sir Harry Luke, who spent part of his career before and after Malta in Cyprus) Britain's oldest colony, and the only one ever to have witnessed a royal wedding.[31] Cyprus' history, however, also provided ample chapters for other national reclaimings. The French in particular focused on the thirteenth- and fourteenth-century Lusignan dynasty, and the Italians on the Venetian occupation after 1489. At the same time, there was not such a direct transmission of property rights as in the case of Malta. Some castles became government property, but most secular buildings were privately owned, while the former Latin ecclesiastical buildings had largely been transformed into Orthodox churches or mosques and were in the hands of the religious authorities (see Figure 2).

Unlike in Malta, both the British authorities in Cyprus and the British public initially paid little attention to the island's architectural treasures. On the contrary, in the 1890s Famagusta's medieval structures were being systematically destroyed to provide stone for the building of Port Said

[29]   On the reclaiming of Rhodes and the restoration of the Hospitaller's heritage between 1913–24 see Mia Fuller, *Moderns Abroad. Architecture, Cities and Italian Imperialism* (London and New York, 2007), 78–9.

[30]   H. Luke, *Malta: An Account and an Appreciation* (1949), (London, 1960), 99-101; Cassia, 'Tradition, Tourism and Memory', 248. On the perception of neglect until Sir Harry Luke's restorations see for instance a paper read by Clarkson to the Society of Antiquaries of London, December 1936. Museum of the Order of St John, London Archives (hereafter MOStJ), Sir Harry Luke Papers, Malta. On the development of conservation in Malta see TNA, WORK 14/2335, Preservation of ancient monuments in Malta. In turn, British interest triggered French curiosity, see CADN, 350PO/3/6 La Valette, 'Autres Affaires'.

[31]   See press clippings, publications and talks in MOStJ, Sir Harry Luke Papers.

Figure 2. St. Sophia, Nicosia. *The Illustrated London News*, 7 September 1878, celebrated the acquisition of Cyprus through a series of special illustrations.

in Egypt.[32] Among the few metropolitan voices that spoke out against this was William Morris' Society for the Protection of Ancient Buildings (SPAB). Founded in 1877 to protest against restorations in England, the SPAB also championed the preservation of buildings all over the world and started to intervene in Cyprus soon after the transfer to British control. The Earl of Wharncliffe, a prominent Conservative member of the Society's Committee, was asked for advice on how to influence the government to initiate a survey of medieval buildings, but efforts to contact Lord Salisbury, the Foreign Secretary, as well as his nephew and private secretary Arthur Balfour, yielded no results.[33]

Interest in Cyprus' architectural heritage was spurred less through English endeavours than through the activities of foreign medievalists. Germany and France simultaneously sent scholars on scientific missions to study Cyprus's Gothic buildings, who in fact met on one occasion after the German scholar

[32] Frank C. Sharp, 'Exporting the Revolution: The Work of the SPAB outside Britain 1878–1914', in Chris Miele (ed.), *From William Morris: Building Conservation and the Arts and Crafts Cult of Authenticity, 1877–1939*, (New Haven, London, 2005), 204.

[33] See ibid and Earl of Wharncliffe to Newman Marks, 4 August 1878, SPAB Archives, 'Cyprus'.

requested to 'know his enemy'.[34] But it was undoubtedly the Frenchman, Camille Enlart, who lastingly put Cyprus on the scholarly map through the publication of *L'Art Gothique et la Renaissance en Chypre* in 1899, which led to international outcries over the British government's failure to protect Cypriot monuments.[35] In France, it fostered the view that French Crusaders had brought Gothic art to the island and that these monuments were therefore part of the national patrimony.[36] At the same time, a number of pieces appeared in the Italian press criticizing the British in Cyprus, in particular in light of the high-handed British campaign to save St. Mark's of Venice from its Italian restorers, which William Morris and the SPAB had led more than twenty years earlier. The *Gazzetino* of Padua, for instance, wrote:

> Some years ago, when the restorations of St. Marks were commenced, and carried on with such care, the English made a devil of a row [sic] with articles in journals, meetings etc. to signify their disapproval. Curiously now the English are selling the stones of ancient Famagusta for the construction of Port Said . . . who in Italy cares for archaeology—and who does not care somewhat— should know what is British respect for the glorious monuments of the Italo-Greeks, and that whilst they are being demolished with the pickaxe, the English soldiers are looting the old cemeteries. The Cypriots murmur 'worse than the Turks!'[37]

The Cypriot murmur soon turned into a loud protest. In reaction to an attempt by Chamberlain to blame the state of monuments on the lack of interest shown by the Cypriots in the preservation of the antiquities of their island,[38] the Legislative Council of Cyprus wrote an address to the High Commissioner, also reprinted by *The Times*:

> With respect of the Cyprus antiquities of universal fame, the council desires to remark that the Cypriotes will be for ever irreconcilable to

---

[34] Archives Nationales, Paris (hereafter AN), F17/2960, Mission de Camille Enlart en Chypre.

[35] Sharp, 'Exporting the Revolution', 204.

[36] On Enlart's place in debates about the origins of the Gothic see Anne-Cécile Celimon-Paul, 'Camille Enlart', in Philippe Sénéchal and Claire Barbillon (eds), *Dictionnaire critique des historiens de l'art actifs en France de la Révolution à la Première Guerre mondiale*", Institut National d'Histoire de l'Art Paris, (2009), http://www.inha.fr/spip. php?article2309 [accessed 27 January 2013].

[37] *Gazzetino* of Padua, 14 April 1901, translated by Jeffery and forwarded to the SPAB from Venice, 25 April 1900, SPAB Archives, 'Cyprus', repr. in Pilides, George Jeffery, II, 589-90.

[38] House of Commons Debate, 26 May 1902 (M. Chamberlain).

the despoliation thereof which has been carried on from the time of the English occupation to these days, for which the Cypriotes consider the Government to be chiefly responsible, because they under their very eyes, have suffered the glorious temples and tombs of the ancestors of the Cypriotes to be despoiled of their most precious objects. The Council is very glad to see that the Government has well perceived the very great interest which is taken by the Cypriotes in their antiquities, which, of course, is not unconnected with their noble descent; and the Council anxiously awaits the efficient measures that will be submitted for the purpose, which will be favoured by the Council with all its attention in the conviction that such measures, which passed by the Council, will, now that the feelings of the Cypriotes have been sufficiently understood, receive the necessary sanction as soon as possible.[39]

Over the following months, as voluntary groups in Britain took a number of measures to highlight the issue, a growing consensus developed in the major British newspapers that the government should do more to protect Cypriot monuments.[40] George Everett Jeffery, architect of St. George's Anglican Cathedral and College in Jerusalem, who had worked as an Inspector of Public Works in Cyprus in 1899-1900 and had assisted Enlart in Cyprus in 1901, was called back to a newly created post of Curator of Ancient Monuments.[41] One of his first acts was to record the danger posed to many prominent medieval buildings and the destruction of structures researched by Enlart. He also approached the SPAB, the National Trust, and other learned and voluntary bodies in Britain, which would eventually lead to collaboration over the next three decades.[42] Mobilizing the political connections of David Lindsay, heir to the Earl of Crawford and Balcarres, a first campaign resulted in the successful demise of plans to demolish Famagusta's medieval seawall to make way for a harbour and the railway.

Over the following years, the collaboration between Jeffery, Balcarres and the SPAB thwarted not only colonial and local vandalism, but also some

---

[39] 'Cyprus and its Antiquities', *The Times* (24 June 1902), 13.

[40] E.g., 'The Neglected Treasures of a British Crown Colony', *Illustrated London News* (hereafter ILN), 11 August 1934, 221; press clippings, SPAB Archives, 'Cyprus'; Sharp, 'Exporting the Revolution', 205.

[41] Despina Pilides, *George Jeffery: His Diaries and the Ancient Monuments of Cyprus*, 2 vols. (Lefkosia, 2009), 83. K. W. Schaar, M. Given, and G. Theocharous, *Under the Clock: Colonial Architecture and History in Cyprus, 1878–1960* (Nicosia, 1995).

[42] SPAB, *Annual Reports* from 1902 onwards; Pilides, *George Jeffery*, I and II.

foreign intervention, in particular a restoration funded by the French government in Famagusta that would have stripped Venetian features from a number of Lusignan buildings in an attempt to restore them to their state under the French dynasty.[43] Jeffery believed that 'the memorials of 100 years of Italian occupation of Cyprus should be religiously preserved and in no case sacrificed to French interests'.[44] Imbued with Ruskinian principles, Jeffery and the SPAB opposed all forms of stylistic restoration and tried to protect all historic remains rather than just those that could serve a particular artistic or nationalist school.

A general shift in attitudes within the government also took place between 1901, when Jeffery complained that 'nothing can be expected from them', and 1904, when Sir W. Heynes Smith, the High Commissioner for Cyprus, 'expressed approval of any scheme for enlisting' voluntary societies in Britain 'in the endeavour to preserve all that remains of the remarkable artistic past of Cyprus'.[45] An Antiquities Law was passed in 1905, which was primarily designed to regulate the excavation and export of archaeological objects, but which also enabled the classification of buildings as ancient monuments. Although it had stronger compulsory clauses than the ancient monuments legislation in Britain, it stopped short of religious buildings. The Gothic cathedrals in Famagusta and Nicosia, as well as many other Latin churches that had been converted to Orthodox churches or mosques, remained under the control of the Moslem Board of Turkish Commissioners for Charitable and Religious Purposes (Evcaf) or the Greek Orthodox bishop. There were also limits due to private ownership, which is well illustrated by the castle of Kolossi, the former headquarters of the Knights Hospitallers. The well-preserved fifteenth-century keep, containing numerous medieval carvings related to Hospitaller sculpture at Rhodes, was owned by the Anglo-Egyptian Allotment Company and used for storage. In 1909, Jeffery learned that the property was available for sale and the SPAB offered £400 for the castle, but was outbid by a local merchant who transformed the castle into a residence. Subsequently, the Venerable Order of St John became interested in this 'ancestral' home, and acquired a small share. Noticing the interest, the main owner sold off parts of the castle among the villagers to drive up the price in case the Order or the government were willing to buy it. As a result, it

[43] Sharp, 'Exporting the Revolution', 207; MAP 81/098/1, 'Ile de Chypre, Antiquités franques de Famagouste'; see also TNA, FO 370/1027, 'Preserving of French monuments by Government of Cyprus'.

[44] Jeffery to Thackery Turner, 16 May 1901, SPAB Archives, 'Cyprus'.

[45] Jeffery to Thackery Turner, 15 June 1901 and 21 Oct. 1904, SPAB Archives, 'Cyprus'.

took decades of negotiations before the Order and the government emerged as sole owners.[46]

In the midst of war in 1915, the SPAB expressed hopes that 'One of the effects of this otherwise disastrous War is that Cyprus has come entirely under the control of the British Government, with the result that the Curator of Ancient Monuments, Mr George Jeffery, will be in a better position to exercise his authority than when the country was under Turkish influence'.[47] Whether one sees the following years as a period of increasing preservation or of continuous vandalism and neglect is a question of perspective, however. The new status as a Crown colony did not bring with it an immediate shift towards the preservation of ancient monuments. Jeffery returned to the Island after a brief English interlude with a bigger salary, but still a very small budget at his disposal. In the early 1930s, Jean Ricard, the French Consul in Larnaca, repeatedly complained to Paris about the neglect of the 'Frankish antiquities' by the British authorities. Throughout his dispatches Ricard continually emphasized the need to improve France's reputation in the region, not least because of an ever greater Italian presence.[48] Given that 'the preservation of these moving vestiges is especially interesting for us, as they pay testament to the grandness of works conceived and executed by French masters',[49] the Consul deplored the lack of repairs, the disfiguration of ancient buildings by modern constructions, and the total abandon of Jeffery's small lapidary museum of Gothic remains. He was especially scornful about Jeffery ('a very old man of somewhat doubtful competence') and hoped that once he retired, better care would be taken to preserve the 'important artistic heritage given to generations of amateurs and scholars by the French dominance in Cyprus'.[50]

The French Foreign Office consulted Paul Deschamps, expert on Crusader architecture and intellectual heir of the recently deceased Camille Enlart, and René Dussaud, curator at the Louvre, about how to approach this diplomatically delicate matter. Both had recently curated the section on the Crusades for the 1931 Colonial Exhibition in Paris. Dussaud pleaded caution, pointing out that the recent tension between the British authorities and the Cypriot population meant that any intervention by the French authorities might not

---

[46]   Sharp, 'Exporting the Revolution', 208–10; CSA, SAI 1242/13/1; MOStJ, Sir Harry Luke Papers, 50/3 C.

[47]   SPAB, *Annual Report* (1915), 32.

[48]   See dispatches 1931–34, CADN, 345 PO1 Larnaca, Consulat et Agence Consulaire.

[49]   Jean Ricard to Président du Conseil, Ministre des Affaires Etrangères, 24 March 1932, Mediathèque de l'Architecture et du Patrimoine, Paris (hereafter MAP), 81/98/1, 'Île de Chypre'.

[50]   Ibid.

be seen for its 'purity of motives'. He assumed that Sir Ronald Storrs, formerly in charge of Palestine and now governor of the island, could surely not be aware of the problems, otherwise they would not have been ignored. He suggested getting a better idea of the situation by asking the archaeologist in charge of excavations near Famagusta, M. Schaeffer, to visit the medieval monuments and record their state of conservation. Schaeffer would then have the necessary authority to signal to the British government which measures were the most urgent to take.[51]

In his comments on the state of the 'monuments erected on the island of Cyprus by the Princes of French stock', Paul Deschamps likewise drew a much less negative picture than Ricard had done. Based on his visit to the island three years earlier, he was full of praise for Jeffery.[52] He also stated that the former cathedrals of Famagusta and Nicosia were in a relatively good state, even if only very modest sums were available. He conceded, however, that 'The English do not seem to exploit intensely the island's resources'.[53] For him this was clearly due to a lack of national interest:

> The English don't have the same immediate reasons to be interested
> in the medieval monuments erected in Cyprus as we do, because
> these monuments are not related to their past, but belong essentially
> to our national history and our national art.[54]

Like his colleague Dussaud, Deschamps was not sure how the British authorities would react to suggestions by foreigners about how to care for the island's ancient monuments. Despite these pleas for caution, the Ministry of Public Instruction in France eventually decided to offer the Cyprus government a considerable sum for the 'preservation and restoration of the French mediaeval monuments in the island'. Although it was coldly rebuffed, it had important consequences.[55] The fact that other European countries perceived a link between medieval remains and modern claims provided powerful ammunition for those who were campaigning for preservation in Cyprus and

---

[51] René Dussaud to Paul Léon (Directeur Général des Beaux Arts) c/c M. le Sous-Secretiare d'Etat des Beaux Arts, Paris, 5 July 1932, MAP 81/98/1 'Île de Chypre'.

[52] Paul Deschamps to Sous-Secretiare d'Etat des Beaux-Arts, 12 July 1932, MAP 81/98/1 'Île de Chypre'.

[53] Ibid.

[54] Ibid.

[55] Sir George Hill to Mogabgab, August 1934, TNA, CO 67 253/2, Doc. 80, quoted in Charlotte Roueché, 'The Prehistory of the Cyprus Department of Antiquities', *British School at Athens Studies*, viii, *MOSAIC: Festschrift for A. H. S. Megaw* (2001), 160.

in Britain.[56] The Colonial Office and the Cyprus Government were forced to react, as British, local, and international voices joined each other.[57] Time and again, the important monuments, 'initiated by our own Richard of the Lion Heart, developed by the French Lusignan Dynasty, and ended by a Venetian hegemony',[58] of which there were 'enough to fill two volumes of Dr. Enlart's great work, "L'Art Gothique et la Renaissance en Chypre"' were now described in the pages of major newspapers along with vociferous calls for the government—'apparently callous in this important matter'—to reconsider its 'negative attitude'. It was 'time that Great Britain, which has inherited this responsibility with the direct control of the Island, should play her part as Italy is doing in Rhodes and Tripoli, and France in Syria, Algeria, and Tunisia'.

Even more strongly than in Malta, one can observe how the international situation motivated preservation in Cyprus. In a confidential report to the Secretary of State for the Colonies, Sir George Hill, Director and Principal Librarian of the British Museum, warned that: 'In the shouldering of such a moral responsibility the Italian administration in Rhodes and the French in Syria offer examples which put the British in Cyprus to shame. The French and Italian governments understand the value in imponderable assets—such as a reputation for enlightenment—of a proper care for the historical monuments of the countries, which they have undertaken to govern'.[59] In the national press the same argument appeared repeatedly. Despite hard economic times, 'the loss of such priceless treasures of antiquity is likely in the long run to lead to a lack of prestige in the world of culture as irreplaceable as are the treasures themselves if allowed to founder'.[60] 'The national reputation for pietas', 'for a decent regard for the noble relics of the ancients, would suffer'.[61] Efforts were redoubled after the invasion of Abyssinia fuelled fears about the aggressiveness of Italian imperialism.[62] In 1933, a 'belated beginning' was thus made with the formation of a Cyprus Committee under the

---

[56] Roueché, 'Prehistory', 155-66.

[57] TNA, FCO 141/2475, 'Cyprus: measures for preservation of historic and pre-historic monuments in Cyprus'.

[58] Norman H. Baynes, William H. Buckler, W. D. Caroe, F. H. Marshall, John L. Myres, Steven Runciman, George Francis, and Harold Gibraltar, 'Antiquities of Cyprus', *The Times* (22 September 1933), 8.

[59] 'Report on the Condition of Antiquities in Cyprus', 9 May 1934, Cyprus State Archives, SAI 728/34, fol. 87.

[60] 'Antiquities of Cyprus', *The Times* (22 September 1933), 8.

[61] 'An Appeal for Cyprus', *The Times* (24 January 1935) (Leader).

[62] Roueché, 'Prehistory', 155-66.

chairmanship of Lord Mersey and with the approval of the Colonial Office and the government of the island. It raised awareness through the press, learned talks, and exhibitions, and started fundraising. The new Cyprus Monument Fund solicited donations from Britain to accomplish the 'very necessary work analogous to that accomplished years ago in Rhodes', where, as the Committee explained in its preliminary appeal, the Italian Government has ' "transformed a city of dirt and ruin into one of the sights of the East" '. The same lesson was drawn from Syria, where ' "a wise but lavish expenditure by the French yearly discovers, restores and preserves the famous relics of the past" '.[63]

The preservation of monuments in Cyprus thus draws attention to the importance of international competition between the French, British, and Italians in the Mediterranean. What, then, are we to make of the many assertions about the differences between French versus British attitudes to the Crusader sites as national heritage? Were the developing preservation policies only reactive rather than based on identification with these sites? Not quite. Those Britons who were not indifferent to monuments altogether showed incontestable interest in the 'English' past of the island. Jeffery strongly romanticized Richard I,[64] and, shortly after starting his post as Curator of Ancient Monuments, wrote to London to encourage more interest in the Latin past and to prevent the control of sites from being passed to a 'native committee'. The sites should be preserved and if possible be acquired 'by the representatives of the race to which they historically belong. In other words, I think that a little English interest of a solid proprietary kind would be a good thing in Cyprus', above all to establish the Englishness of the island against the anti-colonial nationalists' 'imaginary Homeric parentage'.[65] In the 1930s, this idea was taken up by the governor of Cyprus. Soliciting help from the Order of St John for the preservation of Kolossi in 1935, Sir Richmond Palmer suggested that 'the fact that the British Realm of the Order should take an active interest in Cyprus is an asset of very considerable value from an Imperial and National point of view, as cementing further connections of

---

[63] Cyprus Committee for the Preservation of Ancient and Medieval Monuments, *Cyprus. An Appeal to Preserve its Historic Antiquities* (s.d., s.p.), the passage was often reprinted in the later reports of the committee and in the press, e.g., 'The Antiquities of Cyprus. Work of Preservation', *The Times* (14 January 1936), 13.

[64] George Jeffery, *Cyprus under an English King in the Twelfth Century: The Adventures of Richard I and the Crowing of his Queen in the Island* (Nicosia, 1926).

[65] George Jeffery to Hugh Thackeray Turner, 6 January 1911, repr. in Pilides, *George Jeffery*, II, 402-3.

Figure 3. Stamp of Cyprus showing Kolossi Castle and King George VI, *c.* 1938. (Author's collection).

Cyprus with England which dates from the days of Richard I'.[66] During the same years, Kolossi also appeared on the Cypriote stamps (see Figure 3). Overall, however, such blatantly instrumentalist statements were relatively rare. Those people who cared for ancient buildings tended to campaign for monuments of all periods and regardless of their supposed national origin— if anything the Byzantine monuments were perhaps of greater concern to British scholars than the Latin ones.[67] When we place the competition over Cyprus's 'Crusader' buildings in relation to other Mediterranean areas, it also becomes apparent that a more pronounced difference between French and British attitudes concerned acquisition rather than symbolic appropriation. The French state made considerably greater efforts from the late nineteenth century to restore and acquire monuments associated with the 'national' past, regardless of who ruled the territories in which they were found, whether British or otherwise. France's ambassador to Constantinople acquired another monument associated with the Crusades, the Auberge de France in Rhodes, at a moment when control of the island passed from Ottoman to Italian hands, despite Italian, Greek, and Turkish protests against such interference.[68] This acquisition set a precedent for wider interventions after

66   Sir Richmond Palmer to Lord Scarborough, 1 January 1935, Cyprus State Archives (hereafter CSA), SAI 1242/13/1; see also, MOStJ, Sir Harry Luke Papers, 50/3 C.

67   E.g., Cyprus Committee for Preservation of Ancient and Medieval Monuments *Cyprus. An Appeal to Preserve its Historic Antiquities* (s.d, s.l).

68   CADN, 569PO1/16 Rhodes Vice Consulat, 'Auberge de France'.

1920, as the mandatory system of the League of Nations brought a whole range of older and arguably more significant Crusader sites under French control.

Syria: 'national heritage' reclaimed

French interest in the Crusader sites in Syria was long-standing, and had been fostered through a series of scientific missions during the nineteenth century.[69] Given their interventionist policies elsewhere, it is all the more interesting that, when given the Mandate over Syria, French officials underlined the need to be 'very indirect' in the establishment of a French Archaeological Institute and Antiquities Service. In order not to alienate the locals, it was argued, the Institute had to operate almost more indirectly than the French Antiquities Service in Egypt under British dominance.[70]

And yet within the next fifteen years, the most extensive intervention on a Crusader site was to take place, slowly but steadily pushed by the same group of scholars already encountered in Cyprus. Given his expertise in Crusader art on Cyprus, Enlart was invited in 1921 by the High Commissioner General Gouraud to conduct a survey of monuments in Syria and Lebanon that culminated in the publication of *Les Monuments des Croisés dans le Royaume de Jérusalem*, a 'last chapter of a vast inquiry that he began thirty years before on the expansion of mediaeval French art in foreign lands', and a prequel to his earlier work on Cyprus.[71]

After Enlart's sudden death in 1927, Paul Deschamps, a graduate of the École des Chartes and Enlart's assistant at the Museum for Comparative Sculpture in Paris, was simultaneously made his successor at the Trocadéro and in Syria.[72] Setting sail for the Levant ' "very anxiously", as his knowledge

---

[69] Jaroslav Folda, *Crusader Art in the Holy Land: From the Third Crusade to the Fall of Acre, 1187-1291* (Cambridge, 2005), 1–7; AN, F17/2936/A Mission de Louis Batissier en Orient, 1846.

[70] Note 'Sur la Creation d'un Institut Archéologique de Syrie', MAP, 81/98/3 'Syrie, Creation d'un Institut archéologique'. On the Antiquities Service see Pierre Fournié and Jean-Louis Riccioli, *La France et le Proche-Orient, 1916-1946* (Tournai, 1996), 138-68; Rolf Stucky, 'Henri Seyric—Engagierter Archäeologe und Verwalter des Antikendienstes während der Mandatszeit', in Charlotte Trümpler (ed.), *Das Grosse Spiel. Archäologie und Politik zur Zeit des Kolonialismus, 1860-1940* (Cologne, 2010).

[71] Trans. in Mayer Schapiro, Review of 'Les Monuments des Croisés', *The Art Bulletin*, xii (1930), 301-2.

[72] Jean Richard, 'Notice sur la vie et les travaux de Paul Deschamps, Membre de l'Académie', *Comptes-rendus des séances de l'Académie des inscriptions et belles-lettres*, cxxxv (1991).

of medieval military architecture was according to his own account "very modest"',[73] he subsequently turned himself into '"one of our last Crusaders"'.[74] A devout Catholic, he was inspired by a romantic vision of the period and rejected any criticism of the Crusaders.[75] During the Mandate, Deschamps laboured tirelessly for the French government to obtain the Crac des Chevaliers, arguing that this 'essentially French monument' and 'national heritage' needed to be rescued from the indigenous people who used it as a quarry to build houses and lived on the site with their herds.[76]

The French Foreign Office negotiated that the Alawite State would offer the Crac as a gift to the French State, subject to the sum of one million francs as indemnities for the expulsion of the indigenous inhabitants. The sum (plus an additional 2.2 million francs for restoration and maintenance) was initially approved,[77] but then suddenly withdrawn by a subsequent Minister of Finance because of the Depression. In their renewed campaign, Deschamps, the Fine Arts Administration, and the Foreign Office once again underlined not only the importance of the site as French national heritage and the threat posed to it by the indigenous population but also pointed out that failure to acquire it would give way to the possibility of 'the Knights of Malta—that is to say Italy', claiming the site.[78] Given the 'propagandistic value' of the site, the international rivalry argument proved successful and the Crac was acquired. The acquisition was accompanied by a vast publicity effort in France ranging from the Colonial Exhibition, the Colonial Museum, and the Museum of French Monuments, to radio shows, popular

[73] Quoted in Richard, 'Notice sur la vie', 342.

[74] Gustave Dupont-Ferrier quoted in Richard, 'Notice sur la vie', 345. See also *Remise à M. Paul Deschamps de son Epée d'Académicien, le 26 Octobre 1943 au Musée des Monuments Français*, AMN, O30 471 Paul Deschamps.

[75] As late as the 1970s, he replaced critical comments about the Crusaders in a preface to one of his books by ' . . .'. Richard, 'Notice sur la vie', 345.

[76] The expression '*patrimoine national*' is recurrent in the letters Deschamps wrote to the various government agencies involved in the negotiations and was taken up by the Administration des Beaux-Arts, MAP, 81/98/3, 'Syrie, Acquisition du Krak'.

[77] 'Project de loi ayant pour objet l'acquisition par l'Etat du Crac des Chevaliers apparte-nant a l'Etat des Alaouites (Syrie)', MAP, 81/98/3, 'Syrie, Acquisition du Krak'.

[78] Présidence du Conseil, Affaires Etrangères to Sous-Secretaire D'Etat des Beaux-Arts, 8 Dec 1932, MAP, 81/98/3, 'Syrie Aquisition du Krak'. For the details of the acquisition, CADN, 188PO/C/30-33 Damas (ambassade) and Archives des Affaires étrangères, La Courneuve, 50CPCOM/601 Correspondence Politique et Commercial E – Levant, Syrie Liban 1918-1940.

2. *Au moment des Croisades, nos aïeux ont occupé le pays Alaouïte. Il y subsiste des ruines imposantes de leurs forteresses. L'un des châteaux forts les mieux conservés est Qalaat el Hosn : le Krak des Chevaliers.*

Figure 4. Krak des Chevaliers. French postcard from the mandatory period with the caption 'During the Crusades, our ancestors occupied the Alawite land. Impressive ruins of their fortresses still exist. One of the best-preserved castles is the Qalaat el Hosn: the Krak des Chevaliers'. (Author's collection).

books, and reproduction on postcards and even chocolate advertisements (see Figure 4).[79]

The ensuing restoration, which removed the settlers, destroyed their habitation, and restored the site to its 'original' appearance, was extraordinary not only in its scale but also in its invasive nature, which was unusual for the period by international standards. It seems far more reminiscent of mid-nineteenth-century restorations than of the contemporary efforts in interwar France. Nineteenth-century 'stylistic restoration' had followed the idea of resurrecting an ideal state by removing not only later architectural additions from heritage sites but often also their current inhabitants. For instance, in the Roman amphitheatres in Nimes, Orange, or Arles, medieval houses built inside the arenas were removed. Under the influence of Ruskinian thinking, conservation theory had since changed to preserve all elements of a site as part of the historic record rather than privileging an idealized vision of one period. Although the Athens Charter codified these conservation principles as international standards in the interwar period, stylistic restoration remained widespread in a colonial context. The Antiquities Services in Syria, for

---

[79] On the international reception of the acquisition for instance, 'The Crusaders' Greatest Castle Ceded to France for Preservation', *ILN*, 20 October 1934, iv.

instance, similarly decided to demolish a Christian church to free the Roman temple of Baalbek and evacuated the entire population that had settled in the Bel temple of Palmyra.[80] Such thoroughgoing restorations were not limited to the French Empire. Across the border in the British Mandate, Jerusalem had just witnessed a similar stylistic restoration of its medieval city walls under the auspices of the Arts and Crafts designer C. R. Ashbee.[81]

Palestine: no dream come true

The treatment of the Crusades under the British Mandate in Palestine was, however, very different from France's outspoken reclaiming of sites as national heritage in Syria. Preparing the advent of British rule in Palestine, the British authorities issued a confidential D-notice in 1917 explicitly outlawing any reclaiming of the Crusaders in order not to alienate Muslim supporters:

> The attention of the Press is again drawn to the undesirability of publishing any article paragraph or picture suggesting that military operations against Turkey are in any sense a Holy War, a modern Crusade, or have anything whatever to do with religious questions. The British Empire is said to contain a hundred million Mohammedan subjects of the King and it is obviously mischievous to suggest that our quarrel with Turkey is one between Christianity and Islam.[82]

Within days, the satirical magazine *Punch* issued a dissident caricature entitled 'The Last Crusade', showing Richard Coeur de Lion overlooking Jerusalem suspiring 'My dream comes true'. A similar tension marked the official propaganda too. While allusions to the Crusades were downplayed in Palestine they were exploited for a Christian audience in Britain. Yet, while the conquest of Palestine was packaged as a Christian endeavour domestically, the Holy Sites were portrayed to have been liberated not so much from Muslim presence as from the German Kaiser.[83]

The contested nature of all Holy Sites in Jerusalem, and the Kaiser's self-fashioning as a Crusader during his Oriental Visit in 1898, were further

---

[80] Stucky, 'Henri Seyric'. On a much larger scale, the clearing of local inhabitants from these sites relates of course also to the much more coercive removal of Native Americans from US National Parks.

[81] Simon Goldhill, 'The Cotswolds in Jerusalem: Restoration and Empire', in Swenson and Mandler (eds), *From Plunder to Preservation*.

[82] Quoted in Eitan Bar-Yosef, 'The Last Crusade? British Propaganda and the Palestine Campaign, 1917-18', *Journal of Contemporary History*, xxvi (2001).

[83] Ibid.

reasons not to emphasize the Crusader theme through restoration or label-ling. Considerable efforts were made to erase the Kaiser's presence—for instance by bringing the bronze wreath Wilhelm II put on Saladin's tomb in Damascus to the Imperial War Museum in London,[84] or by removing commemorative plaques. The original sites, however, were approached with more caution. C. R. Ashbee, as town planner, transformed and restored Jerusalem right, left, and centre after he was brought there by the first military commander Sir Ronald Storrs, but no attempts were undertaken to emphasize the changes made to the Al-Aqsa Mosque during the Crusades. Crusader-period doorways from the Church of the Holy Sepulchre were taken down for restoration but never put back because of the different owners' quarrels over the prerogative of restoration.[85] The Crusader tombs destroyed in a fire in the nineteenth century were likewise never to be restored. While some sites built during the Crusades were researched, excavated, and restored as part of larger preservation policies, the restorations were not particularly promoted as a reclaiming of the Crusades.[86] Although there was no attempt to stake claims through the ostentatious restoration of Crusader sites, allusions to the Crusades were rarely far from the surface and returned in many guises. According to *Country Life*, the British High Commissioner's Residence, and the Palestine Archaeological Museum in Jerusalem, for instance, much resembled a 'Crusader Castle of Today'.[87]

The Crusades, heritage and empire

What broader questions are raised by these four snapshots for understanding the refashioning of the Crusades and the making of heritage in the imperial period more generally? First of all, across all sites and empires, a number of overarching trends can be observed. An initial phase, starting with the Napoleonic Egyptian campaign and enhanced by the 'defence' of the Holy Sites during the Crimean War, saw a growing interest in Crusader architecture everywhere in Europe. It was intertwined with debates about the origins of Gothic art. Scholars pondered whether the Gothic was engendered though the European encounter with Arab pointed arches during the Crusades, or

---

[84] Siberry, 'Images of the Crusades', 368.

[85] See Raymond Cohen, *Saving the Holy Sepulchre: How Rival Christians Came Together to Rescue their Holiest Shrine* (Oxford, 2008).

[86] Simon Goldhill, *Jerusalem: City of Longing* (Cambridge, MA, 2008) and personal communication.

[87] R. Fuchs and G. Herbert, 'Representing Mandatory Palestine', *Architectural History*, xliii (2000).

whether Arab art was derivative of European architecture.[88] With the colonization of the Mediterranean—the second phase—came a greater focus on preservation. Since the 1870s, preservation was seen increasingly as a marker of civilization, not just in the geographical context discussed here but also more broadly across Europe and the different empires. Given the increased competition between colonial powers, which was apparent in the constant references to each other's failures and achievements, all states saw it as necessary to preserve the monuments of the past to establish themselves as civilized ruling powers. Yet the establishment of policies (rather than piecemeal repairs) was much slower on the Mediterranean islands than in other parts of the empires, especially in India, Egypt, and Algeria. It was only during a third phase, started by the Italian restorations in Rhodes and brought to fruition by French restorations in Syria, that interest in Crusader sites surged, with a mutually enhancing effect on restorations across the region in all empires in the 1930s. It was at this moment too that the 'Crusader sites' and their preservation were increasingly integrated into the culture of metropolitan heritage through colonial exhibitions and museum displays, by which conscious attempts were made to 'bring' the empire 'home', to use Catherine Hall's phrase.

There was an overarching trend to think of the Crusades in national terms, and to efface older interpretations. In contrast to the Early Modern period, where the Crusaders were seen as a pan-European, Christian enterprise, distinct national claims were made from the 1830s onwards. Individual Crusaders became important heroes in various nation-building projects, made visible through new monumental displays such as the history paintings in Versailles or the statue of Richard I in Westminster.[89] At the same time, the Crusades became a template for modern imperialism. This was most noticeable in French imperial discourse. As early as the 1830s, the French historian Joseph-Francois Michaud started to identify Charles X's Algerian campaign with a fulfilment of the Crusades.[90] Subsequently, the Crusader period was used to provide the French empire with a *longue durée* and to claim continuity with 'the unique ability of the Franks to maintain a warm and fair relationship with their subjects'.[91] Less strongly, perhaps, the colonialist approach to the

---

[88] Nabila Oulebsir, *Les Usages du patrimoine: Monuments, Musées et politique coloniale en Algérie, 1830-1930* (Paris, 2004), 145.

[89] Ellenblum, *Crusader Castles*, 18–39.

[90] Ibid., 18–23.

[91] Ibid., 45. The continuity is most explicitly stressed in Exposition coloniale internationale de Paris 1931, Commissariat General, *Les Colonies et la vie française pendant huit siècles* (Paris, 1933).

Crusades could also be found among representatives of other nations and was applied in other regions of Europe's empires. British writers such as Claude Reigner Conder compared British rule in India to Crusader rule in positive terms.[92] These national-colonial narratives left little room for stylizing the Crusades and their sites as a European or a Christian heritage. A rare moment of an almost common European reclaiming occurred during the ceremonial entrance of the Allies into Jerusalem in 1917, but it was a Crusade against the Kaiser that was invoked rather than a war against Islam.[93]

More striking than the nationalization of the Crusader sites is perhaps the relative absence of anti-Muslim rhetoric. British and French preservationists certainly often complained about the danger posed to monuments by local inhabitants, but these laments were little different from their statements about ignorant locals and philistine contemporaries in France or Britain. The French or British usually portrayed each other as worse vandals than the Ottomans, Arabs, Greeks, and Maltese. How, then, did different imperialists deal with the fact that the complicated histories of appropriations and encounters were inscribed in the textures of the monuments themselves? Or, in other words, what do the restorations say about ideas of hybridity? Here again, it seems that more attention was paid to removing the traces of other European histories than of Arab or Ottoman additions, which were sometimes expunged but were also often left in place. Reasons for this varied. As some (especially French and Italian) scholars viewed Arab architecture as derivate of Gothic art, it did not stand in the way of seeing building as national in origin. Other preservationists did not like the later additions, but kept everything in place out of Ruskinian principles. On some occasions, however, later additions were also celebrated as symbols of an ancient and ongoing encounter between cultures,[94] almost eradicating the idea that both the Crusades and modern colonialism were built on war and conflict. For instance, following the restoration of the cathedral-mosque of Famagusta, conducted in collaboration between the Curator of Ancient Monuments and the Evcaf, Jeffery wrote:

> The new minaret at Famagusta may perhaps be regarded as onemore [sic] link in that series of monuments which recalls the amicable relations between Christians and Moslems before and during the earlier Crusades—Charlemagne and his friend Haroun er Rashid,

---

[92] Ellenblum, *Crusader Castles*, 47. The crusader theme also helped to foster German informal imperialism under Wilhelm II and became important for ideas about German *Lebensraum* in the European East.

[93] Bar-Yosef, 'The Last Crusade?'

[94] Exposition coloniale internationale de Paris 1931, Commissariat General, *Les Colonies et la vie française pendant huit siècles* (Paris, 1933).

> Frederick II in the Mosque of Omar, not forgetting the romance of
> Coeur de Lion and Salah e'Din, or the fact that in the Holy City of
> Jerusalem most of the more important shrines are still common to
> both religions as they have been ever since the era of the Hegira![95]

By looking deeper into the administrative archives on restoration work across several local contexts, rather than at the public portrayal of restoration, we find that the degree of intervention was heavily dependent on the importance given to maintaining good relations with either local or global Muslim populations for broader imperial policies. This rationale was at its most explicit in the absence of Crusader rhetoric in Jerusalem, but it was not limited to the city. The Italians, for instance, treated Ottoman architecture with more care in Tripoli than in Rhodes.[96] Hence, while the local meaning of certain sites was often erased in the national and colonial discourses addressed to metropolitan audiences, they were taken into account much more on the ground. Despite the similarities in national reinterpretations of the Crusades and the increasing entanglement of preservation policies within and across empires, there were thus considerable differences with regard to the actual treatment of individual sites in different local contexts.

What then, of differences between the imperial powers? For France, the supposed Frenchness of all the Crusader remains led to more state-sponsored efforts to show the influence of France's art in foreign lands as a means of legitimizing French colonial presence. A similar logic underpinned Italian rhetoric and drove restorations during the Fascist period (and arguably the German restoration of the castles of the Teutonic Order in East Prussia as well). By contrast, the link between restoration and national appropriation of the Crusades appears much weaker in British policies. Where there was preservation at all, it was not so much focused on 'English' Crusader monuments but encompassed all kinds of monuments.

There could be several reasons for these differences. A first is aesthetic: whereas the French heritage institutions involved in the restorations were still influenced by Viollet-le-Duc, who emphasized restoration and purity of style, many of the English preservationists were influenced by Ruskinian appreciation of 'the value of age' and the respect of different periods. A second reason

---

[95]   Report by George Jeffery on 'Famagusta, Cyprus, The Great Mosque', 1934, CSA, SAI/ 992/34.

[96]   On Tripoli and Rhodes see Mia Fuller, *Moderns Abroad*, chapters 1-3. A notable absence of German interest in Crusader sites in the interwar period can perhaps also be explained by a wish not to endanger Germany's position in the region. On the decline of interest in Crusader sites see Hans Eberhard Mayer, *Bibliographie zur Geschichte der Kreuzzuege* (Hanover, 1960).

could be more instrumental: while the argument of a 'return' of 'previously colonised' territories served French and Italian colonial ambitions in the Mediterranean (and German expansion in Eastern Europe), it was of little use to the British. The French and Italians of course used the same logic about reclaiming the territories of the Roman Empire. None of this served a purpose in the British Empire. The only major overlap between the Roman and the British Empires was England,[97] and Richard Coeur de Lion had sold off Cyprus and failed to conquer Jerusalem. For the British Empire as a whole, and especially for the Jewel in its Crown, a discourse about guardianship, based on the respect of all monuments or all religions, which supposedly differentiated British from indigenous rule, was more potent as a tool of indirect rule than the reclaiming of national sites.[98] It could be argued that the principles developed in India were then translated to other colonial contexts.

Can we therefore postulate a fundamental difference between British and other imperial preservation policies? In some ways, a better understanding of different areas of European empires is necessary to answer this question. Judging from the comparisons now available it appears that the treatment of the Crusader sites is only partially representative of imperial heritage politics more generally. The picture gets more complicated when we broaden our view. Not all of French colonialism was built on national 'reclaiming'. Although the money spent on the Crac in Syria was exceptional, most projects by the Antiquities Service in Syria focused on other periods. In the Far East, the civilizing nature of preservation was also much more heavily emphasized. Likewise, not all British preservation policies were based on a universal understanding of heritage. In particular, if we shift our gaze from government-driven policies and the action of elite groups like the SPAB to more popular religious and archaeological movements, reclaiming of heritage (and territories) because they 'are ours' and always 'were ours' can be found. The broad popular interest in Egypt, for example, was largely based on the idea that Egypt was British because it was the cradle of biblical civilization that had found its direct descendants in Protestant Britain.[99] In some ways it was unnecessary to invoke the Crusades in Jerusalem, as British claims to the

---

[97] Mary Beard, 'Officers and Gentlemen, Roman Britain and the British Empire', in Swenson and Mandler (eds), *From Plunder to Preservation*, 49–61.

[98] See Swenson, 'Heritage of Empire', 12–14.

[99] See David Gange and Michael Ledger-Lomas (eds), *Cities of God: Archaeology and the Bible in Nineteenth-century Britain* (Cambridge, 2013); David Gange, 'Unholy Water: Archaeology, the Bible, and the First Aswan Dam', in Swenson and Mandler (eds), *From Plunder to Preservation*.

Holy City were much more widely underpinned by the Archbishop of York's idea that 'Palestine is ours' as a biblical heritage.

Generalizing statements about whether preservation was primarily underpinned by ideas of localism, nationalism, or universalism get even blurrier if we look at the actions of some of the heritage-makers that we observed caring for Crusader heritages in other contexts. While we only saw fierce competition between European powers when it came to restoration or reclaiming, the same individuals co-operated across borders to save 'monuments of universal interest' in Europe and collaborated on rescuing Arab or Ottoman antiquities in Egypt or Turkey.[100] Although this language of universal heritage was hardly mobilized for the 'Crusader sites', there was nevertheless much collaboration and even friendship between scholars and preservationists of different nationalities. The different colonial governments also aided scholarly relations. 'A very good friendship owing to the similarities of our tastes', for instance, connected Jeffery and Enlart after the High Commissioner of Cyprus had first asked Jeffery to assist Enlart with his work in Cyprus, fostered through common work setting up the lapidary museum in Nicosia, and visits and correspondences over the years until Enlart's death.[101] Here, as in other areas of preservation and scholarship, fierce international competition was accompanied by strong international collaboration.[102] Preservationists often tactically used foreign 'superiority' to convince people in their own governments unwilling to provide the necessary funding and infrastructure for preservation. There might even be some evidence that complaints in the foreign press about national neglect were deliberately created in order to provide material to cite.[103]

The history of the preservation of Crusader sites thus enriches what we know about the national and colonial appropriation of the Crusades from historiographic sources, revealing that uses on the ground were often different from the narratives created for domestic audiences. This also helps us understand more general mechanisms in the history of heritage. The

---

[100] SPAB Archives, 'Egypt' and 'Ottoman Antiquities'; Swenson, *The Rise of Heritage*, ch. 5; Donald Malcom Reid, *Whose Pharaohs? Archaeology, Museums and Egyptian National Identity from Napoleon to World War I* (Berkeley, CA, 2002).

[101] George Jeffery, 'Autobiographical Notes' (1920), in Pilides (ed.), *George Jeffery*, I, 83; George Jeffery to Secretary of the SPAB, 24 June 1901, in Pilides (ed.), George Jeffery, II, 596-7. On government assistance to French scholars, AN, F17/2960, Mission de Camille Enlart en Chypre; Heiniker-Heaton (C.S.) to Consul of France, 25 January 1933, CSA, SAI 431/33.

[102] For other examples see Swenson, *Rise of Heritage.*

[103] Pilides, *George Jeffery*, I, 20-1.

examples discussed here show how much the preservation of each individual site was intertwined with the preservation of other sites across national and imperial boundaries. They also draw attention to the dense personal connections that underpinned these entanglements. At the same time, the history of the Crusader sites emphasizes the importance of local context to understand how co-existing and often contradictory notions of heritage were formulated and used. Their history is a case in point for seeing how the nationalization of heritage involves not just the construction of a national heritage but also the effacing of other legacies both above and below the scale of the nation. Yet these erasures were never total or absolute. Personal records and archives of the different colonial bureaucracies reveal that interpretative frameworks were much less consistent than the confident tone of many publications or exhibitions would have us believe. There was rarely a straight progression or replacement of interpretations. Rather, the case studies suggest that a multiplicity of meanings continued to exist for different (and sometimes the same) actors.

In his study on Crusader castles and modern histories, Ronnie Ellenblum concluded that modern categories such as 'colonialism' are often unhelpful for understanding the complex interactions in the period of the Crusades themselves. Paradoxically, the same can be said for the very period that engendered these categories. The preservation of 'Crusader sites' was certainly driven by national and colonial agendas, and it is necessary to understand these agendas. However, these were only some of the complex motives and affective relations which should be unearthed if we want to gain a better understanding of what drove the making of heritage in the modern world.

The Inheritance of Empire and the Ruins of Rome in French Colonial Algeria

Caroline Ford

In 1912 Albert Ballu, chief architect of the Service des Monuments Historiques de L'Algérie, described the 'triple task' of the Service, which had been established in 1880—fifty years after the beginning of France's conquest of Algeria—as that of not only excavating the 'secrets' that the ground contained, but also of 'making them presentable to the public' and of 'preserving them from destruction.'[1] France was not alone in embarking on this archaeological project that sought to explore an antique and more particularly a Roman past in the nineteenth and early twentieth century, but Algeria came to occupy a special place in the French historical imagination.[2]

Archaeologists and architects had early on accompanied the French military on its campaigns in Algeria, and the work undertaken by them was at first the result of initiatives launched by specific individuals, who included Amable Ravoisié, Charles Texier, and Léon Rénier. These early forays paved the way for a more coordinated, state-sponsored effort to unearth the buried vestiges of Algeria's past by those who were formally trained in the science of archaeology and who were employed first by the Service des Monuments Historiques de l'Algérie and then by the Service des Antiquités de l'Algérie, which was established in 1923. Stéphane Gsell, who became, successively, inspector of Algerian antiquities, director of the Museum of Algerian Antiquities and Muslim Art in Alger, and professor of North African history at the Collège de France, not only articulated the parameters of archaeological excavation in terms of method, but he also drew up a precise list of historical monuments and sites that deserved particular attention.[3]

---

[1] Albert Ballu, 'Les Monuments historiques de l'Algérie,' *Revue Africaine*, 56 (1912), 372.

[2] Gábor Klaniczay, Michael Werner, and Ottó Geiser, *Multiple Antiquities, Multiple Modernities: Ancient Histories in Nineteenth-Century European Culture* (Frankfurt, 2011) and Catherine Edwards, *Roman Presences: Receptions of Rome in European Culture, 1789-1945* (Cambridge, 1999).

[3] Stéphane Gsell, *Instructions pour la conduite des fouilles archéologiques en Algérie* (Alger, 1901).

They included Roman temples, baths, churches, and monumental arches as well as mosques and public markets.

French archaeologists embarked on their work in Algeria (and later in Morocco and Tunisia), and in other parts of France's ever expanding empire during the course of the nineteenth century. In 1863, for example, the year that France established a French protectorate in Cambodia, the explorer Henri Mouhot created a sensation when he published one of the earliest descriptions of the ancient Khmer site of Angkor Wat and its temple complex for a European audience.[4] Several years later Louis Delaporte visited the site as a member of the French Mekong Expedition (1866-68) and published his impressions in 1880 in *Voyage au Cambodge, l'architecture khmer*. Archaeological research and restoration was at the heart of the mission of the Ecole Française d'Extrème Orient, and in 1907 the Ecole was charged with the restoration of Angkor Wat. What made the French archaeological forays in Algeria unique, however, was their focus first on Algeria's Roman and Christian antiquities, which came to be appropriated as both a French and Mediterranean *patrimoine*, and which in turn shaped the identity of the growing settler population, before they later turned their attention to a *patrimoine mauresque*.

The French were not alone among Europeans in their search for the physical vestiges of the past on soil that they eventually seized, dominated, or colonized. Sir Alexander Cunningham established the Archaeological Survey of India in 1861, for example, under the British Colonial Administration, and its purview ultimately became all of British India as well as Burma and Afghanistan. While Germany only acquired colonies after German unification in 1871 and did not keep them for very long, Germans nonetheless continued to engage in a variety of archaeological expeditions throughout the world. Moreover, the French were not alone in North Africa. Later, the conquest of Libya by Italy under Benito Mussolini was accompanied by archaeological missions that were guided by the ideology of 'Romanità', which appeared to justify Italy's conquest. Even later in the twentieth century, during the years of Salazar's dictatorship in Portugal (1932-1968) the Portuguese state undertook a number of archaeological excavations in Angola, Mozambique, and Timor in order to acquire a better understanding of the colonies that they possessed and to showcase the artefacts that were excavated back in Portugal.[5]

---

[4] Henri Mouhot, *Voyage dans les royaumes de Siam, de Cambodge, de Laous, et autres parties centrales de l'Indochine* (Paris, 1868).

[5] Tapati Guha-Thakura, *Monuments, Objects, Histories: Institutions of Art in Colonial and Post-Colonial India* (New York, 2004); Suzanne Marchand, *German Orientalism in the*

In recent years both historians and art historians have become increasingly interested in the relationship between European colonial expansion, collecting, and historical preservation in the non-European world. Two of the most impressive recent examples include *German Orientalism in the Age of Empire* by Suzanne Marchand, and Nabila Oulebsir's comprehensive and path-breaking *Les usages du patrimoine*.[6] Much of this historiography has focused on the classification and display of artefacts, the creation of new ethnographic museums in Europe, and on questions of custodianship, which are reflected in the provocative titles of two recent volumes of essays edited by James Cuno, *Whose Museums?* and *Whose Culture?*[7] This essay explores how archaeology in Algeria and the historical narratives that it produced became, in the words of Claire Lyons and John Papadopoulos, 'enmeshed with colonialism, not only in the subject of its investigations and methods of practice but also in the visual, cultural and national representations it engenders'.[8] I will not, however, be concerned with the excavation and collection of so-called 'indigenous' cultural or ethnographic artefacts for museums in Europe. This is a subject that has been fruitfully explored by Nicholas Thomas, Glenn Penny, Annie Coombes, and Nélia Dias in their work on ethnographic museums in Germany, Britain, and France.[9]

Age of Empire: Religion, Race and Scholarship (Cambridge, 2009); Stefan Altekamp, 'Italian Colonial Archeology in Libya, 1912-41' in M. L. Galaty and C. Watkinson (eds), *Archeology under Dictatorship* (New York, 2004), 55-72; and Massimiliano Munzi, 'Italian Archeology in Libya: Romanità to Decolonization of the Past' in Galaty and Watkinson (eds), *Archeology*, 73-101; Mia Fuller, *Moderns Abroad: Architecture, Cities and Italian Imperialism* (New York, 2007), 1-3, 40-1.

[6] Marchand, *German Orientalism*; Nabila Oulebsir, *Les usages du patrimoine: monuments, musées et politique coloniale en Algérie* (Paris, 2004).

[7] James Cuno, *Whose Museums?: Art Museums and the Public Trust* (Princeton, 2006) and James Cuno, *Whose Culture?: The Promise of Museums and the Debate over Antiquities* (Princeton, 2009). For recent discussions of the status of these artefacts and their display in new museums in France see Caroline Ford, 'Museums after Empire in Metropolitan and Overseas France', Contemporary Issues in Historical Perspective, *Journal of Modern History*, 82:3 (September 2010), 625-61.

[8] Claire L. Lyons and John K. Papadopoulos, 'Archeology and Colonialism', in Claire L. Lyons and John K. Papadopoulos, *The Archeology of Colonialism* (Los Angeles, 2002), 2.

[9] Nicholas Thomas, *Entangled Objects: Exchange, Material Culture, and Colonialism in the Pacific* (Cambridge, MA, 1991); Glenn Penny, *Objects of Culture: Ethnology and Ethnographic Museums in Imperial Germany* (2002); Annie Coombes, *Reinventing Africa: Museums, Material Culture, and Popular Culture in Victorian and Edwardian England* (New Haven, 1994); and Nélia Dias, *Le musée ethnographique de Trocadéro, 1878-1908: anthropologie et muséologie en France* (Paris, 1991).

I examine how 'heritage'—or to use the French term *patrimoine*—came to be articulated in the specific context of French colonial Algeria and how it came to be deployed in ways that differed from other parts of France's far-flung empire, by focusing principally on the role of archaeological research and excavation, which linked Rome's ancient past with France's colonial present from the 1880s to the beginnings of decolonization. I will also examine how this research came to be disseminated and popularized by archaeologists, historians, and novelists, while underlining the key role that mass tourism and colonial exhibitions played in linking metropolitan France to what came to be seen as its rightful inheritance in North Africa.

Defining *patrimoine* in metropolitan France and colonial Algeria

Fascination with ruins and empires had, of course, a long history in France, if not in Europe as a whole. They were intimately associated with the cultural current of Romanticism from the late eighteenth century onward, as the popularity of Constantin-François Volney's *Ruins, or Meditations on the Revolutions of Empires*, first published in 1791, attests.[10] He developed an interest in the eastern Mediterranean and the Middle East following a journey to the Ottoman Empire, Syria, and Egypt in the 1780s, where he embarked on the study of Arabic, sparking a new interest in the area, as Napoleon's Egyptian campaign came to affirm. Indeed, French initiatives to preserve a historical heritage on the other side of the Mediterranean began during Napoleon's expedition to Egypt, after which the Louvre and the public spaces of Paris were filled with objects from his Egyptian campaign in the late eighteenth century. As Astrid Swenson argues in this volume, the British and French Empires also came to vie with one another to reclaim the sites built by European Crusaders and their successors between 1798 and 1840.

A word must be said about the meaning of heritage or *patrimoine* and about the history of historical conservation in the French context. *Patrimoine* is derived from the Latin term *patrimonium*. Emile Littré's *Dictionnaire de la Langue Française* of 1859, which is the French equivalent of the British lexicographer James Murray's *Oxford English Dictionary*, defines it as *un bien d'héritage suivant la loi des pères et des mères à leurs enfants*. It is thus defined in material and juridical terms and linked to an ancestral inheritance. As it came to be articulated over time, only those monuments or objects that transmitted a shared tradition and recalled a common past—and which were privileged or venerated as a result—would be considered as

---

[10] By 1821 the book was in its 7th edition. Volney, *Les ruines, ou méditations sur les révolutions des empires*, 7th edn (Paris, 1821). Also see Roland Mortier, *La poétique des ruines en France: ses origines, ses variations de la Renaissance à Victor Hugo* (Geneva, 1974).

such.[11] As Dominique Poulot and the authors associated with Pierre Nora's seven volume *Les lieux de mémoire* have suggested, the French conception of heritage or *patrimoine* has been a work in progress since the French Revolution.[12] France's earliest defence of its *patrimoine* has long been associated with abbé Grégoire's call to protect the nation's pre-revolutionary monuments and religious objects from vandalism during the French Revolution, a call that laid the groundwork for the creation of France's Musée National des Monuments Français in 1795. This museum confined itself early on to the project of historical conservation within the borders of metropolitan France. While André Malraux, France's first Minister of Culture, attempted to broaden the definition of *patrimoine* soon after France's Ministry of Culture was created in 1960, understandings of the term have been intimately bound up with historical 'monuments', and this association was eventually extended to 'natural monuments' on French soil.[13] Indeed, when legislation was passed to conserve and preserve natural landscapes, they were conceived of in terms of 'monuments' by the laws of 21 April 1906 and more especially by that of 2 May 1930, which provided for the conservation of natural monuments and sites, which had an artistic, historical, scientific, legendary, or picturesque interest. Moreover, the French brought this notion of *patrimoine*, which centred on venerated objects and historical monuments, to Algeria in the 1840s when architects, who included Amable Ravoisié and Charles Texier, prepared inventories of various archaeological sites. The French idea of *patrimoine* did not correspond, according to Nabila Oulebsir, to Islamic tradition governing heritage, the closest Arab translation of which was the term 'turâth', which embraced the notion of heritage that was as much spiritual as material, and one in which texts and their transmission had a privileged place.[14]

---

[11] This view was articulated early on by the Viennese art historian Aloïs Riegl, a member of the Royal Central Commission for Researching and Preserving Monuments and author of a work that was to have a considerable impact on the field of historical preservation, *Der Moderne Denkmalkultus, sein Wesen, seine Entstehung* (Vienna, 1903). Dominque Poulot, among others, believes that this conception of heritage is a Western or European phenomenon, which was then exported to other parts of the globe, though this claim is open to question: Dominique Poulot, *Une histoire du patrimoine en occident* (Paris, 2006).

[12] Dominique Poulot, *Musée, monument, patrimoine, 1789-1815* (Paris, 1997); Dominique Poulot, *Patrimoine et musée: l'Institution de la culture*, 4th edn (Paris, 2007); Pierre Nora, (ed.), *Les lieux de mémoire*, 7 vols (Paris, 1984-92).

[13] Herman Lebovics, *Mona Lisa's Escort: André Malraux and the Reinvention of French Culture* (Ithaca, NY, 1999).

[14] Oulebsir, *Les usages du patrimoine*, 14.

Legislation governing the preservation of historical monuments and the protection of a national *patrimoine* was passed slowly during the course of the nineteenth century in metropolitan France. In May 1840 the liberal Catholic Charles de Montalembert argued before the Chamber of Peers that the government should classify historical monuments as having a '*utilité public*' and that they should be subject to expropriation by the state. A ministerial circular of 14 August 1876 called for the publication of a general inventory of '*richesses d'art de la France*'. This circular prompted the creation of a departmental commission in Alger charged with making an inventory there.[15] It wcas at this moment that the Académie de l'Instruction Publique et des Beaux-Arts urged that the Ministry of Public Instruction and Beaux-Arts apply heritage legislation to Algeria that would protect the colony's ancient ruins. The ministry immediately pleaded a lack of financial resources, even though the Chamber of Deputies began to discuss the passage of a law regarding the conservation of historical monuments in France, with special provisions for Algeria and France's protectorates, in June of 1886.

On 30 March 1887 the Chamber passed a law on the conservation of monuments and art objects that had a historical and artistic interest. Article 16 of the legislation made the law applicable to Algeria and to France's protectorates. Once the law was passed, the archaeological service commission as well as the Service des Monuments Historiques de l'Algérie selected very specific sites for classification. They included the palace of Khaznadji and Dar es-Souf, several mosques and minarets, and the triumphal arch at Lambaesis. Although they represented a mix of Roman and Muslim sites, excavations associated with the Roman cities of Tébessa, Lambaesis, and Timgad were privileged from the start, and their excavation began early on. This was no accident. Each of these cities had been the home of the Roman Empire's third legion, whose own history was intimately bound up with that of Africa's Roman past. Tébessa became an important commercial entrepot for the Romans, while Lambaesis became a military centre. Timgad was a thriving city throughout the time of the Roman Empire, and although it was ultimately pillaged by the Berbers, much of the city remained intact. For this reason it became the Service des Monuments' first priority.[16]

Of the three Roman cities, Timgad, which came to be known as 'Algeria's Pompei,' received the greatest attention. What made it unique, according to Albert Ballu, chief architect of the Service des Monuments Historiques, was that much of the city was still preserved, unlike many Roman ruins scattered across the Mediterranean in Italy, Austria, Turkey, and Asia Minor. The

[15] Oulebsir, *Les usages du patrimoine*, 218.
[16] Ibid., 200-16.

ruined city was the subject of discussion among the French military soon after the conquest of Algeria. Curiously, those deported to Algeria during the 1848 revolution in metropolitan France provided labour for the beginnings of archaeological excavations in 1852. But it was only in the 1880s that the site was systematically excavated. By 1892 onwards it had become a stop for government ministers from the metropole, including Léon Bourgeois, then minister of Education and Beaux-Arts, and Jules Ferry.

From the beginning of the twentieth century the restoration and excavation work undertaken by the Service des Monuments extended to the three administrative departments of Algeria: Alger, Oran, and Constantine. In the department of Alger, sites included Cherchell and Tigzirt, but it was in the Constantine that some of the most extensive work was undertaken. In addition to Timgad, Djemila and Lambaesis became important new foci of interest (and all three are currently classified as World Heritage Sites by UNESCO). Many of the directives pertaining to these sites originated in Paris, where René Cagnat of the Institut de France and Maurice Besnier of the Ecole Française de Rome, collaborated with Albert Ballu. From 1906 onward Ballu presented a general report to the Governor General of Algeria on the the progress of various excavations and restoration projects, which were then diffused in the metropole in the *Bulletin Officiel de la République Française.* The ruins of Rome in Algeria ultimately attracted a broader public in this period, when many sites, such as Timgad or Djemila, finally became easily accessible to the French travellers, and some of the sites turned into important tourist destinations.[17]

On 31 December 1913 the Chamber of Deputies passed a second law on historic monuments, which was designed to restrict the rights of individual property owners on whose land sites were identified as having a scientific or historical interest, and that law too was soon applied to Algeria. However, Eugène Albertini, who later became inspector general of antiquities in Algeria, questioned its utility in an Algerian context, as so much of the colony's territory was under the control of the French state. In metropolitan France the legislation was intended for medieval houses and châteaux of the Renaissance, whereas in Algeria it would apply principally to abandoned ruins next to remote villages or *bleds.* Architects, scholars, and curators in Algeria were particularly concerned about Roman antiquities, and their voices were eventually heard in metropolitan France, as evidenced by a decree issued by the Governor General on 16 June 1923 regarding the creation

---

[17] Arnaud Berthonnet, 'Le tourisme en Algérie (de 1880 aux années 1940): Une histoire à écrire', *Revue du tourisme,* (mai 2006), 1-16.

of a Direction des Antiquités whose head would be chosen by the former students of the Ecole Française de Rome and the Ecole Française d'Athènes.

The restoration of 'l'Afrique latine'

While a great number of archaeologists and curators took part in the organized effort to excavate and restore the Roman ruins of Algeria, several figures, most particularly archaeologists, novelists, and historians, were responsible for popularizing these sites. Three of them played a central role in bringing North Africa's Roman heritage alive for a broader French public. They were the archaeologist Stéphane Gsell (1864-1932), the novelist Louis Bertrand (1866-1941) and the historian Fernand Braudel (1902-1982). All of them first came to Algeria as young men in their twenties. All of them were employed first as teachers, and their early encounter with North Africa came to profoundly shape their subsequent work.

Stéphane Gsell was one of the most influential archaeologists of his generation, and he was captivated almost immediately by Rome's rich legacy in Algeria. He was born into a family of artists and grew up in Paris, where he graduated from the Ecole Normale Supérieure. He spent several years at the Ecole Française de Rome before arriving in Algeria in 1890 as a teacher of archaeology at the Ecole Supérieure des Lettres at the age of 26. He immediately participated in an archaeological dig in the ruined Roman coastal city of Tipasa, and was later appointed Inspecteur des Antiquités de l'Algérie. In 1912 he returned to the metropole to take up a chair at the Collège de France and was later appointed inspector general of Algeria's museums.

Gsell wrote a guide to archaeological excavation in his *Chronique d'archéologie africaine,* and he published two important works that brought archaeological excavation in North Africa to the public's attention. His *Monuments antiques de l'Algérie* (1901) systematically described the colony's Roman theatres, baths, temples, and triumphal arches, while his *Atlas archéologique de l'Algérie* (1911) provided a detailed map of all Roman sites in the colony. Finally, between 1913 and 1927 he published his 8 volume *Histoire ancienne de l'Afrique du Nord* which covered its history to the end of the Roman Empire.[18] His writings were not, however, confined to scholarly publications. He also wrote for a more popular audience. In 1896, wishing to capitalize on the growing number of tourists in Algeria, the Alger publisher A. Jourdan put out a series of books on the history of Algeria and on the Arab and Kabyle languages. Gsell participated in the series and penned his

---

[18] Also see Gsell's *L'Algérie dans l'antiquité* (Alger, 1901) and *Instructions pour la conduites fouilles archéologiques en Algérie* (Alger, 1901).

Guide archéologique des environs d'Alger (Cherchel, Tipasa, tombeau de la chrétienne).[19] In his preface, he wrote that 'this little book has no scientific pretension. Responding to a desire which has been expressed to me more than once, it is addressed to tourists who, passing from Cherchel to Tipasa, will wish to have some information on these two localities' past, as well as brief explanations of their ruins and their works of art.'[20] In the same collection he published a revised edition of *L'Algerie dans l'antiquité,* which had been part of a set of brochures edited for the Gouvernement Général de l'Algérie on the occasion of the Exposition Universelle, which was held in Paris from April to November 1900. The work provided an overview of the history of Algeria from the Stone Age to the end of the Roman empire and the Arab invasions of the seventh century. He described North Africa as a 'veritable island—Island of the West, the Arabs say, bordered by the waves of the Atlantic and the Mediterranean and by a desert that has been called the sea of sand.'[21] In claiming the region for the West, he remarked that those who inhabited it before the Arab invasions, the Berbers, bore a striking resemblance to the populations of Spain, Italy, the south of France, Corsica, and Sardinia: 'It is the same dark race, generally small in height, energetic, and dynamic. One also finds in Algeria, as in Morocco, many blonds of a more or less pure type; it is not impossible that their ancestors came from regions to the north.'[22]

In describing the establishment of the Roman Empire and the first Roman armies of occupation, Gsell asserted that most of the troops were born on the other side of the Mediterranean and that under the early emperors of Algeria there were many Gauls.[23] He devoted a chapter to 'the prosperity of Algeria under Roman domination' and contended that it was indisputable that the conquest had 'beneficial effects'.[24] This was a period that saw rapid urbanization and the emergence of towns possessing great wealth, including Lambaesis and Timgad, which left ruins that attested to their prosperity. Gsell argued that it was largely due to a period of peace that the conquest ushered in that Algeria became 'the richest agricultural country in the West', and he cited the density of its population and high life-expectancy as evidence of this prosperity.[25] Indeed, Gsell painted a rosy portrait of the conquest,

---

[19] Gsell, *Guide archéologique* (Alger, 1896).

[20] Ibid., 7.

[21] Gsell, *L'Algérie dans l'antiquité* (Alger, 1903), 18.

[22] Ibid., 19.

[23] Ibid., 49.

[24] Ibid., 59.

[25] Ibid., 61.

arguing that it was relatively peaceful and that this resulted in a broad acceptance of Roman civilization and institutions:

> Berber towns, the inhabitants of the plains, accepted the Latin conquest without revolt. No obstacle seemed to prevent a sincere and durable accord: the ancients did not experience racial hatred; the pagans ignored religious intolerance. Rome knew [how] to respect municipal constitutions, laws, customs, and beliefs. It assured or did its best to assure the peace.[26]

According to Gsell, Rome favoured cultural assimilation without using force and made Latin the official language of the land.

In describing the end of the Roman Empire in Algeria, Gsell admitted that some parts of the region did not accept Roman rule as willingly as others, and he pointed to the serious revolts that occurred between 253 and 260 AD. For him, the evidence of these areas' refusal to embrace Roman culture could be measured in the relative lack of any trace of Roman monuments or inscriptions, as in the Edough, the mountains of El Milia, the Aurès, greater Kabylia, the Atlas, and the Ouarsenis.[27] Citing the French historian of Rome, Fustel de Coulanges, who noted that the Gauls (*les gaulois*) in France had enough intelligence to understand that [Roman] civilization was worth more than barbarism, Gsell contended that many Africans, in contrast, failed to understand this, preferring 'idleness and misery to work and living comfortably'.[28] He described the economic, religious, and military foundations of Rome's decline in Algeria, but for Gsell it was the invasions of the Vandals, and above all of the Arabs that brought this long period of Roman rule and prosperity to an end. Gsell described how the indigenous population was forced to convert to Islam in 717, and how the Arab language soon replaced any use of Latin, although vestiges of it could later be found in certain Berber dialects. Indeed, Gsell noted that it was only among the Berbers that traces of the Roman past survived in terms of local customs and artistic expression: 'the peasants in some cantons in the Aurès and greater Kabyle claim to descend from the *Roumis* or Romans'.[29] For Gsell their surviving artefacts were among the rare

---

[26] Gsell, L'Algérie dans l'antiquité (Alger, 1903), 75.

[27] Ibid., 98.

[28] Ibid.

[29] Ibid., 142. 'Rumi' or 'roumi' was a term that was historically used by Berbers and Arabs to describe Europeans, and it is derived from the Arabic *rum*, that referred to land dominated by Rome. The alleged and ostensible identification of the Berbers with the Romans appears to contradict Gsell's assertion forty pages earlier regarding the rare traces of Rome in Berber mountainous outposts.

vestiges of what he described as the 'great shipwreck' caused by the Arab invasions: the territory over which the West and the Orient had long fought and where Latin Christianity was formed 'belonged from now on completely to the Orient; Mediterranean unity ceased to exist.'[30] For Gsell, after this, hardly anything was left of Roman civilization but 'immense ruins and the memory of the power of the "roumis" '.[31]

Gsell's writing was steeped in nostalgia, and in his brief overview of Algeria's ancient history he acknowledged the frequently invoked comparison between the French Empire and the Roman Empire and the existence of a Latin heritage in North Africa. However, he argued that the conditions under which Roman and French rule were established were 'very different'. Gsell characterized the Algeria that the French first encountered in 1830 as a 'barbaric country', while the Romans, in contrast, had found prosperous cities and a rich countryside. In Gsell's turn of phrase the Romans were faced with the task of developing 'an already healthy body', and not with the burden of resuscitating 'a corpse', as the French were forced to do after their conquest.[32] In a barely veiled justification for colonization, Gsell argued that the Romans had not needed to bring in a large number of settlers to affirm their domination because they had not encountered national and religious hatreds. But Rome's biggest mistake, according to Gsell, was that it did not try assiduously enough to change hearts and minds, which would have been a guarantee of Rome's security. Above all, for Gsell, the Romans were wrong in not 'establishing in Africa a military organization capable of forever discouraging Berber pillages' and blocking 'the road for invaders, Vandals, and Arabs'.[33] As an archaeologist, he devoted his life to unearthing Rome's heritage, and implicitly argued that a close study of it provided the French in Algeria with a cautionary tale. Gsell was neither the first nor the last to look to the Roman Empire in thinking about the French settlement of Algeria. In his 'Second Letter on Algeria', Alexis de Tocqueville wrote, 'at the time of the Western empire's fall, two laws ruled at once: the barbarian was subjected to barbarian laws, and the Romans followed Roman laws. This is a good example to imitate. . . .'[34]

Like Stéphane Gsell, Louis Bertrand came to Algeria as a young man. He was born in the Lorraine in 1866, studied literature at the Ecole Normale Supérieure in Paris and became an *agrégé de lettres* in 1889 at the age of 23.

---

[30] Ibid., 142-3.

[31] Ibid., 144.

[32] Ibid., 144.

[33] Ibid., 144-5.

[34] Alexis de Tocqueville, *Writings on Slavery and Empire*, ed. and trans. Jennifer Pitts (Baltimore, 2001), 23.

He taught at lycées in Aix-en-Provence and Bourg-en-Bresse before becoming a professor of rhetoric at the lycée d'Alger. He would remain in Algeria until 1900, and his experiences there profoundly shaped his subsequent literary work. From 1897 he began to publish a series of novels, which were set in the French colony, including *Le sang des races* and *Le roman de la conquête*. He also published a number of works on the Mediterranean and the Orient: *Devant Islam*, *Le livre de la Méditerranée*, *Le mirage oriental*.

During his nine years in Alger Bertrand met Stéphane Gsell, whom he began to accompany to archaeological sites around the Maghreb.[35] In 1926, on the eve of France's centenary of the conquest of Algeria, Stéphane Gsell published *Promenades archéologiques aux environs d'Alger (Cherchel, Tipasa, le tombeau de la chrétienne)* in which he declared that there were no ruins in the world that compared with those of Tipasa, one of Algeria's most 'seductive' sites: 'Here one becomes an archaeologist, even if one does not have the vocation', and this according to him, gave him the 'pretext for charming walks in one of the most picturesque sites in Algeria'.[36] Gsell's appraisal was one that came to be widely shared. The Roman city on the Mediterranean coast, situated 70 kilometres from Alger, soon became an important pilgrimage destination for a whole generation of writers, including Louis Bertrand and Albert Camus, and a place where the past and the present seemed to be joined together. In 1895, for example, soon after Bertrand arrived in Algeria, he visited Tipasa with Gsell, and he later described it as an emotional moment in terms of making his own personal connection with his Latin past and in making the Algerian landscape and settler population the centre of his subsequent novels, including perhaps his most famous, *Le sang des races*.[37] On first seeing Tipasa's ruins he alleged that he could hear the men 'who spoke his language and believed in his gods'.[38] He saw himself as their descendant, claiming a lost heritage, and admitted to feeling that he was a 'lost Rumi in an Islamic land'.[39] Similarly, about forty years later, the existentialist

[35] L. A. Maugendre, *La renaissance catholique au début du xxème siècle, Louis Bertrand (1896-1941)* (Paris, 1971), 10-11 and Erato Paris, *La genèse intellectuelle de l'oeuvre de Fernand Braudel: La Méditerranné et le monde méditerranéen à l'époque de Philippe II (1923-1947)* (Athens, 1999), 53.

[36] Gsell, *Promenades archéologiques* (Paris, 1926), 93.

[37] For the place of Algeria in Bertrand's novels and self-understanding, see Seth Graebner, *History's Place: Nostalgia and the City in French Algerian Literature* (Lanham, MD, 2007).

[38] Quoted in Patricia M. E. Lorcin, 'Rome and France in Africa: Recovering Colonial Algeria's Latin Past' *French Historical Studies*, 25:2 (2002), 316.

[39] Quoted in Patricia M. E. Lorcin, *Imperial Identities: Stereotyping, Prejudice and Race in Colonial Algeria* (London, 1999), 200. Bertrand, who became a member of the Académie

writer Albert Camus wrote of the site that he came to understand what glory was, and after his death a stele carrying this quote, which is derived from one of Camus's most lyrical texts concerning Tipasa, was erected and still stands at the site.[40]

During the course of his novelistic career Bertrand developed his 'signature concept', the idea of a Latin Africa. The notion emerged slowly in his writings, but it appeared in his first novel, *Le Sang des races*, published in 1895, the year of his epiphany at Tipasa. It describes the exploits of his hero Rafael, the son of Spanish immigrants in Algeria, who worked as a carter and caravan driver and who in his wandering connected with both the Algerian landscape and his Latin past.[41] He celebrated the mingling of the French, Spanish, Maltese, and Neapolitans, who were forging a new invigorated Latin race, to which Arabs were unfavourably compared. He pursued Rafael and his friends in subsequent novels, describing them as the builders, conquerors and civlizers in a new Latin Algeria that needed to be reclaimed from the Arabs and Muslims. The narrative of Rome's decline and its renewal in the hands of a new Latin race haunts the pages of most of his subsequent novels, which are steeped, like Stèphane Gsell's historical writings, in nostalgia. In *Pépète le bien-aimé*, which was published in 1904, for example, he made European farmers and labourers into heroes for their roles in directly contributing to the reconstruction of the empire that the French had inherited from Rome.

Bertrand's concept of 'Latinité' or Latinitude was central to his work as a novelist and as an intellectual. He embraced his identity as a Latin who had a deep connection with the soil of North Africa. He heralded the rebirth of a Latin Africa that harked back to the Roman Empire, which had been restored by the founding of the French colonial empire, and he saw Algeria, in particular, as the nodal centre of a new racial 'melting pot' comprised of the French, Piedmontese, Italians, and Spanish. Bertrand's concept of Latinitude in the 1890s was later taken up by novelists associated with the Ecole d'Alger, who formed the Association des Ecrivains Algériens in 1920, which came to promote a new kind of literature that extolled the virtues of the Mediterranean landscape and climate.

Fernand Braudel followed Bertrand to Algeria some years later. Like Bertrand, Braudel was born in the Lorraine and spent seven formative

---

Française, was also an essayist, writing in 1897 *La fin du classicisme et le retour de l'antique*, and *Saint Augustin* (1899).

[40] Albert Camus, *Les noces* (Paris, 1939).

[41] The Algerian landscape also occupies a central place in Albert Camus's writings. See, e.g., Camus, *L'exil et le royaume* (Paris, 1957).

years in the colony before moving to Brazil and then to back to France, where he took up a position at the Collège de France. The common origin of Fernand Braudel and Louis Bertrand as Lorrainers has elicited little commentary. While neither could be characterized as a settler or *colon*, they arrived in a colony where a significant proportion of settlers hailed from the Lorraine. Early on, between 1845 and 1860 between one fourth and one fifth of the colony's population came from Alsace-Lorraine. Immigration from the region came in two waves between 1830 and 1914. The first followed the agricultural downturn and famine of 1845-55 when close to 7,500 immigrants left France for Algeria. The second came when Prussia annexed Alsace-Lorraine in 1871 when many Alsatians and Lorrainers refused to live under Prussian rule and opted for French nationality. Cardinal Lavigerie, the bishop of Nancy became the bishop of Alger soon after the founding of the French Third Republic, and he made an appeal to his compatriots to follow him, while the French parliament granted land in the colony to those who chose to leave. Between 1871 and the First World War between 12,000 and 15,000 Alsatians and Lorrainers left the metropole for Algeria.[42]

Alsatians and Lorrainers had little affinity with their new environment on the shores of the Mediterranean, but they embraced their new home as exiles. In a curious way the almost emotional attachment that Bertrand, Braudel, and many of the *algérieniste* writers of the early twentieth century had to the climate and landscape of North Africa echoed the right-wing regionalist writers of the same period in metropolitan France, and most notably a fellow Lorrainer, the novelist Maurice Barrès, whom Bertrand succeeded as an *élu* of the Académie Française in 1925.[43] Bertrand himself acknowledged his connection with Barrès in 1938 when he wrote that he 'made Latin and French Algeria as Barrès [made] Lorraine'.[44] While Barrès's 'Culte de Moi' trilogy followed the lives of his *déracinés* (those uprooted from the native soil of their beloved Lorraine) and explored the deleterious consequences of their alienation, Bertrand celebrated a new Latin race and its role in creating a new Latin Africa on the shores of the Mediterranean.

In 1923, a few years after the foundation of the Association des Ecrivains Algériens the 21-year-old historian, Fernand Braudel arrived in Algeria, like Stéphane Gsell and Louis Bertrand before him, to be a professor of history and geography first at the lycée in Constantine and then at the Lycée Bugeaud in

---

[42] Fabienne Fischer, *Alsaciens et Lorrains en Algérie, histoire d'une migration, 1830-1914* (Nice, 1999).

[43] Graebner, *History's Place*, 16. Paris, *La genèse intellectuelle de l'oeuvre de Fernand Braudel*, 41.

[44] Louis Bertrand, *Une destinée: Mes années d'apprentissage* (Paris, 1938), 249.

Alger, before returning to France and fulfilling his military service in the Ruhr in 1925-6. Afterwards he found his way back to Algeria, where he began taking an intellectual interest in the history of North Africa, along with a group of other young teachers. He came under the influence of a number of scholars at the University of Algers, including the archaeologists and historians Stéphane Gsell, Eugéne Albertini, a specialist of medieval Islamic art, Georges Marçais, and Georges Yver, a historian of French North Africa. He ultimately became secretary of the journal *Revue Africaine,* a position he held for five years, until 1932.[45] It was the *Revue Africaine*'s editorial committee that would participate in the organization of the congress celebrating the centenary of the conquest of Algeria in 1930.[46]

While a mountain of books and articles has been published on Braudel and the *Annales* School, it is surprising that so little attention has been devoted to his Algerian years.[47] Braudel wrote warmly about his years in Algeria and acknowledged that 'this spectacle, the Mediterranean as seen from the opposite shore, upside down, had considerable impact on my vision of history'.[48] While he was not of Gsell's or Bertrand's generation, he came under the influence of the existing narrative regarding the inheritance of empire and the reasons for Rome's decline, and he began his doctoral studies when the racial and historical dimensions of the unity or disunity of the Mediterranean were being debated. He was also deeply influenced by the work of Emile-Felix Gautier, a historian and geographer who would teach at the University of Alger for thirty-five years. It was from Gautier that he took the idea of the unity of the Mediterranean, which became central to the core of his own work.[49]

Braudel began to conceive of his doctoral thesis, which was to become *The Mediterranean and the Mediterranean World in the Age of Phillip II* during his early years in Algeria. Lucien Febvre advised him to focus on 'la Méditerranée des Barbaresques' four years later, but he remained steadfast to his original idea, and he ultimately defended the thesis years later in 1947.[50] Braudel had undoubtedly read the historical writings of Gsell, but it is the Belgian historian Henri Pirenne who had the most influence on his subsequent work.

<hr>

[45] The *Revue Africaine* was the principal publication of the Historical Society of Algeria, which was founded in 1856.

[46] Giuliana Gemelli, *Fernand Braudel* (Paris, 1995), 38.

[47] The notable exception is Paris' *La genèse intellectuelle de l'oeuvre de Fernand Braudel.* Also see Giulia Gemelli, *Fernand Braudel* (Paris, 1990), 36-50.

[48] Fernand Braudel, 'Personal Testimony', *Journal of Modern History,* 44:4 (Dec. 1972), 450.

[49] Paris, *La genèse intellectuelle de l'oeuvre de Fernand Braudel,* 70-5.

[50] Fernand Braudel, *The Mediterranean,* trans. Siân Reynolds, 2 vols. (New York, 1966).

Indeed, in his bibliographical essay at the end of *The Mediterranean*, he cites Pirenne's *Les villes du moyen age* (1922) and *Mohamet et Charlemagne* (1937) as the 'top of the list' for the 'general orientation of the book'.[51] Pirenne argued that the Roman empire had essentially been a Mediterranean commonwealth in his *Medieval Cities* and unquestionably the bulwark of its political and economic unity. The central thesis of *Mohamet et Charlemagne*, which advanced what came to be known as the 'Pirenne Thesis', was that Roman civilization in the Mediterranean, including North Africa, was not destroyed in the fifth century by the Germanic tribes, but rather by the Arab invasions beginning in the seventh century. Using numismatic and archaeological evidence, Pirenne demonstated that trade between Mediterranean ports persisted after the fifth century and the economic and social unity of the Mediterranean survived, even after the empire's political collapse. However, for him it was the Arab war fleets that closed off Europe and deprived it of its larger Mediterranean horizons, and paved the way for the rise of Charlemagne, the end of *Romania*, and the Mediterranean trade ties and the economic exchange on which they rested: 'It is therefore strictly correct to say that without Mohammed, Charlemagne would have been inconceivable.'[52]

In 1931 Henri Pirenne gave a set of lectures in Algeria, which Braudel attended, on the 'closure of the Mediterranean after the Moslem invasions', and Braudel described them as 'prodigious': Pirenne's 'hand opened and shut, and the entire Mediterranean was by turn free and locked in!'.[53] While Braudel wrote about the Mediterranean in a period that was much later than Pirenne's, the narrative of Rome's decline informed his book. However, whereas Pirenne focused on the Mediterranean's closure following the Arab invasions of the seventh century, Braudel re-emphasized the Meditrranean's unity and the impact of geography and a common environment in creating that unified world, linking North Africa to the Mediterranean's northern shores.[54] During his years in Algeria Braudel

---

[51] Braudel, *The Mediterranean*, vol. 2, 1273. While the work was published posthumously, Pirenne articulated the central thesis of the work as early as 1916 and put it forward from 1922 onwards. See Peter Brown, 'Mohamet et Charlemagne', *Daedalus*, 103:1 (Winter 1974), 25-33.

[52] Henri Pirenne, *Mohammed and Charlemagne*, ed. B. Miall (New York, 1939), 234.

[53] Braudel, 'Personal Testimony', 452.

[54] Molly Greene, *A Shared World: Christians and Muslims in the Early Modern Mediterranean* (Princeton, 2000), 3.

neither anticipated the rejection of this unity by North Africans nor the growing resistance to French rule:

> At any rate, at that point in my life I did not understand the social, political and colonial drama which was, nevertheless, right before my eyes. It is true that it was not until after 1939 that the North African countryside grew darker, and then, suddenly, the night had fallen. I have my excuses. First of all the need to live when one is twenty, paying attention to oneself alone . . . the difficulty of learning Arabic (I tried seriously and did not succeed). . . And above all it must be said, in 1923, in 1926, and in the years which followed, French Algeria did not appear as a monster in my eyes.[55]

As a young man, then, Braudel enthusiastically embraced the notion of a unified Mediterranean and shared with Gsell and Bertrand an abiding interest in Algeria's Roman heritage. While he chose another period as a focus for his own work, he was a part of a group of scholars who were deeply immersed in Algeria's ancient and more recent history, embracing the idea of a Latin Africa, which, as Frenchmen, they claimed as their own *patrimoine*.

Nostalgia and the political uses of heritage

Patricia Lorcin has argued in a path-breaking article that France's appropriation of Algeria's antique past was not simply a justification for empire, but it served as a means to efface the colony's Arab-Berber presence. Based on the belief that the region had been the 'granary of Rome', and a land of milk and honey, before the Arab invasions that brought the empire to an end, the French saw themselves as the inheritors of that empire and their work as one of both reclamation and restoration.[56] France's first sustained exposure to the glories of the Roman Empire across the Mediterranean had come with Napoleon's Egyptian expedition. Interest in North Africa's Roman past only grew over time, after the translation of the work of the Arab scholar Ibn Khaldun and with the increased presence of European settlers in the colony. By the end of the nineteenth century the narrative of France's inheritance of empire was crystallized in a language that laid claim to North Africa's

[55] Braudel, 'Personal Testimony', 450-1. The English translation of this text cites 1929 as the turning point in error, while the French edition cites 1939. Gemelli, *Fernand Braudel*, 40.

[56] Patricia M. E. Lorcin, 'Rome and France in Africa'. Also see Diana K. Davis, *Resurrecting the Granary of Rome: Environmental History and French Colonial Expansion in North Africa* (Athens, Ohio, 2007) and Caroline Ford, 'Reforestation, Landscape Conservation, and the Anxieties of Empire in French Colonial Algeria', *American Historical Review*, 113:2 (April 2008), 341-62.

Christian and 'Western' (as opposed to the African or Arab) origins, and the region's 'desertification' was laid at the feet of the indigenous population, who were the descendants of Khaldun's Arab hordes.[57] Cardinal Lavigerie, archbishop of Algiers, constantly evoked North Africa's Roman Christian past, making frequent reference to St Augustine.

Initiatives to recover a lost Roman and Mediterranean heritage through the excavation of ruins and monuments dovetailed with attempts to restore the supposed historic landscapes of the Mediterranean, which had allegedly been destroyed and turned into deserts by the Arab invasions that brought the Roman Empire to an end. A campaign took root, which was spearheaded by organizations such as the League for the Reforestation of Algeria.[58] In 1926 two commentators summarized the problem in the following terms:

> Following the prosperous days of the Roman era, Algeria, Tunisia and Morocco . . . vegetated, barely surviving, cultivating piracy. . . One by one, the former riches disappeared . . . all fell into ruin. Of the splendid golden age of Roman Mauretania only a sun-baked rocky desert remained, where the beneficent river had become a devastating torrent, where agriculture had atrophied, where livestock subsisted and perished according to the vagaries of rainfall, and where the native sought to secure by force or ruse what his neighbor had produced instead of producing it himself.[59]

Such views underpinned efforts to conserve Algeria's forests and shaped the implementation of legislation governing the preservation of 'natural monuments' that was passed in 1906 and 1930 respectively. It is perhaps no accident that France's first extensive system of 'national parks' was created in Algeria in the 1920s.[60]

---

[57] See Diana K. Davis, 'Desertification Narratives in French Colonial Environmental History of North Africa', *Cultural Geographies*, 11:4 (2004); Ford, 'Reforestation, Landscape Conservation'; and G. Barker, 'A Tale of Two Deserts: Contrasting Desertification Histories on Rome's Desert Frontiers', *World Archeology*, 33:1 (2002), 288-307.

[58] Ford, 'Reforestation, Landscape Conservation'.

[59] Quoted in Will D. Swearingen, *Moroccan Mirages: Agrarian Dreams and Deceptions, 1912-1986* (Princeton, 1987), 29. See André Fribourg, *L'Afrique latine—Maroc, Algérie, Tunisie* (Paris, 1922); José Germain and Stéphane Faye, *Le nouveau monde français— Maroc, Algérie, Tunisie* (Paris, 1924).

[60] Caroline Ford, 'National Parks and Natural Reserves in French Colonial Africa', in *Civilizing Nature: National Parks in Global Perspective*, ed. Bernhard Gissibl et al. (London and New York, 2012): 69-83.

In a speech given at the congress of learned societies in Alger in 1905, Heron de Villefosse, a curator at the Louvre and member of the Institut de France, remarked that many of those attending the conference had come to Algeria for the first time and could not help but feel a sense of 'pride' and 'joy' in 'putting their feet on African soil', which had become a land that was profoundly French due to the 'heroism of our soldiers and our settlers'.[61] While France's identity as a nation and its place in the world as a colonial power was strengthened by a connection made to its Roman and Mediterranean origins in the past, like Gsell, Heron de Villefosse believed that the past also provided lessons for the present. Quoting from Gaston Boissier's *L'Afrique romaine: promenades archéologiques en Algérie et Tunisie* (1895), 'we are not the first who came from the countries in the north to settle in Africa; on this soil we have had illustrious predecessors who conquered it as we have conquered it and who governed it with glory for more than five centuries'. He thought that the French encountered the same 'resistance' as the Romans and the same opposition of 'warrior races' who occupied the land without wanting to 'share it with anyone'.[62]

The French had an investment in reuniting Algeria with the northern shores of the Mediterranean, and there are some parallels between the valorization of Crusader sites by competing colonial powers and those of Roman antiquity in North Africa, especially after the Italians began to move into Libya in the twentieth century. Archaeology provided a basis for territorial claims and colonial ambitions here as in a number of settler societies historically.[63] For the French settlement of Algeria constituted a kind of resettlement for the French, and Rome's ruins were reminders of a shared past. The vestiges of Rome also gave rise to an emotional connection that began to be forged between past and future, which is ever present in the writings of a Louis Bertrand or an Albert Camus or in the *Ecole Algérianiste*. This Latin *patrimoine* or heritage came to be firmly planted in Algeria's settler society by the 1920s.

In 1930 the French celebrated the centenary of the conquest of Algeria in Algeria. It was marked by parades, speeches, and public displays. While

---

[61] Congrès des Sociétés Savantes d'Alger, *Discours prononcés à la séance générale du congrès le mercredi 26 avril 1905 par M. Héron de Villefosse, Stéphane Gsell, M. Bienvenu Martin* (Paris, 1905), 8.

[62] Ibid., 8-9.

[63] For different perspectives on the political dimensions of landscape, heritage, and landscape archaeology see the essays in Dan Hicks et al. (eds), *Envisioning Landscape: Situations and Standpoints in Archeology and Heritage* (Walnut Creek, 2007) and Gil J. Stein (ed.), *The Archeology of Colonial Encounters* (Santa Fe, 2005).

'L'Algérie Française' was at its centre, the region's Roman and European heritage was evoked at every turn. In addition, many of the novels published around the time of the commemoration made explicit refererence to Algeria's Latin heritage. In Antoine Chollier's *Drusilla, dame d'Alger*, which was published in 1930, one of his characters declares, 'it seems to me that Algeria is an integral part of my homeland, just as, I suppose, the soil of Algeria must in some way be the extension of our Riviera!'. To this another character replies, 'you are right. . . This sea, like all of North Africa, is essentially Latin. Our civilization has gravitated around it and at every moment we find in it the traces of our race.'[64]

The centenary, which was long in the planning, was above all a political festival, which was meant to legitimize France's presence in the colony. It was viewed as a 'glorification of the colonizing methods of the mother country'.[65] The centenary's programme emphasized the region's Roman heritage, as evidenced by the Roman ruins associated with the 'villes d'or', the ancient Roman cities of North Africa that Bertrand popularized so effectively. The organizing committee reserved a significant amount of money for refurbishing the museums of Timgad and Djemila, which housed Roman antiquities. The centenary also showcased the benefits of Roman rule. George Rozet wrote in one of the centenary's publications on the ruins: 'If Rome's cradle was in Italy, if it exerted its new force and put its first splendour there, it is in Roman Africa . . . that she found the true blossoming of [a] civilizing nation.'[66] For the French celebrants in the colony, the Roman ruins were not simply admired; they were an important part of the *patrimoine* or heritage of French Algeria.[67]

In short, France's obsession with Algeria's Roman past was a reflection of a unique territorial claim that did not exist elsewhere in France's far flung empire. It is no accident that Algeria was considered to be a part of *la plus grande France* in a way that French West Africa, Indochina, or Pondicherry in India were not.[68] Although the French certainly settled in other parts of

---

[64] Quoted in Graebner, *History's Place*, 167.

[65] Quoted from the centenary catalogue by Oulebsir, *Les usages du patrimoine*, 261.

[66] Quoted in Ibid., 283.

[67] Ibid.

[68] Braudel notes in his discussion of a certain lack of 'conscience' regarding the impact of colonialism during his years in Algeria, that in 1930, the year of the centenary of France's occupation of Algeria, when Benjamin Crémieux arrived in Algeria to give a lecture, he telegraphed Rudyard Kipling and said, '"Having arrived in Algeria, I begin to understand France". Kipling and England had India—and a clear conscience. And India was the explanation for England.' Braudel, 'Personal Testimony', 451.

France's empire—Indochina, New Caledonia, or the island of Réunion—Algeria was France's only true settler colony, which was populated by a diverse (and self-described) 'Latin race' that included French, Italians, Spanish, Maltese, and eventually, North African Jews. All of them laid claim to French citizenship by the early Third Republic.

The science of archaeology played an important role in creating a new heritage for France across the Mediterranean in North Africa, and this *patrimoine* underpinned claims to nationhood and empire.[69] The early establishment of a Musée d'Archéologie de la Méditerranée in the port city Marseille, which linked Alger to the metropole, was to become a northern extension of a project which was first begun in Algeria. The importance of the Mediterranean as both a unified space and as a value for French 'civilisation' cannot be underestimated. In his novel, *Le jardin de la mort*, Louis Bertrand argued that the ruins of Algeria could only be understood as a living legacy and inheritance: 'They are alive, these African ruins, because the people who move around them, without knowing it, perpetuate the gestures and the thoughts of the ancient men' who created them. For Bertrand, standing among the ruins, almost nothing had changed.[70]

[69] This is a subject that has been hotly contested and explored elsewhere. See Nadia Abu El Haj's *Facts on the Ground: Archeological Practice and Territorial Self-Fashioning in Israeli Society (Chicago, 2001)*.

[70] Quoted in Oulebsir, *Les usages du patrimoine*, 286.

The Ruins of Preservation: Conserving Ancient Egypt 1880–1914

David Gange

The rhetoric of preservation began to suffuse the archaeology of Egypt in the late nineteenth century. Amelia Edwards' best-selling travel narrative, *A Thousand Miles up the Nile*, is sometimes considered to have instigated 'modern' attitudes to the preservation of Egyptian monuments.[1] In some ways this judgement is appropriate: unlike her pronouncements on race (shocking even by contemporary standards), Edwards' attitudes to conservation can be reduced to statements that still sound modern enough:

> The wall paintings which we had the happiness of admiring in all their beauty and freshness are already much injured. Such is the fate of every Egyptian monument. . . The tourist carves it over with names and dates. . . The student of Egyptology, by taking wet paper 'squeezes' sponges away every vestige of the original colour. The 'Collector' buys and carries off everything of value that he can, and the Arab steals it for him. The work of destruction, meanwhile goes on apace. . . The Museums of Berlin, of Turin, of Florence are rich in spoils which tell their lamentable tale. When science leads the way, is it wonderful that ignorance should follow?[2]

Between 1876 and her death in 1892, Edwards did more than anyone else in Britain to popularize Egypt's ancient history and established several of the institutional structures that still dominate British Egyptology today. The continuity of these institutions, in particular the Egypt Exploration Fund/Society (the name was changed in 1919) and the Edwards Chair of Egyptology at University College London, encourages a sense of connection from the

---

[1] For this view see any publication or website on the early history of British Egyptology, from T. G. H. James, *Excavating in Egypt: The Egypt Exploration Society 1882-1982* (London, 1982) to www.digital.library.upenn.edu/women/edwards/edwards.html; for some explanation of Edwards' attitude to the Egyptian people see Billie Melman, *Women's Orients* (Ann Arbor, 1993), 254-75.

[2] A. B. Edwards, *A Thousand Miles up the Nile* (London, 1876), 353.

Past and Present (2015), Supplement 10　　　　　　　　

present back to the moments in the 1870s and '80 s when modern conservatory Egyptology, concerned with the painstaking recovery and recording of
sites rather than acquisition of art for museums, was supposedly born.

This paper deals with the contingencies that subverted preservation: it
concerns the ways in which the creation of disciplines, with the power-
struggles and epistemological competition that involves, can compromise
the development of coherent responses to preservation concerns. Although
the language of conservation entered Egyptological discourse in the 1870s, it
did not define practice until nearly half a century later. For most Europeans,
preservation continued to mean export to Europe, and the spectre of *felaheen*
lime-kilns continued to be used as justification for dismembering ancient
structures. Conservation interests were also consistently over-ridden by the
many ideological crusades that Egyptologists pursued. Indeed, the need to
fund-raise in Britain led Edwards herself to advocate the dismantling of sites
so that donors to her cause might receive items for their private collections.
These were often as mundane as uninscribed bricks from the walls of New-
Kingdom storage buildings. From being the voice of conscience when unin-
hibited by practical interests, Edwards became a manifestation of the problem
itself. The ideological causes that shaped Egyptology, ranging from proofs of
biblical events to evidence for racial or eugenic theories, always trumped the
fragile conservatory principles which hindsight leads us to overestimate as a
driving force behind this Egyptological activity. In fact, the decades that followed the birth of preservation rhetoric were by far the most destructive in
history, and those who voiced preservation concerns most loudly were often
the most culpable. This phenomenon in Egypt has marked parallels with the
development of archaeological practice in other imperial settings, particularly in the troubled movements for preservation in India. The question of
who, whether the tiny Egyptological lobby or the army of administrators
drafted into 1880s Egypt from India, really shaped attitudes to Egyptian
monuments complicates this picture. In fact, it was often not Egyptologists
who travelled the monuments and lobbied administrators for their preservation, but vice versa. Administrators who travelled the length of the country
fulfilling their imperial duties habitually wrote to London periodicals to 'put
Egyptologists on the alert' to the 'museum thieves' and 'stone contractors'
who preyed on the monuments.[3] These correspondents usually note informing local police, who are chastised for their lack of interest; quite what they

---

[3] J. C. Ross, 'The Mutilation of Monuments in Egypt', *The Academy*, 927 (1890), 107; Ross
was Inspector-General of Irrigation in Egypt and was a frequent conduit of information
for Egyptologists.

expected Egyptologists to do, beyond wringing their hands, is not always clear.

There was one striking element of Egyptological discourse in which preservation concerns did predominate. While preservation was not the guiding principle of excavation, it did quickly become the dominant rhetorical theme in Egyptological power struggles. Egyptology, even by the standards of other incipient archaeological disciplines, was intensely factional. This was in part because of national jealousies that intensified after British occupation in 1882. Administrators, engineers, and officers poured into Egypt from British India, where preservation had already become a contentious issue as Upinder Singh describes.[4] Many of these officials became large-scale collectors, founding several of the regional museums in England and Scotland; others became respected Egyptologists in their own right, perpetuating the long-running theme whereby diplomatic postings began archaeological careers (e.g. Henry Rawlinson); yet more donated funds to the new Egyptological organizations. Before long these organizations recognized that it was politic to give administrators or engineers such as Sir John Fowler and even the toxically unpopular retired Proconsul, Lord Cromer, honorific roles on their committees.

The distribution of antiquities was not, in theory at least, a free market. Rudimentary antiquities legislation was first introduced under Mehmed Ali in 1835, endeavouring primarily to restrict export of ancient art works; this had been almost entirely ineffective. The creation of an Antiquities Service in the 1850s, the pet project of the French scholar August Mariette, gave slightly more bite to efforts to control the movement of monumental art. As Elliott Colla has argued, this control of the market did not mean the end of commerce in antiquities, but encouraged the development of new market mechanisms and new commercial discourses. This involved reframing purchases in the non-commodity registers of aesthetic-historical conservation, centralizing antiquities extraction through emergent state agencies, and giving quasi-commercial practices a legitimacy they may not have enjoyed before.[5] It remained, however, very straightforward for even the humblest individuals to continue as before: countless European and American travellers continued to do so.

---

[4] Upinder Singh, *The Discovery of Ancient India: Early Archaeologists and the Beginnings of Archaeology* (Chicago, 2004); see also Robert Tignor, 'The "Indianization" of the Egyptian Administration under British Rule', *American Historical Review*, (1963), 636-61.

[5] Elliott Colla, 'Preservation and Repression: Egyptian Antiquities Law as Doctrine and Practice', 3rd German-American Frontiers of Humanities Symposium (2006); abtsract http://www.humboldt-foundation.de/pls/web/docs/F8284/4_colla.pdf

The British occupation gave the need to protect antiquities intense new urgency. However much the British liked to present themselves as saviours of Egypt's heritage, this event (even more, perhaps, than the burning of the library of Alexandria or Napoleon's brief rampage along the Nile) was a moment of enormous escalation in the destruction of Egypt's antiquities. Once Anglo-Indian administrators, with their sense of imperial entitlement, flooded into Egypt, previous legislation counted for nothing. Techniques for preventing customs officials opening export crates packed with antiquities were discussed openly in archaeological and military circles; the British Museum curator Sir E. A. T. Wallis Budge developed particular renown for his skills in subterfuge.

Several attempts were made to stem the flow. The early 1880s, for instance, saw a string of decrees relating to Arabic art, Antiquities prior to the Arab conquest, and the ailing Museum of Egyptian Antiquities at Bulaq. Those decrees dealing with the ancient world were negotiations between Khedival power and the French antiquities service and were designed with British acquisitiveness in mind. 'All the monuments and objects of antiquity, recognised as such by the Regulation governing the matter, shall . . . be declared property of the Public Domain of the State' insisted a pronouncement of May 1883; this raft of legislation reprised themes of previous decades with no guarantee of greater potency.[6] In response to efforts to curb export, the British launched impassioned criticism of treatment of antiquities that were kept in Egypt. They noted, in particular, the vulnerability of Mariette's museum in Bulaq to flooding during the annual inundation: even improvements carried out after a particularly damaging deluge in 1878 did not end the insistence that preservation was synonymous with export of antiquities to major European capitals. When the collections were moved to new quarters in Giza in 1890 initial enthusiasm was quickly replaced by fresh jingoistic criticism.[7] In the same breath as he demanded that 'politics and political chauvinism' be kept out of discussion of preservation, A. H. Sayce railed against this French-controlled 'incohate institution in a partially civilised community'.[8] Also in the early 1880s, Maspero selected six retired military officers to become an improvised 'inspectorate' of monuments, each assigned

---

[6] For translations of selected antiquities legislation, see Adrienne L. Fricke (trans.), 'Appendix II: Egyptian Antiquities Laws' in J. H. Merryman (ed.), *Imperialism, Art and Restitution* (Cambridge, 2006), 175-92.

[7] For A. H. Sayce's initial, positive, views see 'Letters from Egypt', *Academy*, 937 (1890), 273.

[8] A. H. Sayce, 'How are the Monuments of Egypt to be Preserved?', *Academy*, 1022 (1891), 508.

a particular sensitive region to oversee. Then, in 1891, a marginally more robust decree had the language of preservation at its core. It insisted that 'monuments fixed to the ground, regardless of their state. . . must be conserved in place'; but it also formalized the system of *partage* whereby half of any haul could be exported out of Egypt by an excavator.[9] These were not inconsiderable adjustments, but in comparison to the vast new scale of problems they were small-scale, under-resourced and indecisive.

Until the 1880s field Egyptology had been dominated by a close network of scholars led by the intensely anti-British Mariette, friend and ally of the Paris-educated Khedive Ismail. The abrupt jerk from this French domination, towards British involvement, under the more pragmatic figure of Gaston Maspero, could not be anything but divisive.[10] The most impassioned statements of concern for the preservation of Egyptian antiquities in this period came from French literary figures such as Pierre Loti, and were sustained attacks aimed squarely at the British administration.[11] This was also a period of waxing German imperial interest in regions as disparate as Cameroon and Mesopotamia, and German antiquarians such as Rudolph Virchow were increasingly vocal in their distaste for the activities of British Egyptologists and political leaders. They favoured analogies between British archaeological sites and the chaos of war zones, reminding readers of the close fit between imperial belligerence and British fascination with the ancients.[12] Areas coloured British red on world maps, they implied, marked 'danger' for remains of the past and regional heritage which would be forced violently into new colonial interests.

Yet factionalism was not just determined along national lines. The early history of British Egyptology is riddled with misunderstanding and personal vendetta. The Egypt Exploration Fund's first two excavators, for instance, played out their mutual distrust by enlisting younger scholars to undermine each other's work. Spies were hired, press-campaigns were used to blacken reputations, and physical fights resulted on more than one occasion.

---

[9] This conformed to treatment of treasure trove accepted since Roman Law; for the fullest coverage to date of these developments see Antoine Khater, *Le Régime juridique de fouilles et des antiquités en Egypte* (Cairo, 1960).

[10] Profoundly anti-British sentiments persisted among the French and German archaeological establishment; during Maspero's two spells in charge the British found excavation and export much easier than in the years when others, such as Emil Brugsch sought to revive the spirit of Mariette.

[11] E.g., Pierre Loti, *La Mort de Philae* (Paris, 1908).

[12] See below, p. 97.

Preservation concerns became the primary rhetorical resource in the new vocabulary of Egyptological outrage and insult.

However impossible their application, Egyptologists were at least fantasizing about a world in which conservation would be an overriding concern. Each excavator compared his rivals to exploitative industrial capitalists, concerned only with extracting maximum remuneration from the ground at minimal cost, and presented himself as protector of Egypt's heritage. The history of archaeology has tended to label its protagonists either as 'good' preservationist, record-keeping excavators, or as 'bad' unsystematic and scientifically illiterate ones. In reality no such division could be drawn. The pace of excavation, and therefore of destruction, accelerated rapidly because Egyptologists failed to agree on how preservation concerns should operate; they acquired many more sites than they could excavate responsibly simply to prevent rivals from 'destroying' them. This was a trend in which so-called 'progressive' archaeologists were most culpable. Disagreement about what Egyptology was, rather than leading to slower, more reflective, activity, led to rapid, panicked excavation that bore little relation to the idealistic schemes set out in Egyptology's first pedagogic texts.

Politics of excavation

Sometimes excavation sites were likened to war-zones because that is exactly what they were. This was true of the Egypt Exploration Fund's early excavations in the Nile Delta near the recently opened Suez Canal. The canal remains the biggest generator of income in Egypt, and Ismailia, the city founded by the canal-builders, still carries the memory of de Lesseps in the faded grandeur of a few public buildings. It recalls the period when, after the booming cotton production of mid-century, prices plummeted. Egyptian borrowing from European financial houses ceased to be invested in economic expansion; instead, it was consumed in the service of a national debt that was now more than ten times the size of annual revenue.[13] In the 1860s the Suez Canal Authority had established its headquarters in Ismailia, and it is no coincidence that this city, constructed at the height of Ismail's efforts to emulate Europe, later became an important centre of resistance to British colonial intrusion. Between 1875 and 1936 Egypt received virtually no income from the lucrative canal and Ismailia symbolized this kind of injustice.

---

[13] For these circumstances see several works by Robert Tignor, beginning with 'The "Indianization" of the Egyptian Administration' and culminating in *Egypt: A Short History* (Princeton, 2010).

Where the current, neoclassical, Ismailia museum was provocatively opened in 1932, at the height of nationalist tensions, its smaller predecessor was opened at a similarly contentious moment, the year after British occupation. In 1882, Ismailia had been a key strategic objective for both the British troops of Garnet Wolsey and the Egyptian nationalist forces of General Ahmed Urabi: the diminutive 1883 museum was not just a reflection of historical interest but a small symbol of European victories.[14] It catered for several separate European constituencies and told a story of Egyptian history that began in the pages of the King James Bible and ended with the arrival of a new chosen people. These European constituencies included official travellers between Egypt and India; they also included nonconformist ministers from provincial towns like Leicester and Bedford who made up the bulk of Thomas Cook parties before the occupation, and whose pursuit of the Exodus route has left behind extensive diaries that revel in parallels between modern Lake Timsah and Bible verses.[15] A third constituency was the surprisingly large number of battlefield tourists who descended on Egypt after the occupation and the 1882 defeat of Urabi's Egyptian nationalist forces by Wolsey's British troops.

Outside the museum hawkers sold wares to appeal to each of these classes of visitor. Small artefacts, often strawless bricks from domestic buildings, were sold as biblical relics, supposedly fashioned by the 'bleeding hands' of enslaved Hebrews. Other artefacts were military: a visitor could 'acquire for the sum of one pound sterling a shell which may or may not have been originally picked up on the battlefield'.[16] This military tourism is a feature of British activity in 1880s Egypt that is often forgotten. It was entangled with Egyptology, and was presented by commentators as a far bigger phenomenon than historically inspired travel. Stanley Lane-Poole's gory description of the Egypt Exploration Fund's first site captures this messy relationship between military occupation and Egyptological activity. Far from the idyllic wilderness presented in Egyptologists' press-releases, this is a landscape punctuated by

> a succession of abandoned preserved-meat tins, exploded shells, fragments of clothes and other debris, and by the legs of horses,

[14] For the events surrounding Urabi's uprising against Ishmael's successor, Tewfiq, in 1879, and the way this was used as justification for British military intervention see Tignor, *Egypt: A Short History* (Princeton, 2010).

[15] Cook himself was a Baptist minister and, as Tim Larsen in *Contested Christianity* (Baylor, 2004) has shown, his tours in the Eastern Mediterranean partook as much of the nature of pilgrimage as tourism.

[16] Stanley Lane-Poole, 'The Discovery of Pithom-Succoth', *British Quarterly Review* (July 1883), 108.

and sometimes of men, protruding from the ground where their shroud of sand has been blown away.[17]

The larger of two Thomas Cook boats seen on the Freshwater Canal, Lane-Poole continues, is fitted out for those 'on the trail of the army of '82', the much smaller dahabiyeh is intended 'to be used for the purposes of science' and 'devoted to no sordid gain or vulgar curiosity'.[18]

Egyptologists themselves were more reticent than Lane-Poole concerning politics and empire. They went to extraordinary lengths in the 1880s and '90 s to demonstrate that military and scholarly activity were entirely disconnected, or even that the occupation had problematized, rather than assisted, the activities of British Egyptologists. They were acutely aware of the tightrope they trod between securing the backing of the unpopular political regime, and preventing scholars from around the world from seeing the activities of British Egyptologists as just another arm of imperial power.

Like several other areas of Egyptian administration Egyptology remained nominally under French control, as it had been since the mid-century. British Egyptologists liked to emphasize the threats this posed to their own existence, including the fact that, for fear of upsetting French interests, nervous British administrators hoped to limit or even close down potentially fractious British Egyptological activity. There is some justification for their view. In the 1880s Lord Cromer, at the beginning of his troubled tenure as Proconsul, was deeply concerned by the diplomatic tensions that antiquity hunting could lead to. He vetoed the deployment of an official British Museum representative in Egypt and when a British Museum employee, the exceptionally irresponsible and 'entitled' Wallis Budge, arrived in an unofficial capacity Cromer did all he could to persuade him back to London.[19] Two decades later, Egyptology was still—staggeringly—said to exemplify a science 'remote from politics'.[20] No-one since the mid-twentieth century would claim that Egyptology was not politically entangled, but the extent to which it was tossed around on an ocean of much more powerful interests, unable to develop in any cogent and self-determined manner, is constantly underestimated.

<hr>

[17] Ibid.

[18] Ibid.

[19] See, e.g., Budge's account of his arrival in Egypt, E. Wallis Budge, *By Nile and Tigris*, 2 vols (London, 1920), I, 76ff.

[20] 'Ancient Egyptian Art', *Athenaeum* (1915), 267.

Exploration and conservation

Egyptology in 1882 was still many years away from becoming a coherent discipline. The ideal skill-set of an Egyptologist was not agreed on and disciplinary objectives were not settled, never mind the technical apparatus that might achieve them. Philologist, historian, engineer, draftsman, archaeologist, astronomer, anthropologist, architect, theologian, chemist, physicist, mathematician: each was considered a key component in the identity of the ideal Egyptologist by some of those who popularized or funded the incipient discipline. The Egyptian language and script could be studied in Berlin and other German universities, and several American (but few British) students made their way there in this period. Yet no courses existed anywhere that taught Egyptological skills representative of any combinations that might be used in the field.

The Egypt Exploration Fund embodied this confusion over what Egyptology was. Until after 1900 this organization had similar numbers of members to the more famous societies dealing with British heritage, including the National Trust. Preservation of Egyptian temples and tombs had been central to its founding principles. By the time it actually engaged in its first excavations, however, preservation played little role in the discourse the organization was involved in, still less its practice. The Fund's founders had quickly discovered that preservation of Egyptian monuments did not raise subscriptions: only religion could assure a following on the scale that could fund large excavations. Attempts to map the Exodus route, excavate the Land of Goshen and discover records of Joseph, Moses, and Jeremiah followed. It is indicative of this shift that a rival organization, run by Royal-Academy painters and with a tense relationship with Egyptologists, was soon set up in London to represent the preservation interests the EEF had discarded.[21] It is also no coincidence that this group, the Society for the Preservation of the Monuments of Ancient Egypt, was short-lived.

Dominated by theological interest on its inception, the turnover of EEF committee members was rapid. Combined with rich discoveries at Graeco-Roman sites this led the organization to be transformed within a decade: much to the chagrin of many subscribers, the Fund was quickly wrenched from biblical enthusiasts seeking Hebrew relics from the muddy Delta, by

---

[21] This has usually been presented as a complementary institution to the EEF (their archives are now amalgamated, giving an unhelpful sense of unity). The relationship between the two was never easy: the founder of the SPMAE, Edward Poynter, insisted that it was Egyptologists the monuments needed protecting from. Even after the foundation of this society, however, commentators continued to urge 'the necessity for the preservation of the monuments'.

classicists coveting papyri from the dry Fayum. Amidst such rapid about-turns major projects such as an archaeological survey of Egypt, painstakingly planned, fell apart or were dramatically scaled down. Even on individual projects priorities were so different that excavators failed to work together, undermining each other's schemes. Near Amarna in 1892, for instance, Petrie followed an incongruous set of boot prints in the sand to find junior employees of the archaeological survey sabotaging the work to which they were supposed to be contributing.

Political shocks of the 1890s and early 1900s made Cromer's name a byword for iron-fisted aggression rather than the 'enlightened' leadership he aspired to; this encouraged nationalist sentiment to extend into the Egyptian countryside and further problematized archaeological activity.[22] A handful of administrators did see official archaeology as politically expedient. For instance, Kitchener in Khartoum championed the archaeology of Meroe: this was both a personal agenda, consolidating his identity as 'Avenger of Gordon' by emphasizing the shared archaeological proclivities of the two generals, and a publicity stunt to generate public awareness of the Sudan.[23] Yet the protection of Egyptian monuments remained a staggeringly piecemeal affair. Administrators were much more likely to collect for themselves, or for sale in London, than to support official archaeological bodies or preservation agendas. The British Museum's 1920 document *How to Observe in Archaeology* demonstrates the persistence of this phenomenon. It encouraged administrators, military officers, and travellers in Egypt to collect responsibly: to record, for instance, the provenance of acquisitions, and to consider sale to museums before dispersal among private collectors. Its existence emphasizes the extent to which digging and collecting, despite legal stricture, remained a free market until the creation of an Egyptian parliament in 1922 began to give the law teeth; famously, this new dispensation would be dramatically tested in its very first year when Howard Carter opened the Tomb of Tutankhamun.

[22] On Cromer's use of the classics to emphasize his 'enlightened' status see Donald Malcolm Reid, *Whose Pharaohs? Archaeology, Museums and Egyptian National Identity from Napoleon to World War 1* (Berkeley, 2003).

[23] At this point Gordon's fame rested as much on his supposed discovery of the 'true' Tomb of Christ in Jerusalem (validated by the Anglican Church) as on his martyrdom at Khartoum. For Kitchener's efforts to tie his mythology to the legacy of Gordon, see James Robinson, 'The Heroic Myth of Lord Kitchener', unpublished dissertation, University of Birmingham.

Petrie and *Methods and Aims in Archaeology*

Caught up in the confusion and petty jealousies of the 1880s and '90 s was a young Kentish archaeologist called William Matthew Flinders Petrie. Petrie made two key enemies in the Egypt Exploration Fund which would dog the first decades of his career. One was the Fund's Honorary Secretary, R. S. Poole, a British Museum numismatist, UCL Professor of Classics, and enthusiast for biblical Egypt.[24] The other was the Fund's first excavator, the Swiss Bible scholar, Edouard Naville. The conflict with Poole stymied teaching of the Egyptian language in Petrie's UCL Egyptology course, but it is the conflict with Naville that is of interest here, based as it was on conflicting ideas of how a site should be maintained and recorded.[25] This was a conflict based on disagreement over what an archaeological site was.

In 1885 Petrie was visited at Koptos by an ambitious young classical scholar called David Hogarth; soon Hogarth had been persuaded to infiltrate Naville's large EEF excavation of the Temple of Hatshepsut. Petrie's caricature of Naville was of a clumsy theologian-cum-antiquarian who lacked any conception of the archaeological record, whose idea of scientific excavation was to find a direct route to the biggest monumental remains and extract them for the lowest price, whatever the archaeological cost. Petrie contrasted this with his own interest in unprepossessing remains like potsherds, which could be used to reconstruct cultural development, and his delicate treatment of archaeological strata, applying (as he put it) the techniques of geology to the human past. His celebrated teaching collection at UCL, with its 20,000 pots, makes a marked contrast to Naville's legacy in monumental art scattered around Europe's museums. Following the law that a discipline's history is written by the institutional winners, Petrie's image of the two men has been set down as canonical.

However, the British press did not always see things this way. They presented Naville, working in an official capacity for a British institution, as selflessly reconstructing ancient cities and temples, piece by monumental piece.[26] Petrie, working on his own account, and shipping small items to Europe by the thousand was instead presented as selfishly grubbing in the mud, dismantling sites to feed museums abroad. Within a few months even

---

[24] Poole's particular vision of Egypt is captured in *Cities of Egypt* (1881) in which some of the most important pharaonic cities are not even mentioned, but tiny border outposts receive whole chapters on the basis of a single scriptural mention.

[25] Since Poole vetoed the employment of anyone but himself to teach hieroglyphs, and Petrie refused to work with Poole, Egyptian language classes had to be held irregularly and surreptitiously in the bedsit of Frances Llewellyn Griffith.

[26] E.g. F. L., 'In the Learned World', *Academy*, (1914), 402.

Hogarth had switched sides. In a delicately phrased public apology for his earlier espionage he disowned Petrie and his techniques: where Petrie accused Naville of destroying the archaeological record at Deir el Bahari, Hogarth insisted that the strata had been compromised before Naville arrived. Hogarth had, he insisted, found 'a German newspaper of 1875' sixteen feet down.[27] Naville undoubtedly represented an older model of archaeological practice than Petrie, which placed much less emphasis on detailed recording of sites, or limiting the scope of excavations in order to preserve material for future excavators. But it is important to note that Petrie's progressive archaeology was not considered by many contemporary commentators to offer greater scope for either conservation or the acquisition of knowledge.

The reasons for this are instructive and can be approached through the most important published engagement with preservation concerns in this period. This is the first comprehensive manual of Egyptological technique and practice in any language: Petrie's *Methods and Aims in Archaeology* (1904). It is also one of the first systematic statements of archaeological practice, and therefore an early interrogation of the vexed relationship between destructive knowledge-generation and careful preservation that was the constant conundrum of pre-electronic archaeology. Since 1892 Petrie had been teaching Egyptology at UCL in a decidedly haphazard manner and this text had three main purposes: to set his pedagogy on a firmer footing; to develop his ambitions towards the status of public intellectual; and to win the public and press over to his new archaeological approach. Before exploring the text itself, this section will set out some of the reasons it was needed.

Petrie faced difficult circumstances in the 1880s and '90 s. Firstly, tensions developed in his relationship with museums. He became increasingly frustrated with the pressure museums exerted for the dispersal of artefacts around the globe; yet he remained dependent on their sponsorship. His method of operation was to collect donations, then to give the biggest donors—whether Copenhagen, Boston, or the Ashmolean—first choice from among the items he could secure permission to export.[28] A significant

---

[27] 'Egypt Exploration Fund', *Academy*, (1894), 356.

[28] Under *partage*, the Director General of the Antiquities Service had the real first choice, keeping especially significant items for the Egyptian Museum; most of these were not intended for display but were entered into public auction. Once this share had been taken the remaining material (in practice often much more than half the discoveries) was Petrie's to distribute as he saw fit. Without this distribution there would have been no viable means of funding excavations. The auctions were a significant source of income for the Egyptian museum, and resulted in enormous dispersal of antiquities around the globe, until the mid-twentieth century.

proportion of the current collections of many European and American museums was acquired through Petrie in this way. Although Petrie placed great emphasis on provenance, he worked so quickly that the destinations of his items were often not properly recorded. Several current museological projects such as *Naukratis: the Greeks in Egypt* have spent a great deal of time locating the huge numbers of artefacts that Petrie dispersed around the world.[29]

The case of Naukratis is instructive of other contingencies attached to Petrie's approach. Before *Methods and Aims*, Petrie singularly failed to persuade museum curators of the value of his interests: the results were disastrous. After his first season at this major site of early-Greek iron working, Petrie had enthusiastically, and with a minimum of recording, packed the best iron instruments for immediate transport to the British Museum. When he returned to Britain, one of his first priorities was to visit his Naukratis exhibit in the Museum's Bronze room. To his surprise he found a few pots and statuettes but no metal-work. Enquiring of an attendant, he learnt that the curator, C. T. Newton, had considered the iron items ugly and thrown them away. They were never recovered. The next decade saw several more misunderstandings of this kind, caused perhaps by the art-historical obsession of curators, but exacerbated by Petrie's hasty recording and failure to communicate effectively. The real problem here, responsible for untold destruction, was still lack of agreement on what Egyptology was and who had the right to define its parameters.

Just as damaging as these disjunctions between Egyptologist and museum was Petrie's neurotic disdain for his peers. The suspicion he harboured not just for Naville but for all other excavators explains his failure to adhere, even approximately, to his own strictures. Egypt to Petrie was 'a house on fire': despising 'maggoty' modernity and other excavators with equal intensity he saw his own role as salvage from these twin threats.[30] His first priority was not the patient conservation of sites that *Methods and Aims* suggested; it was keeping sites out of the hands of other excavators. If this meant hastily working-over vast, delicate remains himself, in explicit contradistinction to his own published strictures, this was seen as a small price to pay for keeping them out of other hands.

The disjunctions between archaeologists and their curatorial sponsors combined with the difficulties generated by rapid excavation to inspire some strongly negative coverage of Petrie's publications. Throughout the

---

[29] http://www.britishmuseum.org/research/research_projects/naukratis_the_greeks_in_egypt.aspx

[30] For some of Petrie's railing against modernity and 'maggoty' industrial England see W. M. Flinders Petrie, *Seventy Years in Archaeology* (London, 1931), 125–6.

1880s and '90 s every particular in which the new Egyptian archaeology deviated from the established norms of classical excavation was a source of contention. Petrie insisted on three particular developments. Firstly, in order to leave excavated structures standing, and recover museum-pieces with minimum destruction, the Egyptologist should be an engineer by training and temperament: language and historical scholarship were merely secondary considerations (Petrie even used his inaugural lecture at UCL to insist that 'no greater mistake is made . . . than supposing that an excavator must needs be a scholar').[31] Secondly, he pressed the importance of developing techniques to reconstruct societies and their history from potsherds, weights and measures, and stressed the relative unimportance of high art. Thirdly, he insisted that results must be published within weeks of excavation to make absolutely certain that records of every site, however incomplete, became public.

All three of these considerations were subjected to ridicule. Petrie's insistence on rapid publication was assaulted as unscholarly and embarrassing. *The Athenaeum*'s reviewer took a typical line:

> Mr Petrie should not thrust upon the world a book 'with all its imperfections, its half-gleaned results, its transitory views', upon the principle that 'half a loaf is better than no bread'. When he informs his readers that 'it is a golden principle to let each year see the publication of the year's work', he quite forgets that he publishes a confession of his inability to do work which requires careful deduction or patient research.[32]

This reviewer's assault on Petrie's 'ephemeral' interests and lack of proper training was also typical: the Naukratis volume

> is a most laborious, but wearisome treatise . . . and in spite of all this Mr Petrie declares that 'no finality' can be expected. . . When Mr Petrie began to excavate . . . he should first have had a training in Egyptian and Greek and Roman archaeology [and] some acquaintance with ancient languages . . . most of Mr Petrie's conclusions will have to be altered or modified.[33]

Methods and Aims became Petrie's most substantial attempt to put an end to this kind of criticism. The text is an apology for his approach, intended to win

---

[31] This lecture is reprinted as Appendix A in Rosalind M. Janssen, *Egyptology at University College London, 1892-1992* (London, 1992), 98.

[32] 'Naukratis', *Athenaeum*, (1886), 471.

[33] Ibid.

classicists, philologists, and museum curators over to his scientistic cause.[34] This was his attempt to define, once and for all, what Egyptology should be, and to assure his authority over its development. Petrie set out by establishing a dichotomy. On one side was the world of 'pretty things', fine art, literature, and history which had 'housed' the dilettante archaeology of previous decades (the world of Giovanni Belzoni and A. H. Layard).[35] On the other was an approach to the past that made history subservient to the 'principles of science' and 'real knowledge' in which, Petrie insisted, archaeology's disciplinary future lay. Knowledge of chemistry and physics, he argued, is as important as critical knowledge of ancient languages. By this stage in his career, Petrie was ready to declare war on classical archaeology and the practices of museum curators, and *Methods and Aims* became a text about the practice and ethics of scientific treatment of antiquities and sites.

One of the most striking features of *Methods and Aims* is its detailed proscription of the character, ethical agenda and personal habits of the archaeologist. This character is defined in explicit contrast with contemporary notions of the aesthete: to borrow James Eli Adams' terms it emphasizes 'desert saint' against 'dandy' masculinity.[36] Petrie insists that archaeology is 'better fitted to open the mind, to produce wide interests and toleration', effectively to form character, than any other discipline.[37] His opening chapters are a bold and direct statement concerning this vision of Edwardian masculinity. In keeping with the volume of Epictetus he carried in his overcoat, Petrie presents a Stoic vision of the modern male: eschewing luxury, embracing physical hardship, actively pursuing austerity and militaristic regimentation. This vision was fully realised on Petrie's sites, for which an 'iron constitution' was famously required.[38] Frequently taking up occupancy in tombs, much like second-century Alexandrine ascetics, Petrie as well as his assistants and visitors adhered to long working hours, Spartan conditions and 'the master's' astonishingly strict regimen.

This emphasis on moral rigours rather than formal training gives *Methods and Aims* its intensely remonstrative flavour. Petrie sets out the

---

[34] Its failure to ignite much excitement in 1904 has been explained away by archaeologists such as Roger Summers on the grounds that 'it was in fact twenty-five years ahead of its time and was consequently unpopular', Roger Summers, 'Methods and Aims in South African Archaeology', *South African Archaeological Bulletin* (March 1958), 3-9.

[35] W. M. F. Petrie, *Methods and Aims in Archaeology* (London, 1904), viiff.

[36] J. E. Adams, *Dandies and Desert Saints: Styles of Victorian Masculinity* (Ithaca, 1995).

[37] Petrie, *Methods and Aims*, viii, 1-8.

[38] E.g., Charles Breasted, *Pioneer to the Past* (New York, 1943), 75-6; see also Drower, *Flinders Petrie*, 217f.

responsibilities of excavators: 'gold digging has at least no moral responsibility, beyond the ruin of the speculator; but spoiling the past has an acute moral wrong in it'.[39] He compared archaeology to a laboratory science but emphasized that unlike other experiments Egyptological experiments could be conducted only once: the very essence of this science was destruction. The key to the archaeologist's craft was therefore to be found in the moral judgment that weighed knowledge gained, against evidence annihilated. The archaeologist's true identity was not founded on aesthetic discrimination (like Charles Newton at Halikarnassos) nor courageous adventure (like Layard at Nineveh) nor even inspired discovery (like Schliemann at Troy) but on a kind of discrimination that was ethical rather than artistic: a principle of inspired compromise that balanced the claims of the present to know the past against the claims of future excavators.

The character that Petrie aims to establish is not just a generalized ideal of modern masculinity; it is an attempt to generate an image of himself that can secure him a status as a public figure. This is an endeavour that his eugenicist texts soon followed up.[40] His attempt to acquire the prestige of a latter-day Layard or Schliemann reveals him reshaping the role of celebrity archaeologist for a new political environment. He employs the classic 'anxiety of influence' technique of undermining the basis of his predecessors' popularity which he locates in both aestheticism and the 'romance of adventure'. He casts aspersions on 'gentlemen' and 'businessmen' who had enthusiastically 'squandered [thousands] 'in doing harm' where level-headed experts could do great good 'with a hundred pounds intelligently spent'.[41] The association of archaeology with adventure, he implies, is the cause of its bad name among scientists. The press, of course, demurred, praising Petrie most strongly when he failed to undermine this adventure: even the lofty *Athenaeum* revelled in the fact that Mr Petrie's rigid typologies cannot 'curb the element of Oriental fantasy—neither do we apprehend he would desire to—which bids defiance to all rules of scientific classification'.[42]

---

[39] Petrie, *Methods and Aims*, 1.

[40] These texts, in particular *Janus in Modern Life* (London, 1906) and *The Revolutions of Civilisation* (London, 1911), were both enthused over by figures as eminent as H. G. Wells; as Richard Overy has noted, ideas we usually associate with Spengler were, in the 1910s and '20s often referenced to Petrie's works instead. See also Petrie's chapter 'Archaeology' in Alfred Russell Wallace's collection *The Progress of the Century* (New York, 1901).

[41] Petrie, *Methods and Aims*, 3.

[42] 'Mr Petrie's Forthcoming Exhibition of Egyptian Antiquities', *Athenaeum*, (30 Aug 1890), 297.

Methods and Aims depicts the thrifty expert with a steady hand and level head as an all-powerful puppet-master guiding complex excavations: the archaeologist must inspire the loyalty of scores of local Egyptian workers; sites must become well-oiled machines in which all those present are eyes and ears of the centralized power. The archaeologist is a charismatic man-manager, but also a creature of uncanny instinct. Petrie describes how the buried work of masons dead four-thousand years can be sensed by tiny variations in the feel of earth beneath the feet. Published just as *The Return of Sherlock Holmes* was being penned, this is redolent of the 'animistic reason' that Michael Saler insists was present in so much more than Doyle's fictions at this moment.[43] This unteachable sensitivity and intuition distinguishes the good from the bad archaeologist:

> The power of conserving material and information; of observing all that can be gleaned; of noticing trifling details which may imply a great deal else; of acquiring and building up a mental picture; of fitting everything into place, and not losing or missing any possible clues;—all this is the soul of the work, and without it excavating is mere dumb plodding.[44]

All others on site are mere tools; 'the hands of the master' must be responsible for all delicate work such as clearing soil from antiquities. As Stephen Quirke has pointed out, this glorification of expertise as authority mirrors colonization in miniature.[45] Even Petrie's unusually loyal commitment to the most proficient of his workers (rehiring them year after year even for excavations distant from their homes) neatly parallels certain techniques of colonial rule. The roles of these intermediary agents such as Ali Suefi who quickly developed substantial local power through their access to the archaeologist, echoes the 'go-betweens' of recent scholarship on the borderlands between cultures in imperial zones.[46]

Local knowledge, although rarely acknowledged in excavation reports, was a powerful resource even for the excavations most rooted in the traditions of

---

[43] Michael Saler, *As If: Modern Enchantment and the Literary Prehistory of Virtual Reality* (Oxford, 2012), 25-56.

[44] When Petrie touches on these themes he often employs echoes, surely deliberate, of the language and ideas of Conan Doyle and of T. H. Huxley's 1888 essay 'On the Method of Zadig'; Huxley and Doyle exemplify the kind of public status that Petrie sought.

[45] Stephen Quirke, *Hidden Hands: Egyptian Workforces in Petrie Excavation Archives, 1880-1924* (London, 2010).

[46] Simon Schaffer et al., *The Brokered World: Go-betweens and Global Intelligence, 1770-1820* (London, 2009).

the King James Bible and Herodotus. Archaeology and antiquities tourism were both enormously destructive of small Egyptian communities after 1882, but Egyptologists came to value these communities for unexpected reasons. In works like *Methods and Aims*, which aspired to interest the public not just in the outputs of Egyptological research, but in the day-to-day practice of the excavator, some picture of local communities and the archaeologist's relationship with them began to emerge. At the beginning of the 1880s Petrie, Naville, and other excavators were deeply interested in local traditions. This was not the 'peasant studies' agenda that emerged in the 1930s: excavators before the First World War had little interest in understanding or preserving fellah traditions in their own right.[47] Instead, they worked hard to recover traces of biblical or classical people and locations from Arabic place names and folklore. British periodicals frequently featured images of excavators not as lone explorers, but shepherded by intermediaries who pointed out landmarks to which tradition attached the names of Moses or Rhodopis. And every archaeological instruction manual of this period suggests strategies for appraising the reliability of local knowledge. The Arabic language and local tradition are presented as a veil drawn between the modern European viewer and a crystalline reality called 'ancient Egypt'. From the patterns dimly discerned through this veil the contours of antiquity can be reconstituted. As well as this highly amateurish attentiveness to etymological echoes among local people, observation of the relationship between modern *felaheen* and the Nile was used as a means of accessing the 'ancient Egyptian mind' which was supposedly formed in response to the same environmental challenges and quotidian realities. Amid assumptions of the unchanging nature of 'the East', and despite general lack of interest in modern Egyptian culture in its own right, the Egyptologist became folklorist as well as engineer, engaged in the preservation of cultural traces as well as stone and mortar.

British Egyptology in European perspective

It is a familiar fact that preservation concerns played out very differently in different European states. It is also well known that this related in part to divergent attitudes to professional and amateur approaches (so far as those terms make any sense for this period). To wheel out the cliché, preservation in

---

[47] When this genre did emerge, towards the end of Petrie's career, its exponents usually studied villages with economies that were reliant on archaeology or the tourist trade, where villagers could acquire archaeological expertise themselves or else 'become mysteriously rich in a very short time' by joining in the circulation of antiquities. Nor was this the anthropology of the *felaheen* which usually, for the sake of convenience, studied archaeological workforces (e.g. W. H. R. Rivers).

Germany was less a matter of public interest and more a matter for certificated experts in architecture, art history, or engineering. Preservation concerns in Britain were mobilized through public interest, often open subscription and donation, and organized by celebrities whose institutional affiliations or expert training were not self-evidently those of an incipient heritage industry. This cliché holds more or less true. To all intents and purposes Flinders Petrie, until at least the time when *Methods and Aims* was published, was seen to belong to this amateur tradition. He lacked classical languages and university training. The costs of his early excavations were raised by Amelia Edwards via public subscription and he received no remuneration beyond bare expenses.

The differences this generated between Petrie and European scholars were many. Often university trained, they had access to university resources and authority. Often state-funded, they received official sanction from their own governments and the Egyptian state. Mariette for instance was sponsored from 1849 by his employer, the Louvre, and by 1859 had persuaded Khedive Ismail to found the Department of Antiquities he controlled until his death in 1881. This position also allowed him status as director of Egypt's first museums. Still more dramatically, it permitted him use of *corvée*: he wielded state authority to compel *felaheen* into his workforce. His role as a cultural intermediary between states was demonstrated in his authorship of the libretto of Verdi's *Aida*, commissioned for the opening of the Suez Canal. Other French and German archaeologists partook of Mariette's system to varying degrees, but most sought connections with a system that became increasingly formalized and was tied increasingly closely to state power.

By the time Petrie arrived in Egypt this was (despite the usual institutional jealousies) a well-oiled system with its own pecking-order in which leading French and German Egyptologists knew their place. It carefully controlled permits to excavate, both to limit antiquities leaving Egypt and to attempt to establish a professionalized system whereby only those with appropriate credentials or connections might dig. Like Mariette, its new leaders saw retaining antiquities in Egypt as a primary goal, and like Mariette they aimed to develop a professional system with a clear hierarchical structure.

Mariette's ambition to keep antiquities in Cairo was one that the British continued to oppose. In fact, Petrie, and his peers refused to work within this hierarchy and in so doing they threatened the system. Self-consciously independent and amateur, they rejected French or German leadership, and considered that their own authority trumped that of the Department of Antiquities. To this end, Petrie's claim to a technical archaeological superiority, which used mathematics to record sites and chemistry to preserve artefacts, was crucial. Since he asserted that imperial power was not his justification, Petrie's insistence on an entirely new skill-set, not taught in universities, not 'owned' by Mariette's hierarchy, was the chief grounds that British archaeologists found for justifying their antagonism to the Department of Antiquities. Although he did attack Mariette on the grounds of his treatment of *felaheen*, his chief critique concerned the aesthetic nature of the Department's concerns and their apparent lack of interest in the contributions of chemical and physical knowledge to the development of an archaeological science. The support Petrie did have in the British press thus hit out at French, German, and Greek excavators, deploring the fact that not archaeological judgements, but 'some diplomatic fad' placed the antiquities of Egypt in 'the present utterly incompetent hands'; in the view of this reviewer the French system ('if system it can be called') squandered 'thousands upon thousands of pounds of the public grant' and achieved nothing.[48] Even in the 1890s when all real danger from flooding was long gone, the Department of Antiquities museum was consistently portrayed as the most dangerous place in the world for antiquities.

This drawing of battle lines defined the enmities that developed. Petrie was belittled by German scholars such as Virchow and Schweinfurth in much the same terms as were employed by the cosmopolitan art critics whose work filled the London journals: he was an untrained amateur who showed no flair for those skills that validated the archaeologist's or antiquary's claim to expertise. His enemies could wield the opinions of the most prestigious names of European archaeology when they sought to sully Petrie's reputation. One American lawyer, resident in London, did so when he used Petrie's most celebrated excavation—Hawara—as a case study to damn the amateurism of British Egyptology in general: 'Schweinfurth told me that Virchow had said to him that the horrors of Königgratz had not prepared him for the revolting sight of Petrie's mangled remains of Hawara'.[49] In reality, of course, there were no 'good' or 'bad' figures. Petrie's attitude to the *felaheen*, although deeply orientalist, was fairer than Mariette's; Mariette's attitude to the Egyptian state was more positive than Petrie's.

After *Methods and Aims*

From 1910 onwards the UCL Egyptology course (nominally under Petrie's control but in fact masterminded by Margaret Murray) was finally organized into a certificated qualification, no longer just Petrie's paternalistic finishing school for 'lady artists'.[50] It had soon become the model for archaeological

---

[48] 'Illahun, Kahun and Gurob', *Saturday Review*, (17 Oct 1891), 452.

[49] F. C. Whitehouse to Edward Poynter, 27 September 1888, EES VIIIa.3.

[50] See Rosalind M. Janssen, *Egyptology at University College London, 1892-1992* (London, 1992).

Egyptology education, its elements adapted into similar courses in Britain, Europe, and America. But change was under way before these students reached the field: the vast salvage archaeology projects associated with the building of the Aswan Dam forced international cooperation on an entirely unprecedented scale. At the same time, reorganization of the Department of Antiquities gradually placed some, younger, British Egyptologists within the system. In 1899, for instance, Howard Carter was appointed Chief Inspector of Antiquities for Upper Egypt (some of the many tensions at work here were demonstrated when Carter was forced to resign after siding with Egyptian guards against French tourists in the 'Saqqara Affair' of 1905). The careers of Carter and his replacement, Arthur Weigall, demonstrate the gradual professionalization of British Egyptology. Yet this was all patchy and unsustained development: this new generation of Egyptologists struggled to balance the pressures exerted by the British Government (including those for rapid development of Egyptian irrigation, road, and rail) with the claims of preservation; surprisingly frequently, they sided with industrial modernization and against the cause of antiquities. In this sense, increasing professionalization of British Egyptology did not mean increasingly coherent attitudes to preservation.

Two things changed this. The first was the suspension of archaeological activity during the First World War. The Egyptology that emerged after 1919, long discussed in European cities over five inactive years, was more coherent than its earlier manifestations. Members of the EEF continued to meet irregularly during the war and at their meetings a post-war agenda for the organization was shaped. On 3 October 1916 H. G. Lyons, J. G. Milne, and A. H. Gardiner met and with 'scientific' as their watchword compared the techniques of French, German, and American scholars to attempt to reconcile diverse Egyptological approaches into a coherent disciplinary norm.[51] It was in this wartime fermata that the reputation of Naville was finally challenged, not Petrie but the American Egyptologist George Reisner being praised as the model for progressive recording and preservation techniques. Reisner was soon celebrated as the first Egyptologist to achieve in practice the freedom from museum interests that Petrie had long advocated in theory. His work at Giza was also celebrated as developing photography from an ethnographic and topographic tool into one that could truly be called 'archaeological'.

Yet 1922 was an even more significant year than 1919. It represented the beginning of a new Egyptological order. Under the 1922 Egyptian parliament the plunder of antiquities became much more difficult. Egypt became much less a 'house on fire' and the sense of panicked acquisition receded. Those for

---

[51] EEF Sub-committee Report, 3 October 1916, XVIII 32.

whom this panic had become a way of life, including Petrie and many of his students, now found Egypt an inhospitable place to dig and moved their focus eastward and northward around the Mediterranean. Once again, the archaeologists followed in the footsteps of the imperial regime, taking advantage of the Jerusalem Mandate (1923-48) in much the same way as they made use of British power in Egypt from 1882-1922. The same kinds of practice continued in Palestine far into the twentieth century: Petrie maintained many of his 1890s approaches into the 1930s. Pressures for heritage agendas, it seems, remained localized, the established culture of archaeology continuing to prove resistant to change.

Timothy Mitchell has demonstrated how Egypt under British rule was treated as a playground for technological experimentation, generating approaches and ideas that would then be exported around the globe. The most obvious example is the total restructuring of the flow of the Nile from the 1870s onwards, with the Aswan Dam begun in the 1890s being the first really major event in this. This helped, in Mitchell's words 'inaugurate around the world an era of engineering on a new scale. . . for many postcolonial governments the [ability to rearrange] the natural and social environment' through this new breed of super-dam 'became a means to demonstrate the strength of the modern state as techno-economic power'.[52] Archaeology, on a much more modest scale, followed a comparable pattern. Much like these dramatic engineering interventions, the archaeological practices established in Egypt in the 1890s did not so much adapt to the new circumstances of the 1920s as migrate to places where political developments permitted their operation. Numerous figures who had trained as Egyptologists within Petrie's circle of influence (such as John Garstang) chose to reject the new strictures of Egypt, persisting with established approaches in areas made newly amenable by political and military power. The factors that limited the efficacy of heritage agendas in the 1890s continued to wreak ruin on preservation.

---

[52] Timothy Mitchell, 'Can the Mosquito Speak?' in *Rule of Experts: Egypt, Technopolitics, Modernity* (Berkeley, 2002), 19-53; what Mitchell also shows is that these alterations of the Nile made it a highway for diseases that were new to Egypt. They permitted, for instance, the 1942 invasion of Egypt by mosquitoes carrying particularly virulent forms of malaria, which Mitchell suggests was as momentous an invasion as that by Rommel's panzers in the same year.

The Warden of World Heritage:
UNESCO and the Rescue of the Nubian Monuments

Paul Betts

On 10 March 1980 the long-awaited consecration of two dozen of the most famous Nubian monuments rescued from the waters of Lake Nasser took place with solemn pomp and circumstance. Over 500 people were in attendance, as the desert ceremony unfolded between two colonnades of the famed Isis temple. One witness described the remarkable sunrise spectacle this way:

> In the darkness, well before sunrise, the Cairo Symphony Orchestra, under the wondering eyes of the Nubians, in full evening dress and with their instruments, had filled the Nubian boats to be carried to the re-erected Philae. With them went guests to hear the morning prayer and see the temples first red then golden in the light of the rising sun.

This event crowned the unprecedented twenty-year campaign of the United Nations Education, Culture, and Science Organization to cut, transport, and relocate twenty-three massive Nubian statues to higher ground in order to save them from submersion by Egypt's High Aswan Dam project of the early 1960s. The International 'Save the Nubian Monuments' initiative enlisted the support of dozens of countries and NGOs, along with thousands of archaeologists, engineers, and volunteers, in a common enterprise of fundraising, political will, and technical virtuosity that transcended Cold War division. The Senegalese Director General of UNESCO, Amadou-Mahtar M'Bow, was on hand to pay tribute to the dawning of a global universal heritage: 'our generation is the first in history to perceive the totality of these works as an indivisible whole, each of them being considered as an integral part of a single universal heritage,' concluding that '[i]t will be numbered among the few major attempts made in our lifetime by the nations to assume their common responsibility towards the past so as to move forward in a spirit of brotherhood towards the future.'[1] A similar spirit informed the words of Egyptian President Anwar el-Sadat:

> The success we are celebrating today gives us concrete evidence that when people work together for a good cause they can achieve miracles. We have joined hands in saving an ancient civilization, so let us join hands to save the future of all peoples by strengthening peace.[2]

No event better exemplified UNESCO's abiding mission to build and safeguard what it boldly called 'world civilization,' and as such it constituted an instructive tale of Cold War internationalism. This was no small feat, given that the internationalization of the heritage industry after 1945 (often seen with the national reclamation of monuments, religious sites, and natural parks around the world) was usually so closely tied to projects of state-building and the construction of new national identities.[3] In this way UNESCO flew in the face of international trends, and here and elsewhere made great strides in bringing together international law, historical preservation, and intercultural awareness about the historical emblems of universal humanity. UNESCO's Nubian monument preservation project played a special role in this cultural crusade, hailed as proof that such a global heritage-consciousness could and did exist despite geopolitical antagonism and ideological difference. Given Gamal Abdel Nasser's effort to speed along the Aswan High Dam project in the early 1960s, Nubia played host to a dramatic clash between progress and preservation that attracted worldwide media coverage. As one contemporary commentator wryly put it: 'Thus Nubia, poor, forgotten and now doomed, commanded in its dying days the interest of mankind.'[4] This essay explores the extent to which UNESCO's 'Save the Nubian Monuments' project captured a pivotal episode of post-war universalism based on a distinctly post-war sensibility of humanity's shared and imperilled cultural patrimony.

---

[1] Amadou-Mahtar M'Bow, 'A Single, Universal Heritage', *Unesco Courier*, 33 (Feb/March 1980), 4.

[2] Torgny Säve-Söderbergh (ed.), *Temples and Tombs of Ancient Nubia: The International Rescue Campaign at Abu Simbel, Philae and Other Sites* (Paris, 1987), 185-6.

[3] M. Diaz-Andreu and T. Champion (eds), *Nationalism and Archaeology in Europe* (Boulder, 1996); Philip L. Kohl and Clare Fawcett, *Nationalism, Politics and the Practice of Archaeology* (Cambridge, 1995); and John Schofield and Wayne Cocroft (eds), *A Fearsome Heritage: Diverse Legacies of the Cold War* (Walnut Creek, CA, 2007).

[4] Tom Little, *High Dam at Aswan: The Subjugation of the Nile* (London, 1965), 157.

For starters, Nubia was the name of the land in north-eastern Africa directly south of Egypt, stretching along the banks of the Nile along numerous cataracts. It was the only continuously occupied tract of land that connected sub-Saharan Africa with the Mediterranean world. Nubian culture dates back to 3500 BC, and it is generally agreed that the word Nubia derives from the ancient Egyptian word *nwb*, meaning gold, and defines the region between Aswan and Debba where Nubian languages are spoken.[5] The region is now a sparsely populated area straddling Egypt and Sudan. It was the first and most enduring of the African trading empires, as the Nile corridor represented the safest means of commerce connecting the African and Mediterranean coasts. At times the area fell under the domination of Egypt, at other times it was an independent state. However, the modern history of Nubia has been dominated by Egypt and Sudan; there was an uprising in 1883 under Mohammed Ahmed, the Mahdi, and though he died in 1885, Nubia became for a short time an autonomous Islamic state independent of Egypt and Great Britain. In 1896 a joint Egyptian–English expeditionary force led by Sir Herbert Kitchener began a successful campaign against the Mahdist regime in the Sudan. In 1899 the Sudan and Egypt were amalgamated and placed under the rule of the British Governor-General as Anglo-Egyptian Sudan.[6] The area was known to a number of intrepid Western travellers and colourfully chronicled by European explorers such as Louis Norden, Johann Ludwig Burckhardt, and Amelia Edwards. Nubia was the site of nineteenth-century archaeological expeditions made famous by Jean-Francois Champollion and Karl Richard Lepsius, and the region continued to exert fascination among Western anthropologists and photographers over the course of the twentieth century, ranging from Merian C. Cooper to Rolf Herzog, George Rodger to Leni Riefenstahl.[7]

Nasser's Aswan High Dam project began in 1960, and took ten years to complete. Large dam construction was not new to the region. While ideas of taming the river's flow go back to pharaonic times, the modern era's effort to devise a reservoir to store excess water from the Nile's great floods first began with the building of the first Aswan Dam between 1898 and 1912. It was

---

[5] John H. Taylor, *Egypt and Nubia* (London, 1991), 4-7.

[6] John A. Larson, *Lost Nubia: A Centennial Exhibit of Photographs from the 1905-1907 Egyptian Expedition of the University of Chicago* (Chicago, 2006), vii–x.

[7] Alexandra Ludewig, 'Leni Riefenstahl's Encounter with the Nuba', *Interventions: International Journal of Postcolonial Studies* 8:1 (2006), 83-101. See too Rolf Herzog, *Die Nubier* (Berlin, 1957) and Armgard Grauer, 'Die Architektur und Wandmalerei der Nubier behandelt nach dem ethnographischen Befund vor der Aussiedlung 1963/1964', PhD dissertation, Albert-Ludwigs-Universität zu Freiburg i. Br., 1968.

designed by British engineers, primarily to service cotton cultivation. The dam was raised in 1912 and then again in 1933 in order to meet Egypt's growing demands for water.[8] Its thirty-year construction made it easily the largest civil enterprise of the British mandate in Egypt, and was celebrated as a wonder of technical achievement and British imperial might. But the side effects of the project attracted more and more attention. As the first dam construction was nearly completed, there was growing concern among Egyptologists and others about the fate of the ancient Nubian ruins (both monuments and human remains) and peoples once the area had been flooded.[9] Hasty compromises were struck—the famous Philae monument, for example, was allowed to be half-submerged for five months of the year. In this case, the preservationists were largely overrun by the technocrats, who drove ahead with subjugating the Nile for their agricultural and economic purposes.

The conflict between old and new became even more pronounced in the wake of the Egyptian Revolution in 1952. Regulating the Nile served as the political cornerstone of the fledgling United Arab Republic, and the dam was often described as Nasser's latter-day pyramid in terms of its central political symbolism. One of the overarching goals of his revolution was economic and social progress, and the new regime targeted the High Dam at Aswan for its modernization crusade. It was deemed vital to control the new country's water supply for irrigation and hydro-electricity, as well as to protect the country from droughts and perennial flooding. In 1954 the new republic succeeded in removing British soldiers from the Suez Canal, and later that year looked to the World Bank for a loan to finance the High Dam construction. However, relations with the West were soured by the fact that Nasser had just negotiated an arms deal with Czechoslovakia and then established formal diplomatic ties with communist China, policies openly in conflict with American containment policy. The US thereafter withdrew its initial offer of financial support, as did the World Bank. Undeterred, Nasser announced his intention to nationalize the Suez Canal in July 1956, expecting that revenues generated from this would help underwrite dam construction and the creation of a 300-mile long artificial lake, Lake Nasser. With the outbreak of war later that year, Egypt was in urgent need of support and in 1958 the USSR offered financial assistance for the project, along with requisite technicians

---

[8] Hussein M. Fahim, *Dams, People and Development* (New York, 1981), 7-15.

[9] David Gange, 'Unholy Water: Archaeology, the Bible and the First Aswan Dam', in Astrid Swenson and Peter Mandler (eds), *Between Preservation and Plunder* (London, 2013), 93-114.

and heavy machinery.[10] While the communist dimension of the deal was of little appeal to Nasser, he embraced it for tactical reasons; there was widespread feeling in the West and the Arab world that the US and Great Britain failed to help when they had the chance.[11] The joint dam project became the source of great Cold War theatre as a sign of a new Soviet-African axis, as well as a showcase of Soviet engineering (even if the Soviets simply modified an earlier West German design). In a publicized exchange of letters between Khrushchev and Nasser in January 1960, Nasser proudly confirmed that the Aswan High Dam 'will forever remain a symbol of the friendship between our two peoples. I am also confident that it will remain for all peace-loving peoples a living example of a positive and magnificent work for peace.'[12]

Even so, the High Dam project clearly had its shadow side. The director of Egypt's Antiquities Service, Mustafa Amer, was the first to sound the alarm about the fate of the Nubian monuments residing in the valleys slated to be flooded. Amer enlisted the support of Egyptologists and engineers from around the world in writing a letter of appeal to Nasser's new government to reconsider the plan. Nothing came of it, however, as Nasser's insouciance toward the Nubian monuments was well known.[13] In 1955 Egypt's Antiquities Service quickly published a study by Osman Rostem, *The Salvage of Philae*, which pointed out the rich cache of antiquities still to be excavated in the area, but which would be lost forever were the dam project to move forward. That year UNESCO created the 'Documentation and Study Centre of the History of Art and Civilization of Ancient Egypt' in Cairo so as to document some four hundred private tombs of the Theban Necropolis along with hundreds of other sites, with Louvre director Christiane Desroches-Noblecourt driving the rescue campaign at this early stage.[14] The French Institut Géographique National was called in to carry out a 'photogrammetic survey' of the area affected before it was too late, aided by the Egyptian armed forces. By 1959 the Egyptian Minister of Culture,

---

[10] James E. Dougherty, 'The Aswan Decision in Perspective', *Political Science Quarterly*, 74:1 (March 1959) 21–45.

[11] Leslie Greener, *High Dam over Nubia* (London, 1962), 27. See too the booklet in the Cairo series 'Africa for Africans', *The Aswan High Dam: New Wonder of the Nile* (Cairo, 1960), 13.

[12] Gamul Abdul [sic] Nasser to N. Khrushchev, 17 January 1960, Cairo, reprinted in *The Aswan High Dam: New Wonder*, 66-7.

[13] See the typed confidential letter from Louis-A. Christophe, Centre de Documentation sur l'Egypte ancienne, Cairo, to M. A. Vrioni, 30 Jan 1963, 069 (62) N/Abu Simbel Part I and IV, Box 53, UNESCO Archive, Paris, hereafter UAP.

[14] Säve-Söderbergh, *Temples*, 64-5.

Tharwat Okasha, began to worry about the negative international publicity for both his ministry and the new state, and called a meeting with UNESCO representatives to discuss the matter in earnest.[15]

But why UNESCO? This is not as obvious as it may at first appear, not least because the organization was subject to bitter political wrangling among various factions from the very beginning. Over the decades its history was marred by a series of protests and dramatic walk-outs from various delegations, and in the early 1950s one director-general famously resigned in tears of frustration over further budget cuts. Worse, UNESCO's lofty internationalist mission was routinely ridiculed in the world press as woefully starry-eyed and out of step with a hard-edged world of Cold War power politics. By the late 1950s UNESCO's 'civilizing mission' was pilloried as nothing but a 'cavalry of hobby horses' and 'pork barrel riding on a cloud'.[16] Max Frisch's popular 1957 novel, *Homo Faber*, was a kind of send-up of UNESCO's 'one-world' civilizational ideal and its do-gooder espousal of modernization for all; at one point the novel's protagonist, a normally reserved Swiss UNESCO technical expert en route to South America to help build turbines in Venezuela, remarked to an acquaintance that he met on the trip: 'I only lost my temper when Marcel started to talk about my work, that is to say about UNESCO, saying the technologist was the final guise of the white missionary, industrialization the last gospel of a dying race and living standards a substitute for a purpose of living.'[17] But such a characterization was quite misleading, for UNESCO was as interested in preservation as it was in progress; so much so that the stewardship of ancient ruins and the protection of endangered cultural property across the world was identified as an area where UNESCO hoped to make its international mark.

Of course UNESCO by no means pioneered these ideas. The international safeguarding of cultural property had been devised a century or so earlier, often in reaction to the destructive capacities of war. In the wake of the Napoleonic Wars, for example, plunder became a key moral issue among nations, and international treaties (beginning with the 1874 Brussels 'Project of an International Declaration concerning the Laws and Customs of War') were expressly dedicated to redressing damage and destruction to state property of all kinds in times of war. The respect of cultural property in wartime was made more present in the Hague Conventions for the Protection of

---

[15] Fekri A. Hassan, 'The Aswan High Dam and the International Rescue Nubia Campaign', *Journal of African Archaeology*, 24:3/4 (Sept/Dec 2007), 81.

[16] James Sewell, *Unesco and World Politics: Engaging in International Relations* (Princeton, 1975), 153-9, 119, 135.

[17] Max Frisch, *Homo Faber*, trans. Michael Bullock (London, 1974 [1957]), 55.

Cultural Heritage in 1899 and 1907, respectively, and there were proposals put forward by Switzerland and Belgium during the First World War to set up a Red Cross-like organization entrusted with protecting cultural objects during war.[18] Nevertheless, it was the aftermath of the Great War that saw renewed international attention toward preservation, spearheaded by the League of Nations. The League and its new International Commission on Historical Monuments endeavoured to create new legal instruments to protect cultural antiquities as a step toward international cooperation. The League's first attempt to set up a cultural heritage conservation initiative took place in 1923, on the back of the worldwide coverage and popular excitement associated with the discovery of King Tutankhamun's tomb the year before. The League's International Museums Office was founded in 1926 to carry on the mission, and the final report of its high-profile conference in Athens in 1931 concluded with the words that the 'question of the conservation of the artistic and archaeological property of mankind is one that interests the community of States, which are wardens of civilization.' Likewise, the Pan-American Union signed a Treaty on the Protection of Artistic and Scientific Institutions and Historical Monuments in 1935, and two years later an International Conference on Excavations took place in Cairo infused with a similar claim to save the world's 'common archaeological heritage'.[19] But for all of the rhetoric of universalism, World War II cruelly put paid to this budding internationalist preservation movement.

After 1945 there was a move to rehabilitate and extend this interwar dream, even to the extent of rendering such destruction an internationally recognized criminal offence. At the Nuremberg Trials, for instance, the destruction of cultural property was now declared a crime against humanity. In the proceedings Alfred Rosenberg—infamous Head of the Third Reich's Centre for National Socialist Ideological and Education Research—was singled out for his office's unlawful seizure of cultural treasures.[20] UNESCO sought to build on this new political sensibility. American poet and UNESCO delegate Archibald MacLeish went so far as to say that UNESCO solemnly held the

---

[18] Michael Elliott and Vaughn Schmutz, 'World Heritage: Constructing a Universal World Order', *Poetics* 40 (2012), 262-3; and Astrid Swenson, *The Rise of Heritage: Preserving the Past in France, Germany and England, 1789-1914* (Cambridge, 2013), 220-8.

[19] Sarah M. Titchen, 'On the Construction of Outstanding Universal Value: Unesco's World Heritage Convention (Convention Concerning the Protection of the World Cultural and Natural Heritage, 1972) and the Identification and Assessment of Cultural Places for Inclusion in the World Heritage List', PhD Thesis, Australian National University (April 1995), 15-35.

[20] Eliott and Schmutz, 'World Heritage', 265.

'responsibility of civilization itself' and that its guiding objective should be to stand above state conflict and partisan politics in an increasingly divided Cold War world.[21] But despite its post-Nazi internationalism, UNESCO's early preservation campaign was expressly geared toward Europe, fuelled in particular by the need to shore up Western civilization in crisis. At the famed Council of Allied Ministers of Education Conference in 1944, a meeting of Education Ministers from sixteen countries in London to discuss post-war reconstruction, European education and culture were the main priorities. Shock and outrage were directed toward the Nazi looting and decimation of European treasure and heritage. The conference's newly created Commission for the Protection and Restitution of Cultural Material tipped its hand in declaring that 'a concentrated effort is being made for the immediate protection and ultimate restitution of the cultural heritage of Western civilization'.[22] The early years of UNESCO continued this logic, as it developed an expansive notion of reconstruction.[23] In this case, reconstruction meant books for libraries, materials for schools, scientific equipment for laboratories, the distribution of musical instruments, and the creation of International Youth Camps.[24] Focus fell on the 'Translation of Classics', to the extent that UNESCO was to spearhead translations of 'world's classics in the various languages of the Member States of the UN', together with drafting a Bill of Human Rights.[25] Article 1 of UNESCO's 1946 Constitution stated its mission as 'assuring the conservation and protection of the world's inheritance of books, works of art and monuments of history and science'.[26]

UNESCO's heritage protection mission began to take shape over the course of the next decade. The 1950 earthquake in Cuzco, Peru launched UNESCO's first mission to save archaeological ruins. On this occasion it sent down teams of international archaeologists and technical experts to work with Peruvian locals to save its Aztec ruins, and by all accounts this was a

---

[21] Sewell, *Unesco*, 169.

[22] *Allied Plan for Education: The Story of the Conference of the Allied Ministers of Education* (London, 1945), 29 and 33.

[23] *UNESCO General Conference: First Session, Paris, 1946* (Paris, 1947), 136-47.

[24] *UNESCO Report of the Director General on Activities of the Organisation in 1947*, presented at Second Session in Mexico City, Nov-Dec 1947 (Paris, 1947), 6-7.

[25] Interim Report of UNESCO to the Economic and Social Council of the UN, 11 July 1947, 13, JG Crowther Papers, SxMs29 Box 84, Univ. of Sussex Special Collections, Falmer.

[26] Address Delivered by Dir. Gen. at the Meeting of the International Committee on Monuments, Artistic and Historical Sites and Archaeological Excavations, Unesco House, Paris, 21 May 1951, 1, 069: 72 A02/06 III, UAP.

very successful initiative.[27] Its new global vision found further expression in the 1954 Hague Convention on the 'Protection of Cultural Property in the Event of Armed Conflict', which was explicitly designed as a fortified version of the Hague Conventions of 1899 and 1907.[28] 'Cultural property belonging to any people', so it proclaimed, is 'also the cultural heritage of all mankind'.[29]

Yet these were still pipe dreams, and UNESCO needed a big project to showcase its new role as guardian of world civilization. The timing of the threat to the Nubian monuments could not have been more fortuitous. At a moment when Egypt had just removed British military force after seventy years of occupation, UNESCO was viewed by Nasser as a non-partisan inter-governmental alternative to Western institutions.[30] There was growing interest in the Nubians among *National Geographic* photographers in the early 1950s, and the 'Save the Nubian Monuments' campaign looked to capitalize on this international publicity.[31] In 1955 Luther Evans, the new American Director General of UNESCO, went to the famed site of Abu Simbel, whereafter an agreement was made with Cairo about UNESCO's technical assistance. Now there was a hurried effort to explore, map, and record all sites of 'archaeological importance for the history of Nubia from the beginning of the Egyptian dynasties onwards'.[32] Egypt and the Sudan then entreated UNESCO for assistance, citing its constitutional responsibility for 'the conservation and protection of the world's inheritance'. Proposals were solicited from various quarters of Europe, and eventually the experts selected a Swedish plan to have the temple facades and walls cut into big blocks that could be transported to a safe place and then rebuilt on higher ground. Rock temples were to be hewn from the cliffs and then transported in sections, while free-standing temples

[27] *Cuzco: Reconstruction of the Town and Restoration of its Monuments* (Paris, 1952).

[28] *Records of the Conference Convened by the United Nations Educational, Scientific and Cultural Organization Held at the Hague from 21 April to 14 May 1954* (The Hague, 1961), 6.

[29] Lowenthal, 228.

[30] Hassan, 'Aswan High Dam', 79.

[31] George Rodger, *The Village of the Nubas* (London, 1955). Many of these images first appeared in Robin Strachan and George Rodger, 'With the Nuba hillmen of Kordofan', *National Geographic Magazine*, 99:2 (February, 1951), 249-78. The interwar photographic fascination with the Nubians can be seen in Merian C. Cooper, 'Two fighting tribes of the Sudan', *National Geographic* (1929), 464-86 and Charles and Gabriel and Brenda Seligman, *Pagan Tribes of the Nilotic Sudan* (London, 1932).

[32] Harry S. Smith, *Unesco's International Campaign to Save the Monuments of Nubia: Preliminary Reports of the Egypt Exploration Society's Nubian Survey*, United Arab Republic, Ministry of Culture and National Guidance, Antiquities Department of Egypt (Cairo, 1962), 1, Pamphlet Box 96, S-Z, Sackler Library, Oxford.

were to be dismantled, transferred, and reassembled. To give the temples an 'appropriate setting', so argued the Egyptian government in one of its publicity brochures, 'hills would be built up, which, though not exact copies of the cliffs where the Temples originally had been hewn, would nevertheless preserve their memory'.[33] To further drum up support, the Egyptian government organized an exhibition, 'Five Thousand Years of Egyptian Art', which started its world tour in Brussels in 1960.[34]

In March 1960 UNESCO's new Director General Vittorio Veronese kicked off the international appeal 'to governments, institutions, public and private foundations and all people of goodwill'. UNESCO was careful not to offend the Egyptian government in any way, lest it appeared too partisan in this delicate Cold War climate. Vittorese conceded that this was a difficult issue for the new Egyptian state, and that 'it is not easy to choose between temples and crops'. But then he made his case for the higher cause of universal civilization:

> These monuments, the loss of which may be tragically near, do not belong solely to the countries who hold them in trust. The whole world has the right to see them endure. They are part of a common heritage which comprises Socrates' message and the Ajanta frescoes; the walls of Uxmal and Beethoven's symphonies. Treasures of universal value are entitled to universal protection.[35]

Notably the language of rights and legal protections was gravitating to the centre of this heritage campaign, driven forward by UNESCO. Such views were given additional imprimatur by UNESCO's deputy director, the Swiss René Maheu, who intoned that 'the affirmation of the existence of an artistic heritage that belongs to humanity and the recognition of a duty to international solidarity to ensure its preservation is a human idea in the widest and noblest meaning of the word' and that such a campaign signalled 'the universalization of the human consciousness of values'.[36] Where the early

---

[33] Arab Republic of Egypt, Ministry of Culture, *The Salvage of the Abu Simbel Temples: Concluding Report, December 1971*, prepared by Swedish engineering team of Vattenbyggnadsbyrån (Örebro, 1976), 25.

[34] Little, *High Dam*, 163.

[35] 'March 8 Appeal by Vittorino Veronese, Director-General of Unesco', *Unesco Courier*, 13 (May, 1960), 7.

[36] Statement by Mr. R. Maheu, Assistant Director-General of Unesco, on the progress made in the international campaign for safeguarding the monuments of Nubia, UAR Consultative Committee, Cairo 23-1 June 1960, 3, R1/3, CLT/CIH/MCO Box 29, UAP.

twentieth-century preservation drive to save the famed Nubian monuments was justified by Egyptologists for the study of biblical narratives and theories of racial diffusion,[37] this post-1945 campaign was animated by a decidedly secular ideal of universal civilization that linked ancient past and present around the ideas of science, culture, and peace, best reflected in UNESCO's commissioned six-volume series, *History of Mankind,* that covered prehistory to the present day.[38] For this reason Maheu dubbed the rescue of Abu Simbel a kind of 'spiritual act'[39] in a secular international world.

Internationally, this project offered UNESCO the chance to 'act as the essential intermediary between States and institutions anxious to participate in the great enterprise' of Nubia's archaeological salvage.[40] This was widely seen as UNESCO's moment. Jacquetta Hawkes, co-author of the first volume of UNESCO's high-profile World History series on 'The Scientific and Cultural History of Mankind', concluded an *Observer* (London) article with the question: 'Could any request be more exactly addressed to the ideals of Unesco as we dreamed of them in the high, hopeful, early days?'[41] As such the UNESCO initiative challenged state sovereignty in subtle ways. Until that point all monuments within states were of exclusively national concern and were to be cared for by individual states. This time things were different. As UNESCO's director of the Monuments of Nubia Service, Ali Vrioni, understood at the time: 'For the first time the world has seen organized international action to save monuments of archaeological wealth, which, in law, belong only to the two countries where they are located.'[42] A number of publications in various languages were quickly published by UNESCO to help publicize the urgency of the campaign.[43]

American assistance was also crucial. In 1961 an exhibition of Tutankhamun treasures toured the US, visiting thirteen American cities,

[37]   Gange, *Unholy Water*, 112-14.

[38]   Glenda Sluga, 'Unesco and the (One) World of Julian Huxley', *Journal of World History*, 21:3 (2010), 393-417; and Poul Duedahl, 'Selling Mankind: UNESCO and the Invention of Global History, 1945-1976', *Journal of World History*, 22:1 (2011), 101-33.

[39]   Max-Pol Fouchet, *Rescued Treasures of Egypt*, trans. Michael Heron (London, 1965), 40-1.

[40]   *Philae Resurrected* (Paris: Unesco, 1980).

[41]   Quoted in Sewell, *Unesco*, 253.

[42]   Ali Vrioni, 'Victory in Nubia', *Unesco Courier*, 17 (Dec 1964), 5.

[43]   See, e.g., *Republique Arabe Unie: Centre de Documentation sur L'Egypte Ancienne* (Paris, 1961?); and *Temples de Nubie: Des Trésors menaces*, preface by Christiane Desroches-Noblecourt (Paris, 1961). See too *La Nubie Antique* (Brussels, 1963?) and Louis-A. Christophe, *Abou-Simbel et L'Épopée de la Découverte* (Brussels, 1965).

partly 'organized to publicize and awaken interest in the Nubian campaign'.[44] That same year President John F. Kennedy launched an impassioned plea before Congress on 7 April 1961 to garner American support, and fully subscribed to the UNESCO mission of converting these ancient ruins into world heritage:

> The United States, one of the newest civilizations, has long had a deep regard for the study of past cultures, and a concern for the preservation of man's great achievements of art and thoughts [sic]. . . By thus contributing to the preservation of past civilizations, we will strengthen and enrich our own.[45]

The US thus sought to make up for the failure to support the Aswan Dam project, heeding the call to rescue the ancient monuments by matching Egypt's $10 million financial commitment.[46] Accompanying exhibitions took place both in the US and Europe, and a number of countries (such as Ghana and Nigeria) issued commemorative stamps to keep the campaign in the public eye.[47]

The European dimension was significant too. The original 'Honorary Committee of Patrons' for the Nubian campaign was chaired by King Gustav VI Adolf of Sweden, flanked by other royals (Queen Elizabeth of Belgium, Queen Fredrika of Greece and Princess Mikasa of Japan), the UN Director Dag Hammarskjöld, UNESCO's first director Julian Huxley, and French Culture Minister André Malraux. Malraux waxed lyrical about this great UNESCO mission to undo the corruption of time and to reconceive world history as a new 'family of man' dedicated to peace and concord. He underlined the novelty of the project by saying that '[s]uch an appeal, in the last century, would have seemed fanciful', but now it was 'historic' because 'for the first time, world civilization publicly proclaims the world's art as its indivisible heritage'.[48] On one level having Malraux endorse the project

---

44   20 December 1961, 2, E1/ 168, 1947-1966, Press Review, UAP.

45   Message of Mr. John F. Kennedy, President of the United States of America, Delivered to the US Congress on 7 April 1961 concerning the Participation of the United States of America in the International Campaign to Save the Monuments of Nubia, CUA/107/ Annex II: CLT/CIH/MCO Box 28, UAP.

46   Greener, *High Dam*, 31. Notably, British support was relatively absent, and has sometimes been attributed to rancour following the Suez debacle. Little, *High Dam*, 182.

47   International Campaign to Save the Monuments of Nubia, Executive Committee, Ninth Session, Unesco House, Paris, 17-20 March 1965, 1-2, UNESCO/NUBIA/CE/IX/2, E1/ 144, UAP.

48   Quoted in Rex Keating, *Nubian Twilight* (London, 1962), 16.

might be seen as entirely in keeping with UNESCO's broader brief. After all, UNESCO was based in Paris and was seen as a particularly French institution in terms of its crusade of defining and defending the idea of universal civilization. Yet it is worth recalling that Malraux was hardly a figure associated with universal culture in the 1920s. In 1924 Malraux was scandalously charged with removing and stealing some stone Khmer statues and bas-reliefs from the temple of Bantea-Srei in Cambodia during an expedition to study ancient monuments of Khmer architecture. Apparently he had been warned of the illegality of removing the sculptures, but ultimately justified his archaeological 'recovery' on the grounds that the temple was in a state of total oblivion and disrepair, and thus fell under the category of 'abandoned property' (*res derelicta*) belonging to no one, given that it had not been officially classified by any legal authority at the time. He and his assistant were seized while trying to transport his ton of material across to Saigon en route to Paris, and his trial in Phnom Penh became a major cause célèbre (the so-called Angkor Affair) about the international ownership of heritage, to say nothing of French-Indochinese relations.[49] The stolen pieces were eventually returned to the temple wall (where they are today) and ownership transferred to the state. Such a figure espousing the importance of a world heritage may seem hypocritical to some, but it can also be argued that his conversion to the anti-national universalist cause was thus symptomatic of a changed internationalist sensibility (at least among Unescan Europeans) after 1945. Malraux's shift of attitude dramatically demonstrated that this UNESCO project was in large measure an effort to move archaeology (and indeed civilization itself) beyond the sphere of imperialism and nationalism once and for all. The whole enterprise, as Malraux slyly summed it up later, was 'a kind of Tennessee Valley Authority of archaeology. It is the antithesis of the kind of gigantic exhibitionism by which great modern states try to outbid each other.'[50]

For its part, the Egyptian government funded around one-third of the project, even if its ideas diverged from UNESCO's in subtle ways. Publications were quickly prepared to raise awareness, and the internationally renowned Egyptian singer Oum Kalthum gave a concert in the shadow of pyramids to generate support for the cause.[51] To assuage sceptics who feared that this was nothing more than velvet-gloved imperialism in a new guise, Sarwat Okasha,

---

[49] Walter G. Langlois, *André Malraux: The Indochina Adventure* (London, 1966), 3–51. See too Herman Lebovics, *Mona Lisa's Escort: André Malraux and the Reinvention of French Culture* (Ithaca, 1999).

[50] André Malraux, 'TVA of Archaeology', *Unesco Courier* 13 (May 1960), 10.

[51] John Bulloch, 'Pearl of Ancient Egypt Preserved', *Daily Telegraph* (London, 31 July 1969), unpaginated.

Egyptian Minister of Culture and National Guidance, made clear that the international response 'is a testimony to the bonds that can unite our race in brotherly concord and in friendly cooperation'. Nonetheless, it was also emphasized that these monuments belonged to Egypt first. As Okasha insisted, the United Arab Republic has done its 'utmost to preserve its ancient inheritance which links the past to the present and which is the foundation of both present and future'.[52] Nasser—who showed no interest in the issue a few years before—now changed his spots, and made clear to whom the ruins belonged:

> We pin our hopes on the High Dam for the implementation of our plans of economic development; but likewise we pin our hopes on the preservation of the Nubian treasures in order to keep alive monuments which are not only dear to our hearts, we being their guardians, but dear to the whole world which believes that the ancient and the new components of human culture should blend in one harmonious whole.[53]

The national dimension of this international rescue mission was underscored by Sudanese officials as well, to the extent that the mission was lauded for having 'sparked interest among the Sudanese in their own past and cultural heritage'.[54] The international rescue mission to instil a post-national sense of humanity also worked to spur new national concern with national heritage.

But these funding bids were still not enough. To secure the necessary funds, UNESCO struck a curious deal with the Egyptian and Sudanese governments about the terms of excavation. Egypt agreed to cede to excavators in threatened areas 'at least half the proceeds of their finds, with the exception of certain items which are unique or essential for completing the national collections'. The host countries also authorized excavations elsewhere (such as the Royal Necropolis of Sakkara) and promised to cede 'with a view to their transfer abroad certain Nubian temples and various antiquities from the State

[52]   Statement of Dr. Sarwat Okasha, Minister of Culture and National Guidance, on the Occasion of the Opening of the Second Meeting of the Unesco Executive Committee for the Preservation of the Nubian Monuments, Cairo, 18 April 1962, 1-2, Nubia/2/CE/2,E1 143, UAP.

[53]   Statement by Pres. Gamal Abdel Nasser on the Safeguarding of the Nubian Monuments, 5 June 1961, CUA/107/ Annex 1: CLT/CIH/MCO Box 28, UAP. For background, Donald Malcolm Reid, *Whose Pharoahs? Archaeology, Museums and Egyptian National Identity from Napoleon to World War II* (Berkeley, 2002), esp. 292-7.

[54]   Negm-el-Din Mohamed Sherif, 'Victory in Nubia: The Sudan', *Unesco Courier*, special issue on 'Victory in Nubia', Feb-March 1980, 19.

reserves, on the understanding that all such items would be assigned to museums or scientific organizations open to the public'.[55] UNESCO was then granted the 'scientific, technical and financial responsibility for the missions which are sent to undertake excavation work'.[56] Egypt also offered 'many objects from the State reserves', including tables, alabaster vases, earthenware, and jewellery. The Sudanese government added a rather wistful and despondent plea for help in light of this uncomfortable historical relationship with Western excavators. Aiada Arbab, Sudan's Minister of Education, entreated the international community accordingly:

> In our country every excavator has always been, and is still, entitled to fifty per cent of the objects discovered by him; but this is the only counterpart we can offer. We do not possess important reserves in our museum which we could cede, [so the] only hope that is left to us [is that] the prehistory, history and archaeology of the area endangered in our territory are much less known than Egyptian Nubia and for this reason might attract enough scholars to help us to undertake [further excavations].[57]

The ruins were photographed and advertised with captions, much like a sales catalogue for international prospectors and adventurers.[58]

In this race against time and scramble for antiquities, some twenty-five countries sent archaeological teams to Nubia 'in a frantic effort to record, relocate, or salvage the monuments of Nubia before the waters of the Nile destroyed them'.[59] With it Northern Nubia 'became the most thoroughly excavated area in the world before it was submerged beneath Lake Nasser'.[60] Shifts worked frantically day and night to record and save the monuments, turning 'the temples into film studios' of study and documentation.[61] Spectacular photographs recording the herculean engineering task were widely circulated, most notably regarding the dismantling and relocation of Abu Simbel (see Figures 1 and 2). At this site one could hear Arabic, English, German, French, Spanish, Italian, Swedish, and Polish being spoken,

---

[55]   *A Common Trust: The Preservation of the Ancient Monuments of Nubia* (Paris: UNESCO, 1960), 4.

[56]   *A Common Trust*, 27-8.

[57]   Greener, *High Dam*, 52.

[58]   *Common Trust*, 29-31. See too Rex Keating, *Nubian Rescue* (London, 1975).

[59]   Säve-Söderbergh, *Temples*, 68.

[60]   *Nubia: Africa in Antiquity: The Arts of Ancient Nubia and the Sudan*, expo. catalog, Brooklyn Museum, 1978, unpaginated, Pamphlet Box 113, Sackler Library, Oxford.

[61]   Little, *High Dam*, 164.

Figure 1. Abu Simbel, 1965. Photograph [©] UNESCO.

Figure 2. Abu Simbel, 1965. Photograph [©] UNESCO.

as archaeologists and engineers worked together in apparent harmony and good will in the name of world heritage. Archaeological teams hailed from Spain, Scandinavia, Ghana University, the University of Chicago, a Joint French-Argentinian Mission, as well as key missions from Great Britain, West Germany, and Italy. Significantly, support came from across the Cold War blocs, with teams from the USSR, East Germany, Hungary, Czechoslovakia, Poland, and Yugoslavia. The expedition from the Polish Academy of Sciences and National Museum of Warsaw made some of the greatest discoveries, uncovering an eighth-century cathedral that was built on the site of an ancient church, whose excavation yielded over 100 frescoes made between the eighth and eleventh centuries.[62] Yugoslav newspapers generously covered the Nubia campaign, with special reference to the country's experts in Sudanese Nubia.[63] In numerous publications the East European missions (such as the GDR's in the Sudan) proudly boasted of their contribution.[64] Added lustre derived from the on-site presence of Crown Princess Margrethe of Denmark, who arrived in 1962 as part of the Scandinavian Mission, and reportedly impressed everyone by refusing the luxury accommodation of the Nile Hotel in favour of living with members of the mission so as to get a taste of the 'Nubian way of life'.[65] But it was less the glamour than the anti-Cold War spirit of international cooperation that struck international journalists at the time. One *New York Times* reporter in 1961 marvelled at the way that the project brought together countries that officially did not recognize each other (such as Spain and the USSR) or were in political conflict (India and Pakistan); as he put it, 'there seemed to be no Cold War in the Land of Kush', as Moscow and Washington, 'so feverishly contesting the future of all Africa, are working hand in hand to protect its past'.[66]

This whole project seemed like a UNESCO dream come true of overcoming Cold War antagonism in the name of common purpose and cooperation. It was 'an exemplary occasion for demonstrating the international solidarity which Unesco has been striving to make a reality in all domains'.[67] This was all the more important, given that UNESCO's assistance initiatives in the late 1940s and early 1950s—such as in UN Trust Territory of Tanganyika (later

---

[62]   IES Edwards, 'Archaeological Consequences of the High Dam in Nubia and Egypt', *Probe* (Johannesburg, 1965), 44-7.

[63]   17 March 1964, 4, E1/ 168, 1947-1966, Press Review, UAP.

[64]   Friedrich W. Hinkel, *Auszug aus Nubien* (East Berlin, 1978).

[65]   Hassan, 'Aswan High Dam', 320.

[66]   C. L. Sulzberger, 'No Cold War in the Land of Kush', *New York Times* (20 March 1961), 28.

[67]   Veronese, 'Message', 3.

Tanzania) and Haiti—were widely condemned as failed endeavours.[68] Even Nasser—who just a few years earlier with the dam construction had turned his back on the West and joined forces with the USSR—came around to this international ideal. At the UNESCO project launch in March 1960 Nasser exhorted:

> This action will constitute, we have no doubt, a happy precedent for the generation of the United Nations, that generation which is trying to make the Charter [of Human Rights] a living reality, a belief and a faith which affirms its confidence in the value of human cooperation and seeks a better knowledge of civilizations and cultures despite differences of time and place.[69]

UNESCO made much of its success in having found a way to exorcise the spectre of violence from this land, both in the ancient past and Cold War present. Indeed, UNESCO Director Vittorio Veronese could not resist plugging UNESCO's achievement, rejoicing that 'from a land which throughout the centuries has been the scene of—or the stake in—so many covetous disputes should spring a convincing proof of international solidarity'.[70] Other international commentators—including those from communist Eastern Europe—made a similar point. One article in the Prague publication, *New Orient*, mouthed UNESCO ideals: 'The Nile Valley, where so many battles had been fought, destroying human lives and great cultural values, will now see peaceful international co-operation for saving the cultural heritage of the past. There are, indeed, few nobler tasks.'[71]

Still, there were problems. A 1959 French report revealed growing tension between Egypt and the Sudan. Apparently, the Sudanese felt that Egypt was not consulting them properly, and that Egypt had much to gain with the High Dam while Sudan had much more to lose.[72] And not everyone was convinced of the project's virtues or even necessity. A March 1962 piece in the Italian daily *Corriere della Sera* by Cesare Brandi, Professor of Art History at

---

68 Marian Neal, 'United Nations Technical Assistance Programs in Haiti', *International Conciliation*, 468 (February 1951), 102-11; and Glenda Sluga, *Internationalism in the Age of Nationalism* (Philadelphia, 2013), 108-11.

69 'Unesco's Nubian Campaign is Launched', *Unesco Courier* 13 (May 1960), 5.

70 'March 8 Appeal by Vittorino Veronese, Director-General of Unesco', *Unesco Courier* 13 (May, 1960), 7.

71 Zbynek Žába, 'Ancient Nubia Calls for Help', *New Orient: Journal for the Modern and Ancient Cultures of Asia and Africa* 1:3 (June 1960), 6-9, quotation p. 9, Pamphlet Box 96, S-Z, Sackler Library, Oxford.

72 Typed Report from Jean Thomas, Sous-Directeur General to JK van der Haagen, Chef de la Division des Musées et Monuments historiques, 6, MUS/6063, 20 Oct 1959, 069 (62) NUB, UAP.

University of Palermo, predicted that the massive statues may end up as a 'floating wreck', lamenting the ways these monuments are brazenly 'dismantled and thereby falsified and destroyed, put together again like copies of themselves in alien sites, lost by a civilization thousands of years old . . . and all of this at a time when atomic energy is about to substitute, more advantageously, energy produced by water. . .'. Another piece in *Die Welt* (Hamburg) remarked that UNESCO should not be involved in the project since there is 'neither interest nor money for the safeguarding of the temples'.[73] A *Sunday Times* science correspondent was even more damning:

> For many archaeologists believe that the attempt to save the temples by removing them from their original position is scientifically worthless. 'They will be no more than a tourist attraction', one archaeologist told me. 'They have been photographed and measured and examined in every detail so, from an archaeological point of view, it is not very serious if they are now submerged.'[74]

Funding was also slow, and the international press did its best to ratchet up the rhetoric. One 1962 article in *News* (Chicago) by an US Egyptologist associated with the University of Chicago's Oriental Institute wrote that this is the 'biggest artistic crisis that the world has ever known'.[75] By 1962 press articles appeared with such titles as 'Drowning Antiquity'; one *Herald Tribune* piece from that year complained that the 'most prominent hold-outs are the United States and the Soviet Union. And the deadline is approaching fast',[76] while an *Observer* piece concluded that the publicity calling for a timely rescue may turn out to be 'an advance obituary of a fascinating land which Progress is about to do to death'.[77] Frustration (and suspicion) was mounting in Egypt too. An article of 11 February 1962 in the *The Egyptian Gazette* wondered whether the slow international response was a 'politically-inspired drive to slow down the construction of the High Dam'.[78] The carnivalesque atmosphere was also a favourite theme of journalists. In one 1962 piece in *Art News*, the area south of Aswan was described as a 'gargantuan beehive of men and machines' encompassing both the outsized dam construction and archaeological salvage operation. In this 'Alice-in-Wonderland anomaly in the totalitarian United Arab Republic',

[73] 6 April 1962, 5, E1/ 168, 1947-1966, Press Review, UAP.

[74] 15 October 1962, 3, E1/ 168, 1947-1966, Press Review, UAP.

[75] 14 November 1962, 5, E1/ 168, 1947-1966, Press Review, UAP.

[76] 16 August 1962, 4, E1/ 168, 1947-1966, Press Review, UAP.

[77] 7 May 1962, 2, E1/ 168, 1947-1966, Press Review, UAP.

[78] 15 March 1962, 6, E1/ 168, 1947-1966, Press Review, UAP.

the article went on, there were potential dangers everywhere:

> even if no UAR official originally thought enough of Abu Simbel to provide for it in the High Dam agreement with the Soviets, the temple has now become a symbol of a sort of national Irredentism which says that if the Western world would not help to build the High Dam it now ought to pay for the consequences. . . For the moment Abu Simbel remains a test, a test of whether civilization is more than skin deep.[79]

But there was one particular issue that was most awkward of all: the evacuation of the Nubian peoples themselves. Some 100,000 Nubians were removed over a painful period of nine months starting in October 1963. This dimension of the project is not so well integrated into UNESCO's broader success story of relocating the monuments, and remained relatively invisible. Still, its jarring presence could not be glossed over so easily. Amid the 1980 celebrations of the end of the project chronicled in the UNESCO *Courier*, the Egyptian Minister of Culture, Shehata Adam Mohamed, sheepishly admitted that

> nothing could be done to prevent the waters of the lake from engulfing every aspect of Nubian life, both in Egypt and the Sudan. . . The Nubians tearfully gathered together their belongings, beasts of burden and chickens, and set off for a new life in another town, Kom Ombo. But they really gave up all hope of being able, one day, to return to their dear homeland on the banks of the lake.[80]

In the same publication, Negm-el-Din Mohamed Sherif, director general of the Sudanese Antiquities Service and director of Sudan National Museum in Khartoum, conceded that the decision to build Aswan Dam 'had meant the loss of their fatherland for good, and on the other hand it entailed the complete disappearance of the cultural remains of their ancestors', and that they were 'deeply concerned about the known and the unknown archaeological remains which would ultimately be lost under the waters of the proposed Dam'.[81] The debit side of the High Dam project was captured by a *National Geographic* photographer covering the rescue mission:

> The new bustle struck me with special intensity, contrasting as it did with the dying land around us. Nubia had always been mostly empty

<hr>

[79] Alfred Frankfurter, 'Is Abu Simbel lost?' *Art News* (Summer Issue, 1962), 24-9.

[80] Shehata Adam Mohamed, 'Victory in Nubia: Egypt', *Unesco Courier*, special issue on 'Victory in Nubia', (Feb-March 1980), 5-12, here 12.

[81] Negm-el-Din Mohamed Sherif, 'Victory in Nubia: The Sudan', *Unesco Courier*, special issue on 'Victory in Nubia', (Feb-March 1980), 16.

space, and the Nubians had ever felt themselves to be denizens of the horizon. But after the modern Nubians were relocated to save them from the rising flood, the area lost its last trace of life. Not a soul, not a sail.[82]

It is well to remember that this evacuation of the Nubians was hardly the first. They had been forced to relocate three times already before the 1963 resettlement—in 1902, 1912, and then again in 1933. This time an estimated 100,000 Nubians were relocated from Lower Nubia northward to Kom Ombo in Egypt, losing their ancestral land and social fabric with it. In the Sudan, riots broke out when the news was announced, and local Sudanese authorities were even taken hostage at one point. They were deeply anxious about the health conditions of the new sites, insufficient compensation, and the spiritual dangers resulting from submerging the tombs of local saints.[83] The deportation ran more smoothly in Egypt, mainly because the government there began evacuation plans earlier. Both governments tried to accommodate the Nubians in areas christened 'New Nubia,' but the Egyptian scheme was better provisioned. Compensation for land lost was to be paid in cash, and new houses and land prepared by local governments 'were to be given free'. A model house was erected, but Nubian visitors criticized and modified it. Some 25,000 homes were to be built, and the government planned irrigation channels, pumping stations, and electricity supply. There was to be training in new agricultural techniques and village handicrafts as well. One report finished by saying that Nubians had adjusted to the last two dam extensions by rebuilding homes on higher ground, and therefore could do it again.[84] According to one estimate, the Egyptian state built some 25,000 houses, 138 stores, 33 mosques, and 36 schools.[85] While some Nubians, especially young men, were often in favour of resettlement,[86] confusion and anger on the part of the Nubians were rife. In a 1955 letter Jean Vercoutter, Commissioner for Archaeology in the Sudan just before the Nubian restoration campaign, wrote: 'The attitude of the Nubians themselves was bitter. "We would be better looked after if we were statues", was a remark

---

[82]   Georg Gerster, 'Saving the Ancient Temples at Abu Simbel', *National Geographic Magazine*, 129:5 (May 1966), 694-742, here 709.

[83]   Little, *High Dam*, 135-9.

[84]   Chetata Adam and K. Van Der Haagen, 29.9.1962, enclosed 6 page typed report in English called 'The Evacuation and Resettlement of the Nubians', undated, 069 (62) NUBIE/A 114/133 (436), Box 40, UAP.

[85]   Hassan, 'High Dam', 85.

[86]   Hussein M. Fahim, *Egyptian Nubians: Resettlement and Years of Coping* (Salt Lake City, 1983), 40-1.

often heard.'[87] American archaeologist Leslie Greener bitterly summed up the sentiment in 1962, a year before the evacuations:

> Yesterday, little was known of Nubia, even by the archaeologists. Today there is world-wide interest in Nubia. But it too is largely theatrical: the dramatic threat of drowning; last-minute United Nations effort at rescue; the spectacular attempt to elevate spectacular Abu Simbel. It is enough to make you forget that people lived in Nubia too.[88]

While the UNESCO archive contains little on the evacuation, other sources captured the upheaval of the Nubian people in great detail. The Sudanese administrator, Hassan Dafalla, lived with the Nubians for six years in the northern part of Wadi Halfa District during the long resettlement, and in 1975 published a diary about the deportation, *The Nubian Exodus*. Dafalla was responsible for evacuating some 50,000 people (there were some 70,000 Nubians in Egypt) and to compensate them for lost homes and trees. He had to cope with opposition, and to address myriad issues arising from relocation, including those associated with the twenty-two archaeological excavations going on at the same time and the reburial of the 'illustrious dead' of tribal heroes in higher ground. He chronicled the sense of people being 'perplexed and confused' and 'sunk in a mire of gloomy thoughts', as the elderly 'with no future to live for met the news with a groan and envied their dead colleagues in their graves'. Individuals were reported as 'seen walking alone in the streets, talking aloud to themselves looking left and right, gazing in astonishment'.[89] A number of citizens reacted by writing petitions to the local courts, and sought redress and compensation, mainly in the form of freehold property rights.[90] And once they had moved, they needed to cope with the fact that the new area was essentially without trees, had to learn new cultivation techniques, and to live in new Sudanese style homes designed to suit the weather conditions of the new environment. Many Nubians even wanted the reconstruction of the old cinema house in Wadi Halfa (which had been built during World War II to provide entertainment for troops on the way to North Africa) in the new area, which was done in 1973. Already after a few years Dafalla observed changes in the Nubians—young women had given up traditional costume, and men wore more Western clothes. Weddings featured

---

[87]   Säve-Söderbergh, *Temples,* 73.

[88]   Greener, *High Dam,* 187. See too Alan Cowell, 'The Ancient Temples Shine, but the People Suffer', *New York Times* (15 December 1990), 4.

[89]   Hassan Dafalla, *The Nubian Exodus* (Uppsala, 1975), 90.

[90]   Dafalla, *Nubian Exodus,* 187.

modern music and dancing, whilst beds were no longer made from date branches and instead featured steel frames with wire springs; food dishes had changed, and they began to use the Coptic and Arabic stellar calendar. Even so, he acknowledged that adaptation was very slow and painful.[91]

Nevertheless, UNESCO's Save the Nubian Monuments campaign can certainly be counted as a great success in archaeological terms. For one thing, it set in train broader ideas and practices of international heritage protection. Reclaiming ancient ruins around the world as the property of humanity (and managed by UNESCO) found formal expression in the organization's 1964 International Charter for the Conservation and Restoration of Monuments and Sites, known as the Venice Charter, which stated that 'people are becoming more and more conscious of the unity of human values and regard ancient monuments as a common heritage'.[92] By the late 1960s, the new concept of World Heritage Sites as a common language of universal patrimony was fuelled by the growing belief that defending 'world cultural heritage' would help promote tolerance and thus international peace.[93] Such ideals of world civilization gained further credence with UNESCO's formal passing of the 1972 Convention concerning the Protection of the World Cultural and National Heritage, which boldly proclaimed that each country 'holds in trust for the rest of mankind those parts of the world heritage that are found within its boundaries' and that the international community 'has an obligation to support any nation in discharging this trust if its own resources are not equal to the task'.[94] This led to the formation of a canon of designated World Heritage Sites around the world placed under international protection. While in 1978 there were only 12 sites inscribed on UNESCO's inaugural World Heritage list, today there are over 900 listed sites. With time the world heritage concept was expanded beyond material artefacts toward the environment. In 1965 the UNESCO Director General René Maheu dramatically claimed that the world's oceans were becoming 'a gigantic ditch into which man discharges the waste from his organic exchanges and the detritus, as it were, of his civilization'.[95] By the end of that decade, the UN declared the seabed and ocean floor as 'the common heritage of mankind'. Several years

---

91 Dafalla, *Nubian Exodus*, 294. See too Hussein M. Fahim, *Egyptian Nubians: Resettlement and Years of Coping* (Salt Lake City, 1983).

92 Titchen, 'On the Construction of Outstanding Universal Value', 50-2.

93 Helaine Silverman and D. Fairchild Ruggles, *Cultural Heritage and Human Rights* (New York), 3-22. See too H. Cleere, *Approaches to the Archaeological Heritage* (London, 1984).

94 Säve-Söderbergh, *Temples*, 220-1.

95 Cited in Sewell, *Unesco*, 246.

later the moon and its resources (as stipulated in the UN's so-called Moon Treaty) were designated as part of this universal common heritage, followed in the early 1980s by proposals to place Antarctica on the list.[96] Like its sister concept of human rights, the post-war universalist mission slowly but surely made its long march through international institutions, and UNESCO had done much to put the old dream of universal civilization in a new post-imperial and even post-European key. World culture, in its post-1945 incarnation, now had now its 'ornamentalist' moment.

What is more, UNESCO's success in this project also helped shore up the legitimacy of its claim to be the new warden of world civilization. The *Indian Express* (Delhi) reported in 1966: 'The moral responsibility of Unesco is clear. It is the guardian of the artistic heritage of the entire world and has rightly taken the lead in Nubia.'[97] The success of the Save the Nubian Monuments Project also inspired salvage operations in other lands. Soon thereafter the Greek government invited UNESCO experts to give advice about preserving the Parthenon, and Florence and Venice recovered from their respective floods in 1966 thanks in large part to UNESCO's international fundraising campaign. Further afield, the Buddhist temple of Borobudur in Indonesia was cleaned and restored between 1970 and 1983 under UNESCO auspices, and related restoration projects took place in Venice and Athens around the same time. The Nubian Monuments project was also a remarkable consciousness-raising event. By the end even Nasser had been brought around to declare that the 'preservation of the legacy of mankind is no less important than the construction of dams, the erection of factories and the greater prosperity of the people.'[98]

Even so, the marriage of universalism and ruins also prompted renewed interest in national claims toward material heritage. In 1970 UNESCO passed the 'Convention on the Means of Publicizing and Preventing Illicit Import, Export and Transfer of Ownership of Cultural Property' at the General Assembly (16th Session), which concerned the restitution of taken objects by former imperial powers. This harked back to some of the international agreements on the restitution of objects of art and science stolen by Napoleon's army,[99] but this time UNESCO aimed to go much further. Indeed, the 1970s witnessed a range of claims from smaller countries against 'ex-colonials' to have their cultural treasures returned to them; this trend

[96]   Kemal Baslar, *The Concept of the Common Heritage of Mankind in International Law* (The Hague, 1998), xix-38.

[97]   25 Feb 1966, 4, E1/ 168, 1947-1966, Press Review, UAP.

[98]   Säve-Söderbergh, *Temples,* 90.

[99]   Swenson, *Rise of Heritage,* 31-46.

augured a certain move away from world heritage and toward the repatriation of cultural resources, akin to the national management of World Heritage Sites. Already a decade before it was reported in the London weekly *West Africa* that the Nigerian Department of Antiquities stepped up its contribution to the Nubian rescue project on distinctly regional, pan-African grounds, to the extent that its contribution was seen as reflecting a 'Nigerian awareness of Africa's cultural heritage of which it considers the Nubian monuments to be among the richest'.[100] In October 1975 a Restitution of Works of Art to Countries Victim of Expropriation was put forward to the UN General Assembly by Burundi, Dahomey, Equatorial Guinea, Egypt, Ghana, Greece, Guinea, Mali, Mauritania, Nigeria, Somalia, Uganda, Cameroon, Upper Volta, and Zaire.[101] To its credit, UNESCO worked to accommodate this growing antagonism, declaring in 1976 that 'the promotion of national culture can enhance a people's ability to understand the culture and civilization of other peoples and thus can have a favourable impact on international cooperation'. This may not have been a full renunciation of the world heritage concept in favour of a defence of national culture, but it did show that material artefacts had become a site of struggle between internationalist and nationalist agendas, be it for nation-building or tourism.[102] World Heritage sites now served as vehicles of national self-promotion often in spite UNESCO's initial intentions.[103]

The campaign saved more than twenty massive Nubian temples and archaeological treasures, including Abu Simbel. By the end, the Egyptian government donated four temples as tokens of appreciation—Debod to Spain, Taffa to Holland, Dendur to the US, Ellesiya to Italy—to be housed overseas as part of the 'open air' worldwide Nubian museum.[104] The University of Chicago's Oriental Institute played a key role, and most of the Nubian antiquities now in its collection were excavated by its archaeologists at that time.[105] The Egyptian government built the Nubian Museum in Aswan and the

---

[100] *West Africa*, 14 March 1964, in Press Round-Up, 6 April 1964, 4, E1/ 168, 1947-1966, Press Review, UAP.

[101] The text and claims of restitution of works of art to lands of origin from 1973 to 1977 can be seen in the file ED 245/41, National Archives London (NAL).

[102] Alma Robinson, 'Art Objects in Foreign Hands', *FESTAC* (Africa) 59 (July 1976), 118-23; Pearson Phillips, 'The BM May Lose its Loot', *The Observer* (23 May 1976); 'Plea for 'Plundered' Treasures', *Sunday Times* (22 May 1976).

[103] J. E. Tunbridge and G. J. Ashworth, *Dissonant Heritage* (London, 1996); and B. Graham and G. J. Ashworth, *A Geography of Heritage* (London, 2000).

[104] Shehata Adam Mohamed, 'Victory in Nubia: Egypt', *Unesco Courier*, 33 (Feb/March 1980), 12.

[105] Larson, *Lost Nubia*, x.

National Museum of Egyptian Civilization in Cairo as a result of the project. Furthermore, these 1960s excavations helped unearth much about the early history of Africa and the development of modern humans.[106] No less important is that given its size, scope, and international participation, this rescue mission was commonly seen to have changed the general attitude toward international salvage programmes.[107] By the late 1960s, the Nubia campaign led to the 1968 adoption by UN member states of the 'Recommendation Concerning the Preservation of Cultural Property Endangered by Public or Private Works,' in which it was stipulated that preservation costs must be included in all major construction budgets, which helped pave the way for the World and National Heritage protection laws in 1972. In a very real sense, the Nubian rescue mission changed 'forever the practice of archaeology on a global scale'.[108] One American journalist in 1961, observing the remarkable spirit of cooperation during the Nubian project, could not help but wonder about its long-term legacy beyond the Cold War present:

> If the habit of cooperation can be established to share in the world's common cultural heritage, maybe someday statesmen may take a cue from archaeologists and devise formulas to insure its legacy. Otherwise, it is a grim thought to contemplate possibly scientific teams, under similar auspices, labouring perhaps a century hence to unearth the shards of our own throbbing time.[109]

Leaving such utopianism aside, it is worth noting that the universalism invoked to overcome Cold War antagonism effectively outlived the Cold War, and has framed the way that heritage sites are managed around the world ever since. No doubt this really was—as one 1966 *Guardian* article put it—the 'most spectacular archaeological rescue the world has seen', and as such rescued the idea and legitimacy of global civilization itself.[110] Today Abu Simbel and Philae still stand as 'symbols and the monuments of a new type of international solidarity' that have survived their reconstruction as one of the very touchstones of world heritage.[111]

---

[106] Fred Wendorf (ed.), *The Prehistory of Nubia*, 2 vols (Dallas, 1968).

[107] Torgny Säve-Söderbergh, *The Scandinavian Joint Expedition to Sudanese Nubia* (Det Kongelige Danske Videnskabernes Selkab Historisk-filosofiske Meddelelser, 49:3 (Copenhagen, 1979), 8, Pamphlet Box 96, S-Z, Sackler Library, Oxford.

[108] Hassan, 'The Aswan High Dam', 81.

[109] Sulzberger, 'No Cold War', 28.

[110] 11 Feb 1966, 3, E1/ 168, 1947-1966, Press Review, UAP.

[111] Säve-Söderbergh, *Scandinavian Joint Expedition*, 52-3.

Japan's Monument Problem: Ise Shrine as Metaphor

Jordan Sand

In Japan there is a shrine that is rebuilt every twenty years. A new shrine, identical to the old one, is built on a site next to it. The sacred objects are transferred from old to new and the old shrine is razed to the ground. The main building of the shrine thus moves back and forth between two adjacent sites. The practice dates back to the late seventh century.

The shrine in question is the Grand Shrine of Ise (*Ise Dai Jingū*), a name that is in fact a loose designation for two large Shinto shrine complexes, the Inner Shrine, dedicated to Amaterasu Ōmikami, the sun goddess and mythical ancestor of the Japanese imperial line, and the Outer Shrine, dedicated to Toyouke no Ōmikami, a deity of agriculture and industry. The two are located several kilometres apart, and there are 123 minor subshrines in the vicinity. Not only the main buildings but all of the structures at these 125 shrines undergo the same periodic reconstruction. Ritual objects and priestly vestments are also made anew every twenty years.

The periodic renewal at Ise Shrine is probably the single best known fact about any architectural monument in Japan. It is even something of a 'meme': type the words 'rebuilt every' into Google and the search engine will finish your phrase with 'twenty years' and provide a list of sites making reference to Ise (Figure 1). A large scholarly literature treats the history of the shrine and offers a variety of theories on why the practice of renewal began, since this question is unanswered in the shrine's earliest documents.[1] An even larger literature, scholarly and semi-scholarly, interprets the distinctive practice of periodic renewal in cultural terms. This essay contributes to neither of these

---

[1] For historical and architectural studies of Ise Shrine, see Yasutada Watanabe, *Shinto Art: Ise and Izumo Shrines,* translated by Robert Ricketts (New York, 1974); William Coaldrake, *Architecture and Authority in Japan* (London, 1996), 16-51; Fukuyama Toshio, 'Jingū no kenchiku to sono rekishi' in *Jingū: dai rokujukkai* (1975); Inagaki Eizō, 'Kodai, chūsei ni okeru jingū no shikinen sengū', in *Jingū: dai rokujukkai* (1975), 173-94. For a study of the changing interpretations of Ise Shrine's architectural form, see Inoue Shōichi, *Ise Jingū: Miwaku no Nihon kenchiku* (Tokyo, 2009).

Past and Present (2015), Supplement 10

Figure 1. Ise Shrine in Google Maps, September 2013. In preparation for renewal ceremonies in October, 2013, new shrine buildings stand on the left while the old shrine buildings stand on the right. The buildings on the right were dismantled in early 2014. Image [©] DigitalGlobe; map data [©] Google, Zenrin.

literatures. Instead, I will present a history of how the renewal has been interpreted. Since the end of the nineteenth century, Ise Shrine has provided an unusually versatile metaphor in discourses of Japanese culture, of Asian culture, and of heritage and architectural monumentality. The shrine raises in particularly pure form a classic question in the preservation and restoration of monuments: how does replacement of material elements affect our perception of the antiquity of a monument? Repeatedly, in multiple variations, talk of Ise has been accompanied by interpretive problems concerning newness and age, modernity and antiquity.[2]

Although native Shinto tradition has defined Ise Shrine's religious meaning, the metaphoric meanings of the shrine's renewal that I will be discussing are a product of international dialogue. I will briefly review perceptions of the shrine before the establishment of the modern state and Japan's emergence on the international stage in the mid-nineteenth century. It happens, however, that the evolution of Ise Shrine as a metaphor fits tidily into the century from the 1890s, when Japan joined the club of imperial powers with its victory in the Sino-Japanese War and the termination of unequal treaties, to the 1990s, when Japan signed the Convention for Protection of World Heritage. The 1890s happens also to be when Japan established its first national architectural preservation law, the Law for the Preservation of Ancient Shrines and

---

[2] The question is an ancient one. Randolph Starn recounts the story from Plutarch of a debate in ancient Athens over whether to regard Theseus' ship as the original ship or not, since it had been preserved for generations by replacing the planks as they decayed. Randolph Starn, 'Authenticity and Historic Preservation: Towards an Authentic History', *History of the Human Sciences*, 15:1 (2002), 2.

Temples. And in the 1990s, at the same time that Japan signed the World Heritage Convention, the case of Japan played a key role in a global rethinking of the definition and boundaries of 'cultural heritage'.

The historical record indicates that Ise's periodic renewal was begun on a twenty-year cycle by Emperor Tenmu in 690. Scholars' explanations for the practice have clustered around three areas of emphasis: (1) Shinto rituals of purification and the associated belief that the god should be periodically welcomed in a new structure—as has been practised in the Shinto rituals performed at the time of imperial enthronements (*daijōsai*); (2) the dependence on ephemeral materials in Shinto architecture—thatch, untreated wood, and posts sunk directly in the ground rather than set on foundation stones; and (3) the value of periodic renewal on a cycle of slightly less than one generation for perpetuating the craft knowledge necessary to keep the buildings in their original form in perpetuity. These explanations are of course not mutually exclusive; it seems likely that some combination of all of them lay behind the decision of Emperor Tenmu and the early custodians of the shrine to initiate the cycle of renewal.

Already at the time that the periodic renewal cycle began, Ise's architectural style was an anachronism (or an invented archaism). Continental building techniques and ornament had been used in Japanese palaces and Buddhist temples since the sixth century. These buildings were also post-and-lintel wooden structures, but stood on foundation stones and used complex bracketwork to support heavy tile roofs. These features made them both more sophisticated and more permanent than the buildings at Ise. Since the earliest recorded period in the shrine's history, therefore, Ise represented an intentionally backward-looking style of architecture, like the Gothic Revival in nineteenth-century England. More importantly, just as the Gothic Revival was championed as an indigenous response to sophisticated but alien architectural styles, the primitive architecture of Ise asserted indigeneity. Its significance was defined partly in the context of a dialectic between the native and the foreign. This pattern would reemerge twelve hundred years later vis-a-vis architectural styles and thinking introduced from Europe.

The origins of the tradition of renewal are one question, but why it persisted in subsequent centuries is a distinct and equally important question. The critical factor here was surely patronage. Although the structures are simple, rebuilding the entire shrine complex and replacing all of the implements of worship every twenty years cost extravagant sums.[3] The same

---

[3] For costs and funding of the renewal in the modern era, see Rosemarie Bernard, 'Ise Jingū and Modern Emperorship', in *The Emperors of Modern Japan*, ed. Ben-Ami Shilloney (Brill, 2008), 87-8.

practice of periodic renewal was seen at several other major shrines in Japan before the Meiji Restoration, when the new imperial government limited it to Ise, primarily for financial reasons. All of these shrines enjoyed imperial patronage. Under the manorial system that developed in the ninth century, Ise was granted provincial lands whose taxes were sufficient to sustain the rebuilding. Not surprisingly, when the country was engulfed in civil war after the breakdown of that system, shrine coffers emptied, and the buildings were left to the ravages of time and the elements. There was no renewal between the late fifteenth and late sixteenth centuries. Little was left standing when the shrines were revived in 1583 with the aid of military hegemon Oda Nobunaga.[4] The continuity of patronage and craft having been broken for so long, builders in the late sixteenth and early seventeenth-century renewals were compelled to reconstruct the shrines on the basis of past documents. The shrine has thus not seen perfect continuity throughout its thirteen-hundred-year history. Scholars have also noted several significant changes in site plans and in the ornament of the buildings over the course of time.[5] Nor were the builders always from the same lineage or guild.[6] Nevertheless, as long as either the imperial court or a military ruler with the imprimatur of the emperor was able to guarantee the shrine's sources of income, the buildings were renewed, each time affirming the continued power of the imperial system of patronage and ritual. This system was greatly enhanced with the Meiji Restoration of 1868, which transformed the emperor into a modern sovereign and made Ise into the high church of a state cult.

'Nothing to see and they won't let you see it'

Writings about Ise for Japanese and for foreign audiences naturally differ due to their different contexts and audiences. The *Jingū gishikikai*, the most detailed native text on the shrine written before the modern era, described periodic renewal and related what the ancient religious texts recorded about how it was to be performed, but included no interpretation of its meaning. Meanwhile, the few Western texts mentioning Ise before the 1870s, when foreigners began to enjoy free rights of travel in Japan, relied on hearsay, and presented garbled explanations that suggest a puzzle over whether to regard the shrine as new or old, probably derived in part from misunderstanding of explanations from Japanese interlocutors. The German doctor Engelbert Kaempfer, physician at the Dutch factory in Nagasaki between 1690 and 1692 and author of the best foreign account of the country published

---

[4] Fukuyama, 'Jingū no kenchiku to sono rekishi', 126-7.
[5] Coaldrake, *Architecture and Authority*, 16-51.
[6] Inagaki, 'Kodai, chūsei ni okeru jingū no shikinen sengū,' 186-7.

during the Tokugawa era, wrote that 'all those who have visited it say that the temple is situated in flat country, is poorly built of wood and not very high, and is covered with a low roof of hay. It is maintained with great care in the image of the original poor temple of early times, built in their poverty by the first inhabitants and founders of this nation.'[7] Kaempfer, who makes clear that he did not visit the shrine himself, grasped that the shrine buildings were carefully maintained, but apparently not that this was done through periodic reconstruction. Carl Thunberg, who visited Japan in 1775-6, seems also to have heard of the shrine's antiquity and humble architecture, but misunderstood the nature of the renewal, understanding the care devoted to the buildings as a sign of their dilapidation: 'This temple is most ancient in the whole empire and at the same time in the worst condition, being now so exceedingly decayed with age that it can scarcely be kept together with the greatest care and attention.'[8] Phillip Franz von Siebold, resident physician in the Dutch factory from 1823 to 1829, also never visited the shrine and seems to have heard similar stories or cobbled together his own understanding on the basis of his predecessors' writing, but closed with a note of scepticism: 'The Isye temple is a peculiarly plain, humble, and unpretending structure, and really of great antiquity, though not quite equal to that which is ascribed to it.'[9] It is impossible to know what Siebold understood of the periodic renewal, but this scepticism about the shrine's antiquity hints at the dilemma of whether to consider buildings reconstructed every twenty years as old or new.

Beginning in the 1870s, foreigners were able to visit Ise themselves. By the 1880s, visits had been described in several English-language travelogues; by the turn of the twentieth century, full instructions for visiting, including rail travel times, could be obtained from an English-language guidebook. Yet as Ise Shrine became part of the Western tourist itinerary, the dominant adjective that characterized the shrine in one description after another was 'disappointing'. Lacking either elaborate ornament or monumental scale, its innermost precincts off-limits to all but priests and royalty, Ise Shrine struck Victorian tourists as arid and unrewarding. As Basil Hall Chamberlain warned readers in a 1902 guidebook, the 'disappointed tourist' might conclude "there is nothing to see, and they won't let you see it".[10]

---

[7] Englebert Kaempfer, *Kaempfer's Japan: Tokugawa Culture Observed*, ed. and trans. Beatrice Bodart-Bailey (Honolulu, 1999), 117.

[8] Carl Peter Thunberg, *Japan Extolled and Decried: Carl Peter Thunberg and the Shogun's Realm, 1775-1796*, annotated and introduced by Timon Screech (Routledge, 2005), 206.

[9] Phillip Franz von Siebold, *Manners and Customs of the Japanese* (London, 1852), 343.

[10] Basil Hall Chamberlain, *A Handbook for Travellers in Japan*, 6th edn (London, 1901), 302.

By the time that Chamberlain wrote these words, the sentiment was already almost cliché. British diplomat Ernest Satow, the first European to write a first-hand account of the shrine, described it in an 1874 publication as 'disappointing in its simplicity and perishable nature'. For Satow, the shrine's periodic renewal served as part of the explanation for this let-down: 'The perishable nature of Japanese architecture of course renders it impossible that the original buildings should have lasted down to the present day, and in fact it seems to have been the rule from time immemorial to rebuild the temple once every twenty years, alternately on each of two sites which lie close to each other.'[11] American adventurer Isabella Bird, who visited in 1878, pressed the point further, describing her encounter with the shrine in detail, but in a sarcastic tone, as if in revealing the shrine's failure as a tourist site she were demonstrating that the emperor had no clothes: 'there is nothing, and all things . . . lead to NOTHING. . . . here too there is nothing but disappointment . . .'. Like Satow, she concluded her discussion with the note—almost an after-thought—that the sanctuary was rebuilt every twenty years.[12]

Phase I: Japan's ephemeral abode

The disparagement of Victorian tourists toward Japan's holiest of holies was in itself probably of little consequence domestically, yet it was symptomatic of a broader dilemma that vexed Japanese architects in the first generation after Western architectural education was introduced to the country. Expressed in crude terms—and these were the terms of several Western writers—Japan possessed no architecture. The country lacked a tradition of masonry construction, therefore lacked permanent monuments—and without monuments, one architect judged, the Japanese had 'no architecture as we understand it . . . no lasting style, have never been able to realize any grand conceptions that would last for ages.'[13] Japanese, architecture historian James Fergusson declared in 1876, 'do not belong to one of the building races of mankind'.[14] Josiah Conder, the Englishman who instructed the first

---

[11] Ernest Satow, 'The Shinto Temples of Isé', *Transactions of the Asiatic Society of Japan*, series 1, no.2 (1874), 121, 126.

[12] Isabella Bird, *Unbeaten Tracks in Japan* (1881; London, 1971), 275-7. Inoue Shōichi cites other disappointed Westerners' accounts of Ise. One noteworthy exception in this era was the Scottish designer Christopher Dresser, who visited Japan in 1877-8, and referred to the periodic renewal and the shrine's long history of pilgrimage as 'singularly impressive'.

[13] R. Phené Spiers, in 'Discussion of Mr. Conder's Paper: Notes on Japanese Architecture', *Sessional Papers Read at the Royal Institute of British Architects, 1876-77* (1877), 210.

[14] James Fergusson, quoted in Don Choi, 'Domesticated Modern: Hybrid Houses in Meiji Japan, 1870-1900' (PhD dissertation, University of California, Berkeley, 2003), 3.

generation at the Meiji state's new architecture academy, shared the view that Japan's entire architectural tradition was peculiarly 'fragile', as evidenced by the frequent conflagrations in the capital as well as the lack of stone monuments. Conder himself was an enthusiast for Japanese traditions, but regarded Buddhist architecture derived from the continent as more significant historically.[15] As Gregory Clancey has observed, it was partly the misfortune of late nineteenth-century Japanese to have adopted a British-dominated architecture curriculum, since North America, for example, still had many wood-built cities.[16] Several of Conder's students wrote graduation theses on the problem of creating a more permanent architecture for Japan.[17] Even Itō Chūta, the doyen of Japanese architectural history and modern Japan's first restoration architect, looked forward to the time that Shinto shrines too would be built of brick and stone.[18] By 1899, the government had embarked on construction of a steel-frame and brick neo-baroque palace modelled on Versailles. Since the very nature of the profession of architect in the new system was to design durable structures for the state, it is not surprising that before the twentieth century Japanese architects had little to say about Ise.

The first interpretations of Ise Shrine to address the cultural meaning of periodic renewal came not from native architects explaining Japanese building traditions but from cultural interpreters explaining the new imperial Japan to Western audiences. Lafcadio Hearn and Okakura Kakuzō, two of the most popular Japan apologists writing in English at the turn of the twentieth century, both turned to Ise in their explanations of Japanese culture. Both authors made reference to Ise in writings published when Japan was in the flush of war victory, and both reread the lack of permanent architecture

[15] Josiah Conder, 'Notes on Japanese Architecture', *Transactions of the Royal Institute of British Architects* series 1, vol. 2 (1877-78), 179-80, 186.

[16] Gregory Clancey, *Earthquake Nation: The Cultural Politics of Japanese Seismicity* (Berkeley, 2006), 16-17.

[17] Clancey, 16, 58-9; Choi, 'Domesticated Modern', 53-5. These architects did not condemn Japanese wood construction. They saw brick and masonry as essential to the nation's modernization, however.

[18] Maruyama Shigeru, *Nihon no kenchiku to shisō: Itō Chūta shōron* (Tokyo, 1996), 121. Itō switched to advocating traditional wood construction when he was commissioned to design the Meiji Shrine in 1914. At the time of the 1909 renewal, the Home Minister and Imperial Household Minister expressed concern that there would soon be a shortage of large timbers for the Ise renewal and proposed rebuilding the shrine on a concrete foundation so that the structures would last for two hundred years instead of twenty. The Meiji emperor rejected this proposal. Kunaichō, *Meiji tennōki dai 10 kan* (Tokyo, 1974), 802.

that had presented a dilemma for architects to make impermanence instead the country's great virtue. Hearn's essay 'The Genius of Japanese Civilization', published in the *Atlantic* in October 1895, opened with the question of how to explain Japan's victory in the Sino-Japanese War, and found the answer in national character, which he called the 'race ghost'. Despite the country's sudden and surprising accession to military dominance, Hearn assured readers, little had changed in Japan at its core. Japanese were innately frugal, and accepted the ephemerality of life. Hearn presented Ise Shrine's periodic renewal as exemplary of this, and found that ultimately, not only was this the strength of the Japanese people, but it revealed 'weaknesses in our own civilization'.[19] In effect, Japan and its humble, regularly rebuilt shrine offered a new model of civilization, a virtuous antithesis to the West. A decade and another imperial war later, Okakura Kakuzō similarly pointed to Ise as an example of a peculiarly Japanese—or, in Okakura's pan-Asianist rhetoric, 'Eastern'—sensibility toward life. Okakura's classic, *The Book of Tea*, written in English based on lectures the author had given to audiences in Boston, and published in New York in 1906, also sought to explain a militarily ascendant Japan in terms of race and culture. Okakura related Ise's periodic renewal to the ephemerality of the Japanese tea hut (which he called the 'abode of fancy'), finding them both rooted in a Shinto practice of abandoning a house upon the death of its master and the accompanying belief that 'everyone should have a house of his own.'[20] A canny reader of his audience, Okakura thus turned an exotic-seeming and 'disappointing' architectural practice into evidence for a claim that Japanese placed a high value on home-ownership: an ethic that would have had reassuring familiarity for New Englanders.

In the rhetoric of 'national character' that these apologists deployed to defend Japanese imperialism, Ise Shrine could serve as the ephemeral 'abode' for Japan as a whole, and a lesson to the West about 'who' the Japanese really were. This was a new way of reading the shrine. The logic was metonymic. Although the metonym remained implicit, in the context of an explanation of the rising imperial power, Hearn's cultural interpretation in effect proposed that 'Japan does not engage in imperialism in the manner of the West, simply to acquire territory, she is not grasping and acquisitive'. And Okakura implied, on the other hand, 'everyone must possess his own home; Japan's home is Asia'.[21]

---

[19] Lafcadio Hearn, 'The Genius of Japanese Civilization', *Atlantic* (October, 1895).

[20] Okakura Kakuzō, *The Book of Tea* (1906; Rockville, Maryland, 2009), 46.

[21] Ise Shrine today is renowned for its unspoiled natural setting and austere beauty, but in the years that Hearn and Okakura were writing, the site also presented visitors with tangible evidence of Japan's imperial wars. The 1914 edition of *Terry's Guide to the*

In the same years that Hearn and Okakura were turning Ise Shrine into a metaphor for the national character, architecture history was emerging in Japan as an independent field and the state was establishing an institutional framework for conservation of historic structures. Itō Chūta, who would become the country's first professor of architecture history in 1903, began tracing the historical lineage of Japanese architectural styles in the early 1890s.[22] Itō's two-part study, 'The Development of Shinto Architecture,' published in 1901, was the first systematic treatment of the subject. In this study as in the travelogues of Victorian visitors, Ise Shrine's periodic reconstruction is described with a subtle note of disappointment. Itō regretted that since Shinto shrines in general were frequently rebuilt, it was difficult to classify them by period. He pointed out that the present structures at Ise were an imperfect gauge of the style of their ancient predecessors, noting frankly: 'indeed, if we compare what is written in the Enreki ritual records with what stands today, we can easily find the difference.' In later writing, Itō would come to champion the renewal as a unique feature of Japan's imperial tradition, but the more pressing issue for him at the turn of the century was how to establish that Japan possessed a history of indigenous stylistic development that would put it in the company of the progressive nations, escaping the status of a stagnant 'Asiatic' nation, a short branch low on the evolutionary tree of world architecture.[23] Cyclical reconstruction served poorly in a progressive evolutionary model.

Other early twentieth-century Japanese intellectuals writing in the domestic context did find Ise Shrine a useful metaphor for the nation. In modern Japanese imperial ideology, Ise readily served as a national symbol, since it was the shrine of the imperial house and the nation was regarded as inseparable from the unbroken imperial line. As the ideology of the *kokutai* (often translated to English as 'national polity' but signifying the eternal unity of emperor and people) became a more prominent part of intellectual life in the first decades of the twentieth century, interpretations of Ise frequently

---

Japanese Empire describes a Krupp gun captured at Port Arthur and other 'grim relics of Japan's titanic struggles with the Muscovites and Chinese' displayed at the entrance to the Inner Shrine.

[22] On Itō Chūta and architectural preservation, see Cherie Wendelken, 'The Tectonics of Japanese Style: Architect and Carpenter in the Late Meiji Period', *Art Journal*, 55:3 (Autumn, 1996), 30-4; Coaldrake, *Architecture and Authority in Japan*, 245-9; Stefan Tanaka, *New Times in Modern Japan* (Princeton, NJ, 2004), 173-5.

[23] On Itō's reconfiguring of Bannister Fletcher's evolutionary scheme of world architecture, see Muramatsu Shin, 'Jūgun kenchikushika no yume', *Gendai shisō*, 21:7 (July, 1993), 181-95.

presented the shrine as the ideal embodiment of the emperor-centred nation. These interpretations did not usually extrapolate a message about the nation from the phenomenon of periodic renewal in the manner of Hearn and Okakura, however. In a 1915 tract on Ise Shrine and the *kokutai*, for example, Shinto theologian and moral philosopher Hiroike Chikurō found the essence of the shrine and of the Japanese empire in Japan's 'spiritualism', which stood in contrast to Western materialism. Yet he did not connect this explicitly to the practice of renewal, which he described instead with the same historian's caution as Itō, acknowledging that 'the process and attending rituals have evolved somewhat since ancient times', but concluding that 'generally speaking it has remained fairly similar'.[24] Hiroike stressed the spiritual importance of the shrine, but treated periodic renewal as a minor impediment to historical knowledge rather than a value in itself.

Kokutai ideology subsequently became a more prominent feature in architecture historical discussion of the shrine and of renewal. The name for Ise's architectural style in Itō's schema came in the 1920s to be prefixed by the word 'unique', indicating that no other shrines belonged to the same classification as the august imperial shrine.[25] Itō's colleague Sekino Tadashi, writing in the late 1920s, would describe Ise as exhibiting in living form 'humanity's first construction'. Its periodic renewal reflected 'the preservation of a primitive form of building belonging to our ancestors . . . a miraculous thing not found elsewhere in the world, a gift of our august *kokutai* (national polity)'.[26] This view required emphasizing that the shrine had been unchanged over the centuries, despite the historical evidence to the contrary. As a loyal imperial subject, Sekino understood the shrine as a manifestation of the unbroken imperial line, while at the same time, as an architecture historian, he saw the significance of the reconstruction in what it revealed about ancient architecture.

Phase 2: A duck-rabbit problem (1929-1945)

The periodic renewal of 1929 came at a time when the various earlier strains of discourse surrounding the shrine were fully developed and the dialogue

---

[24] Hiroike Chikurō, 'Ise jingū to waga kokutai', in *Hiroike hakase zenshū dai 4 satsu*, by Hiroike Chikurō (Kashiwa-shi, 1937), 42, 277. Hiroike's description of Ise's stability over time is in fact more mealy-mouthed than my translation here implies.

[25] On Itō's nationalist reading of the reconstruction, see Jonathan Reynolds, 'Ise Shrine and the Modernist Construction of Japanese Tradition', *Art Bulletin*, 83:2 (June, 2001), 322-3. On the circumstances in which the architectural style of Ise Shrine came to be designated as 'unique Shinmei style' see Tsunoda Mayumi, 'Shinmeizukuri to iu shinwa' in *Fukugen shisō no shakaishi*, ed. Suzuki Hiroyuki (Tokyo, 2006), 60-71.

[26] Sekino Tadashi, quoted in Inoue, *Ise jingū: miwaku no Nihon kenchiku*, 133.

between Japanese and non-Japanese interpretations of the shrine was becoming more intimate. This is glimpsed in the treatment of the renewal ritual by the *Japan Times*, the country's leading English-language newspaper, which reported the events prominently on its front page. An editorial offered a fuller elaboration of the ethos of impermanence that Hearn and Okakura had proposed earlier.

Previous renewals had also received notice in the English-language press, but without commentary on the cultural meaning of the renewal. At the time of the renewal in 1889, the weekly *Japan Mail*, a precursor of the *Japan Times*, had reported that the emperor would be going to the shrine to make offerings, whose extravagant cost, the newspaper noted, gave 'some idea of the solemnity of the occasion'.[27] The *Mail* did not mention that the shrine had been rebuilt. At the time of the 1909 renewal, the *Japan Times* reported on the ceremonies at Ise in a detailed series of articles, but paid little attention to the rebuilding itself. In fact, it would have been difficult for a reader not already familiar with the practice to know from these articles that the shrine was rebuilt entirely every twenty years. Nowhere was it indicated that the new structures were identical to the structures being razed.[28]

As Hearn and Okakura had drawn upon the Ise metaphor in the aftermath of war, the *Japan Times* editorial printed at the time of the 1929 renewal ceremonies, titled 'Permanence in Impermanence', also interpreted the renewal in relation to a recent violent event. In this instance, the event was the Great Kanto Earthquake of 1923, which had cost 100,000 lives. Reconstruction was still under way in Tokyo at the time. The editorial explained that Japanese people recognized the 'permanence of the life spirit' and therefore had no need for permanent structures, either for the enthronement of their sovereign or for their most sacred shrine. 'This spiritual insight of the Japanese', it concluded, was 'the secret of their resiliency . . . . To a people who appreciate that the material is but an expression of the essence, the entire destruction of Yokohama and Tokyo at the time of the Great Disaster was but a tempest withering the flowers which, with the rain and spring, would again bloom. If the building of the Ise Daijingu only lasts twenty years, what matters it if a city or two are destroyed?'[29]

This use of the Ise renewal to express a national spirit of resilience and a casual concern for the physical world (not to mention for the massive loss of

---

[27] 'The Approaching Ceremony in Ise', *Japan Mail* (28 September 1889), 281.

[28] 'Removal of the Ise Daijingu', *Japan Times* (1 October 1909), 3; 'Ancient Festivals at the Ise Shrines', *Japan Times* (3 October 1909), 2; 'Festivals at the Ise Shrines', *Japan Times* (5 October 1909), 2; and (6 October 1909), 2.

[29] 'Permanence in Impermanence', *Japan Times* (3 October 1929), 4.

life in the 1923 earthquake) fleshed out the 'impermanence' idea expressed in earlier English-language interpretations. This time, the idea spoke to a Japanese audience too. An article by Shinto scholar Kobayashi Kenzō published in the historical journal *Shien* a few months later quoted the *Japan Times* editorial at length, and commented approvingly. Yet even as the English and Japanese interpretations seemed to coincide completely in this article, ultimately they subtly diverged. For whereas the *Japan Times* editorial took Ise as evidence of a general national culture of impermanence, Kobayashi found greater significance in the editorial's emphasis on the uniqueness of the imperial shrine itself. Following quotation of the *Japan Times*, he turned to an anecdote about Chinese and Koreans failing to understand why the Japanese emperor had no grand monumental display of his authority. What they could not see, Kobayashi asserted, was that the emperor had no need for such things. The periodic renewal of Ise Shrine transmitted the throne's ancient character and expressed in ideal form the Japanese spirit of ancestor worship. Thus for Kobayashi, periodic renewal affirmed a spiritual link between the Japanese nation and sovereign that other Asians could not appreciate, and this sacred national tradition was affirmed by outsiders (meaning Westerners), as represented in the *Japan Times* editorial.[30]

With the arrival in Japan of Bauhaus architect Bruno Taut in 1933, the East-West dialogue over reading Ise Shrine would return to the field of architecture and become yet more intimate. Since international-style architecture was making inroads in the Japanese academy at the time, Taut was welcomed and his opinions were valued. In several lectures between 1933 and 1935 and in publications in Japanese and English, Taut praised Ise along with the Katsura Palace in Kyoto as Japan's greatest architectural achievements. His admiration was not unprecedented—and it is clear that he was influenced in part by the opinions of his hosts—but the endorsement from an eloquent representative of the high church of modernism was influential. Through Taut's remarks and subsequently through his publications, Ise Shrine came to be widely regarded among architects both Japanese and foreign as a masterpiece. The shrine buildings' simplicity of structure and form were reread through the tenets of modernism as examples of functionalist beauty. In 1935, Itō Chūta quoted Taut's opinion of Ise and noted the 'fine irony' that Victorian visitors had reviled the shrine and Japanese had agreed; now Taut praised it and Japanese agreed again. Later the same year, Taut quoted

---

[30] There is no certainty that the anonymous *Japan Times* editorial was written by a Westerner. Oddly, at one point in the editorial reference is made to 'our ancestors', despite references to the Japanese elsewhere in the same editorial as 'they'.

Itō, admiring his 'Oriental irony'. In 1941, Itō would retell the story in the context of a lecture and urge his audience to buy Taut's book.[31]

Taut praised the renewal as well as the buildings themselves, but he did so with a different intent from previous interpreters. In *Houses and People of Japan*, published in English by a Japanese press in 1937, he began by dismissing what most Japanese authors on Ise had stressed, remarking 'actually, the theological side of the matter seems to be entirely unimportant'. He concluded the same paragraph describing the renewal: 'Not only are the religious rites and the everlasting stream of worshippers a living presence, the shrines have yet another vital quality, which is entirely original in its action, intention and perception. It is the fact that the shrines are always new.' Appropriate to the perspective of a modernist, Taut's reading swept aside tradition and placed freshness and originality at the heart of the renewal. This view of Ise as ever new stood in precise opposition to the view of architecture historians like Sekino and Itō, for whom the renewal's importance lay in the fact that it transmitted ancient forms, meaning in essence that the shrine was ever *old*.

Naturally, 'ever new' and 'ever old' can be seen as two sides of the same coin. Yet in these years, when the antiquity of the *kokutai* formed the core of national ideology, it was difficult to comprehend the two perspectives at once. Rather than two sides of a coin, Ise Shrine in the 1930s and 1940s presented something like the 'duck-rabbit' problem discussed by Wittgenstein: a picture that could be read as representing either of two things but not both at once.[32]

Japanese translations of Taut's writing did not include the remark that theology was irrelevant. Nor did they state that the shrine was 'always new', at least not in quite the same terms. Instead, reflecting an emerging view of Ise as the 'people's shrine', they described the shrine buildings' freshness as a reflection of the Japanese nation's efforts to maintain it.[33] In his 1941 lecture, Itō reported that Taut had told him the value of the building lay in the beauty

---

[31] Itō Chūta, *Kenchiku yori mitaru Nihon no kokuminsei* (Tokyo, 1941), 25-7. On the exchange between Itō and Taut, see Jaccqueline Eve Kestenbaum, 'Modernism and Tradition in Japanese Architectural Ideology, 1931-1955' (PhD dissertation, Columbia University, 1996), 91-2; Inoue Shōichi, *Ise Jingū*, 150-3.

[32] Travis J. Denneson, 'Wittgenstein on Seeing', *The Secular Web* http://www.infidels.org/library/modern/travis_denneson/seeing.html

[33] Bruno Taut, *Nippon*, trans. Hirai Hitoshi (Tokyo, 1934) , 19-20; Bruno Taut, *Nihonbi no saihakken*, trans. Shinoda Hideo (Tokyo, 1939), 19-21. Taut appears not to have published writing on Japanese architecture in his native German, and I have not seen his manuscripts, so I cannot say what he himself said precisely either in writing or in the lectures he gave.

of the materials and purity of form. He made no mention of Taut's remarks on the renewal. Itō's lecture was titled 'Japanese National Character as Seen in Architecture', but rather than speaking of the Japanese love of impermanence or the freshness of the rebuilt shrine buildings, Itō presented the renewal as evidence of the unique longevity of the Japanese imperial line, in contrast with China, where dynasties had changed several times.[34] Hence even as he wrote in approving terms of Taut's interpretation of Ise, it appears that Itō continued to see a duck where Taut saw a rabbit.

Phase 3: The people's shrine (1940s-1980s)

The new democratic nationalism after World War II made it possible for the first time to bundle duck and rabbit together in a single portmanteau. Post-war architects repudiated the wartime ideology of the emperor-state.[35] Once one severed Ise Shrine from *kokutai* ideology it became possible to imagine the site's antiquity and modernity in symbiosis. With the official history based on imperial myths and chronicles delegitimized in mainstream dis-course, historians and archeologists strove to construct a new history that would rejuvenate the injured nation by showing the continuity of a people's culture from the prehistoric past to the present.[36] Ise after the war thus became part of a nationalism that rooted itself not in the arcana of imperial lineage but in the conception of a national identity that needed no lineage, because it had always been and would always be.

The first post-war renewal came in 1953. Delayed because of war and oc-cupation, the renewal took place in a national and international climate quite different from 1929. Imperial tradition and the *kokutai* were now tainted by association with militarism. Yet a wide segment of the Japanese public desired cultural symbols reaffirming the nation in the wake of defeat. For the first time in its history, the renewal was paid for entirely by public contributions rather than taxes or government and imperial household funds.[37] Mass media

---

[34] Itō, *Kenchiku yori mitaru Nihon no kokuminsei*, 28.

[35] Reynolds, 'Ise Shrine', 324. The central figures in pre-1945 architecture history them-selves came in for criticism.

[36] For discussion of an excavation that played a key role in this post-war reimagining of Japan's prehistoric past, see Walter Edwards, 'Buried Discourse: the Toro Archeological Site and Japanese National Identity in the Early Postwar Period', *Journal of Japanese Studies*, 17:1 (Winter, 1991), 1-23.

[37] At the same time that the 1953 renewal mobilized the support of a post-imperial national public, the timbers for this reconstruction may have been partly from Japan's former colonies. At least this is what is implied by a remark from MoMA curator Arthur Drexler, who visited Japan in 1953 in preparation for an exhibit of Japanese architecture in New York. Drexler, *The Architecture of Japan* (New York, 1955), 35. Since timbers are

showed less enthusiasm than in the past, however. The leading English-language newspaper provided only brief notice of the renewal ceremonies, referring to the object of the rites as 'mythical'.[38] On the first day of the renewal, the Japanese newspaper *Yomiuri shinbun* ran an op-ed piece by a former Home Minister about the importance of separation of church and state, along with an article about the rites stressing the fact that this was the first time they had been citizen-sponsored.[39] An earlier editorial had registered concern, however, that contributions to the public campaign were being raised by means that bordered on coercion.[40]

The populist revision to interpretations of the renewal emerged in the years following, again in the context of an international dialogue. Taut's view of Ise and Katsura as triumphant demonstrations of the modernist principles in Japanese tradition became architectural orthodoxy worldwide after the Japanese house exhibition held in 1955 at the Museum of Modern Art in New York. MoMA curator Arthur Drexler's *The Architecture of Japan*, published to accompany the exhibition, devoted more space to these two buildings than to any others. Of the renewal, Drexler emphasized both modernity and the continuity of tradition, referring to Ise's 'perpetual youth', and noting that 'each time the buildings are consecrated anew', the new shrine was 'identical in every respect to the old one, except for its polished, golden freshness'.[41] By this time, appreciations like this one were familiar to architects outside as well as inside Japan. But since the English version of Taut's book had been published by a Japanese press at a time when views of Japan in the Anglophone world were generally not sympathetic, Drexler's work, accompanying as it did the international architectural debut of a rehabilitated Japan, introduced Ise Shrine and its unique tradition to a large new audience that knew nothing of Taut.

Although the fundamental ideological tension around Ise's antiquity and modernity disappeared after the war, interpretations of the shrine for native

---

cut at least seven years prior to the renewal, and the 1953 renewal was originally to have taken place in 1949, this seems quite possible. Securing large timbers domestically was already a matter of concern at the turn of the twentieth century, as noted above.

[38] 'Ceremonies Held at Ise Inner Shrine', *Nippon Times*, (3 October 1953), 3. The *Nippon Times* was formerly called the *Japan Times*. The name reverted to *Japan Times* in 1957.

[39] 'Koyoi hare no ongi: Ise jingū hatsu no min'ei sengū', *Yomiuri shinbun* (2 October 1953), 7; Kanamori Tokujirō, 'Shikinen sengū ni yoseru: kokka to shūkyō no bunri ni tsuite', *Yomiuri shinbun* (2 October 1953), 2.

[40] 'Shasetsu: Gyaku kōsu e no hansei', *Yomiuri shinbun* (15 November 1951), 1.

[41] Arthur Drexler, *The Architecture of Japan*, 35. An advocate of Bauhaus modernism, Drexler also published a book on Mies van der Rohe.

and for foreign audiences continued to differ in emphasis, as evidenced by the Japanese and English versions of the landmark volume of photographs *Ise: Prototype of Japanese Architecture* (Japanese, 1962; English, 1965).[42] Architecture critic and theorist Kawazoe Noboru contributed essays to each. Kawazoe was spokesman for the Metabolist movement, which advocated the development of a new architectural language for the continuous organic growth of cities.[43] In both editions, Kawazoe surveyed the historical origins of the shrine and discussed the meaning of the shrine's architectural form and the renewal. However, the English and Japanese essays under Kawazoe's name were different texts. Kawazoe's Japanese text, reflecting the post-war climate of cultural roots-searching, revolved around the claim that Ise's design represented a people's architecture, while his English text stressed the idea of a Japanese ethos of impermanence. In his Japanese introduction, Kawazoe noted how highly regarded the shrine was outside Japan, but insisted on its special spiritual importance to Japanese people: 'Particularly for us, Ise Shrine is a treasury that arouses images of the ancestral home of the Japanese people.'[44] Since as early as the 1909 reconstruction, when a public subscription was raised to build a new road between the Inner and Outer Shrines, some writers had spoken of Ise as the people's shrine, noting the increasing involvement of ordinary citizens as sponsors and spectators of the renewal, but prior to 1945 these authors invariably wrote of the shrine as a gift bestowed on the people by the emperor.[45] Kawazoe claimed not simply that the Japanese people shared in the cost of rebuilding the

[42] Kenzo Tange and Noboru Kawazoe, *Ise: Prototype of Japanese Architecture* (Cambridge, MA, 1965). *Ise* reproduced photographs of the shrine buildings taken by Watanabe Yoshio at the time of the 1953 reconstruction. Shrine authorities had permitted Watanabe special access to photograph the inner sanctuaries for promotional purposes, and several of the photographs had already appeared in publications at home and overseas, including in Drexler's book. Essays by architect Tange Kenzō and by Kawazoe accompanied Watanabe's photographs in both the Japanese and the English editions. Jonathan Reynolds discusses the circumstances of Watanabe's photographing the shrine in 'Ise Shrine and the Modernist Construction of Japanese Tradition', 325-9.

[43] On Metabolism, see Zhongjie Lin, *Kenzo Tange and the Metabolist Movement: Urban Utopias of Modern Japan* (Routledge, 2010).

[44] Kawazoe Noboru, 'Ise bunkaron', in Tange Kenzō et al., *Ise: Nihon kenchiku no genkei* (Tokyo, 1962), 68.

[45] To offer one fulsome example: 'It is a thing for which to be extremely grateful not only that this greatest of state rituals is to be performed, but that it is becoming more and more a great ceremony for the nation [*kokumin*] as well. It has no comparison on earth. This is really the quintessence of our unique and unsurpassed *kokutai*.' Miyachi Naokazu and Sakamoto Kōtarō, *Jingū to shikinen sengū* (Tokyo, 1929), 116.

imperial shrine, however, but that ordinary people had originally created it. The farming folk of the Ise region, in Kawazoe's interpretation, built the shrine on the model of a rice storehouse, in response to emperor Tenmu's command but 'according to their own traditions and aesthetic sense'. Kawazoe thus made the shrine the pinnacle of Japanese folk architecture.[46]

On the world stage, however, impermanence as a Japanese cultural virtue had more cachet than claims for Ise's status as indigenous folk architecture. The trope of impermanence already had a long lineage in English-language writing on Japan and seemed only strengthened by Japan's wartime destruction and rapid recovery. In place of discussion of Ise's significance to the nation, the English text of Kawazoe's essay explained that Japanese people valued the spirit rather than the actual structures, and concluded that Ise Shrine, 'ever new, yet ever unchanging', reversed the Western dictum 'life is short, art eternal'. Kawazoe's Japanese text had no corresponding passage.[47]

The people's shrine and the abode of impermanence did not stand in opposition. Whether the passages on Ise renewal and impermanence in this English text accurately translated words from a different manuscript by Kawazoe or represented the interpolation of a translator, the two could easily have been the work of the same Japanese author. In fact, the 1962 revised edition of the standard Japanese textbook in architecture history, published in the same year as Kawazoe's original Japanese essay, began with a chapter on the 'Japanese view of architecture' that asserted an innate national feeling for impermanence in much the same language as the English text of Kawazoe's essay. The author also asserted that the Japanese people regarded themselves as a single 'organism'—the term *yūkitai*, meaning 'organism' or 'organic body', substituting neatly for *kokutai*, the now-taboo term for the national body.[48] The imperial versus the popular and the ancient versus the modern were two different axes of interpretation, not conflicting sets of claims. Interpretations of the shrine in the post-war, post-*kokutai*, intellectual environment could combine degrees of each. Ephemerality and anti-monumentality undergirded the philosophy of the Metabolist movement, which was the vanguard of Japanese architectural thought in the 1960s. Metabolism saw Japanese tradition as a model for a new modernism based on organic self-renewal rather than planned regularity. Flying back into

---

[46] Kawazoe, 'Ise bunkaron', 93.

[47] Kawazoe Noboru, *Ise: Prototype of Japanese Architecture*, 206.

[48] Ōta Hirotarō, *Nihon kenchikushi josetsu* (revised 2nd edn, 1962), 18. The first edition of this text, penned in 1939 and published in 1947, lacked this chapter, which Ōta first published elsewhere in 1954.

Tokyo after his visit to Ise, Kawazoe found in the chaotic cityscape of Tokyo below the 'fierce, primitive power' that he sensed in the architecture of Ise's Outer Shrine.[49] The idea of Ise as autochthonous, primordial, and self-renewing gave it special evocative power for Kawazoe and the Japanese architects of his generation.[50]

Phase 4: Pandora's Box, the globalization of the Ise metaphor (1990s–present)

In 1972, UNESCO's Convention Concerning the Protection of the World Cultural and Natural Heritage launched the World Heritage List and a new era of global heritage. From this time on, not only were there shared international guidelines for determining what deserved conservation as heritage, there were powerful incentives to identify sites that could make 'the List', bringing prestige and potential tourism revenues to the listing country. Japan did not sign the Convention until 1992, but the country's conservation establishment showed an intense interest in UNESCO's guidelines. National institutions for architectural preservation had been in place in Japan since the enactment of the Law for the Preservation of Ancient Shrines and Temples in 1897, and a set of standards together with a complex code of practice had developed. The source of concern for Japanese preservationists—and one reason that Japan was late to sign the Convention—was UNESCO's language concerning authenticity. The UNESCO Venice Charter of 1964 had enshrined criteria for authentic restoration that prohibited moving any part of the monument and called for preservation of all possible original material and 'the valid contributions of all eras' in the life of the building or site. Since 1897, preservationists in Japan had made it a practice to completely dismantle state-designated architectural monuments, study the condition of wooden structural members, then reassemble them, usually restoring the building to its earliest documentable form. This practice of dismantling calls to mind the periodic renewal at Ise. The two were related in the broad sense that both belonged to systems of maintenance for Japanese post-and-lintel wood buildings, but they were ultimately distinct. Partial or complete dismantling had been used as a means to extend the longevity of structures, including Buddhist temples, palaces, and ordinary houses as well as Shinto shrines like Ise. The 1897 law, however, altered the significance of the practice by making revival of the original historical form rather than simply maintenance its motive, and

---

[49] Kawazoe Noboru, 'Dentōron no shuppatsu to shūketsu: Ise jingū no zōkei ni tsuite', *Bungaku*, 27:7 (July, 1959), 793.

[50] See the remarks of Kawazoe Noboru and Kurokawa Noriaki in Rem Koolhaas and Hans Ulrich Obrist, *Project Japan: Metabolism Talks* (Taschen, 2011).

making complete dismantling the sine qua non of proper restoration, based on a positivist faith in the possibility of determining the unique original state of a site through scientific analysis of structural members.[51] This modern practice of dismantling and restoration potentially conflicted with the standards suggested by the Venice Charter.

Debate about the language of the Venice Charter began before the birth of the World Heritage Committee and continued as a growing list of nations joined the convention during the 1970s. Eventually in 1977, a four-part test for world heritage authenticity was introduced, calling for authenticity of 'design, material, setting, and workmanship'.[52] Beginning the same year, UNESCO co-sponsored a series of international meetings held in Japan on issues of wood conservation. Led by architecture historian Sekino Masaru (son of Sekino Tadashi, mentioned earlier), the Japanese hosts used these meetings to voice their complaint that the institutions of world heritage and the list's terms of eligibility were Eurocentric. Sekino addressed the first of these gatherings with a plea for recognition that each country had its own history of preservation techniques. He defended Japan's restoration approach by claiming that it was necessary for wood buildings, but assured his audience that it was all done 'in accordance with the Venice Charter'.[53]

Since Japan was not at this time a signatory to the World Heritage Convention, Sekino and his colleagues were worrying in advance, or acting preemptively, so that when the time came, Japan's heritage practices would receive the international recognition they sought. In doing so, they played a role that had been played by Japanese experts in a variety of fields since the late nineteenth century, acting as a wedge in a Western dominated system of

[51] Shimizu Shigeatsu, 'Shikinen zōtai to kaitai shūri: Nihon no dentōtekina kenchiku keishō shuhō wa ika ni kindaika sareta ka', in *Savants and Batisseurs: Patrimoine and Architecture* (proceedings of a conference sponsored by the Institut Franco-Japonais du Kansai and the Japan Foundation, April 2005), 10-12. Shimizu notes that Itō and Sekino were probably influenced in their choice of an approach that emphasized the restoration of ancient forms rather than the conservation of existing ones in part by reading Viollet-le-Duc. Viollet-le-Duc himself had written in his *On Restoration* (1860s) of a custom of rebuilding temples and palaces in Asia, describing it in a manner that suggests he may have been influenced by some version of the story of Ise's renewal.

[52] Herb Stovel, 'Origins and Influence of the Nara Document on Authenticity', *APT Bulletin*, 39:2-3 (2008), 12.

[53] Sekino Masaru, 'Principles of Conservation and Restoration Regarding Wooden Buildings in Japan', in *International Symposium on Conservation and Restoration of Cultural Property: Conservation of Wood* (Tokyo, 1978), 128, 130-1. Sekino's position suggests the way that European masonry haunted late twentieth-century Japanese preservationists much as it had haunted late nineteenth-century Japanese architects.

knowledge—a Westernized but anti-Western cultural vanguard seeking exceptions and expanded interpretations within the terms of the Western field of discourse. In reality, they may have been fretting unnecessarily. Japan's first two listings were approved promptly after the country became a signatory in 1992. Comparatively broad notions of what should constitute material authenticity were already bruited about by European officials in the heritage field in the 1970s. UNESCO expert Michel Parent, who would become chair of the World Heritage Committee in 1981, wrote in a 1979 report that, 'a wooden temple in Kyoto which has been perfectly maintained, and whose timbers have been replaced regularly as and when they decayed—without any alteration of the architecture or of the look of the material over ten centuries—remains undeniably authentic'.[54] Parent's example here, like many examples given by non-Japanese observers of preservation practices in Japan, conflated the Japanese preservationists' logic of dismantling for repair with the ideal of perfect continuity of form that Ise's ritual renewal was imagined to embody. The fact that no Kyoto temple matching Parent's criteria actually existed was irrelevant: as in the past, Japan served the purpose of general antithesis to European conceptions of the monument.

The question of authenticity persisted, however. Eventually, the debate led to a major conference, again sponsored by UNESCO together with Japan's preservation agency and other institutions domestic and international, held in the Japanese city of Nara in 1994, and to the publication of a new set of UNESCO principles in the form of the 'Nara Document on Authenticity'. Although its effects were not immediate, the Nara conference is generally credited with opening up world heritage to a multicultural approach. Many writers—both advocates and critics—have also described it as a 'Pandora's box'. Once the experts at Nara had opened that box, a panoply of new claims to heritage status on the basis of more vaguely defined criteria would emerge.

Ise Shrine was an uneasy presence at the Nara Conference. Japan had been chosen as the conference venue because Japanese had led the campaign against Eurocentrism in the world heritage system, yet the Ise renewal, the Japanese conservationists' most powerful rhetorical tool against that Eurocentric system, which had been honed in an East-West dialogue that now extended over a century, undermined the scientific positivism of their

---

[54] Michel Parent, 'Item 6 of the Provisional Agenda: Principles and Criteria for Inclusion of Properties on World Heritage List', *Third Session of the World Heritage Committee* (Luxor, Arab Republic of Egypt, 23-27 October, 1979), 19. See also Christina Cameron, 'From Warsaw to Mostar: The World Heritage Committee and Authenticity', *APT Bulletin: Journal of Preservation Technology*, 39:2-3 (2008), 19-22.

own official conservation methods. Several Japanese participants laboured to convey to the assembly that Japanese architecture was not all Ise Shrine and that official practice of dismantling for study and restoration was distinct from the ritual of periodic renewal.[55] Nevertheless, Ise's power as a metaphor proved hard for both Japanese and non-Japanese participants to resist.

Architecture historian Itō Nobuo's keynote address derived a broad cultural message from Ise. In order to demonstrate the distinct conditions of Asian wood architecture and the difficulty of defining authenticity in an Asian context, Itō presented to the audience a theory of the origins of Japanese and other wet-rice cultivating Asian societies, which he claimed yielded distinct attitudes toward the sacred and a distinct conception of heritage, both exemplified by Ise. Following this story of cultural genesis, he described the country's contemporary restoration policy, stressing that wood members were preserved to the greatest degree possible, unlike at Ise. He thus implicitly presented modern Japanese preservation practice as out of sync with the essential character of the Asian building culture that he was seeking to defend.[56]

French architecture historian and theorist Françoise Choay spoke of Ise at the Nara Conference too, but refused to treat it as peculiarly Japanese or Asian. Instead she interpreted it as the best example of a particular paradigm of monumentality seen around the world, in which historical significance takes preeminence over material form. The force of the idea of periodic renewal seems to have permitted her to overlook the fact that Ise itself was anomalous within Japan, however, since in her *Invention of the Historical Monument*, published first in 1992 and reprinted several times after the Nara Conference, she referred to the Japanese habit of 'rebuilding their monuments every twenty years,' as if it were general.[57]

Ise Shrine thus remained off the official agenda at Nara yet present as a master metaphor, no longer peculiarly Japanese. After Nara, others less constrained by conservation science than Japan's preservation officials would

---

[55] See Masuda Kanefusa, 'Kaigi hōkoku: Sekai isan jōyaku to sekai bunka isan Nara konfarensu', *Kenchiku shigaku dai* 24 *gō* (1995), 49-51; Inagaki Eizō, 'Bunka isan no Ōsentishiti o meguru sobyō', *Kenchiku shigaku dai* 24 *gō* (1995), 84; also Stovel, 'Origins and Influence of the Nara Document'.

[56] Nobuo Ito, ' "Authenticity" Inherent in Cultural Heritage in Asia and Japan', in *Nara Conference on Authenticity (Proceedings)*, ed. Knut Einar Larsen (UNESCO World Heritage Centre, 1995), 35-45.

[57] Françoise Choay, *The Invention of the Historic Monument*, trans. Lauren M. O'Connell (Cambridge, 2001).

take this metaphor and run with it. Reflecting the open, multicultural mood among participants in the Nara Conference, the Nara Document proposed a new conception of authenticity based on a 'great variety' of sources of meaning, including 'spirit and feelings'.[58] This reached far beyond the restoration issues that had been primary on the Japanese participants' agenda. The Nara Document was formally adopted by UNESCO in 1999. Although its practical results were not immediately evident, more than fifty UNESCO-sponsored workshops and other events followed in the 1990s and 2000s, pursuing the newly liberated conception of authenticity further.[59]

It became common in these years to claim Ise as representative of an 'Asian' attitude toward heritage.[60] It was equally common, even among scholars and heritage professionals, to make erroneous statements about the shrine, sometimes repeating previous misunderstandings, sometimes revealing new misunderstandings: for example, that it had been perfectly replicated every twenty years since its founding, that its rebuilding was typical of Japanese conservation practices generally, that it was denied world heritage status because it was rebuilt, or that it was located in the former imperial capital of Kyoto.[61] The frequency of these casual and often mistaken references to Ise

[58] 'Nara Document on Authenticity', in *Nara Conference on Authenticity (Proceedings)*, xxiii.

[59] Sophia Labadi has examined 106 nomination dossiers for sites nominated to the World Heritage List between 1994 and 2004 and found only a handful treated authenticity 'as a dynamic process'. See Labadi, 'World Heritage, Authenticity and Post-Authenticity' in *Heritage and Globalisation*, ed. Sophia Labadi and Colin Long (London, 2010), 72-81. It may still be too early to tell where the opening up of world heritage criteria will lead, however. The perception in the field seems to be that Nara's impact has indeed been substantial—as suggested by the frequent references to a Pandora's Box having been opened by the Conference. Stovel reports that in 2007, the Vice President of ICOMOS China announced that China was holding a conference in Beijing to do for China what Nara had done for Japan—although it was not in fact clear what the Nara Conference had done for Japan.

[60] See John H. Stubbs, *Time Honored: A Global View of Architectural Conservation* (Hoboken NJ, 2009), 263-7; Jennifer Ko, 'Regional Authenticity: An Argument for Reconstruction in Oceania', *APT Bulletin* 39:2-3 (2008), 55-61. David Lowenthal cites examples of Chinese claims that non-Western cultures value 'authenticity of thought', rather than material form. Lowenthal, *The Heritage Crusade and the Spoils of History* (Cambridge, 1998), 20.

[61] Dawson Munjeri 'Tangible and Intangible Heritage: from Difference to Convergence', *Museum International*, 26:1-2 (2004); Choay, *The Invention of the Historic Monument*; Ralph Pettman, 'Anti-globalisation discourses in Asia', in *Critical Theories, International Relations, and the 'Anti-Globalisation' Movement*, ed. Catherine Eschle and Bice

reveals both the symbolic status of the shrine's ritual renewal and the versatility of the symbol. Using Ise as a metaphor required little actual knowledge of the history or contemporary situation of the shrine.

Authors citing the case of Ise Shrine in the heritage field seldom did so with the intent to undermine the edifice of world heritage itself. They called rather for opening it up. The conception of a more open type of 'authenticity' that accommodated Ise's ritual renewal (and the attitudes it was presumed to represent) made Ise more than a touchstone for claims of Asian difference: Ise became the universal property of the non-West. After 2000, UNESCO introduced a series of measures to protect cultural diversity, including the Convention for the Safeguarding of Intangible Cultural Heritage (2003).[62] The category of 'intangible heritage' had served in Japanese and Korean national conservation policies for decades as a rubric for the protection of performance and craft traditions by official designation of the traditional practice or of the practitioners themselves. The 2003 convention translated this into the terms for a new international classification system. Dawson Munjeri, former representative for Zimbabwe on the World Heritage Committee, participated in the drafting and passage of the 2003 convention. He regarded the convention as a means to fuse the categories of tangible and intangible heritage. Toward this end, Ise offered a vital case, Munjeri claimed, since it was '100 percent original' in design, workmanship and setting, yet 'zero percent original' in materials. Ise had led the way to a rethinking of the categories, yet in Munjeri's eyes, the rethinking did not go far enough. Voodoo temples in Benin, for example, presented a case in which a tradition was not bounded by a stable site, and the buildings and implements used constantly changed. Preserving the 'intrinsic values' of traditions like this had impelled UNESCO forward from Nara to the embrace of intangible heritage.[63] The Ise Shrine metaphor thus contributed to a transformation of

---

Maiguashca (London, 2004) 82; Jukka Jokilehto, 'Preservation Theory Unfolding', *Future Anterior: Journal of Historic Preservation, History, Theory, and Criticism*, 3:1 (Summer, 2006), xii.

[62] For analysis of the significance of UNESCO's change of mission toward protecting cultural diversity, see Witkor Stoczkowski, 'UNESCO's Doctorine of Human Diversity: A Secular Soteriology?' *Anthropology Today*, 25:3 (June 2009), 7-11. UNESCO representatives and conservation experts returned to Nara in 2004 for a conference to discuss interpretations of 'intangible heritage'.

[63] Dawson Munjeri, 'Tangible and Intangible Heritage: from Difference to Convergence', 15-16.

world heritage that would come to encompass everything from coal mines to national cuisines.[64]

'Spirit and feelings' implied a new measure, a new type of authenticity that was both more difficult to define and more difficult to refute when claimed. This was a different spiritualism from the Eastern spiritualism of the Victorian era. It demanded no mystical system of belief, simply the specific claim that the keepers of a particular heritage object valued something invisible within it rather than its materiality. Turning one of the oldest of Western philosophical claims—of the superiority of spirit over matter—against the West itself, the demand from non-Western heritage advocates for recognition of the 'spirit of the place' challenged the UNESCO-centred preservation establishment to make explicit wherein lay the ultimate value of a monument. And in a multicultural age, who could deny the value of 'spirit' anywhere?[65] To espouse the alternative—that material form alone should be the criterion for heritage value—risked descent into fetishism, 'the brute worship of objects', which post-Enlightenment Western thought treated as the basest of human attachments.[66]

At the Nara Conference in 1994, German conservationist Michael Petzet had suggested that in the late twentieth century, the 'monument cult' might reflect a 'longing for survival' in the face of environmental crisis. In this sense, Ise Shrine offered a suitable monument for the era.[67] Several writers since the 1990s have reimagined Ise Shrine in ecological terms. In a popular English-language essay, Shinto ethicist Tokoro Isao presented the shrine's reconstruction as a model example of long-term forestry management.[68] More recently,

---

[64] This most recent phase in the history of Ise as metaphor is also treated in an effective analysis of the depoliticization of the shrine by Tze Loo, who covers some of the same material. See Loo, 'Escaping Its Past, Recasting the Grand Shrine of Ise', *InterAsian Cultural Studies*, 2010.

[65] For a rare opinion advocating a purely materialist approach to authenticity, see Wim Denslagen, 'Authenticity and Spirituality', in *Concepts of Authenticity in Architectural Heritage Preservation, an International Workshop of the Cluster of Excellence, Heidelberg University, 16 June 2008*, http://www.asia-europe.uni-heidelberg.de/en/news-events/events/archive/event-view/cal/event//tx_cal_phpicalendar////workshop_concepts_of_authenticity_in_architectural_heritage_preservation.html.

[66] See David Murray, 'Fetishism and the Hierarchies of Race and Religion', in *Conversions: Old Worlds and New*, ed. Kenneth Mills and Anthony Grafton (Rochester NY, 2003), 199-217.

[67] Michael Petzet, ' "In the Full Richness of their Authenticity": The Test of Authenticity and the New Cult of Monuments', *Nara Conference on Authenticity* (Proceedings), 97.

[68] Isao Tokoro, 'The Grand Shrine of Ise: Preservation by Removal and Renewal' in *Historic Cities and Sacred Sites: Cultural Roots for Urban Futures*, 22-9.

North American ecologist William Jordan III has cited Ise to prove the parochialism of Western thinking about what constitutes landscape restoration.[69] If indeed heritage philosophy since the late twentieth century reflects contemporary environmental concerns, the fascination with Ise Shrine may represent not only a longing for survival, but a longing for perpetual renewal: a wish that careful custodianship might allow humans to inhabit a self-sustaining ecosystem, despite the pervasive signs of irreversible damage.

In cultural terms, Ise also served the seductive idea that outside the fetishistic West, replicas were valued no differently from originals. Writing in the *New Yorker*, journalist Alexander Stille treated Ise's renewal as part of an Asian tradition of copying, which, considered together with the contemporary Chinese government's use of replicas in museum displays and archeological sites signified an alternative authenticity for a post-authentic age: the perfect replica. Stille's use of the Ise metaphor partook of a popular late twentieth-century stereotype of traditional Japan as post-modern *avant la lettre*.[70] Anti-preservationist architects, meanwhile, found in Ise's renewal a cultural rationale for questioning the preservation of built form generally: Rem Koolhaas, for example, spoke admiringly to an interviewer of the Japanese ability to maintain a national tradition in architecture paradoxically by *not* valuing heritage, mentioning Ise and claiming that the Japanese 'do not hang onto things'. Koolhaas' thinking, in turn, echoed that of the Metabolist group, whom he profiled in a volume of interviews published in 2012.[71]

Thus, in a protracted international dialogue, the metaphor of Ise Shrine has continued to grow and ramify, carrying it far from its origins as the ancestral shrine of Japan's imperial family. Yet what about the site itself? The term *heritage* implies a property relation. When UNESCO declares a site to be part of the 'common heritage of humanity', humanity acquires some form of controlling interest in it. States participating in the World Heritage Convention accept the responsibility to protect their heritage sites on behalf of the rest of us, who are the hypothetical inheritors. Here lies a further irony about Ise: while it has become the icon of a broad reconception of cultural heritage associated with Japan and embraced by countless conservationists worldwide, the shrine itself is neither listed as a world heritage site nor even protected by the Japanese government under the country's cultural

---

[69] William Jordan III, *Sunflower Forest: Ecological Restoration and the New Communion with Nature* (Berkeley, 2011), 117-22, 224 fn.

[70] Alexander Stille, 'Faking It', *New Yorker*, (15 June 1998), 36-7. See also Alexander Stille, *The Future of the Past* (Picador, 2003).

[71] 'Reinventing the City: An Interview with Architect Rem Koolhaas', *Christian Science Monitor*, (20 July 2012).

properties law. The shrine's custodians have vigorously defended it from the intervention of any branch of the secular state. They consider it sacrosanct, and perceive heritage designation as a compromise with outside institutions that might diminish the sacred imperial aura.[72] Although forgotten by most of the country, *kokutai* ideology—a vision of the polity embodied in an unbroken line of sacred emperors—is alive and well at Ise. Chief priests and priestesses come from among members of the imperial family. When Allied Occupation Forces compelled the Japanese government to separate church and state in 1946 by ending Shinto's official patronage, the shrine priesthood created the National Association of Shinto Shrines to preserve the vestiges of the old system, including a national hierarchy of shrines with Ise at its pinnacle. The association's regulations state explicitly (in apparent conflict with national law) that Ise Shrine is the property of the emperor, which the association maintains in custody temporarily.[73] Thus the persistence of pre-war imperial nationalism prevents Japan's culture bureaucrats from touching the country's most famous architectural monument, whose listing by UNESCO might be thought highly desirable in global heritage competition. Ise Shrine has been a political site for the duration of its long career. It remains a political site today, although the fact is seldom noted outside Japan.

Conclusion

Ise Shrine has come to play the role of master metaphor because it elegantly articulates paradoxes at the foundation of our attachments to the things of the past. Is the ethos of architectural preservation fundamentally spiritual? Is it material fetishism? Or is every invocation of a 'culture' to be protected itself a form of fetishism? Ise has lent itself to such questions—and more often than not in recent years, it has been treated as offering redemption for heritage discourse, but within an expanded definition of heritage.

This essay has traced the modern trajectory of Ise as a metaphor. In the course of roughly a century, the shrine passed through at least four different symbolic incarnations: from Japanese abode of impermanence, to ancient-yet-modern 'duck-rabbit', to people's shrine, to global master metaphor. One site, multiple readings: my mode of argumentation is a familiar one in cultural criticism. A seemingly simple singularity is shown to contain multiplicity. And with this, usually, an essentialist myth is debunked. I am not

---

[72] In this, Ise has taken a different strategy from the Vatican, which was listed as world heritage in 1984, the only state to be listed entire.

[73] *Sengo no jinja, Shintō: Rekishi to kadai*, ed. Jinja Honchō Sōgō Kenkyūjo (Jinja shinpōsha, 2010), 141. On the contemporary role of the National Association of Shinto Shrines, see John Breen and Mark Teeuwen, *A New History of Shinto* (Chichester, 2010), 199-220.

claiming, however, that Ise Shrine's unique tradition of periodic renewal is a myth. Nor do I mean to deny that it may offer lessons for the heritage conservation field. But with its closely tended historical relationship to a single dynasty and its protectors, Ise is probably not usefully understood as a general cultural archetype, either Japanese or Asian. Additionally, the anti-materialist meanings often attributed to it today find no support in texts pre-dating the end of the nineteenth century, when those meanings appeared in writing much of which was intended for foreign audiences.

If this narrative of changing interpretations had been confined only to the field of architectural history (or conceivably of Shinto theology), the multiplicity of meanings I have sketched might still be interesting in itself, but the true power of the Ise metaphor lies in its reach beyond any one field. In fact, architecture historians have played second fiddle through most of the metaphor's evolution. And the meanings at each stage resonated with events and issues far beyond the shrine's architectural form or religious significance. In the late nineteenth and early twentieth centuries, the idea of a special Japanese love of impermanence helped win foreign sympathy for imperial Japan through aesthetic claims that were at the same time ethical ones; in the first half of the twentieth century, the Ise metaphor split, and the site became proof of both the empire's antiquity and architectural modernism's universal validity; in Japan after World War II, it took on a populist cast, representing native folk tradition; then finally, from the late twentieth century, in an era of global culture, it was taken in hand by conservationists, architects, ecologists, and others worldwide as the key to a Pandora's Box, from which would emerge a liberated, multicultural future for our conceptions of the past. From the first years of modern conservation practice in Japan to the present day, commentators both native and foreign, addressing different audiences with different emphases, yet often in dialogue with each other, have invented and reinvented the essential meaning of the shrine's renewal. Each reinvention injected the shrine into the politics of its time. And all the while, the shrine remained tightly bound to one family, whose members had nothing to say to the world at large about its meaning.

Culture-keeping as State Action: Bureaucrats, Administrators, and Monuments in Colonial India

Indra Sengupta

Late Victorian and Edwardian preservationist lobbies in early twentieth-century Britain, keen to put pressure on the government to become more actively involved in preserving Britain's ancient monuments, were not unsatisfied with the way such matters were being dealt with in Britain's premier colony, India. Christiana Herringham, the noted Edwardian art copyist and member of the Society for the Protection of Ancient Buildings (SPAB), who visited India in 1906, reported, '(as) I saw a great deal of what has been done recently by the Archaeological Department there during a journey last winter. . ., I should like to express my pleasure at finding that the neglect of which the English have often been accused is becoming rapidly a thing of the past'.[1] On the newly enacted Ancient Monument Preservation Act (AMPA) of 1904,[2] the art historian Gerard Baldwin Brown remarked: 'It is noteworthy that it is fully equipped with clauses, prohibitions, and penal sanctions, of which people in the mother country are so shy.'[3] While much work still needed to be done, what preservationists found worthy of note in India was something that Britain seemed to lack: an energetic state, unequivocally committed to the preservation of the country's ancient architectural heritage. Most importantly, it was a state driven by a sense of public duty, free of the need to protect private property, which so hindered the state's effectiveness in preserving Britain's historic architecture.

In this article I shall take a closer look at the preservation of monuments and heritage in India in the early twentieth century as state action, but as a particular kind of state action, which was only possible, as the Edwardian preservationists themselves approvingly noted, in a colonial context. Baldwin Brown rather benignly summed up his satisfaction with the AMPA 1904 thus: 'This illustrated once again the fact already noticed, that in less advanced

---

[1] Christiana Herringham, Extract from letter of Christiana Herringham to SPAB. *Annual Report of the SPAB*, 1907.

[2] Henceforth to be referred to as AMPA 1904.

[3] G. Baldwin Brown, *The Care of Ancient Monuments* (Cambridge 1905, repr. 2010), 235.

communities it is far more easy to pass stringent monument laws than in states where the individual citizen is accustomed to stand stiffly by his rights.'[4] For such 'less advanced communities' where the rights of subjects were largely subsumed by the compulsions of colonial rule, it was the state in its role as custodian of culture that increasingly in the second half of the nineteenth century became the prime mover behind preservation measures. But how did the state manifest itself in the making and implementation of preservation policy? This task fell upon the Department of Archaeology, set up as the Archaeological Survey of India between 1863 and 1871, which worked as a department of government and was run not by antiquarians or architects but by scholar-administrators of the Empire: usually, a body of military surveyors and engineers. This left plenty of room for policy to be made by single, influential personalities in government, who focused on whatever aspect of archaeological activity they fancied at any given time and used the vast realms of the British Empire in India to experiment with their ideas.[5] At the turn of the twentieth century, when the protection and preservation of monuments became of central importance to the Archaeological Department and sweeping changes were introduced by means of the AMPA of 1904, the driving force behind these initiatives was provided by two men: Lord Curzon, appointed Viceroy of India in 1899 and John Marshall, appointed Director-General of Archaeology in 1902.

Of course, the colonial context of India in the early twentieth century was not an isolated one, and debates and policy in India were a part of the global circulation of ideas of heritage and legislation on the preservation of ancient monuments. In her work on the history of preservation in Britain, France, and Germany, Astrid Swenson has emphasised the transnational origins of ideas of heritage in modern Europe.[6] Corey Ross and Paul Basu and Gita Damodaran have argued in their chapters in this supplement that ideas and legislation on preservation of both nature and ancient, manmade structures enjoyed a wide circulation and considerable transregional exchange within the European empires that in the late nineteenth and early twentieth centuries spanned large parts of the globe.[7] Certainly, as Basu and

---

[4] Baldwin Brown, *Ancient Monuments*, 235.

[5] For a more detailed discussion on the various personalities of colonial archaeology, see Upinder Singh, *The Discovery of Ancient India: Early Archaeologists and the Beginnings of Archaeology* (New Delhi, 2004), esp. 1-76.

[6] Astrid Swenson, *The Rise of Heritage. Preserving the Past in France, Germany and England, 1789-1914* (Cambridge, 2013).

[7] See Corey Ross, 'Tropical Nature as Global Patrimoine: Imperialism and International Nature Protection in the Early Twentieth Century' and Paul Basu and Vinita

Damodaran have shown and I have argued elsewhere,[8] Curzon and Marshall were well connected to a large network of preservationists in England and Europe. Nevertheless, and despite the broad consensus on heritage philosophy, legislation, and practice, specific colonies were associated with specific problems of preservation and thus required legislation that, while sharing many of the broad concerns of legislation in large parts of the world, had to address these specific, local problems. I have shown elsewhere that the major challenge for preservationists in colonial India was the complex question of protection of ancient historical buildings (deemed monuments) which were also religious in character and use.[9] For a preservation policy developed almost entirely by bureaucrats in government departments of archaeology the implementation of ideas of heritage management stemming from a largely secular European context could be an extremely difficult task, as any perceived threat of state intrusion into cultural practice could have the potential to throw the full range of the activities of the colonial state into question and thus threaten colonial order.

As a result, preservation in India in the early twentieth century had to conform to the compulsions of colonial rule and the preservation of order. This meant that there was a certain mundane 'everydayness' about the practice of preservation which, as I shall show, was governed largely by rules and regulations, much like the military handbooks and manuals that were used in the early days of the Empire in India to carry out archaeological surveys, with close attention being paid to sentiment on the ground. Thus, even while looking at the ideological framework of state action in culture-keeping, the chapter focuses on the work of the functionaries, especially middle-ranking functionaries, of the state, and looks at the ambiguities and limitations of state action in attempting to carry out preservation. While aware of the colonial rhetoric of the Empire as custodian of culture in the colonies, the chapter also examines the ways in which the intervention of the colonial bureaucracy in

---

Damodaran, 'Colonial Histories of Heritage: Legislative Migrations and the Politics of Preservation', Ch. 8 and 9 respectively in this supplement.

[8] See Basu and Damodaran in this supplement, Ch. 9. See also Indra Sengupta, 'A Conservation Code for the Colony: John Marshall's *Conservation Manual* and Monument Preservation between India and Europe', in Michael Falser and Monica Juneja (eds), *Archaeologizing Heritage?*, (Berlin, 2013), 21-37.

[9] See Indra Sengupta, 'Monument Preservation and the Vexing Question of Religious Structures in Colonial India', in Astrid Swenson and Peter Mandler (eds) *From Plunder to Preservation. Britain and the Heritage of Empire, c.1800-1940* (Oxford, 2013), 171-85.

monument-making practices was mediated both by its own inconsistencies and by local communities on the ground.

On the face of it, an argument about an interventionist colonial state might seem to be an obvious point to make. However, this article takes as its starting point the historiography of colonialism in India that since the 1980s has tried to understand India's colonial experience and its postcolonial legacy in terms of the power of the colonial state over indigenous culture and the ability of colonized peoples to exert their own agency. Any discussion of a state-sponsored project of preservation of cultural heritage thus must address the mutually interrelated question of the ability of a state, which was by no means homogenous, to enforce its much-advertised rhetoric of cultural custodianship and the power of indigenous groups of various ilks to challenge, contest, engage with, and become constitutive of the process of heritage-making.[10] However, in order to understand the practice of preservation by the colonial state not only as part of a broader, global story of heritage-preservation, but also as an administrative practice related to the day-to-day business of governing, it is necessary to examine the nature of bureaucratization of preservation discussions, policy, and practice. The Archaeological Survey of India, under the Ministry of Culture and headed by a civil servant, remains today the main agent of the protection of monuments in India.[11]

Colonial archaeology as a knowledge project

The cultural dimension of colonialism in India has since the early 1980s generally been studied within the analytical framework of colonial knowledge.[12] Following from Foucauldian notions of power in civil society and Gramscian and Marxian ideas of class conflict, and more immediately, from Edward Said's influential study *Orientalism* (1978) and his later work *Culture and Imperialism* (1993) this approach focuses on the centrality of the relationship between the colonial state's knowledge of its subjects on the one

[10] I have argued this point at length elsewhere. See, e.g., Indra Sengupta, 'Monument Preservation'.

[11] Although the ASI is no longer the sole arbiter of India's heritage, especially since the setting-up of the Indian National Trust for Art and Cultural Heritage (INTACH) by professional architects in 1984, it nevertheless commands large public funds and continues to exercise great influence by means of the satellite departments of archaeology and regional archaeological circles in all states of India.

[12] For a broad survey of historiography on colonial knowledge see Tony Ballantyne, 'Colonial Knowledge', in Sarah Stockwell (ed.), *The British Empire. Themes and Perspectives* (Oxford, 2008), 177-98. See also Introduction, in *Knowledge Production, Pedagogy, and Institutions in Colonial India*, ed. Indra Sengupta and Daud Ali (New York, 2011), 1-15.

hand and the ideology and structures of domination that constituted the core of colonial state power on the other. Thus, the production and dissemination of knowledge of India were inseparable from political control of the subcontinent. While there is little dispute on the centrality of colonial knowledge as an analytical category for the understanding of the operation of colonial rule in India, a fundamental question that has divided scholarship on the subject is the relative importance of state-sponsored knowledge projects, such as in the fields of linguistics, law, social formations such as caste, religion, history, and archaeology, and indigenous knowledge/information. Thus, the Sanskritist-historian Ronald Inden and historical anthropologists such as Bernard Cohn and Nicholas Dirks have focused on the deployment of knowledge by the colonial state to further imperial power.[13] By contrast, historians such as Christopher Bayly have highlighted the agency of indigenous informants and the role of indigenous information networks in the growth of colonial power in India.[14]

Colonial archaeology developed as a direct result of the colonial state's engagement with two knowledge projects, both of which were designed to provide the East India Company with crucial information for the conquest and rule of India: the first was driven by an interest in India's past, in the history of its religions and social formations, and of its existing legal structures and ancient legal tradition. This led to the interest in Indian languages, in particular languages such as Sanskrit, which were believed to hold the key to knowledge of India's ancient custom and tradition. The result of this was an early preoccupation of the officials of the East India Company with ancient Indian texts in manuscript form and, following the tradition of historical philology, the drive to collect, emend, and interpret these. The pioneer of early colonial linguistic studies was William Jones (1746-1794) who went on to become the driving force behind the foundation of the Asiatic Society of Bengal in 1784. By the early nineteenth century the search for sources of Indian tradition began to move beyond the text to the study of coins and stone relics from the past, and led ultimately to the interest in ancient building structures as sources that could throw light on the mysteries of India's historical past, as it was believed that the old, predominantly religious texts that

---

[13] Ronald Inden, 'Orientalist Constructions of India', *Modern Asian Studies*, 20 (1986), 401-46, and *Imagining India* (Oxford, 1992), Bernard S. Cohn, *An Anthropologist Among the Historians and Other Essays* (Oxford, 1987) and *Colonialism and its Forms of Knowledge* (Princeton, 1996); and Nicholas B. Dirks, *Castes of Mind* (Princeton, 2001).

[14] C. A. Bayly, *Empire and Information. Intelligence Gathering and Social Communication in India, 1780-1870* (Cambridge, 1996).

the Company's scholar-administrators had come upon were inadequate for this purpose.

The means to locate and study these structures and indeed artefacts from the past was provided by a second knowledge project of the East India Company: the survey project. The imperatives of territorial conquest and empire-building right from the early days of Company rule in Bengal led logically to the undertaking of extensive information-gathering and survey projects, especially cartographic projects, of which the largest and most well-known was the cartographic survey of Bengal by James Rennell (1742-1830), who in 1767 was appointed Surveyor-General of the newly conquered territory of Bengal, and who conducted what was the first regional cartographic survey of India from 1765 to 1771.[15] Rennell's mapping project was equalled by the extensive statistical surveys conducted by Colin Mackenzie—with considerable help from native assistants—between 1800 and 1810 in South India.[16] Mackenzie's surveys, along with those of Francis Buchanan in Mysore and Bengal became significant repositories of historical and archaeological knowledge gathered by the East India Company, as they, especially Buchanan, recorded significant historical sites and monuments and recognised the need for detailed plans and measurements of sites and monuments.

In fact, the birth of the foremost institution for the management of India's ancient built heritage, the Archaeological Survey of India, can be traced to a frenetic programme of surveys that was initiated by the colonial state in the course of the nineteenth century. As in the course of the nineteenth century the military domination of the East India Company became paramount, the imperative of government gradually took over from the imperative of conquest. The result was an intensification of surveys which, although often resulting in unexpected consequences, had the main purpose of gathering information on the country and its people in order to facilitate its governance by an alien power. The momentum to these knowledge gathering surveys picked up especially after the revolt of 1857, when the British crown took over from the East

---

[15] On colonial mapping projects see Matthew H. Edney, *Mapping an Empire: The Geographical Construction of British India, 1765-1843* (Chicago and London, 1997) and the much later work by Ian J. Barrow, *Making History, Drawing Territory. British Mapping in India, c.1765-1905* (New Delhi, 2003). Colonial surveys as knowledge have been discussed in Cohn, *Colonialism and its Forms of Knowledge*, 80-8.

[16] See Nicholas B. Dirks, Colonial Historiographies and Native Informants: Biography of an Archive, in Carol A. Breckenridge and Peter van der Veer (eds), *Orientalism and the Postcolonial Predicament* (Philadelphia, 1993), 279-313. Cohn, *Colonialism and its Forms of Knowledge*, Ch. 4; see also Jennifer Howes, *Illustrating India. The Early Colonial Investigations of Colin Mackenzie (1784-1821)* (New Delhi, 2010).

India Company as ruler of India and even more information came to be required to answer questions like why the revolt took place in the first place, and why the Company raj's intelligence network failed to detect its outbreak, as well as to prevent a repeat of the events of 1857. In 1856 the Geological Survey, in existence since the 1840s, was put on an organized footing; the Indian Meteorological Department was established in 1875; by 1876 the basic triangulatory measurements of the Trigonometrical Survey of India, which had started in 1802 and had run into great difficulty, were completed. The Marine Surveys Department began its early surveys between 1875 and 1882, and a systematic recording of tidal observations began in 1877. Most significant for the study of state-sponsored colonial knowledge projects, the first census was undertaken in 1871-2, followed by a more extensive and systematic one in 1881.[17] In 1871, after about a decade of archaeological surveys conducted by the retired military engineer Alexander Cunningham, the Archaeological Survey of India officially came into being as a department of the colonial government.

Monument preservation and custodianship

Except for sporadic efforts, focusing mainly on the Mughal ruins in the Delhi-Agra region, the government of the East India Company took little interest in the preservation of India's architectural heritage.[18] On the contrary, it became common practice to raze ancient structures if they stood in the way of the great road- and railway-building projects of the empire in India or modernize them beyond recognition, so that they could be used as administrative offices of the Company. The reason for this was not merely a general apathy of the Company towards anything other than revenue collection and the maintenance of law and order in order to maximize revenue collection; it was also the result of prevailing opinion among the scholar-administrators of the East India Company that the sources of Indian history and tradition were to be found in ancient Indian texts. Hence, from the beginning of Company rule in Bengal in 1765 to the early years of the nineteenth century, the efforts of the Company officials to recover India's past focused on the recovery of ancient Indian manuscripts, written mostly in Sanskrit. The activities of the only centre of orientalist learning in colonial India in the eighteenth century,

---

[17] Upinder Singh, *The Discovery of Ancient India*, 2-6.

[18] Scholars such as Anne-Julie Etter have explained this as a conscious choice on the part of early colonial administrators, driven by the political imperative to be seen as both the allies as well as the natural successors of the Mughal rulers of India. See Anne-Julie Etter, 'Antiquarian Knowledge and Preservation of Indian Monuments at the Beginning of the Nineteenth Century', in *Knowledge Production, Pedagogy, and Institutions in Colonial India*, ed. Indra Sengupta and Daud Ali (New York, 2011), 123-46.

the Asiatic Society of Bengal, for instance, focused primarily on textual sources of India's history. This preoccupation with literary sources began to change as the survey reports of Colin Mackenzie and James Buchanan, referred to earlier, appeared and documented a vast array of historical sites and monuments, in various states of ruin. Notwithstanding this and despite early regulations on the conservation of historical monuments (in 1810 and 1817 by the Madras and Bengal governments respectively), archaeological activity till the 1870s remained by and large wedded to the principle of the surveys: information gathering, measurement of buildings, location of historical sites, and mapping of historical geography. The preservation of historical monuments was not high on the agenda of either the Company government or the post-1857 colonial state. The work of the Archaeological Survey of India in its early days tended to follow this pattern, with the task of monument preservation being delegated to the seat of colonial technocracy, the Public Works Department, which had been set up in 1855.

Half-hearted measures, consisting of some legislation on monument preservation, and their wholly inadequate implementation characterized the attitude of the ASI and the colonial state to conservation. The frenetic phase of state-driven conservation came with the appointment of George Nathaniel Curzon, Marquess Curzon of Kedleston (1859–1925) to the office of Viceroy of India, which he held from 1899 to 1905. As has been adequately documented, Curzon not only had a deep interest in preserving India's architectural heritage, he saw this as the fundamental, divinely ordained duty of the colonial government and thus outlined a clear line of archaeological policy to be pursued by the state.[19] In addition to using India's pre-colonial, Mughal public buildings to stage elaborate imperial rituals of state power, and vigorously insisting on the employment of the so-called Indo-Saracenic building style in order to create the illusion of British rule in India as a natural and legitimate successor to Mughal rule,[20] he also radically restructured the Department of Archaeology, appointing a Director-General of Archaeology

[19] See, e.g., the many speeches of Curzon on the subject, both in India and in Britain. Probably the most famous, and certainly most often quoted of these is the speech he gave to the Asiatic Society of Bengal in 1900, in which he rather grandly proclaimed that India's architectural heritage was 'a part of the heritage which Providence has committed to the custody of the ruling power'. Lord Curzon, Speech before the Asiatic Society of Bengal, 7 February 1900. In *Lord Curzon in India, being a Selection from his Speeches as Viceroy and Governor-General, 1898-1905*, vol. 1 (London, 1906).

[20] On Curzon's attempts to use India's architectural heritage for staging imperial power see Thomas R. Metcalf, *An Imperial Vision. Indian Architecture and Britain's Raj* (New Delhi, 2002).

who would implement a new policy of centralization.[21] The man chosen for the position was a young scholar of the classics and archaeology, aged 25 and with no previous experience of India. Nevertheless, he was the personal choice of the viceroy, who wished to entrust the task of India's monument management to a classicist and European archaeologist rather than a philologist and Orientalist. That man was John Marshall.[22] Curzon also dramatically increased the government's expenditure on archaeology and succeeded in passing the Ancient Monument Preservation Act in 1904.[23]

The AMPA of 1904 was the most comprehensive piece of legislation on the subject in colonial India. Introduced in a climate of intense debate and criticism of the colonial state's apparent apathy towards India's ancient monuments, the Act was modelled on the Ancient Monument Protection Act of 1882 that was passed for the protection of monuments in Britain and was subsequently adapted in 1892 for Ireland and then amended in Britain in 1900. However, one major point of difference between the Indian and British Acts was that the former was far more sweeping in character and gave the state much more wide-ranging powers to enforce monument preservation. Section 3 of the AMPA, for instance, gave the local government (i.e. the governments of the provinces and presidencies) independent authority to 'declare an ancient monument to be a protected monument within the meaning of this Act'.[24] The government was given the power to acquire the right of purchase or lease or guardianship of a protected monument, albeit in agreement with the owner.[25] Much to the delight of preservationist lobbies in Britain (such as the Society for the Protection of Ancient Buildings and the Royal Institute of British Architects) the colonial state in India was willing to adopt a much more interventionist approach to the preservation of monuments than the national government of Britain.

---

[21] For the restructuring of archaeology by Lord Curzon see Dilip K. Chakrabarti, *A History of Indian Archaeology from the Beginning to 1947* (New Delhi, 2001); Sourindranath Roy, *The Story of Indian Archaeology 1784-1947* (New Delhi, 1996).

[22] On the background to Marshall's appointment see Nayanjot Lahiri, 'John Marshall's Appointment as Director General of the Archaeological Survey of India: A Survey of the Papers Pertaining to his Selection', *South Asian Studies*, 13 (1997), 127-39.

[23] For instance, in 1898-99 the total expenditure of the Government of India and all provincial governments on archaeology was a total of £7,000 a year; by 1904 this had gone up to £37,000. IOL, IOR/L/PJ/6/674 File 803, President of the Council of the Governor General, or Viceroy Curzon, 18 March 1904, Proceedings of the Legislative Council, Ancient Monuments Preservation Act, Act VII, 1904, Judicial and Public Dept.

[24] AMPA 1904, Section 3.

[25] AMPA 1904, Sections 4-10.

This kind of excessive and, seen from a metropolitan British perspective, unusual degree of state involvement in culture-keeping was of course the product of the colonial relationship between India and Britain. More specifically it was an integral part of the self-fashioning of the colonial state in the high noon of the British Raj in the early twentieth century as custodian of India, until its own people acquired the political maturity to be self-reliant. But custodianship meant more than political guardianship. In the realm of culture it meant that the colonial state bestowed upon itself the responsibility of preserving India's culture, history, and heritage. There was no better mouthpiece for what custodianship meant for the preservation of Indian monuments than the Viceroy who had made archaeological activities a keystone of his rule in India. In his fabled address to the Asiatic Society of Bengal in 1900 he spelt out the fundamental principles of colonial custodianship in relation to protecting India's built heritage:

> If there be any one who says to me that there is no duty devolving upon a Christian Government to preserve the monuments of a pagan art, or the sanctuaries of an alien faith, I cannot pause to argue with such a man . . . Indeed, a race like our own, who are themselves foreigners, are in a sense better fitted to guard, with a dispassionate and impartial zeal, the relics of different ages, and of sometimes antagonistic beliefs, than might be the descendants of the warring races or the votaries of the rival creeds. To us the relics of Hindu and Mohammedan, of Buddhist, Brahmin, and the Jain are, from the antiquarian, the historical, and the artistic point of view, equally interesting and equally sacred. . . . Each represents the glories or the faith of a branch of the human family. . . . Each is a part of the heritage which Providence has committed to the custody of the ruling power.[26]

If one looks beyond the elevated rhetoric of imperial ideology it is difficult to ignore the seriousness with which the idea of cultural custodianship of India was taken by high colonial officialdom. In this kind of self-fashioning of the mission of British rule in India Curzon was not alone; it was a belief that was shared by colonial officials in general. In a note to the Secretary of State for

---

[26] Lord Curzon, speech before the Asiatic Society of Bengal, 7 February 1900, in *Lord Curzon in India, being a Selection from his Speeches as Viceroy and Governor-General, 1898-1905* (London, 1906).

India in 1905, John Marshall explained the peculiarity of India's situation that had virtually forced the state into the role of culture-keeper:

> In India the genius of the people has not yet turned in the direction of the scientific archaeology or of veneration for the monuments of the past.[27]

The onus of discharging the mission of the colonial state and ensuring proper implementation of the Ancient Monument Preservation Act of 1904 to save India's historical monuments from decay and ruin fell chiefly on the ASI. However this was no easy task. The logic of colonial government meant that the execution of centrally drawn policy was left to a bureaucratic mire at the local level, with a complex bureaucratic machinery, including the officials of the ASI, the PWD, and the local government, getting involved in the execution of the newly enacted monument preservation policy. Curzon himself referred to this complexity of administrative procedure and its damaging effects for archaeology and the preservation of monuments in general. Before he took over as Viceroy, there was no system in place for monument preservation, with matters being left to the local or provincial government and as such, standards varied sharply across the country. 'There was neither co-ordination, nor system, nor control.'[28]

Custodianship in practice: the bureaucracy of conservation

In order to sort out the chaos in the preservation of historical buildings that the colonial state under Curzon was confronted with, and to put into practice the ideology of cultural custodianship, colonial archaeology, like other colonial knowledge projects, was dependant on a group of scholar-administrators nestled in the various government departments that were concerned with monument preservation. Essentially, the Archaeological Survey of India was a department of government and, like all government departments, it was run by a bureaucracy that was to act as culture-keeper and custodian of India's monumental heritage. Like the archetypal government official in colonial India since the days of the Company, the bureaucrats of the ASI were scholar-administrators or gentlemanly civil servants.[29] Usually possessing

---

[27] John Marshall to the Secretary of State for India, Simla, 26 May 1905. WBSA, *Proceedings of the Honourable Lieutenant-Governor of Bengal during June 1905, Genl. Dept. (Mis.).*

[28] Lord Curzon to the Legislative Council at Calcutta, March 18, 1904. In *Lord Curzon in India, being a Selection from his Speeches as Viceroy and Governor-General, 1898-1905*, London, 1906.

[29] P. J. Marshall, 'British-Indian Connections *c.*1780 to *c.*1830: The Empire of the Officials', in Michael J. Franklin (ed.), *Romantic Representations of British India* (London, 2006), 45-60.

no specific expertise on India upon arrival, but equipped with some training in Indian languages, the colonial official in India usually immersed himself in colonial knowledge projects (such as surveys, measurement, and statistics) so that in course of time he became an expert on a particular field of knowledge on India. The reports of colonial officials form the bulk of state-sponsored information-gathering projects of the colonial state. Their association with the state provided them with the resources, connections, and legitimacy to conduct in-depth research on historical monuments and sites. As newly-appointed Director General of Archaeology, John Marshall set out to frame an elaborate set of rules and regulations that were designed to manage the chaotic business that monument preservation had become by the end of the nineteenth century and bring it under the direct control of the state. These rules and regulations were enshrined in the *Conservation Manual* (1923) that Marshall spent almost two decades compiling. Marshall's vision of heritage-management in India expressed itself in the form of the centrally dictated, detailed rule-book and the code of practice, which in many ways summed up the way in which the colonial bureaucracy in India functioned. In theory at least, the management of culture, just as the management of the empire in a vast and diverse country like India, had to be conducted with strict discipline aimed at uniformity of practice and maintenance of order by the colonial state.[30] As I have discussed elsewhere the *Conservation Manual* became the single authoritative handbook in colonial India that sought to foresee and provide for every possible exigency in the conservation of ancient struc-tures.[31] It was the self-conscious assertion of the highly centralized nature of policy that the colonial state had adopted in the late nineteenth and early twentieth centuries. The final point of reference for all preservation work was the Director General of Archaeology himself, and all except routine conser-vation work had to be cleared by the Director General before it could be implemented.

On the face of it, the manual reads like a handbook for conservation pro-fessionals laden with detailed technical instructions regarding historical building preservation. It is committed to the principles of conservation of historical buildings so as to retain their historical character, containing clear rules and regulations pertaining to the technicalities of this task, laying down aesthetic principles (for instance the beautification of monuments by

---

[30] For an early and seminal analysis of the need of the colonial state for order and its employment of cultural tools for this purpose, see Bernard S. Cohn, *Colonialism and its Forms of Knowledge* (Princeton, 1996).

[31] Indra Sengupta, 'A Conservation Code for the Colony'.

surrounding them with gardens), and ensuring that their character as monuments was preserved (for example, by erecting fences and setting up notice-boards to keep the visiting public at a distance).

It is equally clear, however, that the intended user was an official of the government: bureaucratic procedure—a rather complex one at that—occupies a major part of the first section of the manual, and this is what singles out Marshall's manual from other, similar manuals that were in circulation in contemporary Britain and Europe. The precise role and duties of the officers of the Archaeological department, the Public Works Department and the Government, at the central and local/provincial levels respectively are specified. Thus, the officers of the Archaeological Department were responsible for drawing up conservation plans and the supervision of the work to be done, which along with the task of making regular and systematic inspections, was the responsibility of the officials of the PWD. However, as mentioned above, all preservation proposals had to be approved the Director General's office, which essentially meant the Director General himself. In fact, the central importance of the Director General's office was highlighted by the addition of injunctions such as that proposals for conservation initiated by Archaeological Officers in the Provinces were not to be treated as ordinary correspondence, but had to be 'printed and submitted in proof in the first instance to the Director General',[32] upon whose approval the notes would be returned to the Provincial Officers, who only then could submit these to the local (provincial) government. The keeping of detailed conservation notes which would then be passed on either to the provincial or central government was stressed.

This emphasis on a clear and stringently applied set of rules and regulations as well as the particular importance of state intervention in defining and preserving monuments was peculiar to the colonial state and its self-fashioning as custodian of India's built heritage. At the heart of the notion of custodianship in the colonial context was the assumption that Indians were not yet ready: the state that the historian Dipesh Chakrabarty has famously described as being confined to an 'imaginary waiting room of history'.[33] While this lack of readiness, rooted in a historicist notion of progress, in the first instance related to the ability of Indians to rule themselves, it could be stretched to include a perceived inability to appreciate their ancient history and heritage. In 1905 John Marshall explained India's special

---

[32] John Marshall, *Conservation Manual* (New Delhi, 1990; (first published 1923)), 5.

[33] Dipesh Chakrabarty, *Provincializing Europe. Postcolonial Thought and Historical Difference* (Princeton, 2000), 8.

needs, as opposed to the situation in Europe, to the Secretary of State for India thus:

> ... there (*in Italy and Greece*) the regulations in force are the outcome of long experience; here it will take many years for them to be developed and reduced into a systematic form, and whereas in those countries expert advice is ready at every turn, if the Government requires it, in India there is no agency through which it can be obtained, except the Archaeological Department.[34]

Ahistorical and childlike, unlike Europe, and waiting to be trained in self-rule and historical consciousness, Indians had a future that was held in trusteeship by the colonial state in India. This, as Curzon had emphasized in his speech of 1900, was the essence of Britain's custodianship of India.

Marshall's approach is thus indicative of two common features of high bureaucratic practice in colonial India: first, the colonial ideological compulsion to see British rule in India as something akin to a divinely ordained civilizing mission with a clear pedagogical goal; and second, the framing of an elaborate and complex set of rules to realize this goal.

But the management of culture by a bureaucracy in the vast and complex culture that India in the heyday of the Raj had become meant that the process was slow and complex. Hamstrung by the rigidity of its rules and regulations and by the complexity of its own bureaucratic structure, and often alienated from the population at large by assumptions of cultural superiority, grand schemes of monument conservation could often have limited effect. In the following section I shall, with the help of a case-study on the preservation of temples in the eastern Indian state of Orissa, show how the practice of custodianship by the colonial bureaucracy was fraught with tensions and how, despite the force of rhetoric at the level of centralized policy-making, monument preservation on the ground, in the provinces and localities of colonial India often did not conform to the uniform policy that the Archaeological Survey was keen to implement.

Control and its limits in the temples of Orissa

One of the fundamental principles of the conservation of historical monuments in Europe that was uncritically accepted by colonial administrators in India was the clear and physical demarcation of space for monuments. According to the principles of monument conservation that were laid

---

[34] John Marshall to the Secretary of State for India, Simla, 26 May 1905. WBSA, *Proceedings of the Honourable Lieutenant-Governor of Bengal during June 1905*, Genl. Dept. (Misc.).

down in the wake of the AMPA 1904, the need to define clearly the space of the monument was central to the creation of a monument. This could be done by means of acquiring the land around it, its beautification, its protection from possible damage by means of fencing, and defining its territory by means of notice-boards. In his *Conservation Manual* John Marshall set down specific instructions for setting a clear distance between monuments and their potential visitors, which included 'delimitation, clearance, drainage, fencing and lay-out of the site' as well as 'erection of notices warning the public against damaging a monument'.[35]

In a colonial context and, especially in the context of India, where religion occupied a more ubiquitous place in society than in contemporary Europe, demarcating the space of monuments could pose complex problems. It was difficult enough to put into practice in the case of non-religious buildings. The application of such ideas to religious structures was an even more complicated affair, as the case of a pillar at the Jagannath Temple at Puri (Orissa) would show. The seaside town of Puri together with the shrine of the Hindu god Jagannatha forms one of the most sacred sites for Hindus from all over India.[36] At the same time, the cult of Jagannatha has historically formed an essential component of the regional identity of the Oriya-speaking Hindus of Orissa and the local kings of Puri/Khurda were traditionally regarded as the representatives of Jagannatha on earth. The sanctity of Jagannatha and his abode in the Puri Temple as well as the administrative authority of the king of Puri as the autonomous head of the Temple were accepted by the East India Company at the time of Orissa's annexation to Company territories in India in 1803. Nevertheless, in the course of the growth of the British Empire in India throughout the nineteenth century, the political dimension of the administration of the Jagannatha Temple became an increasing irritant to British rule and several attempts (including the abortive Puri Temple Act of 1880) were made by the colonial government of the Bengal Presidency to

---

[35] John Marshall, *Conservation Manual*, 7-8.

[36] The sacredness of the Jagannatha cult has been the subject of many popular historical tracts. Two kinds of such writing stand out: first, the writings of Christian missionaries for whom the cult represented a trope of degenerate Hinduism, and second, the writings of Oriya-speaking public intellectuals and political activists in the nineteenth century, who used such writings to argue for the creation of a political entity (a separate province) with its own distinctive culture centred on the cult of Jagannatha. For the first category of literature, see e.g., William F. B. Laurie, *Orissa. The Garden of Superstition and Idolatry* (London, 1850). Of the latter category, see e.g., Bulloram Mullick, *Lord Jagannatha in Indian Relgiious Life* (Calcutta, 1892; repr. 1985).

interfere in matters related to the administration of the Temple.[37] The perception of a colonial government that seemed determined to interfere in Orissa's ancient traditions remained strong among the Oriya-speaking Hindu community and relations between them and the colonial government remained uneasy even before colonial preservation practices became a contentious issue. But the fact that the Jagannatha Temple dated back to the eleventh and twelfth centuries and was, along with other Orissan temples, regarded by the most famous architectural historian of colonial India, James Ferguson, as the purest example of the 'Indo-Aryan' temple style,[38] made it an object of interest for preservation as a historical monument in the run-up to the passing of the AMPA of 1904 as well as its aftermath.

For a period of some three years between 1905 and 1908, the Aruna Pillar of the Jagannatha Temple became the focus of a controversy that brought the issues of historical monument conservation, religious belief, and community rights into direct conflict with each other. The pillar originally belonged to the Sun Temple of Konark, not far from Puri, but was uprooted from there and placed in front of the Lion's Gate of the Jagannatha Temple at Puri by the Marathas in the late eighteenth century. In terms of sacral tradition, therefore, the Aruna Pillar was not part of the shrine of Jagannatha. Nevertheless, in course of time, the pillar, by virtue of its location, came to acquire an extended sacral meaning and the undefined, open area surrounding it came to be considered sacred by the local community. As a result, in keeping with Hindu tradition, stepping on this space with shoes on was regarded as a violation of the religious sanctity of sacred sites.

Nevertheless, when the bureaucrats of the Department of Archaeology arrived in Puri to survey the Temple and its precincts, there was no physical, visible evidence of sacrality: the pillar was neither enclosed nor fenced. This absence of a clear boundary demarcating the area that was regarded as sacred became the cause of much annoyance to the officers of archaeology, as they repeatedly found themselves stepping on to this space and consequently being subjected to the ire of the locals. The accounts of colonial officials visiting the site are replete with such experiences. John Marshall, for example, who visited the Jagannath Temple in Puri in the course of his inspection

---

[37] Nivedita Mohanty, *Oriya Nationalism. Quest for a United Orissa 1866-1956* (Jagatsinghpur, 2005); see also Yaaminey Mubayi, *Altar of Power. The Temple and the State in the Land of Jagannatha* (New Delhi, 2005).

[38] James Fergusson, *History of Indian and Eastern Architecture*, vol. II (New Delhi, repr. 1998; (first published 1876)), 92.

tour of Orissa in 1904, made a note of consequences of his crossing that invisible boundary:

> In front of the east gate of the Jagannath Temple, and standing in the middle of the high road, is a well-known pillar from the Black Pagoda at Konark. Around it is a small pavement of rough stones, across which one naturally steps when wishing to look at the carving on the pillar. I myself did so without a suspicion that I could be giving any offence, and was at once subjected to a great deal of abuse and threats from a gang of pestilential natives, who had been lying about, backed afterwards by the Temple police. There was no notice or indication of any kind to show that the pavement was sacred ground, and I saw no reason, therefore, for paying regard to their threats. Indeed, I think it was only by being firm with them that we avoided personal violence. . . . If the Government decide that the pavement is sacred and belongs indisputably to the temple, then it should be fenced and a notice warning people not to step on it should be posted up. But if, on the other hand, there is no real sanctity attached to the pavement, and if it is mere perversity and ill-nature on the part of the Hindus that induces them to obstruct Europeans in this way, . . . then the rights of Europeans should be insisted on. Surely it is enough that the Hindus close the compound of their temple to Europeans? Or must they go further and usurp the high road too?[39]

This, and similar assertions made by officials of the Archaeological Department are indicative of the general sense of annoyance and frustration that colonial officials felt when confronted with the difficulty of policy-implementation on the ground. Marshall's annoyance and frustration at having to kowtow to the demands of sacrality in an area he believed was not marked out as sacred is evident. Equally apparent is the irritation at the absence of any visible sign of sacrality, in the form of 'notice or indication of any kind to show that the pavement was sacred ground'. Marshall was not alone in his view. His opinion seems to have been shared across the board by the officers of the regional Archaeological Department. In 1906-07, Theodor

[39] Note by Director-General of Archaeology on archaeological remains in Bengal. J. H. Marshall, Simla, 28 February 1905. Proceedings of the Hon. Lieutenant-Governor of Bengal, March 1906, File 9A-13, pp.41-56, West Bengal State Archives (henceforth WBSA). Also DGA Files, Archaeological Survey of India Calcutta Circle (henceforth ASICC), Serial No. 109, Lot 31, 1905, National Archives of India, Eastern Regional Centre, Bhubaneswar (henceforth NAIERC).

Bloch, Superintendent of the Eastern Circle of the Archaeological Survey of India, reported on the pillar and its users:

> . . . the beautiful green chlorite column standing unprotected in the middle of the high road immediately in front of the eastern entrance to the Temple enclosure should be repaired, and the few square feet of sacred ground surrounding its base should be railed in, both as a protection to the column and in order that visitors may know how far they are allowed to approach the monument without being subject to the annoyance and insults of excited and infuriated Hindus, who are generally to be found sitting and loafing about the base of the column on the so-called sacred ground.[40]

A. H. Longhurst, Officiating Superintendent of the Eastern Circle, went a step further. In 1907 he wrote to the Secretary of the Government of Bengal, expressing his displeasure:

> Although the pillar stands on the high road and some yards from the temple gateway, the priests claim the few feet of paved ground on the four sides of the base of the column as their own sacred property. If they have any legal right to the ground, a railing should be erected, enclosing it, and thus save visitors, who do not know, and who do not expect to find, sacred spots unenclosed on the high road, from the insults and annoyance of infuriated Hindus.[41]

The similarity of sentiment and language in the three extracts cited above is strongly indicative of a common discourse on indigenous culture and the colonized subject that seems to have been shared by colonial archaeologists in India. The language and the description of the Hindus correspond very closely to the othering of India that formed the core of British colonialism's civilizing mission in India. The 'natives' in these descriptions are always superfluous to the enterprise of archaeological conservation in India (Marshall thus calls them 'pestilential'): they are indolent and perverse and by definition, have little regard for the order that was essential to the enterprise of creating a space of beauty and historicity that a historical monument stood for. Not only are they unfit to determine for themselves what is sacred ground

---

⁴⁰ T. Bloch, Notes on Places visited in 1906-07, Annual Report of the Archaeological Survey Eastern Circle for 1906-07.

⁴¹ A. H. Longhurst, Officiating Superintendent of Archaeological Survey, Eastern Circle, to Secretary to Govt. of Bengal, General Department, Calcutta, 4 May 1907. General (Misc.) Proceedings of the Hon. Lieutenant-Governor of Bengal, File 9A-5, No. 50-51, March 1907, WBSA.

and what is not, but they are also capable of conjuring up a questionable sacrality to obstruct the efforts of a government that were directed at preserving the past of a people who were incapable of doing so themselves.

But perhaps the most significant part of these statements is the shared view of the questionable legitimacy of community action in denoting sacred space which seems to have united the senior officials of the Archaeological Department. The statements of Marshall and Longhurst, in particular, indicate that the matter of legal rights, established through government action and the courts, needed to be settled first, and that this was the business of the government, in which the community was to play a role decided upon by the government. The above accounts all convey the impression that the 'Hindus' had in some way simply taken over the pavement around the pillar and signified it ipso facto as sacred space. Marshall makes his view on this very clear: the action of the local community was clearly tantamount to usurpation of rights that belonged to the state. It was the state that, in Marshall's view, had the sole authority to determine whether the pavement was sacred or not and whether it was a part of the Temple itself. And, having established sacrality, it was the government's job to legislate on this and erect fences, put out notice-boards and take all measures necessary to make the distinction between sacred and secular space visible and public. The role to be played by the Archaeological Department to establish the authority of the state by determining the status of historical monuments and spaces deemed sacred by the community was clear. All this was part of the custodial duty of the colonial state, not merely to ensure that sacred space was clearly marked out, but also that the state itself drew the boundaries.

State control over religious spaces was part of a long history of fear of losing control over India that had haunted the colonial state for at least half of the nineteenth century. As shown above, official reports tended to view the Hindus not only as lazy and chaotic, but also volatile and potentially violent. It is hardly difficult to see that this was a reflection of the topos of the violent native that had dominated colonial discourses at least since the revolt of 1857. The impression of colonial officials actually being threatened with bodily harm by local Hindus runs through these accounts. In all of them, the Hindu's religious zeal was not something that the colonial state could afford to ignore as in its alleged aggressiveness it manifested a direct threat to the authority of the state itself. Marshall wrote: 'Indeed, I think it was only by being firm with them that we avoided personal violence'.[42] Much of these accounts can be understood in terms of control and subjugation, in order to maintain colonial power relations in India. In the particular case of the temple

---

[42] Ibid.

in Orissa, the restrictive rights of entry for non-Hindus meant that European, colonial officials were not allowed to enter the temple precincts. The inability of the colonial government to control the activities of the Jagannatha Temple in Puri had, as I have discussed above, a long history. In the high-noon of monument preservation in the early years of the twentieth century such apparently extensive rights for the community meant that European officials of the Department of Archaeology, but also the Viceroy Lord Curzon himself, did not have the authority to access these temples nor to see for themselves what kind of preservation work was necessary to keep these ancient temples from ruin, even when the government itself had provided some funds for the purpose.[43] More importantly, it meant that sacred sites were beyond the pale for the colonial state and the limits of colonial control ended at the boundary of places deemed sacred by indigenous communities. The insistence on fencing or railing the pillar at Puri was an attempt to assert control over a situation that, in the absence of clear boundaries, had the potential to get out of hand and could challenge the authority of the colonial state.

The incident of the Jagannatha pillar, as it was called, is significant as an example of the limits of colonial power on the ground. Despite the rhetoric of control that emanated from the seat of power in central government, the colonial state, when confronted with a situation concerning religious sentiment and posing a potential threat to order, found itself in a frustratingly helpless situation. Between 1905 and 1908 the officials of the Archaeological Department made several attempts to put a fence around the Jagannatha pillar, failing each time due to the unhelpful, even hostile attitude of the local community and the management committee of the temple at which the pillar stood. Finally, in 1908 the Government of India gave in to the pressure of strong local feeling in Puri against fencing the Aruna Pillar and decided to abandon the project.[44]

It is easy to treat this incident as a narrative of colonial state power being thwarted by indigenous resistance. There is no doubt that this is the main story. Nevertheless, there is a corollary to this story: an immediate objection to the tone and content of John Marshall's report on the Jagannatha pillar was

---

[43] I have discussed the question of temple entry and its relationship to the preservation of religious monuments elsewhere. See Indra Sengupta, 'Sacred Space and the Making of Monuments in Colonial Orissa', in H. R. Ray (ed.) *Archaeology and Text: The Temple in South Asia*, (New Delhi, 2009), esp. 178-81.

[44] Extract from the Progs. of the Govt. of Bengal in the PWD for August 1908. Home Dept., Branch Archaeology and Epigraphy, Part B, Proceedings May 1909, Nos. 7-10, NAI.

voiced not by the Temple authorities or the local elite. It came from J. R. Blackwood, the Collector of the district of Puri and went thus:

> . . . I would point out that the Director-General of Archaeology appears to have absolutely no sympathy for native feeling and appears to consider that the interests of his own Department should take precedence of every other consideration. This attitude is in conflict with the declared policy of Government and is in my opinion to be very much deprecated. Archaeology may be a very interesting and important subject, but there are other things in the world of still greater importance. I would respectfully submit that sympathy with the feelings of the people among whom our lot is cast should take precedence of every other consideration and should govern our policy generally. I protest against the expression 'pestilential natives'. As far as they are known to me they are not 'pestilential'. Such expressions are unnecessary and give avoidable offence.[45]

Thus, the case of the Jagannatha or Aruna pillar also helps to throw light on the nature of the colonial state and its operative power in India. The colonial project of monument-making in the early twentieth century was repeatedly faced with the complicated question of sacrality and sacred space in the conservation of India's pre-colonial architectural heritage. However, this was not a problem of heritage-management or monument-making alone, but a problem that had haunted colonial policy-making and bureaucratic control of India since the early days of Company rule in the late eighteenth century. Caught between the reluctance to intervene in the practice of culture and the need to exercise bureaucratic and revenue control over wealthy organizations—such as temples—in the style of the European nation-state, the colonial bureaucracy in India until the middle of the nineteenth century was compelled to draw the distinction between the sacred (cultural) sphere and the secular (revenue and administrative) spheres in the management of Hindu temples. The problem was that, in trying to determine the sacred, the Company officials relied almost exclusively upon ancient Indian textual tradition, rather than the more fluid practices that prevailed on the ground, which rendered the sacred rather more difficult to pinpoint. From the outset, the officials of the East India Company looked for the sources of Indian tradition in scriptural texts and set out policy and laws on the assumption that these formed the basis of the practice of law, government, and religion in contemporary India. As a result, until the second half of the nineteenth century and,

---

[45] JR Blackwood, Collector, Puri, Memo no. 1593, Puri 25 July 1905. WBSA General (Misc.) Proceedings of the Hon. Lieutenant-Governor of Bengal, Oct 1908, File 9A-5, No. 62-67.

to a lesser extent, even later, the colonial state found itself locked in an endless series of conflicts with temple trusts over their management and drawn willy-nilly into disputes involving religious ritual practice.[46]

The architectural preservation of religious structures was not left untouched by such contradictions and conflicts, as any attempt to protect or preserve ancient buildings meant the invasion of cultural practice. The passing of the Religious Endowments Act in 1863 in the aftermath of the revolt of 1857 was an attempt to appease religious sentiment, which was believed to be a cause of popular dissatisfaction with the rule of the East India Company. By means of the Act of 1863 government—in an attempt to enforce its goal of religious neutrality—handed over its previous, often highly controversial practice of managing religious endowments to local area committees that it set up for the purpose. Nevertheless, by continuing to reserve for itself the right to intervene in the case of ancient religious structures that in the considered opinion of the colonial bureaucracy required government aid and by enshrining this right in the AMPA of 1904, the colonial state found itself in the unhappy position of constantly trying to negotiate the tricky path between what it saw as sacred space, the realm of culture, best left to indigenous communities, and the realm of centralized bureaucratic control.[47] Taken together, the AMPA of 1904 and the framing of strict rules of conservation and monument-making, which tried to demarcate clearly the rights of government (state-sponsored archaeology) and those of religious communities, succeeded no more in keeping the boundaries between the sacred and the secular separate than their antecedents in other areas of law-making with regard to temples had done. In practice, as the conflict over the Jagannatha pillar indicates, it was not always possible to maintain religious neutrality. In fact, the story of the Jagannatha pillar indicates that sacred space, which the colonial officials were so keen to demarcate and treat as a distinct sphere that the state consciously left to the community, was itself being constantly redefined and thus co-constituted, by indigenous communities, who often challenged the colonial bureaucratic definition of sacred space and drew colonial monument-makers, against their will, into engaging with religious practice.

Nayanjot Lahiri has addressed the fear of invasion of the religious sphere that was generated by the archaeological enterprise of conservation, which

---

[46] A number of studies on the bureaucratization of temple control under colonial rule dwell on this point. See, in particular, Arjun Appadurai, *Worship and Conflict under Colonial Rule. A South Indian Case* (Cambridge, 1981) and Yamini Mubayi, *Altar of Power. The Temple and the State in the Land of Jagannatha* (New Delhi, 2005).

[47] For a detailed argument about the problem of sacred space in managing monuments after 1904, see Sengupta, 'Monument Preservation', 171-85.

often entailed highly intrusive practices such as surveying, measuring, and documentation of structures (Lahiri 2000: 691). The temples of Orissa were a test-case for the conflict and negotiation of secular and sacred space, of the rights of a state that sought to place itself in India's history as its civilizer and the rights of traditional communities to their tradition. In the case of the Orissa temples, the fear of invasion of the religious sphere was often outweighed by considerable ability to negotiate the religious rights of the community from possible interventions by colonial archaeology. As the case of the Jagannatha pillar has shown, it was the state that ultimately gave in. Thus despite the mechanisms of control that were set in motion as a result of the AMPA 1904 and the new rigidly controlled rules of monument-preservation, the actual exercise of control on the ground was often considerably circumscribed and much more agency accrued to the 'colonised' than the rhetoric of colonial archaeology suggests.

However, it was not just the resistance of the local population that circumscribed the will of the state officials. The nature of the colonial state in the early twentieth century, with its complex bureaucratic structure and elaborate culture of rules and procedure, often turned out to be a source of weakness in implementing policy decisions. The historiography of the colonial bureaucracy has tended to see it as a homogenous body, driven by the impulse of empire building. In the context of early twentieth-century India the size and complexity of administrative procedure and bureaucratic machinery rendered such harmony of opinion difficult. As the case of the Jagannatha pillar has shown, officials of the Archaeology Department often found themselves locking horns with functionaries of the local government, who were motivated by imperatives that were rather different from those of the Archaeological Department. Within the system of procedure for the conservation of monuments that John Marshall created, archaeological officials were nevertheless compelled to work with local and provincial administrators.

Conclusion

This story of what may be described as the failure of the colonial state in the face of indigenous resistance on the ground and the inconsistencies of its own bureaucratic apparatus sits somewhat uneasily with the praise that preservationist lobbies in Britain heaped on the colonial state in India for being interventionist in enforcing monument conservation. There can be no doubt about the ability of the colonial state to push through radical legal measures for the conservation of historical monuments without being unduly restricted by the rights of private landowners. With the exception of religious monuments, the Ancient Monuments Preservation Act of 1904 gave the state the legal instrument to compulsorily acquire privately-owned historical structures, should the owners be reluctant to undertake preservation measures; in the case of endowments, the Act gave the state the right to move the courts to enforce implementation of the Act. The codification of the rules of conservation in the form of a manual of government procedure armed the officials of state archaeology with a detailed code of practice that was expected to rule out room for uncertainty. Such measures, adopted unquestioningly in the colonial state, could only be of limited use in a nation-state, which was obviously more closely bound to the interests of the propertied classes. Realities on the ground, as we have seen, were rather different, and state-driven archaeology often had to make compromises on its programmes of monument conservation, as it came up against opposition from both within its own ranks and the local community. Does this however suggest weakness, or indeed failure on the part of the colonial state? Judging by the flurry of applications for grants for the preservation of historical structures and the scramble to get into the government's list of protected monuments in the immediate aftermath of the enforcement of the AMPA in 1904, clearly conservation measures were not per se regarded as an act of epistemic violence on the part of the colonial state, especially since they were accompanied by substantial grants for the maintenance of monuments. In fact, so successful was the perception of Curzon's preservation measures that preservationist lobbies in England used the case of India as an example of the beneficial effects of state intervention in the preservation of ancient monuments in the metropole. Asked to report on the Indian Act in the parliamentary debates on extending a monument protection act for England in 1912, Curzon himself stated that the operation of the Act had given rise to not 'one murmur of opposition, no case of injustice, nothing but satisfaction at the operation of the Act' even in a country known for its extreme sensitivities regarding religious buildings.[48] Obviously this was not entirely true, as we have seen, and cases of friction between the officials of archaeology and local communities abound in the files of the ASI. However, even allowing for some exaggeration, it is clear that the measures proposed by the Act and the mode of their enforcement had by and large been successful.

What explains this peculiar combination of the general success of preservation measures enforced by the state and the numerous instances of the state stepping back from measures in the face of persistent opposition? How can the general satisfaction with the Act and its enforcement be reconciled with the many instances of suspicion, hostility, and conflict that preservation measures on the ground often led to? What analytical tools can help to explain

---

[48] Curzon, Parliamentary Debates, House of Lords, Tuesday 30 April 1912, vol. II, no. 24, Official Report Col. 883.

the near-coterminous operation of the power of colonial, state-sponsored knowledge projects and the agency of indigenous groups to resist, negotiate, and determine the suitability as well as the limits of operation of such projects?

In his work on governmentality and aesthetics, *The Bureaucracy of Beauty*, Arindam Dutta provides an analysis of British (metropolitan and colonial) administrative practice in relation to education in the arts and crafts in the nineteenth century, which is useful for understanding how the cultural custodianship of the colonial state in India operated. The absence of direct political representation in the colony meant that the colonial state was essentially engaged in the day-to-day task of administration. It was thus 'sheer bureaucracy', saddled with 'the task of negotiating the gap between constitutional minimalism and the heterogeneous demands of custom, that is, culture'.[49] But it was also 'thin' bureaucracy: its driving force was no grand ideology, but a general tendency to 'muddle along' with an extra sensitivity to 'situational circumstance'.[50] In this fundamentally open-ended approach to administration, failure in the face of crisis on its part did not so much mark an undoing of its power as an opportunity to change and evolve, and thus ensure its continued survival, even strength. The failure of the officials of the Department of Archaeology to push through their proposals to demarcate the sacred ground belonging to the Aruna Pillar of the Jagannatha temple was, in the bigger scheme of the enforcement of modern practices of heritage-management in colonial India, a small step back for the colonial state. It was a concession that was essential to contain the kind of antagonism of indigenous groups that a fundamentally bureaucratic state could ill-afford to confront for a sustained period. Such steps ensured that the management of India's cultural heritage by the colonial state did not lead to a perception of colonial policy as a purely invasive set of practices, but in fact it also provided the tools of stabilization and control of disorder, which in the long run ensured the success of the colonial management of religious monuments in India.

Seen in this analytical framework colonial practices of preservation appear to have gained acceptance, not because they gave force to the ideology of rule that permeated the rhetoric of custodianship of the men of empire such as Curzon, nor because they reflected the cultural arrogance evident in the many reports and letters of John Marshall, but because they had the ability to adapt to local circumstances.

[49] Arindam Dutta, *The Bureaucracy of Beauty. Design in the Age of its Global Reducibility* (New York, 2007), 68.

[50] Dutta, *Bureaucracy*, 11-12.

Contentious Heritage: The Preservation of Churches and Temples in Communist and Post-Communist Russia and China[1]

S. A. Smith

Writing of Chinese temples in 2000, Vincent Goossaert commented: 'From 1898 until today there has unfolded a century of continuous destruction, destruction by every means, which will remain as one of the greatest annihilations of a patrimony in human history'.[2] It is true that there were few more alarming instances in the twentieth century of governments waging war on their built heritage than the destruction of temples and other ancient monuments that took place in the People's Republic of China (PRC), particularly during the Great Leap Forward of 1958-60 and, above all, during the Cultural Revolution of 1966-76. Yet a grim precedent for this had already been set in the Soviet Union, when in 1928-32, and again in1959-1964, a government campaign of closure and demolition of churches took place. This essay compares the policy of the two Communist states towards the maintenance of religious sites; it argues that notwithstanding bouts of annihilation, the policy of both the Soviet Union and the PRC towards these sites was rather more complex, indeed less consistently negative, than Goossaert's comment suggests. In principle, both regimes were committed to the preservation of cultural heritage—if not steadfastly—and both recognized that religious buildings were a major element in that heritage. At the same time, the preservation of places of worship posed a particular challenge to these regimes, since it was precisely in this area that the commitment to maintain the national patrimony collided with the invariably stronger desire to build an industrial, urban, and socialist society freed from all religious belief. The first half of the essay compares the shifting policies of the Soviet Union and the PRC towards the preservation of religious buildings; the second half examines the extraordinary revival of churches and temples—as religious sites and as national monuments—that has taken place in the former Soviet Union since 1991 and in China in the so-called 'reform era' since

---

[1] My thanks to Catriona Kelly, Emanuela Grama-Neamtu, Aurélie Gfeller, and Geoffrey Hosking.

[2] Vincent Goossaert, *Dans les temples de la Chine* (Paris, 2000), 101.

　　　　　　　　　　© The Past and Present Society

the 1980s. The paper thus turns on a double comparison: a comparison between the respective policies of the Soviet and Chinese Communist governments towards the preservation and destruction of churches and temples; and a comparison between the policies of the Communist era and those that have typified post-Communist times. It focuses solely on religious sites of ethnic Russians and Han Chinese.

In a seminal essay published in 1985, Maurice Meisner argued that 'perhaps the most radical difference' between Lenin and Mao Zedong concerned 'the relationship of the new society to the cultural legacy of the past'.[3] Repeating Richard Stites's claim that Lenin believed it 'essential to grasp all the culture that capitalism had left and build socialism from it', Meisner contrasted this approach to that of Mao who, he averred, rejected traditional Chinese culture *tout court*, condemning it as a product of the literati that had nothing to contribute to the building of a socialist society.[4] This counterposition captures something of the difference in attitudes between the two leaders, but it is too absolute a distinction. Mao, for example, loved traditional opera and vernacular novels and had real talent as a calligrapher and as a poet. Conversely, Lenin was unmoved by the religious elements in Russian art, music, and literature. More pertinently, one cannot read off policy towards cultural heritage in the two regimes from the statements of their founding fathers, however influential these may have been. In practice, the policy of both regimes towards the cultural legacy of the past was more divided and contested than Meisner's account suggests.

Within both the All-Union Communist Party (as the Bolshevik party became known from 1925) and the Chinese Communist Party (CCP) there was from the first a tension between those who appreciated the intrinsic value of the national heritage, regardless of its class origins, and who sought to place it at the disposal of workers and peasants, and those who took a more negative view of that heritage, at best favouring its selective, class-based appropriation, at worst inclined to welcome its destruction. Within Bolshevik ranks, Proletkult—the movement to develop a 'proletarian culture', to which Lenin and Trotsky both gave short shrift—was inclined to the iconoclastic pole, although even in this movement a selective appropriation of past culture was more typical.[5] Representative of the iconoclastic position was the

---

[3] Maurice Meisner, 'Iconoclasm and Cultural Revolution in China and Russia' in Abbot Gleason et al. *Bolshevik Culture: Experiment and Order in the Russian Revolution* (Bloomington, 1989), 289.

[4] Meisner, 'Iconoclasm', 290.

[5] Lynn Mally, *Culture of the Future: the Proletkult Movement in Revolutionary Russia* (Berkeley, 2000).

proletarian poet, V. T. Kirillov, who vowed, in a typically loud, Futurist gesture, to 'burn Raphael, tear down the museums and trample on the flowers of art'. By contrast, Lenin hoped that every Soviet citizen would come to appreciate Tolstoy yet was not convinced that they needed to appreciate the finer points of icon painting. In the CCP, attitudes towards China's cultural heritage were similarly mixed. Whereas Mao was hostile to Confucius, Guo Moruo, the poet, historian, and archaeologist who went on to become the first president of the Chinese Academy of Sciences, wrote an essay in 1925 entitled 'Marx Enters the Confucius Temple' in which he argued that Marx's 'thorough affirmation of life in this world' was 'completely identical' to that of Confucius.[6] Major leaders of the CCP, such as Liu Shaoqi and Chen Boda, a key architect of Mao Zedong Thought, were inclined to agree with him. In China, too, Communist policy depended on the particular strand in the cultural heritage that was at stake: the CCP was unremittingly hostile to popular religion, for example, while broadly positive towards traditional practices such as landscape painting or calligraphy.

In both regimes, although to different degrees and in differing combinations over time, policy towards cultural heritage oscillated between an exclusivist 'class' or 'proletarian' pole and a more inclusivist, 'national' pole. Notwithstanding his animosity to notions of proletarian culture, for example, Lenin broadly exemplified the 'class' approach to cultural heritage.[7] Yet the attempt to substitute a class-based approach for a 'national' approach was never very successful.[8] Following the turmoil unleashed by forced collectivization and the First Five-Year Plan from 1928 to 1932, the Stalin leadership fretted about the weakness of national identity among the Russian people, fearful that it constituted a source of weakness in the Soviet state. Turning against what it called 'sociologizing' approaches to the past, which stressed class struggle, it gave its blessing to a patriotic narrative that focused on the rise of the Russian state, exalted the role of great men and heroic events, and looked more positively on the inherited culture of the past.[9] On 8 August 1936, *Pravda* declared:

> Great artists of the past belong to the labouring people who have
> inherited all the cultural values of the preceding classes; it is not in

---

[6] Xiaoming Chen, *From the May Fourth Movement to Communist Revolution: Guo Moruo and the Chinese Path to Communism* (Albany, 2007), 100.

[7] V. I. Lenin, 'On the National Pride of the Great Russians', *Collected Works* (Moscow, 1974), vol. 21, 103.

[8] S. A. Smith, *Revolution and the People in Russia and China* (Cambridge, 2008), 178-80.

[9] David Brandenberger, *National Bolshevism: Stalinist Mass Culture and the Formation of Modern Russian National Identity, 1931-1956* (Cambridge MA, 2002), 54.

our interests to keep these values under a bushel, to disperse them or to transform them into historical rags, as vulgar sociologists seek to do'.[10]

Similar tensions were evident in the CCP. Even during the Cultural Revolution, when an extreme 'class' approach to cultural heritage was dominant, themes of national pride and national unity were seldom far beneath the surface. In February 1966, Jiang Qing addressed the forum on work in literature and art in the People's Liberation Army, and called for a 'heroic and tenacious offensive against the literature and art of the feudal class, the bourgeoisie and the modern revisionists'. She even censured Stalin for uncritically taking over 'what are known as the classics of Russia and Europe'.[11] Nevertheless the central point of her speech was to call for the revolutionizing of traditional cultural forms such as Peking opera, rather than for their repudiation. Indeed the model operas that she sponsored, though replete with the language of class, served in practice to undermine the localism of cultural forms in China and to promote a simulacrum of a united nation in struggle, purged of class, ethnic, and gender divisions.[12] Moreover, once the backlash against Maoism was in full swing in the 1980s, CCP leaders shifted rapidly and relatively uncritically towards exploiting the cultural heritage for purposes of nation-building.

So far as policy towards the preservation of religious buildings was concerned, one sees the same tension between 'class' and 'national' approaches, but in this sphere the 'class' approach was particularly prominent. In both the Soviet Union and the PRC, a relatively moderate policy of preserving churches and temples was pursued initially but soon came under frontal attack. The Communist state, however, was not a unified agency. Different institutions, notably those responsible for culture and religion, battled for influence with more powerful institutions responsible for industrialization, collectivization, and urban planning.[13] Among the wider public, moreover,

[10] A. S. Shchenkov (ed.), *Pamiatniki arkhitektury v Sovetskom Soiuze: Ocherki arkhitekturnoi restavratsii* (Moscow, 2004), 14.

[11] *Peking Review*, 23, (2 June 1967).

[12] Paul Clark, *The Chinese Cultural Revolution: A History* (Cambridge, 2008).

[13] The policy of preservationists was very much influenced by aesthetic judgements. Catriona Kelly shows that in Leningrad in the pre-war period policy was directed towards preserving baroque and, above all, neo-classical buildings in the city and that so-called 'eclectic' style of the second half of the nineteenth century was happily consigned to destruction. Catriona Kelly, 'From "Counter-Revolutionary" Monuments to "National Heritage": the Preservation of Leningrad Churches, 1964-1982', *Cahiers du monde russe*, 54:1-2 (janvier-juin 2013), 1-34.

attitudes towards the preservation of churches and temples were equally contested. Believers, who comprised a large section of the population, invested their churches and temples—usually of no great historical or architectural significance—with sacred meaning through legend and ritual. Many who were not particularly religious looked on their village church or temple with affection as a symbol of the local community, as the place where key community and family celebrations took place, as the place where the dead were remembered. Yet there were also vocal minorities in the populace who were politically opposed to anything that smacked of support for religion. Many workers and some younger peasants in Russia and China strove to distance themselves from the 'old society' (a term much favoured by the CCP) and sometimes enthusiastically backed the destruction of places of worship or their conversion to 'socially useful' purposes.

Churches and heritage in Soviet Russia

Even as war and revolution brought destruction to Russia's architectural heritage—and gave rise to vandalism in some quarters—the first years of soviet power were characterized primarily by a concern to ensure that historic and cultural monuments were preserved unscathed. As early as 2 November 1917, Anatolii Lunacharskii, the Commissar of Enlightenment, tendered his resignation when he learned (wrongly) that in the course of the Bolshevik attempt to seize the city of Moscow, St Basil's Cathedral and the Cathedral of the Dormition in the Kremlin had been destroyed. Two days later, his Commissariat called for the 'vigilant preservation of the patrimony of people'.[14] Such thinking was in line with a European tradition of preservationism that can be traced back at least to Abbé Grégoire during the French Revolution. This tradition arrived in Russia around 1826, when Tsar Nicholas I ordered a register of architectural 'antiquities' to be compiled and forbade the demolition of historic 'castles, fortresses and ancient buildings'.[15] Following the October Revolution, the task of preserving the architectural and artistic patrimony became the exclusive responsibility of government, as aristocratic estates, royal palaces, and private art collections and museums passed into state ownership. A Department for Museum Affairs and Protection of Landmarks was set up under the Commissariat of Enlightenment, and the painter Igor E. Grabar headed the new Central State Restoration Workshops. These institutions provided a gathering

---

[14] Shchenkov (ed.), *Pamiatniki*, 5.

[15] Interest in Russia's pre-Petrine heritage emerged remarkably late, towards the end of the nineteenth century. James Cracraft, *The Petrine Revolution in Russian Architecture* (Cambridge MA, 2004), 10.

place for conservationists such as Petr D. Baranovskii (1892-1984), who would enjoy a long career in the preservationist movement after a stint in the camps, establishing the museum of wooden architecture at Kolomenskoe in 1923 and the Andrei Rublev icon museum in 1960.[16]

Under the Decree on Separation of Church and State of 20 January 1918, churches technically became state property, but the group of twenty (*dvadtsatka*) responsible for running each parish was enjoined to 'treat with due care the national heritage that has been assigned to us'.[17] Where churches were important enough to be granted the status of monuments (*pamiatniki*) they were subject to regulation by the museum departments of the city or oblast administrations, and later by the bureaux for the protection of monuments. In Moscow in 1913 there were 9 cathedrals, 15 monasteries, 10 convents, 292 Orthodox and 40 Old Believer congregations, 98 in-house chapels, and 20 other places of worship.[18] The resources of the city's museum department were quite insufficient to look after so many churches, many of which in any case it considered to be devoid of aesthetic or historic merit. Many in more powerful departments of the city administration objected to spending scarce resources on 'buildings of the old world'.[19] So from the first, there was a move to close churches and this steadily gathered momentum in the first decade of Soviet power. The first closures came at the end of 1917 as many private chapels attached to palaces or estates were confiscated, along with churches attached to state institutions, military units, and educational establishments. More important was the closure of monasteries, which the Bolsheviks considered institutions that had grown fat by exploiting the masses. Out of 1253 monasteries and convents in Russia at the beginning of 1918, 673 passed into state ownership by 1921.[20] Sometimes, this led to bitter clashes, such as that which took place at the Troitse-Sergiev monastery in Sergiev Posad, the largest and wealthiest monastery in the country. This was the focal point of the cult of St Sergy of Radonezh and had for centuries been linked to the ruling dynasty. In 1919 a clash flared up when the Bolsheviks ordered the removal of

[16] Timothy J. Colton, *Moscow: Governing the Socialist Metropolis* (Cambridge, MA, 1995), 111.

[17] Catriona Kelly, 'Socialist Churches: Heritage Preservation and "Cultic Buildings" in Leningrad, 1924-1940', *Slavic Review*, 71: 4 (2012), 802-3.

[18] Colton, *Moscow*, 39.

[19] Shchenkov (ed.), *Pamiatniki*, 14.

[20] M. V. Shkarovskii, 'Monastyri severo-zapada Rossii v 1920-1930-e gody', *Tserkov' v istorii Rossii*, sb.1 (Moscow, 1997), 18; Boris Kandilov, *Monastyri-muzei i antireligioznaia propaganda* (Moscow, 1929) 78.

the relics of St Sergy.[21] In November the local board of church organizations declared:

> For five centuries the Russian people has gathered at the tomb of St Sergy. During the struggle against the Tatar yoke, in the terrible years of this evil period, the people drew moral strength from this place which helped it to preserve face and become a great people. Invested with such memories, the remains of St Sergy became a precious national shrine.[22]

The statement typifies what religious heritage could mean for believers.

The major monastic churches that passed into state ownership were subject to a policy of 'museification' (*muzeefikatsiia*), a policy whose origins can be traced back at least to the French Revolution, but which Soviet experts systematically developed through experimental forms of exhibition in the course of the 1920s and early 1930s. Moscow was a trail-blazer in this regard, Leningrad being slower to turn its churches into museums.[23] The policy was motivated, on the one hand, by a desire to protect historical monuments and artefacts—in 1921 the second largest monastery on the outskirts of Moscow, Novoierusalimskii, had been robbed by the bandit brothers Polezhaev[24]—and, on the other, by a desire to use the monasteries to make anti-religious propaganda. All heritage, according to Barbara Kirshenblatt-Gimblett, is about the excision of artefacts from their original context and their exhibition in a new discursive context, as knowledge, performance and museum display.[25] Museification of churches thus entailed the displacement of the sacred meaning and history of the site and its resignification as a historic and aesthetic site set in the new discursive context of anti-religious propaganda. The policy was facilitated by what Adam Jolles has called the 'invasion of the didactic text' into the church-museum. The Convent of the Passion (Strastnoi) in Moscow was turned into the Central Anti-Religious Museum in 1929, its front adorned with a huge banner that proclaimed: 'Religion has always been an instrument of working-class

---

[21] S. A. Smith, 'Bones of Contention: Bolsheviks and the Struggle against Relics, 1918-1930', *Past and Present*, 204 (2009), 163.

[22] Vladimir Vorobev (ed.), *Sledstvennoe delo Patriarkha Tikhona: sbornik dokumentov* (Moscow, 2000), 538.

[23] M. E. Kaulen, *Muzei-khramy i muzei-monastyri v pervoi desiatiletie sovetskoi vlasti* (Moscow, 2001), 44, 58.

[24] Kaulen, *Muzei*, 38.

[25] Barbara Kirshenblatt-Gimblett, *Destination Culture: Tourism, Museums, and Heritage* (Berkeley, 1998), 18, 149.

exploitation'.[26] Soviet curators at this time experimented with the 'self-explanatory' (*samogovoriashchii*) museum, which aimed to give uneducated visitors an unambiguous understanding of exhibits through the liberal use of texts. The Central Anti-Religious Museum, for example, interspersed idols, fetishes, Christian images, and black-magic objects with 'pejorative dioramas, incriminating documents and defamatory didactic panels'.[27] Exhibits included a statue of Galileo in chains, a miraculous weeping icon, in which schoolchildren were shown how a little pump behind the icon caused the Virgin to cry, and a painting of a black man carrying a capitalist drinking whisky.[28] Despite this ideological onslaught, believers often displayed ingenuity in inscribing their own meanings onto exhibits to the vexation of the authorities. In the Vologda museum the display of the relics of St Feodosy was said to have encouraged 'among the dark, unconscious masses . . . the illusion that they have been exhibited for the purpose of religious worship'.[29] And an irritable writer complained that tour parties to the Troitse-Sergeev monastery were still taking off their hats when entering the cathedral and still kissing the sarcophagus containing a 'rotten skeleton with dried up skin and decaying rags'. 'Must the historic treasures of the churches inevitably provoke reactions of religious worship?', he asked in frustration.[30]

The onset of collectivization in 1928 unleashed a ferocious assault on places of worship. Article 26 of the Decree on Religious Associations of 1929 permitted the executive committee of a provincial or republican soviet to 'liquidate a place of worship' if this was 'essential to the needs of state and society'. It triggered a wave of demands—often from factory workers, egged on by local officials—for churches to be turned into libraries, clubs, canteens, and warehouses, or for them to be obliterated from the landscape of the 'model socialist city'. Typical was a resolution of March 1929 by workers of the Red October factory in the Middle Volga who announced: 'We consider this church a breeding ground for religious intoxicants that is not necessary to us. We instruct the city soviet to close the church immediately and use the premises as a school'.[31] In 1928, 534 churches were closed and in 1929 1,119.[32] The Cult Commission of the All-Russian Executive Committee of

---

26   Adam Jolles, 'Stalin's Talking Museums', *Oxford Art Journal*, 28:3 (2005), 434, 436.

27   Jolles, 'Stalin's Talking Museums', 446.

28   Jolles, 'Stalin's Talking Museum', 446.

29   Smith, 'Bones', 174.

30   *Antireligioznik*, 7 (1928), 71.

31   Kursovaia istoriia gosudarstva i tserkov'. http://works.tarefer.ru/33/100990/index.html [accessed 9 April 2012].

32   V. Tsypin, *Istoriia russkoi pravoslavnoi tserkvi, 1917-1990* (Moscow, 1994), 92.

Soviets in fact allowed some subsequently to reopen, but the sharp decline in the number of churches was never reversed. In this period preservationists in the museum departments of city and provincial governments lost out completely to economic and urban planners and industrial managers. In Moscow the number of buildings on the heritage register was slashed from 474 to 74 between 1925 and 1935 (the number of listed buildings for the whole of the RSFSR was cut from around 3,000 to 1200).[33] Perhaps the most famous casualty was the Cathedral of Christ the Saviour, conceived by Alexander I to mark Russia's victory over Napoleon, which was blown up in December 1931 to make way for a Palace of Soviets, a building planned to be higher than the Empire State Building and to be topped by a colossal statue of Lenin.[34] But there were many other examples. The distinguished restorer, Baranovskii, supervised the restoration of the Kazan Cathedral on Red Square from 1929 to 1932, but in 1936 it was bulldozed to clear the space for military parades.[35]

How did the millions of believers, whose numbers easily outstripped the zealots of socialist construction, respond to this attack on their religious heritage? Believers, of course, made no distinction between churches listed as historic monuments and the ordinary churches where they worshipped. For them every church was a house of God, a sacred space set apart from everyday life, a site venerated by their ancestors. The most revered churches were said to be 'prayed over' (*namolennye*), that is, places where God's grace had accumulated over generations by dint of the prayers of the faithful. The arbitrary closure of churches and the cutting down of bells which accompanied this was thus experienced as an assault not only on the sacred but also on the identity of the local community. The OGPU reported that in 1929 there were 307 'mass actions' against church closures and the removal of church bells (23.5% of the total number of mass actions); and in 1930 1,487 similar actions (10.8% of the total). In most of these, women took the lead, reminding us of the fact that religious identities and consequential perceptions of heritage are in part shaped by gender.[36] In Verovka in Artemovskii district in the Donbass, villagers petitioned the soviet executive committee as follows:

> The militia from Rykov . . . along with the secretary of the communist cell and the local Komsomol broke into the church, smashed

[33] B. G. Fedorov, *Khroniki unichtozheniia staroi Moskvy, 1990-2006* (Moscow, 2006), 9.

[34] Andrew Gentes, 'The Life, Death and Resurrection of the Cathedral of Christ the Saviour, Moscow', *History Workshop Journal*, 46 (1998), 63-95.

[35] Colton, *Moscow*, 269.

[36] N. A. Ivnitskii, *Repressivnaia politika sovetskoi vlasti v derevne (1928-33gg.)* (Moscow, 2000), 192.

the iconostasis, the icons, and defiled the altar and sacred vessels. This pogrom was carried out in the presence of believers who, weeping, begged them not to profane the sacred items.[37]

Yet even as this wholesale destruction of churches was underway, the Stalinist regime was beginning to reconfigure cultural heritage in less strident class terms. The promotion of a Soviet-patriotic narrative from the mid-1930s allowed for a rather more positive evaluation of the role of the Church in Russian history. In 1936, when discussing the revision of school history textbooks, Andrei Zhdanov opined that the monasteries had played a progressive role in Russian history insofar as they had contributed to the growth of the state. The outbreak of the Second World War reinforced this change of tone, when the Orthodox Church was granted limited toleration as a means of stiffening Russian patriotism. Some churches were allowed to reopen, mainly in the territories of Ukraine and Belorussia liberated from the Nazis, but the scale of this should not be exaggerated. In July 1945, the Council for Russian Orthodox Affairs reported that it had received 5,770 petitions to reopen churches, of which only 414 had been granted, whereas 3,850 had been refused by local soviets.[38] Nevertheless the war strengthened the idea that Russia's churches were an inseparable part of a *national* heritage. According to the Ministry of Culture, some 3,000 architectural monuments were destroyed in the war, among them cathedrals in Kiev, Chernigov and Vitebsk.[39] In 1947 when the Council of Ministers of the RSFSR drew up a list of 600 major monuments and ensembles scheduled for preservation, the list was dominated by religious buildings. Nevertheless when an ambitious programme of restoration got under way from the late 1940s the reconstruction of churches was not the regime's priority. Though the many churches of Novgorod and Pskov—both cities that had suffered appalling damage— were painstakingly rebuilt, in Leningrad the priority was given to the restoration of the eighteenth-century imperial palaces in the city's suburbs, possibly suggesting that it was easier ideologically for the Stalin regime to associate itself with the imperial tradition of the tsars than with the Orthodox idea of Holy Russia.

Just as it seemed as though the fortunes of the preservationists were recovering, the proponents of a class approach to religious heritage suddenly

---

[37] *Russkia Pravoslavnaia Tserkov' i bol'shevistskoe gosudarstvo v 1925-27gg.*, 12. http://kref.ru/infopolitologija2/59641/12.html [accessed 10 April 2012].

[38] Steven Merritt Miner, *Stalin's Holy War: Religion, Nationalism, and Alliance Politics, 1941-45* (Chapel Hill, 2003), 147.

[39] Albert J. Schmidt, *The Impact of Perestroika on Soviet Law* (Dordrecht, 1990), 352.

found themselves in the ascendant, as Stalin's successor, Nikita Khrushchev, launched a new anti-religious crusade from 1959 to 1964. Though less violent than the campaign during collectivization, its effect on the number of active churches was no less devastating, especially in rural areas. Of fifty-eight monasteries and convents open in 1959, only sixteen were still operating by 1964. In Moscow, at exactly the same time as the Central Restoration Workshop was lovingly restoring the Spasso-Andronikov monastery, founded in 1357, thirty of the city's remaining fifty churches were being shut down, six of them demolished.[40] But public sentiment was changing, in part precipitated by this latest episode in the state-sponsored attack on the national patrimony.[41] The sight of so many churches mouldering as brickyards, garages, small factories and administrative offices helped spur one of the most remarkable developments in late-Soviet society, namely, the emergence of a civic movement to campaign for the preservation of Russia's historic monuments. In May 1964, six months before Khrushchev's ousting, students founded the Rodina (Motherland) club 'to promote the study of historic monuments and to study ancient art and history'. A year later, a letter signed by the sculptor Sergei Konenkov, the writer Leonid Leonov and the painter Pavel Korin, condemned the ongoing demolition of churches, especially in Moscow. *Molodaia Gvardiia*, journal of the Young Communist League, an organ that increasingly espoused a thinly disguised nationalism, explained: 'Churches are the foundation stones around which national consciousness is built' and pointed to the patriotic role they had played in the Second World War.[42] It was not long before this burgeoning movement won support among certain members of the Politburo, and in July 1965 the Council of Ministers of the RSFSR set up the All-Russian Society for the Preservation of Historical and Cultural Monuments (VOOPIK), a mass heritage organization, albeit one under the control of the party. It proved extraordinarily successful, raising funds and organizing volunteers for various renovation projects. By 1985 it had 15 million members.[43]

The preservationist movement is commonly tied by historians to the emergence of conservative Russian nationalism, and though the connection is strong—for example, those around *Molodaia Gvardiia* argued that neglected

---

[40] http://en.wikipedia.org/wiki/Russian_cultural_heritage_register

[41] As early as 1956, *Literaturnaia gazeta*, flagship newspapers of the intelligentsia, published an open letter deploring the destruction of ancient monuments. Kelly, 'From "Counter-Revolutionary" Monuments', 8.

[42] Yitzhak M. Brudny, *Reinventing Russia: Russian Nationalism and the Soviet State, 1953-91* (Cambridge MA, 1998), 68.

[43] Brudny, *Reinventing Russia*, 70.

churches were a sign that Russia was losing her 'civilization of the soul'[44] —
many of the activists in VOOPIK were apolitical, concerned to safeguard the
cultural heritage and the natural environment, the two issues being closely
aligned at this time. Nowhere was this new sensibility more apparent than in
the North, where the astonishing wooden churches of Arkhangel'sk, Karelia,
and Vologda were being left to rot as people deserted the countryside.[45]
Preservationists campaigned to create a museum-reserve out of the multi-
domed churches on Kizhi island in the middle of Lake Onega in Karelia, and
in 1966 this was designated a museum of national importance. In 1990 it
would become a UNESCO World Heritage site.[46] The guidebook of the new
museum described the churches of Kizhi as a 'bright reflection of the artistic
genius of Russian people... All were created by the hands of the simple people,
although they were ordered to build them by princes, monasteries and
churches'. Comments in the visitors' book reflected a different sensibility:
'Without faith, we cannot live. It is the foundation that makes life and makes
the building of life steady and keeps it safe from catastrophe'.[47]

In 1976 the Soviet government finally passed all-union legislation to protect historical and cultural monuments, and the following year the new constitution declared it was a duty of all Soviet citizens to preserve them.[48] Yet the
political success of the preservationist movement should not be exaggerated.
Its capacity to raise revenue was never impressive. It is reckoned that in
Moscow the budget for preservation remained under 0.5% of capital investment.[49] In 1982 the renowned literary scholar, Dmitrii Likhachev, lambasted
official efforts, claiming that at best one-third of the Soviet Union's estimated
180,000 historic monuments were listed, a protest that spurred the Council of
Ministers to order the listing of the monuments he had mentioned.[50] It was
only with the onset of perestroika that the preservationist movement began to

---

[44] Brudny, *Reinventing Russia*, 76.

[45] Schmidt, *Impact*, 354.

[46] William Brumfield, 'The churches of Kizhi', http://rbth.ru/articles/2011/01/28/the_
      churches_of_kizhi_russias_sacred_island_12318.html. The continued state of decay
      of many of the wooden churches is emphasized in Richard Davies and Matilda
      Moreton, *Wooden Churches: Travelling in the Russian North* (London, 2011).

[47] Sanami Takahashi, 'Church or Museum? The Role of State Museums in Conserving
      Church Buildings, 1965-85', in *Journal of Church and State*, vol. 51:3, (2009), 502-17,
      509, 508.

[48] F. J. M. Feldbrugge, 'Monuments in Soviet Law' in F. J. M. Feldbrugge (ed.), *Soviet
      Administrative Law: Theory and Policy* (Dordrecht, 1989). Cited in Schmidt, *Impact*,
      335.

[49] Colton, *Moscow*, 559.

[50] Schmidt, *Impact*, 338; Brudny, *Reinventing*, 142.

acquire political clout. In 1986 a Soviet Culture Fund was established, with Likhachev as president and Raisa Gorbacheva as a member of the board, and millions of roubles were budgeted for restoration of monuments. Many complained that this was too little and too late. In the context of perestroika, the class approach to heritage finally began to fade, although the official discourse of heritage remained essentially Soviet-imperial rather than Russian nationalist. In 1988 the Orthodox Church returned to something like a focus of national identity as celebrations to mark the 1000th anniversary of the adoption of Christianity by Prince Vladimir got under way. This proved to be the start of a move to hand back important religious sites to the Church, such as the Optina Hermitage and the Danilovskii monastery, the oldest in Moscow and a former juvenile detention facility.[51]

Temples and heritage in Republican and Communist China

China has the longest enduring written documentation of its past and a civilization characterized by deep fascination with history. Nevertheless it has shown relatively little interest in preserving the built environment. Buildings, being made of materials that decayed rapidly, required frequent reconstruction, and this may have been a factor that made the literati less concerned about the continuity and authenticity of the built environment than their western counterparts.[52] If a historical monument collapsed or burned down, it could always be replaced. The Taiping insurrection in the mid-nineteenth century wrought havoc on China's architectural heritage, yet much was rebuilt and seen to be none the worse for that. The dominant tradition thus held the purely physical traces of the past in small regard, showing far more interest in words than in things. A natural beauty spot or a historic monument only became significant once it was written about, preferably eulogized and thereby committed to social memory. As F. W. Mote observed, 'the past was a past of words not of stones'.[53] Consequently, authenticity was of little account. A building such as the Yellow Crane Pagoda in Wuhan,

---

[51] Christopher Marsh, *Religion and the State in Russia and China* (New York, 2011), 113.

[52] Zhang Liang reminds us that the Chinese used stone in memorial stelae and were familiar with such architectural features as the arch. Zhang Liang, *La naissance du concept de patrimoine en Chine XIX-XXe siècles* (Paris, 2003), 12.

[53] Cited in Pierre Ryckmans, 'The Chinese Attitudes towards the Past', (1986) in Simon Leys (Pierre Ryckmans), *The Angel and the Octopus: Collected Essays* (Sydney, 1999), 23. This seminal essay is also online at http://www.chinaheritagequarterly.org/articles.php?searchterm=014_chineseAttitude.inc&issue=014; Wang Gungwu, 'Loving the Ancient in China' in Isabel McBryde (ed.), *Who Owns the Past?* (Melbourne, 1985), 175-95.

founded in 223CE, was restored many times over the centuries and in 1981 was entirely rebuilt—in a much more elaborate style—one kilometre away from its original site.

Within Asia Chinese nationalism was distinguished by its broadly negative attitude towards the cultural heritage. Compared with nationalists in India or Japan, early Chinese nationalists showed little interest in reinventing elements in their tradition in order to meet the challenges of forging a nation-state. The generation of intellectuals formed by the May 4th Movement of 1919 viewed the Confucian tradition as an incubus that had stifled national self-awakening, and looked to science and democracy as keys to national progress. In 1924, the eminent writer, Lu Xun, hailed the sudden collapse of the Leifeng Pagoda in Hangzhou, one of the celebrated Ten Vistas of West Lake, seeing in it a blow to feudalism, and wistfully imagining that the tragic snake-woman who, according to legend, had been imprisoned in the pagoda, had finally been set free. Two years earlier, his younger brother, Zhou Zuoren (1885-1967) had written an essay arguing that nostalgia for the past should never justify conserving ancient ruins. Yet Zhou himself alerts us to the fact that attitudes to the past were more complex than the preceding generalization suggests, for although Zhou condemned the Chinese classics as an expression of 'unnatural thinking', 'harmful to the people', he was himself steeped in the classical tradition and would go on to become a pioneering scholar of Chinese folklore.[54]

So despite the strong connection between Chinese nationalism and cultural iconoclasm, the 1920s was also the decade when a western ideology of heritage began to percolate into China—above all in the new field of archaeology. The Nationalist (Guomindang) government (1928-49) seized on the latter as a means whereby a newly reunified China could create a historical narrative that no longer centred on the cycle of imperial dynasties but on the supposed five-thousand-year history of a homogenous Han people expanding out of its Yellow River base into the four corners of the country. In a more scholarly register, the discovery of Peking Man at Zhoukoudian in 1929 and the excavations at Anyang in Henan, the centre of the Shang dynasty (1600-1046 BCE), helped to undermine the diffusion theories then influential among archaeologists, which assumed that all civilizations emanated from the Middle East.[55] Yet while the Nationalist government supported

---

[54] Eugene Y. Wang 'Tope and *topos;* The Leifeng Pagoda and the Discourse of the Demonic', in Judith T. Zeitlin and Lydia H. Liu with Ellen Widmer (eds), *Writing and Materiality in China: Essays in Honor of Patrick Hanan,* (Cambridge, MA, 2003); Susan Daruvala, *Zhou Zuoren and an Alternative Chinese Response to Modernity* (Cambridge MA, 2000), 49.

[55] Diana Lary, *China's Republic* (Cambridge, 2007), 64, 92.

archaeological excavation, it proved relatively indifferent to preserving the built environment. In 1928 it issued a law to protect antiquities, but initiative in this sphere came from the educated public.[56] In 1929-30, Zhu Qiqian and Liang Sicheng, son of the late-imperial reformer Liang Qichao, founded the Society for the Study of Chinese Buildings, (*Zhongguo yingzao xueshe*) which drew up a list of 2,738 monuments of historical significance. In 1937, Liang led a team to carry out a scientific survey of the 52 monasteries on Mount Wutai in Shanxi province, one of the four sacred mountains of Chinese Buddhism, some of which had survived since the Tang Dynasty (618-907).[57] Yet the war with Japan would disrupt these endeavours. No-one knows exactly how much of the cultural heritage was destroyed by war — only that it was very considerable.[58]

The average temple in China was very different from the elaborate temples on the sacred mountains. Most were modest in structure, with little claim to architectural distinction, and their significance was purely local. Although broadly similar in architecture and liturgical accoutrements, temples fell into different types: those in the Buddhist tradition, which were were called *si* (寺); those in the Daoist tradition, known as *guan* (观); those dedicated to Confucius or prominent scholars which were usually called *miao* (庙), a term also used for the great majority of temples associated with the religion of the majority of Chinese, which was neither Buddhist, Daoist, nor Confucian, but an essentially local and syncretic mix. A village temple might house bodhi-sattvas, a statue of Guandi, the god of war, one of Guanyin, goddess of mercy, and gods of flood-control or earth gods. The village cult, however, centred on a god—sometimes a historic personage who had been deified—who was the special protector of the locality.[59] Unlike Buddhist or Daoist temples, village temples did not usually have resident clergy. Finally, there were the temples to ancestors (lineage halls), generally known as *ci* (祠), which by the nineteenth

---

[56] I leave aside the question of whether the terms used to translate the western vocabulary of heritage created equivalences. 'Heritage' is generally today translated as *wenwu* 文物 in the PRC, but as *guwu* 古物 in Taiwan. The term *wenwu*, however, is often back-translated into English as 'cultural relics'. This term was adopted in the 1930s and includes any listed building, archaeological or historic site. *Wenwu jianzhu*, the term closest to a 'historic building', appeared towards the end of the 1940s. Zhang Liang, *La naissance*, 63-4.

[57] Zhang Liang, *La naissance*, 66, 83.

[58] In the first year of the war it was estimated that 2,118 libraries, 835 schools, 42 museums, and 54 historic sites were destroyed. Jocelyne Fresnais, *La protection du patrimoine en République populaire de Chine, 1949-99* (Paris, 2001), 53-4.

[59] Stephan Feuchtwang, *Popular Religion in China: The Imperial Metaphor* (London, 2003).

century were probably the most numerous of all, with most villages having at least one. Temples were understood to be the residences of gods, and villagers would go there to make offerings and seek favours. The wooden, metal, or jade statues and scroll depictions of the gods were understood to be their embodiments and mattered more to worshippers than the fabric of the building.[60] Each temple had at least one major annual fair (*miaohui*) in which the image of the principal deity would be carried through the streets. Such temple festivals were joyous occasions, featuring opera performances, dancing, matchmaking, fortune telling, spirit possession, and markets where peasants could buy manufactures, sell farm produce, or buy and sell animals. As Gao Youpeng reminds us, these fairs also had a 'mystical dimension' (*shenmi xing*) which 'caused people to look up to the gods reverently and obtain a sense of inner happiness and relief'.[61] A dense web of story-telling and ritual served to communicate the meaning of a local temple and its periodic festivals. In Shangbao township in Chongyi county in Jiangxi, legend said that a temple perched high on a 1,755m peak had been founded by three hunters, returning empty-handed after a day's hunting. When they alighted on a deer, they chased it to the peak of the mountain, where it turned into three gods, who explained that they desired that a temple be built in their honour. The hunters agreed that they would build one for 1,000 catties. On their way down the mountain they bagged a tiger, a boar, and a goat, the proceeds from which went to build the temple. The legend is still widely known today by the inhabitants of Shangbao who celebrate the temple's foundation on the first *jiazi* day of spring and autumn.[62]

Modern nationalists looked down upon temple religion. From the late Qing there was a steady drive to turn local temples into 'useful' buildings such as schools, granaries, and government offices. It is reckoned that in 1900 there were at least one million temples in China, yet by the outbreak of the Sino-Japanese war in 1937 there were only half that number.[63] In the rural reconstruction area of Ding county in Hebei, there were 435 temples in

---

[60]   Goossaert, *Dans les temples*, 24.

[61]   Gao Youpeng, *Zhongguo miaohui wenhua* (Shanghai, 1999), 77; Adam Yuet Chau, 'Expanding the Space of Popular Religion: Local Temple Activism and the Politics of Legitimation in Contemporary Rural China', Y. Ashiwa and D. Wank (eds), *Making Religion, Making the State: the Politics of Religion in Modern China* (Stanford, 2009), 216-17.

[62]   John Lagerwey, *China: A Religious State* (Hong Kong 2010), 139. The *jiazi* refers to the 60 combinations of 10 heavenly stems and 12 earthly branches that were used to mark time.

[63]   Vincent Goossaert, 'Le destin de la religion chinoise au 20ème siècle', *Social Compass*, 50:4, (2003), 436.

62 villages in 1882 and just 104 by 1928.[64] In November 1928, the new Nationalist government issued 'Rules to decide whether temples are to be preserved or destroyed', which decreed that temples dedicated to 'sages' (*xianzhelei*) and 'religious' (*zongjiaolei*) gods—those whose teachings were 'pure and true'—might be preserved, but temples dedicated to gods worshipped before the development of science (*gushenlei*) or to licentious spirits (*yincilei*), such as the cow goblin and snake god, were to be destroyed.[65] A government sponsored anti-superstition campaign from 1928 to 1930 targeted city-god temples, and 'beating the city god' for a while became a favourite pastime of political activists.[66] Since temples were run by a local committee and usually supported by popular subscription, however, the agreement of villagers was usually required before a temple could be converted into something more 'useful'. Yet the evidence suggests that it was not too difficult to secure such agreement: in Ding county in 1928, of 135 temples that had been converted to other uses, 57 were schools, 25 village offices or public storehouses and 47 were in private hands.[67] At the same time, villagers were often reluctant to dissolve temples held in high regard and could be ingenious in evading official pressure, turning 'temples to be destroyed' into government-approved 'Confucius temples'.[68]

The coming to power of the CCP in 1949 did not initially signal a radical change in policy towards the maintenance of ancient monuments. A State Bureau for the Administration of Cultural Relics (*Guojia wenwu shiye guanliju*), set up in November 1949, had a remit to preserve artefacts, develop archaeological sites, and expand the network of museums. Cultural bureaux were established within provincial and municipal governments to implement this policy. As with the Nationalist government, archaeology occupied pride of place in Communist efforts to preserve the nation's heritage. In the course of the 1950s and 1960s, work resumed at Zhoukoudian and Yinxu and large-scale field surveys and excavations were carried out at prehistoric sites, work that did not stop during the Cultural Revolution. In 1953 an Institute for the Preservation of Ancient Buildings was set up, which advised provincial and

[64] Li Jinghan, *Ding xian shehui gaikuang diaocha* (Beijing, 1986; orig. 1933), 422.

[65] Rebecca Allyn Nedostup, *Superstitious Regimes: Religion and the Politics of Chinese Modernity* (Cambridge, 2009), 79-86; Yoshiko Ashiwa, 'Positioning Religion in Modernity: State and Buddhism in China', in Ashiwa and Wank (eds), *Making Religion*, 51.

[66] Shuk-wah Poon, 'Religion, Modernity, and Urban Space: The City God Temple in Republican Guangzhou', *Modern China*, 34:2 (2008), 247-75.

[67] Li Jinghan, *Ding xian*, 422.

[68] Shuk-wah Poon, 'Religion, Modernity', 268.

county bureaux on issues of conservation.[69] That efforts to preserve heritage frequently remained a dead letter, however, is suggested by the issuance in 1961 of new regulations by the State Council which specified that all buildings under government protection were 'normally to be used only as sites for museums, sites for institutions for the protection and care of cultural objects, or places of interest to tourists'. Appended was a list of 180 monuments directly under the control of the Ministry of Culture, 30 of these being temples and monasteries (six of them in Tibet): 'They have the precious use of teaching patriotism and revolutionary traditions to the people and of presenting the riches of the cultural life of the people'.[70]

During the 1950s, the religious policy of the PRC was rather different from that of the Soviet Union. Whereas the Soviets pursued an 'anti-religious' policy, China crafted a 'religious' policy, primarily intended to uphold a patriotic united front and foster good relations with ethnic minorities. As a way of demonstrating good will towards Tibetans, Mongols, and others, as well as of winning favour with Buddhists outside China, the government invested scarce resources into restoring showcase temples. Between 1951 and 1958, over 100 monasteries and pagodas underwent repair: not a large number, given that in 1949 there were 230,000 temples with resident monks and nuns, yet not an insignificant financial commitment either.[71] The government spent US$400,000 in restoring the temples on Mount Wutai, a site of great importance to Tibetan Buddhists, and US$200,000 on the Lingyin temple in Hangzhou. The Xuanzhong temple in Shanxi, birthplace of the Pure Land sect of Buddhism and a site of particular veneration for Japanese Buddhists, was rebuilt at a cost of US$110,000.[72] Moreover, the new government even funded the building of a handful of new temples, notably the Buddha's Tooth temple outside Beijing, a policy that would have been unthinkable in the Soviet Union. Such cultural diplomacy appears to have paid off at least for a time, since in 1964, following a tour of the tooth relic through Burma, Buddhist delegations from eight countries attended the inauguration of the temple and passed a resolution condemning US imperialism in Vietnam.[73]

More in line with Soviet precedent was the CCP's policy of 'museification' of the major temples. On 17 May 1950, the *Hangzhou Daily* published an

---

[69] Fresnais, *La protection*, 78.

[70] Fresnais, *La protection*, 87, 92.

[71] Holmes Welch, *Buddhism under Mao* (Cambridge MA, 1972), 150. This figure seems too high.

[72] Welch, *Buddhism*, 147.

[73] Welch, *Buddhism*, 153.

article on the reconstruction that was taking place at the West Lake in Hangzhou:

> West Lake is world renowned for the beauty of its landscape; it is a place with numerous famous sites and ancient remains. But these were all the doings of the so-called literati. . . We are preparing to transform a place of luxurious indulgence for the select few into a pleasure park for the enjoyment of the labouring people. There are over 140 temples and shrines in the vicinity of West Lake. For this reason, the majority of people who visited the Lake in the past were pilgrims who 'used the Buddha as an excuse to go on spring outings' . . . Some 49% of the pre-existing buildings in the West Lake Landscape Zone are in a state of disrepair or collapse. . . Apart from retaining a certain number of temple structures that served feudalistic superstitions, the rest will be converted and will become commemorative structures, museums, displays, libraries, as well as exhibition spaces and sales points for provincial manufactures.[74]

This policy of converting major temples into museums was pursued nationwide. In Shandong province, for example, the Pingdu Museum, the Qingdao City Museum and the Provincial Museum were all installed in former Daoist monasteries and in Zibo the city museum was housed in a former ancestral hall.[75] However, none of these museums was an anti-religious museum of the Soviet type, even though class critiques of religion were to be found in the way that artefacts were selected and captioned.

As in the Soviet Union, the cultural bureaux and religious affairs bureaux were much less powerful players than the institutional agencies committed to economic development. The latter did not blanch at the thought of a wholesale recasting of the built environment, although the impact of the modernizers was less than in the Soviet Union if only because urbanization was relatively restricted under Mao. The political weakness of preservationists was most visible with respect to the debate about the development of Beijing. Liang Sicheng, founder of the Society for the Study of Chinese Buildings in 1929 and joint director for planning in Beijing by the 1950s, fought hard to preserve the capital's ancient centre, but was easily outflanked by a combination of Soviet advisers, party bosses, and urban developers who clamoured for the capital to become a 'productive' and industrial city. As a

[74] Translation by Geremie R. Barmé. http://chinaheritagenewsletter.anu.edu.au/features. php?searchterm=028_liber.inc&issue=028.

[75] James Flath, 'Managing historical capital in Shandong: Museum, Monument, and Memory in Provincial China', *The Public Historian*, 24:2, (Spring 2002), 48-9.

result, a large part of the old city was razed to make way for Tiananmen square, the city walls were torn down, and historic buildings, such as the twin pagodas of the Qingshou monastery (constructed in the Jin dynasty, 1190-1209), were demolished to make way for the Chang'an boulevard. Mao Zedong allegedly commented that he looked forward to the day when a forest of factory chimneys would be visible from Tiananmen square.[76]

So far as the great mass of local temples was concerned, the 1950s presents a mixed picture. The end of war and land reform allowed millions of villagers to garner resources to make repairs to their local temples; and although there were exceptions, they were largely left to practise religion, since local authorities had more pressing tasks on their hands, such as land reform and cooperativization.[77] For bigger, especially monastic temples, the situation was less rosy. Communist discourse condemned monastic temples as sites of feudal exploitation, even though the average temple owned relatively little land, and such land as it owned was often worked by the monks themselves.[78] Land reform weakened the already tenuous economic base of the larger temples by reducing their land-holdings and depriving them of rental income. Moreover, if central government was relatively cautious in its religious policy, local officials sometimes behaved recklessly. On 16 June 1951, the Central Committee warned that temples should not be occupied without the agreement of resident clergy; that no damage should be done to temples; and that historic relics should be preserved. If temples were confiscated, they should be ordinary temples without abbots (*zhuchi*)—these were the vast majority in fact—or be given up voluntarily by monks, or be in places where temples were numerous.[79] That local officials frequently paid little heed to these directives is indicated by the fact that further orders to protect temples and historical monuments followed in 1954 and later. On 21 March 1960, for example, the Political Section of the Red Army reminded soldiers not to use temples for target practice.[80] With the Great Leap Forward of 1958, moreover, central policy lurched in a much more radical, 'class' direction: temples were now earmarked for demolition or conversion in order to expedite large-scale economic projects and the construction of communes. In Beijing over 2,000 temples were destroyed or converted to other uses, most of

[76]   Zhang Liang, *La naissance*, 116, 136, 139.

[77]   S. A. Smith, 'On not Learning from the Soviet Union: Religious Policy in China, 1949-65,' *Modern China Studies*, 21:3 (September 2014) (forthcoming).

[78]   Goossaert, *Dans les temples*, 148.

[79]   Chen Jinlong, *Zhongguo gongchandang yu Zhongguo de zongjiao wenti*, (Guangdong, 2006), 129.

[80]   Chen Jinlong, *Zhongguo gongchandang*, 185.

them very small.[81] In Anhui province there were 3,158 Buddhist temples in 1949, many of them in a parlous state, housing 3,933 monks, 2,797 nuns and 3,500 lay officers. By 1955, there were 1,942, of which only about 800 were fully functioning, with 4,962 monks and nuns, and close to 1,000 lay officers. By 1962 the number had shrunk to 700 temples with 560 monks, 889 nuns and less than 200 lay officers. In the same province there were 120 Daoist temples in 1949 with 800 monks. By 1958, there were just 19, six of them on the sacred mountain of Huangshan, and a mere 130 monks. In the early 1960s, the number rose slightly only to plummet with the Cultural Revolution.[82] Chen Jinlong cites an amazing statistic to the effect that by the end of 1961 only 8 per cent of places of worship that existed in 1949 were still operational, and says that in some areas the percentage was as low as 1 to 2 per cent.[83]

In the wake of the atrocious famine (1959-61) caused by the Great Leap Forward, a spontaneous resurgence of popular religion occurred. Many of the tens of thousands of temples closed during the Great Leap were reopened by villagers acting in disregard of the commune authorities. During the Four Clean-ups (1963-66), work teams sent into the villages to wipe out corruption among officials looked askance as villagers lavished time and money on temple reconstruction and temple festivals. The revival was particularly marked in the coastal regions of the south. In seventeen counties and cities of Zhanjiang (Tsamkong) in south-west Guangdong, 2,173 temples were rebuilt in 1963.[84] In Gaohe county in the same province it was reported that 'in many localities peasants are organizing collectively to raise funds and do volunteer labour to repair temples'. The Dengxin keng brigade in Hecheng commune built an altar of four rooms to which hundreds flocked to burn incense. When confronted by officials, they retorted: 'This is freedom of belief and you cannot interfere with it'.[85] But temple building was not confined to the south. In Yulin prefecture in Shaanxi an astonishing 460,000 yuan plus 5,500 jin of grain was spent on restoring temples and building altars for gods.[86] A temple built by miners in the Xiaobojian coal mine in Handan in

---

[81]　http://www.chinaheritagenewsletter.org/features.php?searchterm=001_beijing.inc&issue=001

[82]　*Anhui difangzhi.* http://61.191.16.234:8080/was40/pdf/shzh/63/ [accessed September 2011].

[83]　Chen Jinlong, *Zhongguo gongchandang* 233.

[84]　Guangdong Provincial Archive, 217-1-133.

[85]　*Neibu cankao,* 25 December 1962, 6.

[86]　Hubei provincial archive: SZ 123-2-346.

Hebei cost 1,370 yuan.[87] Frustrated in their efforts to prevent peasants from taking such action, the work teams sometimes resorted to violence: in the Yangshulin commune in Nongan county in Jilin they smashed 2,700 images of the earth god, kitchen god, Goddess of Clear Sight (*Yanguang niangniang*), Zhang Xian, the protector of children, and the Yellow Beard Immortal (Hu Huang). Elsewhere in the county, officials tore down temples and smashed ancestral tablets. Yet people told them: 'Pull it down, we will rebuild it later'.[88]

This resurgence of popular religion may have been an indirect cause of the assault on the 'four olds' that was to become such a defining feature of the Cultural Revolution. When Mao called for a struggle against religion, old ideas, old culture and old customs on 20 August 1966, Red Guards responded with alacrity, although the Chairman's intentions were far from clear.[89] Between mid-August and the end of September 1966, at least 4,922 of Beijing's 6,843 listed historical sites were damaged or destroyed. Classical texts, paintings and antiques were seized from 33,695 households and fed to the flames. In Shanghai zealots were even more fanatical, raiding no fewer than 84,222 households.[90] On Mount Wutai in Shanxi 24 out of 62 temples were destroyed and the rest were turned into offices of official organs.[91] On Putuo island in Zhejiang, forty-eight of the huge complex of Buddhist monasteries were wrecked.[92] For the first time since 845 CE, barely a single monastery functioned in China. Nor were village temples immune. Statues, wood carvings, stone inscriptions, and scrolls were smashed or effaced, and revolutionary slogans daubed on them, a symbolic assertion of red values over feudalism and capitalism. In Qufu, the ancient seat of Confucius, a statue of the sage was toppled and paraded through the town, and some 2,000 graves in the Kong family cemetery were desecrated. The Revolutionary Rebel Liaison Station to Annihilate the Kong Family Business delightedly announced:

> The raging torrent swept into the Confucius Cemetery where stelae were smashed and the Kong tombs dug up. Let all those saintly

---

[87] *Neibu cankao*, 19 July 1963.

[88] *Neibu cankao*, 15 August 1963.

[89] Denise Y. Ho (2011), 'Revolutionizing Antiquity: The Shanghai Cultural Bureaucracy in the Cultural Revolution, 1966–1968', *The China Quarterly*, 207, 691.

[90] Dahpon David Ho, 'To Protect and Preserve: Resisting the Four Olds Campaign, 1966-67', in Joseph W. Esherick, Paul G. Pickowicz, and Andrew G. Walder (eds), *The Chinese Cultural Revolution as History* (Stanford, 2006), 64-5.

[91] Chen Jinlong, *Zhongguo gongchandang*, 235.

[92] Fresnais, *La protection*, 100.

> people in their finery and with their solemn bearing kneel before
> Old Kong's grave and eat dirt! The grave of the 76th-generation
> descendant of Old Kong, the big landlord and evil tyrant Kong
> Lingyi has been dug up. The poor and lower-middle peasants
> split open the coffin and dismembered the corpse. They burnt the
> dead dog till he was nothing but ash.[93]

This particular action may have had the blessing of Chen Boda of the Cultural Revolution Leadership Group in Beijing, but it is clear that some in the party leadership, and not only Zhou Enlai, had serious reservations about such vandalism and rallied to minimize the destruction. Zhou issued orders for the protection of the lamasery (*Yonghegong*) in Beijing, the Han tombs at Mawangdui, the relics at Mount Tai, Hangzhou's Lingyin temple, the Banpo prehistoric site, and the Han tombs at Mancheng. Careful to praise the campaign against the four olds, he nevertheless emphasized respect for the artistic achievements of the Red Guards' forebears.[94] On 14 May 1967, the Central Committee issued a directive, 'Regarding Several Suggestions on Protecting Cultural Relics and Books during the Great Proletarian Cultural Revolution', which appealed to pride in China's long history and claimed that cultural relics were part of the nation's glorious 'revolutionary tradition'. It reminded the Red Guards that cultural relics were state property (in fact, many had been seized from private homes) and argued that 'feudal' buildings, religious sculptures and the like should be preserved so that they could be used as 'public spaces for condemning the crimes of the ruling classes and the imperialists and for educating the masses in class struggle and patriotism'. Similarly, 'poisonous books' were not to be burned, but preserved as 'negative educational materials for further criticism'.[95] Despite the risks, villagers often hid temple furnishings, statues and ancestral tablets, and were sometimes able to preserve the actual buildings by the simple expedient of plastering them with revolutionary slogans.

Temples and heritage in post-Communist Russia and China

The collapse of Communism in the Soviet Union in 1991, together with the rapid moves to privatize and deregulate the state economy in China in the 1980s, led to a dramatic reversal in policy towards the preservation of

[93] Sang Ye and Geremie R. Barmé, 'The Fate of the Confucius Temple, the Kong Mansion and Kong Cemetery' http://www.chinaheritagenewsletter.org/scholarship.php?search term=020_confucius.inc&issue=020 [accessed 28 July 2011].

[94] Ho, 'To Protect', 68-9.

[95] Ho, 'To Protect', 69-70.

churches and temples: once vilified as emblems of class oppression, these places of worship were rapidly reconfigured as towering examples of national heritage, potentially available to contenders for political and economic power as symbolic capital to exploit in their struggles for power. At the same time, central government in both countries, though spearheading the recalibration of religious sites as cultural heritage, found itself less able to control religious activity on the ground, as new political and economic actors unleashed by the market and by the opening up of society to transnational forces, became involved in the restitution and reconstruction of religious sites. In both countries, the number of agencies shaping policy towards the preservation of the national patrimony thus multiplied in comparison with the Communist era.

The implosion of the Soviet Union in 1991 raised the acute issue of what it meant to be Russian. The essentially imperial identity that had typified the Soviet era was suddenly undone, and new and old elites struggled to master a discursive field in which different versions of national identity—ethnic, imperial, and civic—vied with one another.[96] National monuments, memorials, and museums were a key stake in this struggle, as contenders for power sought to tap into their symbolic capital in the hope of bolstering their pursuit of broader projects.[97] How far could Soviet sites of memory be reconfigured to fit an emerging capitalist society? How far could Russian identity be recast in a non-imperial form in a Russian Federation that remained a multi-ethnic polity in which Russians were in the majority? How far could political leaders formed by an entirely secular culture, or 'oligarchs' not notable for their moral probity, attach themselves to a deep-seated religious idiom of Russian national identity, exemplified by the Orthodox Church? It soon became clear that civic renditions of national identity could not compete with long-standing renditions that played on themes of a strong state, patriotic wars, Russia's historic vulnerability to foreign invasion and, increasingly, on the theme of Holy Russia. In the presidential elections of 2012, Putin promised swifter restitution of the Church's real estate and 3.5 billion roubles for renovation. In his words, 'Orthodoxy has always had a special role in shaping our statehood, our culture, our morals'. His rival in the elections, Gennady Ziuganov, leader of the Communist Party, was not to be outdone: 'The army and the Orthodox faith are the two essential pillars that haters of the Russian people and of Russia will strive to cut down after the liquidation

---

[96] Geoffrey Hosking, *Rulers and Victims: the Russians in the Soviet Union* (Cambridge MA, 2006).

[97] Benjamin Forest and Juliet Johnson, 'Unraveling the Threads of History: Soviet-Era Monuments and Post-Soviet National Identity in Moscow', *Annals of the Association of American Geographers*, 92:3 (2002), 524-47.

of Soviet achievements, since their aim is to destroy our spirituality and our traditions'.[98] As this suggests, the alliance between state and Church became increasingly the axis around which a hegemonic version of national identity was constructed, with political elites enhancing their public standing through support for Orthodoxy, and the Church gaining economic and political benefits from what it calls the 'simfoniia' between church and state.[99] The most recent poll by the Levada Centre, an independent polling organization, suggests that the percentage of Russians who consider themselves Orthodox has risen from 44 per cent in 1996 to 69 per cent in 2011; yet only 1 per cent of these are active members of parishes.[100]

Against this background, it is not surprising that by far the most dramatic expression of the drive to revive Russia's cultural heritage has been in respect of restoring and rebuilding her churches. In 1991, the Orthodox Church had 12,000 parishes, 117 monasteries and convents, 2 theological academies, 7 theological seminaries, 16 theological colleges and 4 schools. By 2011, it had 30,675 parishes, 29,324 priests, 3,850 deacons and 805 monasteries and convents.[101] In December 2010, Patriarch Kirill announced that 23,000 churches had been restored since 1991. By far the most significant was the rebuilding of the Cathedral of Christ the Saviour in Moscow, which had been blown up in December 1931 to make way for the Palace of Soviets. The latter had never been built, owing to war, lack of funds, and flooding from the Moscow River. Central to its rebuilding was Yury Luzhkov, the canny mayor of Moscow from 1992 to 2010, whose aim was to transform 'socialist Moscow into a civilized world capital' by 1997, the date of the city's 850th anniversary.[102] The Cathedral was completed on time, although not to budget (the estimated cost is more than US$400 million). The reappearance on the north bank of the Moscow river of what had been the largest architectural project of the nineteenth century served to reconnect post-Communist Russia to the tsarist past. Concomitantly, it represented a triumphant negation of Stalin's will and

---

[98] *Wall Street Journal* (18 December 2007); *Interfax-Religion* (10 April 2012).

[99] Zoe Knox, *Russian Society and the Orthodox Church: Religion in Russia after Communism* (London, 2005).

[100] http://www.globalpost.com/dispatch/russia/100209/russian-orthodox-church [accessed 11 April 2012]; *Interfax-Religion* (8 September 2011).

[101] *Interfax-Religion* (11 January 2012); *Interfax-Religion* (31 October 2011).

[102] Katherine Eady, 'The Reconstruction of the Cathedral of Christ the Saviour: Public Space and National Identity in Post-Soviet Moscow', *University of Toronto Art Journal*, 2 (2009), 11, http://jps.library.utoronto.ca/index.php/UTAJ/article/view/6659.

thereby implied that the Soviet era was an aberration in Russia's history.[103] When in 2000 the Cathedral became the stage for the canonization of Nicholas II and the imperial family, it attested, in the words of Metropolitan Mefody of Voronezh, to the 'return of our fatherland to that historical path of development which was halted by the bloody madness of "militant materialism" '.[104] In fact, the symbolism of the Cathedral is multi-layered. Originally built as a memorial to the war against Napoleon, it continues to commemorate those who lost their lives in both the first and second 'patriotic' wars (the second being against Nazi Germany). For Luzhkov, the successful completion of the Cathedral served to link him to a rendition of national identity that played on the idea of Moscow as the beating heart of a religiously defined imperial nation.

How the financing of church rebuilding has been achieved remains rather murky. The Church claims that it has been funded largely by the faithful, but that seems implausible, given the destitution into which millions—especially the elderly—sank during the wild privatization and deregulation of the 1990s. To a substantial degree, banks, firms, and wealthy donors contributed to the project, since donations were tax deductible.[105] Contributions had the additional benefit of helping burnish the public image of business people, since the names of contributors who donated more than 1 per cent of the overall cost of the Cathedral of Christ the Saviour were inscribed on a golden plaque.[106] The federal government also contributed to the rebuilding programme not only by providing tax breaks, but by awarding the Church in the first half of the 1990s the right to import cigarettes free of duty as well as a lucrative stake in a partnership responsible for exporting oil.[107] The Church no longer enjoys these concessions—indeed it denies that it ever benefited from them—but in the meantime it has acquired substantial property holdings and commercial operations of its own, including a number of banks, all of which are tax exempt.

---

[103] Dmitri Sidorov, 'National Monumentalization and the Politics of Scale: The Resurrections of the Cathedral of Christ the Savior in Moscow', *Annals of the Association of American Geographers*, 90:3 (2000), 548-72.

[104] Wendy Slater, *The Many Deaths of Tsar Nicholas II: Relics, Remains and the Romanovs* (London, 2007), 107.

[105] Nikolai Mitrokhin, 'Ekonomika Russkoi Pravoslavnoi Tserkvi', strana-oz.ru ⟩ ?numid=1&article=104

[106] Kathleen E. Smith, *Mythmaking in the New Russia: Politics and Memory during the Yeltsin Era* (Ithaca NY: Cornell University Press, 2002), 122-3.

[107] Nathaniel Davis, 'Tribulations, Trials and Troubles for the Russian Orthodox Church', *Religion and Eastern Europe*, 20:6 (2000), 39-50.

An innovative dimension of church restoration, indeed one that genuinely relied on the donations and the voluntary labour of the faithful, has been the effort by the Village Church charity to restore abandoned or dilapidated churches in the countryside. Many rural parishes have miserably low revenues, around two-thirds of which come from the sale of candles, so the cost of undertaking something like a roof repair is prohibitive. Village Church works with volunteers, such as the carpenter Yury Chekalov, who helped restore the church in the village of Romanovo near Tver' where his great-grandfather had been parish priest until he was hauled off in Stalin's purges.[108] The project has the support of the Russian Culture Fund, the largest NGO in Russia, whose president, Nikita Mikhalkov, the Oscar-winning film director, has said of it:

> The spiritual and moral core of Russia always has been, still is, and will always be Holy Orthodoxy, the symbol and figure of which remains the village church. Lost in the vast expanses of the Russian countryside, it is vivid, alluring, and always giving consolation to the faithful.[109]

The issue of who owns religious property confiscated during the Soviet era has generated friction between the Church and heritage organizations. Already in the early 1990s, a storm blew up in Yaroslavl over the Church of Elijah the Prophet, when preservationists demanded that the Church 'not be permitted to assert a new ideological monopoly over the meaning of Russia for Russians'.[110] During the 1990s, tens of thousands of buildings were returned to the Church, but in only about 100 cases did it receive full legal title to the buildings. However, in 2006 President Putin announced that a law would be passed to allow the church to regain all buildings, land, and treasures it had owned prior to the October Revolution, a move that caused consternation among preservationists. In February 2010, 150 museum directors appealed to President Medvedev not to sign a new law that allowed federal, regional, and municipal authorities two years in which to hand over property to the Church for rent-free use or into full ownership. They argued that the Church does not have the financial means or expertise to maintain more than 12,000 works of art, and cited in evidence the alleged deterioration of the iconostasis in the Troitse-Sergeev monastery in what used to be called

---

[108] www.village-church.ru/HIST.HTM [accessed 9 April 2012].

[109] www.village-church.ru/HIST.HTM [accessed 9 April 2012].

[110] Blair A. Ruble, 'Architecture, Urban Space, and Post-Soviet Russian Identity', in James Cracraft and Daniel Rowland (eds), *Architectures of Russian Identity, 1500 to the Present* (Ithaca, 2003), 209.

Zagorsk. The museum directors, of course, are not disinterested parties, since they stand to see the depletion of their collections and a loss of revenue as buildings and treasures are taken out of their hands.[111] In November 2010, this law was ratified, although the government has promised to indemnify museums against losses. It remains to be seen what the outcome will be.[112]

The overall record in post-Communist Russia with regard to the preservation of the architectural heritage is, to say the least, mixed. It has suited the federal government to be seen to be active in preserving Russia's artistic and historical sites and to work with UNESCO. Currently, there are twenty-four World Heritage Sites in the country, fifteen of which are cultural and nine natural. They include the Troitse-Sergeev monastery, the church of the Ascension at Kolomenskoe, the Ferapontov monastery in Vologda, the Novodevichii convent in Moscow, the historic centres of Yaroslavl and Novgorod, Kizhi, Solovki, Vladimir and Suzdal'. At the same time, there has been massive investment in urban development on the part of municipal, regional, and federal government and the private sector, driven by a desire to realize the commercial potential of valuable real estate. All too often, regional and local governments have been happy to do deals with aggressive developers and investors. In Moscow Yury Luzhkov kept a strict eye on this, yet he connived in the demolition and reconstruction of historic buildings rather than in their restoration, since this was a much cheaper option.[113] According to the Moscow Architectural Preservation Society, in the five years up to 2007 at least 200 listed buildings disappeared from the city.[114] In other cities, too, listed buildings have proved easy prey to the wrecking ball. In the words of Minister of Culture Alexander Sokolov, there has been a 'bacchanalia of uncoordinated construction' since 1991. Public support for preserving heritage remains strong, and there have been a few victories, such as the relocation of the Gazprom tower to the outskirts of St Petersburg. Nevertheless, in general, preservationists have proved no match for developers. Capitalism thus poses as many threats to the built heritage of Russia's cities as did state socialism.

At the start of the reform era in China, one of the first pieces of legislation passed by the government of Deng Xiaoping in 1982 was a law on the protection of cultural relics:

[111] *RIA Novosti*, 24/05/2010 http://en.rian.ru/russia/20100524/159132306.html.

[112] http://www.themoscowtimes.com/opinion/article/giving-the-church-what-belongs-to-the-people/405651.html#ixzz1rkGxXklw

[113] http://en.wikipedia.org/wiki/Russian_cultural_heritage_register#cite_ref-64

[114] Andreas Schönle, 'Introduction', *Slavic Review*, 71:4 (2012), 740.

to strengthen state protection of cultural relics, to contribute to the development of scientific research, to maintain the splendid historical and cultural legacy of our nation, to conduct education in patriotism and in the revolutionary tradition, and to build a socialist society with an advanced culture and ideology.[115]

The State Administration of Cultural Relics (*guojia wenwu ju*), re-established in 1973 and placed under the Ministry of Culture, was tasked with responsibility for ensuring that cultural bureaux at provincial, county, and municipal level carried out these duties.[116] In the same year, the Committee for the Study of the History of Architecture persuaded the government to publish a list of 'towns of historical and cultural value . . . particularly rich from the point of view of our patrimony . . . that have historic value and a very important revolutionary significance' and are endowed with 'stylistic physiognomy' (*fengmao*).[117] By 2005, the list of protected sites had grown to 1,271 national sites, around 7,000 provincial-level sites, and about 60,000 local sites.[118]

In 1980, in an astonishing reversal of government policy, the State Council issued a circular requiring that all religious property confiscated since 1949—that is, not only property confiscated during the Cultural Revolution—be returned to the appropriate religious associations, and that they be paid compensation for their losses. This was a gesture on a par with the Russian government's concessions to the Orthodox Church, but it was not as sweeping as it appears, since worshippers were required to prove that they had need of a place of worship and had reputable leaders to manage it.[119] Nevertheless it was the spur to a huge wave of temple rebuilding and renovation. By 1994, the government was so concerned that it tried to put a brake on this by requiring all religious associations to register with the authorities. Temples now had to apply for a licence to operate for public use and the licence was made conditional on the size and history of the congregation, the number of worshippers, and the leadership and management of the association.[120] Some

[115] http://www.china.org.cn/english/environment/34304.htm

[116] Fresnais, *La protection*, 206.

[117] Zhang Liang, *La naissance*, 157-8.

[118] Marina Svensson, *In the Ancestors' Shadow: Cultural Heritage Contestations in Chinese Villages* (Lund, 2006), *www.ace.lu.se/images/Syd. . ./M_Svensson.pdf.*

[119] Mayfair Mei-hui Yang, 'Spatial Struggles: Postcolonial Complex, State Disenchantment, and Popular Reappropriation of Space in Rural Southeast China', *Journal of Asian Studies*, 63:3 (2004), 719-55.

[120] Hong Qu, Religious Policy in the People's Republic of China: An Alternative Perspective, *Journal of Contemporary China* 20:70 (2011), 437.

bodies, notably Christian house churches, refused to register; but the number of registered religious sites rose from 85,000 to about 110,000 by the early 2000s.[121] This, however, should not be read as evidence that central government has imposed control of religious sites at the grass roots. The political dynamics involved in temple building are complex, involving not only local communities and township and municipal governments but also higher-level cadres in united front and religious bureaux, cultural relics bureaux and, not least, commercial tourist companies.

During the 1980s and 1990s, the rebuilding of temples and ancestral halls in rural areas provided an arena in which villagers could express their religious devotion and honour their ancestors. Elderly and uneducated women spearheaded the revival of temples, while older men with some education, such as teachers and officials, took the lead in refounding ancestral halls, mostly in single-surname villages and in south-east China. The rebuilding of village temples and ancestral halls was largely funded by small donations and carried out by the voluntary labour of community members, although in some regions, such as Fujian in south-east China, overseas Chinese also made significant contributions.[122] As central government withdrew from ensuring guaranteed jobs, housing and medical care, the temple became for many a focus of moral order in an increasingly anomic world. Participation in temple life also offered social contact at a time when many villages were haemorrhaging young people.[123] Villagers not only rebuilt temples, they revived and invented rituals that expressed local identity, actively weaving legends and organizing colourful festivals in honour of the local gods. In Jinhua municipality in Zhejiang, the Daoist god, Huang Daxian, hardly known before 1990, became a new focus of veneration after local people discovered that he was one of the most popular gods in Hong Kong: at least nine new temples and one major shrine were built in the provinces of Zhejiang and Guangdong in an attempt to attract pilgrims from Hong Kong.[124] These temples were established at the behest of local officials, but villagers spontaneously

---

[121] Hong Qu, 'Religious Policy', 437.

[122] Svensson, *In the Ancestors' Shadow.*

[123] John M. Flower, 'A Road Is Made: Roads, Temples, and Historical Memory in Ya'an County, Sichuan', *Journal of Asian Studies,* 63:3 (2004), 649-85; Xiuhua Wang, 'The Collapse of Social Capital and Religious Revival in Rural China', *Interdisciplinary Journal of Research on Religion,* vol. 9 (2013), Article 4.

[124] Graeme Lang, Selina Ching Chang and Lars Ragvald, 'Folk Temples and the Chinese Religious Economy', *Interdisciplinary Journal of Research on Religion,* 1 (2005), article 4, 8.

resurrected a long-forgotten version of the cult that centred not only on Huang but also on his brother. They discovered a holy well used by Huang and advertised a local glutinous rice dish said to cure skin disease as well as a vegetable peculiar to the region, all said to have been brought to Zhejiang by the god himself.[125]

In taking the initiative to rebuild large temples, local officials have sometimes borrowed millions of yuan to do so. They hope that a large and attractive temple will attract tourists, especially from overseas, and thus bring in investment for regional development. In Changsha the municipality has renovated the area around the Kaifu temple as a means to 'improve the quality of urban services and the environment, increase the level of culture, and promote the development of local commerce and religious tourism'.[126] This desire to attract pilgrim-tourists from overseas is paramount in the case of major Buddhist temples, and officials have successfully solicited donations from Buddhist Associations in Japan, Taiwan, and South East Asia. In the case of the restoration of the temples on Mount Wutai contributions came from donors in Thailand.[127] In some cases, officials have even persuaded foreign investors to fund public works projects, thus easing straitened local budgets. Nevertheless, the calculation that temple building will boost the local economy had not always paid off: some township and municipal governments have found themselves burdened with heavy debts where temples have failed to attract visitors. The motivations of local officials are not only mercenary, however. Some support temple building out of religious devotion, while probably more do so in the expectation that this will strengthen their legitimacy in the eyes of the local populace.[128] In northern Shaanxi, for example, temple building has created what Adam Yuet Chau calls a 'temple-village political nexus', in which temples gain political acceptance by involving local officials in their dedication ceremonies, while officials gain face by showing support for popular religion.[129]

Between 1985 and 1996, China's annual domestic tourist arrivals increased from 240 million to 640 million, and this has risen exponentially since

---

[125] Selina Ching Chan and Graeme S. Lang, 'Temple Construction and the Revival of Popular Religion in Jinhua', *China Information*, 21:1 (2007), 49.

[126] Zhe Ji, 'La nouvelle relation Etat-bouddhisme', *Perspectives chinoises*, 84, (2004), 9.

[127] Goosseart, *Dans les temples*, 112.

[128] Gareth Fisher, 'The Spiritual Land Rush: Merit and Morality in New Chinese Buddhist Temple Construction', *Journal of Asian Studies*, 67:1 (2008), 143-70.

[129] Adam Yuet Chau, *Miraculous Response: Doing Popular Religion in Contemporary China* (Stanford, 2006), 198.

then.[130] In seeking to exploit religious sites commercially, local officials often depend on the expertise of tourist companies to landscape sites, provide amenities, advertise them and, not least, to transport visitors to the site. Tourist companies, however, often show little regard for the needs of local residents and this can lead to clashes over compensation, ownership, and land use.[131] In relation to religious sites specifically, conflicts arise when worshippers are charged fees to enter temples, when priests are reduced to being bit players in a theme park, or when believers are deprived of any say in temple management. The religious affairs bureau, often located at a higher level than the municipality, often looks with disfavour on such touristification, insisting that religious sites are intended for religious activities. Sometimes they condemn as 'superstitious' some of the activities that go on in temples, such as healing via spirit mediums, exorcism, fortune telling or animal sacrifice, activities to which local officials may turn a blind eye if they bring in tourist income or increase their own legitimacy in the eyes of local people.[132] If pressured by religious affairs bureaux, local officials may justify such activities as 'popular beliefs' (*minjian xinyang*), that is, as cultural expressions of local identity, rather than as 'feudal superstition'.[133]

Officials in the cultural relics bureaux may also look askance at much of what is packaged as heritage for tourists.[134] In Qufu the 'dead dogs' once vilified by the Red Guards have long since been reburied in the Confucius cemetery, but the site now features Confucian Temple gourmet tours, a daily *son-et-lumière* entitled 'Confucius's Dream', and Confucius Study Tours designed to promote respect for parents and teachers and appropriate etiquette in relationships.[135] Cultural officials, increasingly influenced by notions of authenticity propagated by UNESCO, find themselves drawn into adjudicating what may or may not be considered 'authentic' heritage.[136] In Quanzhou, for instance, the cultural bureau looks down on the lively festivals staged for

---

[130] Tim Oakes and Donald Sutton, 'Introduction', in Tim Oakes and Donald Sutton (eds), *Faiths on Display: Religious Revival and Tourism in China* (Lanham, 2010), 12.

[131] Svensson, *In the Ancestors' Shadow*.

[132] Lang, Chang, and Ragvald, 'Folk Temples', 25.

[133] Oakes and Sutton, 'Introduction', 16.

[134] Svensson, *In the Ancestors' Shadow*.

[135] Ma Aiping, Si Lina, and Zhang Hongfei, 'The Evolution of Cultural Tourism: The Example of Qufu, the Birthplace of Confucius', in Chris Ryan and Gu Huimin (eds), *Tourism in China: Destination, Cultures and Communities* (London, 2009), 190.

[136] Robert Shepherd, 'Cultural Heritage, UNESCO, and the Chinese State: Whose Heritage and for Whom?', *Heritage Management*, 2:1 (2009), 72.

the gods by small neighbourhood temples (*pujing*) because these are patent recent inventions. Instead it promotes more ancient forms of culture such as Nanyin ('southern sound') music, but this is not entirely to the liking of locals or tourists.[137] At the same time preservationists may be drawn into the invention or reinvention of traditional forms. In rural Hebei a local cult known as the Dragon Tablet Association could not have emerged without the active support of the Chinese Folklore Association.[138] In so acting, the cultural bureaux are in effect *making* folk culture through sponsoring certain cultural practices and rejecting others. At the same time, UNESCO's idea of 'intangible cultural heritage' allows cultural bureaux to drop the pejorative notion of 'feudal superstition'—although this is still a staple of official ideology— and permit the recrudescence of cultural practices once condemned as backward and unworthy of modern China.[139]

In China today, then, a Communist government continues to insist that religious belief is incompatible in the long run with a modern socialist society, yet it presides over a country in which a gamut of religious practice flourishes in ways that are beyond the control of Beijing. However, this situation is not as paradoxical as it may seem, since despite their different interests the various agencies of the state—in contrast to the mass of believers—are unified in a belief that religious practice is best dealt with by discursively transforming it into an aspect of national heritage.[140] Just as the Russian government has endorsed a national idea rooted in a notion of Holy Russia, so the Chinese government now attaches its colours to the mast of cultural nationalism, from which any reference to class exploitation or the despotism of Confucianism has been expunged. It hopes that religion, preferably in its 'higher' forms, can be mobilized to create more solidarity in society as China negotiates the choppy waters of capitalist modernization. From this perspective, the preservation and display of heritage boosts economic modernization, serves as a form of cultural diplomacy, particularly vis-à-vis overseas Chinese, and, above all, serves to foster pride in China's ancient heritage and to promote

[137] Wang Mingming, ' "Great Tradition" and its Enemy', *Southern Fujian: Reproduction of Traditions in Post-Mao China.*

[138] Gao Bingzhong, 'Zhishifenzi, minjian, yu yige simiao bowuguan de dansheng', *Minjian wenhua taolun* (2004), 13–18.

[139] Gloria Davies, Geremie R. Barmé, and Timothy Cheek, 'Chinese Visions: A Provocation', http://www.chinaheritagenewsletter.org/scholarship.php?search-term=016_provocation.inc&issue=016

[140] Rubie Watson, 'Afterword' in Tim Oakes and Donald Sutton (eds), *Faiths on Display: Religious Revival and Tourism in China* (Lanham, 2010), 266.

national values approved of by the state. Moreover, in a new twist to the Confucian ideal of ruling through culture, the government hopes that by exposing its citizens to the civilizing effects of China's heritage it will improve their quality (*suzhi*) and advance the creation of a harmonious and prosperous society.[141] Though formally still deprecated, then, religion can be enlisted to serve these goals: gods can—to an extent, at least—be reconfigured as embodiments of a national patrimony, rather than as expressions of particularistic identities, and temples can become sites of patriotic education.[142] As we have indicated, religious practice on the ground remains far more conflictual than this official vision supposes, but it nevertheless represents an ideal to which the many different parties can sign up.

Conclusion

During the Communist era the debate over the value of the heritage of the past swerved between 'class' and 'national' poles, reflecting deeper uncertainty about the relationship of national identity to socialism. Even for the militant advocates of a class approach, this was seldom a matter of rejecting the cultural legacy of the past *in toto*, more one of appropriating it selectively and repackaging it in ideologically acceptable forms. Yet Communist leaders such as Stalin and Liu Shaoqi quickly perceived that a stridently class-based appropriation of cultural heritage closed off elements of potential value to the regime that fostered identifications with the state as representative of the people's history, elements that could be mined for purposes of building a national socialism.

If there are strong similarities between the Russian and Chinese cases in the Communist era, there were always important differences in government policy towards the inherited culture of the past. First, if the role of the state in dictating the terms of heritage discourse and practice was overwhelming in both countries, a preservationist ethic was more deeply embedded in Russia than in China, one which had considerable public support, especially in the post-Stalin era. In the PRC there was nothing similar to the civic movement that campaigned to preserve the monuments of Russia's past prior to the twenty-first century.[143] Second, the place of religious buildings in the public

---

[141] Tim Oakes, 'Heritage as Improvement: Cultural Display and Contested Governance in Rural China', *Modern China*, online publication 12 July 2012.

[142] Oakes and Sutton, 'Introduction', 15.

[143] Concern with cultural heritage in China has grown hugely in the past decade, and serves as yet another illustration of the maxim that the impulse to preserve appears precisely when the heritage of the past seems fated to vanish. For one example, see the Old Beijing website, http://www.oldbeijing.net (in Chinese).

understanding of heritage was not equivalent in the two countries. Churches, particularly the great monastic churches, were central to the heritage of Russia in a way that temples were not in China. True, there were the much-venerated temple complexes associated with China's sacred mountains, as well as temples of national importance in Beijing or Nanjing, but in China it was archaeological sites, the textual heritage, and visual arts such as calligraphy that carried greater symbolic weight in the national imaginary than the built heritage. Third, the modes of attack on places of worship differed somewhat in the two societies. Even during what Sheila Fitzpatrick called the Soviet 'cultural revolution' of 1928-32, there was nothing akin to the splenetic attack on the 'four olds', evinced in the destruction of art collections or the pulping of historic books. The decision to close or demolish a Russian church was a bureaucratic decision, usually initiated by a local soviet and subject to ratification by the centre. By contrast, the destruction of a local temple in China was often decided by local officials without any consultation with higher authority, and during the Cultural Revolution hot-headed Red Guards carried out the destruction of temples very much in a movement 'from below'. Fourth, oscillations in heritage policy were much more extreme in China than in Russia, ranging from the government actually building temples in the 1950s (something inconceivable in the Soviet Union) to their acquiescing in their outright vandalization in the late 1960s.

In the era since state socialism, the national construal of cultural heritage has triumphed unequivocally over the class construal in both societies. With respect to religious sites, there has been a dramatic reversal of symbolic polarities, in which places of worship once vilified as symbols of class oppression and superstition have been reconfigured as symbols of cultural continuity and national particularity. In Russia a regime that once viewed religion with fierce animosity has been replaced by one that opportunistically seeks to exploit the symbolic capital of Orthodoxy for purposes of political legitimation. And the rebuilding of churches has been crucial to the construction of an ethnically based, still somewhat imperial form of national identity, rooted in ideas of Holy Russia and the 'simfoniia' between Church and state. In China temples, always less central to the cultural patrimony, have been less central to the reconfiguration of notions of Han identity but are nevertheless lauded as monuments that testify to the richness of China's indigenous culture and to its capacity to absorb and transform transnational religious traditions of Buddhism, Islam, and Christianity. The regime, though still defining itself as Communist, seeks legitimacy through bringing economic prosperity to its citizens and by playing on a nationalism that is essentially cultural (though more chauvinistic renditions of national identity compete within it in the wider society). The official discourse of cultural heritage serves to connect pride in China's civilization with loyalty to the CCP as the protector of that heritage. And as in Russia, the discursive connection to *world* cultural heritage allows the Chinese government to 'enter into the world' at the same time as it presents itself as the defender of the nation.[144]

[144] Kirk A. Denton, 'Museum, Memorial Sites, and Exhibitionary Culture in the People's Republic of China', *China Quarterly*, 183 (2005), 570.

Tropical Nature as Global *Patrimoine*: Imperialism and International Nature Protection in the Early Twentieth Century

Corey Ross

In the late nineteenth and early twentieth centuries, the swelling appetite for heritage increasingly expanded beyond the realm of human artefact to regard the land, its flora and fauna as important legacies in need of preservation. In industrializing Europe and North America, the relentless rationalization of the countryside nourished a growing sense of the need to safeguard historic landscapes, 'wildernesses', and endangered species, whether as natural resources or as treasures of unusual beauty. The fact that these shifting sensibilities coincided with the largest land-grab in human history meant that encounters with the colonial landscapes of Europe's burgeoning empires were bound to impinge on ideas about nature and its preservation more broadly. In recent years scholars have explored various facets of this relationship, from the colonial roots of environmental thought to the misapprehensions engendered by European land management models in unfamiliar tropical environments.[1] We have also acquired a better appreciation of how the spread of conservationist ideas and practices involved complex exchanges between metropoles and colonies, as well as between and across colonial boundaries themselves.[2] If the 'scramble' for overseas territory was

---

[1] Richard H. Grove, *Green Imperialism: Colonial Expansion, Tropical Island Edens and the Origins of Environmentalism, 1600-1860* (Cambridge, 1995); Richard H. Grove, *Ecology, Climate and Empire: Colonialism and Global Environmental History* (Cambridge, 1997); William Beinart and Joann McGregor (eds), *Social History and African Environments* (Oxford, 2003); David Arnold and Ramachandra Guha (eds), *Nature, Culture, Imperialism: Essays on the Environmental History of South Asia* (Delhi, 1995).

[2] Generally, Roy MacLeod (ed.), *Nature and Empire: Science and the Colonial Enterprise, Osiris* vol. 15 (2000); David Anderson and Richard H. Grove (eds), *Conservation in Africa: People, Policies and Practice* (Cambridge, 1987); Helen Tilley, *Africa as a Living Laboratory: Empire, Development, and the Problem of Scientific Knowledge, 1870-1950* (Chicago, 2011); Donal P. McCracken, 'Fraternity in the Age of Jingoism: The British Imperial Botanic and Forestry Network', in Benedikt Stuchtey (ed.), *Science across the European Empires, 1800-1950* (Oxford, 2005), 49-62; John M. MacKenzie (ed.), *Imperialism and the Natural World* (Manchester, 1990). On parks specifically: Bernhard

driven by intense national rivalries, imperialism was also a powerful globalizing force that furnished new spaces for cross-border interaction.

By the turn of the twentieth century nature conservation was one of the key realms of such trans-imperial and international coordination. These preservationist efforts were driven by a variety of ideas and objectives, ranging from a utilitarian interest in resource conservation to a more ethically oriented desire to preserve colonial 'nature' for its own sake. Though often regarded as rival agendas, what bound them together was the increasingly prevalent conceptualization of tropical wilderness as a global heritage to be held in trust for all humankind. This article briefly explores how this concept crystallized in the early twentieth century out of the interplay between long-standing ideas about nature and history, the emergence of international nature advocacy, shifting scientific perspectives, and the structures of colonial domination to furnish a potent legitimating rationale for worldwide conservationist intervention—one that powerfully moulded nature preservation for the remainder of the century.

Nature preservation in industrial Europe: ideas and organization

The idea of protecting a 'natural heritage' from the threat of ruin has a remarkably complex genealogy. At one level it is a universal notion: the protection of revered sites and other expressions of 'sacred ecology' are common to most rural cultures and have functioned for millennia to set limits on the human transformation of nature.[3] Yet even within modern Europe, its lineage is messy. While certain elements are rooted in elite enthusiasm for hunting and natural history, others arose more recently out of humanitarian concerns for animal welfare. And while cameralist traditions of rational, state-centred forest management informed many preservation efforts, some of the earliest cases of landscape preservation (Drachenfels am Rhein, Forêt de Fontainebleau) grew from Romantic notions about the spiritual need for unspoiled landscape. From the middle of the nineteenth century, this potpourri of concerns gave rise to an equally diverse sct of civic movements: some rooted in the discovery of the countryside for recreational purposes, others concerned with protecting endangered species, still others with guarding the aesthetic landscape from advertising and other excrescences of modern life. Common to most, however, was a determination to preserve

---

Gissibl, Sabine Höhler, and Patrick Kupper (eds), *Civilizing Nature: National Parks in Global Historical Perspective* (New York, 2012).

[3] Fikret Berkes, *Sacred Ecology*, 2nd edn (London, 2008).

cherished landscapes and their rustic denizens against the advance of industrial modernity.[4]

As scholars have long recognized, these budding concerns about landscape and 'nature' formed a central plank in nineteenth-century programmes of cultural nationalism. Rooted in Romanticism, the idea of a close association between a people and its indigenous nature was commonly evoked to generate a sense of connection to the biophysical homeland. Nature, for many contemporaries, furnished not only a crucial foundation of identity but also a source of moral strength. For societies increasingly living in dirty cities and subjected to the dehumanizing rhythms of industrial work, an idealized countryside—whether the pastoral landscapes of Merrie England or the primeval German *Urwald*—represented a fount of physical and spiritual renewal. At the same time, the notion of 'wilderness' was subtly evolving from an object of conquest to one of veneration, a repository of untrammelled authenticity in which the individual could escape the pressures of social conformity and where an elemental virility could still assert itself against the effeminizing constraints of industrial society. As a complementary mirror of civilization, wilderness represented a sublime heritage that anchored the nation in time and space.[5]

By the late nineteenth century, nature protection associations had been established in nearly all industrialized countries. Though often steeped in nationalist rhetoric, they were well aware of developments elsewhere. Shortly after the turn of the century many became more conscious of the international dimension of the preservation cause. The work of Hugo Conwentz, a senior forester in Berlin, was an important catalyst. As commissioner of the Prussian *Staatliche Stelle für Naturdenkmalpflege*—established in 1906 as the world's first state-supported office for nature protection—he travelled widely throughout Europe to promote his concept of the *Naturdenkmal*, or natural

---

[4] A good recent overview is Charles-François Mathis, 'Mobiliser pour l'environnement en Europe et aux États-Unis. Un état des lieux à l'aube du 20ᵉ siècle', *Vingtième Siècle. Revue d'Histoire*, 113 (Jan-Mar. 2012), 15-27. For national studies: David Evans, *A History of Nature Conservation in Britain*, 2nd edn (London, 1997); Friedemann Schmoll, *Erinnerung an die Natur. Die Geschichte des Naturschutzes im deutschen Kaiserreich* (Frankfurt a. Main, 2004); A. Cadoret (ed.), *Protection de la Nature: Histoire et Idéologie* (Paris, 1985); Henny J. van der Windt, 'Biologists Bridging Science and the Conservation Movement: The Rise of Nature Conservation and Nature Management in the Netherlands, 1850-1950', *Environment and History*, 18:2 (May 2012), 209-36.

[5] See generally Max Oelschlaeger, *The Idea of Wilderness. From Prehistory to the Age of Ecology* (New Haven, 1991). On nature and nation, see esp. Thomas M. Lekan, *Imagining the Nation in Nature: Landscape Preservation and German Identity, 1885-1945* (Cambridge MA, 2004).

monument. As explained in his 1904 book that first gained him international notoriety, the idea was based on the simple observation that a 'monument' as a vehicle of commemoration could apply to nature as readily as to anthropogenic artefacts, and that natural monuments should therefore 'be given the same care and attention as has long been successfully expended upon the memorials of earlier art'.[6] The concept clearly struck a chord, and gave a new impulse to nature protection groups across much of Europe.[7]

For all their differences, the common purpose of these organizations was to identify natural monuments and ensure that they were safeguarded. In deciding what to preserve and how, most followed the broad guidelines set out by Conwentz, who defined a natural monument as 'an original—that is, entirely or almost entirely untouched by cultural influences—and characteristic feature of the landscape or an original and characteristic natural living condition of extraordinary, general, patriotic, scientific, or aesthetic interest'.[8] It was a fuzzy concept open to all manner of interpretation. But two aspects of this 'conwentzional nature protection' (as critics called it)[9] are worth highlighting. First, the terminology of a monument focused attention on individual areas or objects of natural history rather than larger biophysical systems or communities. This was symptomatic of the concern of early nature protection—quite unlike environmentalism in the late twentieth century— with symbols of nature rather than matters such as pollution or health. Second, and more fundamentally, nature was associated with the 'untouched' and 'pristine'; it resided only where people did not.

This created a problem for conservationists inasmuch as there was little 'untouched nature' left to salvage in Europe. As Conwentz himself explained, his broad definition of a natural monument derived from the recognition that

---

[6] Hugo Conwentz, *Die Gefährdung der Naturdenkmäler und Vorschläge zu ihrer Erhaltung* (Berlin, 1904), 206.

[7] Conwentz was particularly influential in Britain, where his 1907 lecture to the British Association for the Advancement of Science formed the basis of his widely cited book *The Care of Natural Monuments with special reference to Great Britain and Germany* (Cambridge, 1909). Among the principal nature organizations of the period were the Société pour la Protection des Paysages de France (1901), Bund Heimatschutz (1904, of which Conwentz was a founder member), Vereeniging tot Behoud van Natuurmonumenten (1904), Ligue Suisse pour la Protection de la Nature (1909), British Society for the Promotion of Nature Reserves (1912).

[8] Conwentz, *Gefährdung*, 186.

[9] For critics: Friedemann Schmoll, 'Schönheit, Vielfalt, Eigenart. Die Formierung des Naturschutzes um 1900, seine Leitbilder und ihre Geschichte', in Hans-Werner Frohn and Friedemann Schmoll (eds), *Natur und Staat. Staatlicher Naturschutz in Deutschland 1906-2006* (Bonn, 2006), 13-84, here 59-60.

'completely untouched landscapes, here as in other civilized countries (*Kulturstaaten*), hardly survive any longer'.[10] For most nature advocates, as for other heritage enthusiasts, the prime culprits of this despoliation were obvious: modern industry, economy, and finance, the same forces that were responsible for all the other unwanted side-effects of modernity (alienation, artificiality, the destruction of tradition, etc.). But if the basic problem was the 'advance of civilization' itself, then the aim for the future was to ensure that the same mistakes were not repeated as 'civilization' spread. One could still take solace in the thought of vast stretches of wilderness in other parts of the world, especially in the recently colonized tropics. These exotic lands represented an opportunity to experience a pristine nature long since disappeared from the domesticated and defaced landscapes of Europe. But first of all they required protection. The spread of European sovereignty into the tropics provided nature conservation with an enormous field of action.

Tropical nature as imperial trust

The idealized image of tropical Edens that underpinned these preservationist concerns was by no means new around the turn of the century. Anxieties about the destruction of island paradises stretched back centuries, and travelogues of explorers had long conjured primeval wildernesses brimming with exotic creatures and sparsely populated by primitive tribes.[11] Nonetheless, a number of developments around the turn of the century intensified these perceptions. For one thing, the 'new imperialism' coincided very closely with the rapid expansion of communications and commercial entertainments—mass-circulation papers, cinema, urban leisure industries—that helped to assemble and popularize these stereotypes. Moreover, this was also the heyday of 'social evolutionism' during which it was taken for granted that the technical mastery of nature was what separated the civilized from the primitive and legitimated European rule over those more subservient to nature.[12] In this respect, the 'untamed wilds' of the tropics represented both a foil to a domesticated Europe as well as a reflection of its own past. The use of terms such as 'Eden', 'original' or 'authentic' reflected the current evolutionist tendency to temporalize spatial differences.[13] The vocabulary is revealing: the 'primeval' forests in Sumatra or the 'aboriginal' herds in

---

[10] Conwentz, *Gefährdung*, 5-6.

[11] See generally Grove, *Green Imperialism*; Oelschlaeger, *Idea of Wilderness*.

[12] See Michael Adas, *Machines as the Measure of Men: Science, Technology, and Ideologies of Western Dominance* (Ithaca, 1989).

[13] See Johannes Fabian, *Time and the Other: How Anthropology Makes its Object* (New York, 1983).

East Africa were perceived not merely as different geographic environments but as throwbacks to an earlier stage of history before the advent of civilization. In this sense, tropical savannahs and jungles became landscapes frozen in time, relics of human heritage.

At the same time, the closing of the 'global frontier' under the impact of steam and telegraph made nature seem less vast and more vulnerable than ever before. Whereas human history since the dawn of time had been dominated by the struggle against nature, it was, as one contemporary put it, 'first since the close of the nineteenth century that civilized peoples are becoming fully aware not only that humanity requires protection against the forces of nature, but also, conversely, that nature requires protection from human activity'.[14] The recent spate of well-publicized extinctions or near-extinctions—from the South African quagga to the American bison—was already encouraging a more global perceptual framework of environmental decline.[15] With the massive overseas extension of European authority, the threat to tropical Edens posed by capitalist trade and technical progress generated a powerful urge to 'salvage what could still be salvaged' of the primeval purity that had already been extirpated in the industrial world.[16]

In addition, the formal extension of European sovereignty itself made a difference, for the direct stake in governing overseas territories furnished a clearer opportunity to pursue conservation through appeals to national pride or imperial obligation. As the self-proclaimed guardians of their tropical dependencies, governments could be called upon to protect wildernesses as a matter of imperial stewardship. In the realm of nature as in the realm of culture, imperialism and heritage preservation became mutually reinforcing enterprises.[17] While protecting a threatened inheritance against human exploitation served to legitimate imperial intervention, ensuring the adequate

[14] Max Haushofer, *Der Schutz der Natur* (Munich, 1906), 3.

[15] The strident warnings of William T. Hornaday were influential not just in the United States but also in Europe: *The Extermination of the American Bison* (Washington DC, 2002) (originally 1889); more generally, William T. Hornaday, *Our Vanishing Wildlife: Its Extermination and Preservation* (New York, 1913). On the decline of the bison generally, Andrew C. Isenberg, *The Destruction of the Bison: An Environmental History, 1750-1920* (Cambridge, 2000); on South Africa, William Beinart, *The Rise of Conservation in South Africa: Settlers, Livestock, and the Environment 1770-1950* (Oxford, 2003), here 196.

[16] Quote from F. B. v. Schellendorf, *Internationaler Wildschutz in Afrika* (Munich, 1900), 7.

[17] Astrid Swenson, 'The Heritage of Empire', in Astrid Swenson and Peter Mandler (eds), *From Plunder to Preservation: Britain and the Heritage of Empire, c.1800-1940* (Oxford, 2013), 3-28, esp. 8-14; also William H. Rollins, 'Imperial Shades of Green: Conservation and Environmental Chauvinism in the German Colonial Project', *German Studies Review*, 22 (1999), 187-213.

preservation of nature became a badge of imperial credibility, a measure of a nation's fitness to rule abroad.[18] Paradoxically, the threat posed by the 'advance of civilization' meant that nature protection became part of the civilizing mission.

The 1890s and 1900s thus witnessed a flurry of nature conservation efforts throughout the colonized tropics as scientists and hunter-naturalists grew increasingly alarmed over the fate of threatened plant and animal species. In Malaysia and the Dutch East Indies, the mounting disquiet prompted piecemeal measures to protect large mammals and colourful birds before crystallizing into legislation in 1909-11. A similar process took place in India, where regional measures were gradually combined into uniform legislation by 1912.[19] Yet it was undoubtedly in east and central Africa where the bulk of attention was focused, establishing a perceptual pattern that persisted for decades to come. This reflected not only the rich wildlife of the region but also the combined impact of commercial hunting and disease. Following an 'elephant scare' in the 1880s, a far-reaching Rinderpest epizootic in the early 1890s generated a profound sense of environmental crisis. German and British observers gave vivid accounts of collapsing herds of domestic cattle as well as wild ungulates such as buffalo, eland, and giraffe. Although game numbers rebounded significantly by the end of the 1890s, many onlookers nonetheless drew parallels to earlier bouts of wildlife destruction in the American West or southern Africa and concluded that only strict game laws would halt the slaughter. The first to sound the alarm were generally the big-game hunters themselves, 'penitent butchers' like Hermann von Wissmann, governor of German East Africa, or Harry H. Johnston, first commissioner of British Central Africa, who were determined to ensure a continued supply of game.[20] At their urging, colonial governments

---

[18] On heritage preservation as cultural 'yardstick' more generally, see Astrid Swenson, *The Rise of Heritage: Preserving the Past in France, Germany and England, 1789-1914* (Cambridge, 2013), 273-328.

[19] On Malaysia, Jeyamalar Kathirithamby-Wells, *Nature and Nation: Forests and Development in Peninsular Malaysia* (Honolulu, 2005), 195-200; on the Netherlands Indies, Peter Boomgaard, 'Oriental Nature, its Friends and its Enemies: Conservation of Nature in Late-Colonial Indonesia, 1889-1949', *Environment and History*, 5 (1999), 257-92, here 264-5; J. H. Westermann, 'Wild Life Conservation in the Netherlands Empire: Its National and International Aspects', in Pieter Honig and Frans Verdoorn (eds), *Science and Scientists in the Netherlands Indies* (New York, 1945), 417-24; on India, Mahesh Rangarajan, *India's Wildlife History* (Delhi, 2001), 46-58.

[20] On British territories, see John M. MacKenzie, *Empire of Nature: Hunting, Conservation and British Imperialism* (Manchester, 1988); on German East Africa see the superb study by Bernhard Gißibl, *The Nature of Colonialism: Hunting, Conservation and the Politics of*

introduced closed seasons and licensing from the early 1890s; in 1896 the German East African government established the first game reserves along the Rufiji river and west of Kilimanjaro. Together, these measures helped set African wildlife conservation on a course of indigenous hunting suppression that persisted throughout much of the twentieth century.

But given that neither ivory smugglers nor migrating animals showed much concern for colonial boundaries, it soon became apparent that some degree of trans-border coordination was necessary. By the time von Wissmann suggested an international agreement in 1897, he was pushing on an open door in London. His efforts, strongly backed by the British Foreign Office, eventually culminated in the 1900 London Convention for the Preservation of Wild Animals, Birds, and Fish in Africa. Widely recognized as the 'first ever "international" environmental conference', the 1900 Convention is a vivid illustration of 'imperial internationalism' around the turn of the century, an attempt to realize colonial aims via closer trans-imperial cooperation.[21] Involving all of Africa's major colonial powers, its basic aim was to establish a set of uniform game regulations including gradated lists of protected species, licensing, closed seasons, and common tariffs on traded animal carcasses. There is no need here to describe the convention in detail.[22] For our purposes, a handful of points deserve recognition. The agreement it reached was essentially a hunting treaty, based on a utilitarian desire for the sustainable management of game (especially the ivory trade) rather than the transference of an emergent metropolitan notion of 'nature protection' to the colonies.[23] Moreover, apprehension about the loss of ivory revenue (especially on the part of the French and Belgian governments) ultimately prevented the treaty's ratification by the signatories. The 1900 convention thus highlighted both the appeal and the limits of trans-imperial cooperation. Nonetheless, it marked an important milestone in the history of global nature preservation in several respects. First, it established a key point of reference for wildlife conservation until at least the early 1930s, as nearly every colonial government in Africa came to observe the agreements over

---

Wildlife in the German Colonial Empire (PhD Dissertation, Universität Mannheim, 2009); quote from the official history of the FPS, Richard Fitter, *The Penitent Butchers: The Fauna Preservation Society, 1903-1978* (London, 1978).

[21] Quote from Ramachandra Guha, *Environmentalism: A Global History* (New York, 2000), 45; on the convention as 'imperial internationalism', see Gißibl, *Nature*, 416-27.

[22] This has ably (if rarely) been done elsewhere: Mark Cioc, *The Game of Conservation: International Treaties to Protect the World's Migratory Animals* (Athens OH, 2009), 34-40; MacKenzie, *Empire*, 207-12; Gißibl, *Nature*, 416-27.

[23] The utilitarian motivation is emphasized in particular by Cioc, *Game*, 34-40.

the following years. Second, it created a set of internationally recognized norms and methods—closed seasons, licenses, endangered species lists, and the concept of reserves—as vehicles of conservation whose implementation increasingly required 'expert' input. Most fundamentally, it firmly established wildlife protection as an arena of international concern. Despite the failure to ratify the convention, the principles it espoused were vital: namely that threatened species should be preserved from destruction, and that preventive action formed part of an international standard for civilized behaviour.[24]

Ironically, it was perhaps the very lack of ratification that gave the greatest impulse to the cause of global nature preservation. As advocates grew impatient with the inadequacy of colonial conservation efforts, this notional standard of enlightened rule provided them with additional political leverage. Throughout the 1900s, the preservationist lobby increasingly availed itself of the rhetoric of 'imperial heritage' to pressure governments into enhancing protective measures. Although much of the prodding continued through elite contacts, advocates increasingly sought wider public support as well. What lent the cause an attraction beyond its original hunting circles was the emphasis on the teeming savannahs and jungles of the colonies as 'wonders of nature'. The charismatic megafauna in particular—giraffes, elephants, rhinoceros—served as icons of pristine wilderness and faraway paradises (the same qualities that made them prized hunting trophies). Amidst the concurrent campaigning by metropolitan conservationists, these species and the landscapes they roamed were increasingly presented as 'natural monuments', symbols of a precious inheritance entrusted to the colonial powers.

During the decade before the First World War, this rhetoric of a global heritage became a central element of conservation advocacy. It was evident not only in lobbying for African wildlife but also in a wide range of conservationist causes. This included what was arguably the most self-consciously international wildlife cause of the day, the campaign to protect birds-of-paradise from the ravages of the plumage trade. The iridescent feathers of these beautiful birds had been traded from New Guinea for centuries, reportedly reaching Europe after Magellan's first circumnavigation in the early sixteenth century. What catapulted the issue into a conservationist cause was the introduction of guns from the 1870s and regular steamship service in the 1890s, both of which stimulated exports to London, Amsterdam, and Paris.[25] Attention naturally focused on the Dutch and German governments

---

[24] MacKenzie, *Empire*, 207-9; Cioc, *Game*, 39-40; Gißibl, *Nature*, 425-7.

[25] Estimates of exported pelts range from 30,000-80,000 per year for the early twentieth century, the majority apparently from the Dutch half of the island: Reichskolonialamt,

that nominally governed New Guinea. Deploying a humanitarian rather than utilitarian critique, activists across Europe and North America sought to shame them into action by enlisting scientific evidence (such as it was) in support of a hunting ban and by portraying the unregulated slaughter of these creatures as a woeful breach of international standards of behaviour, both for animal welfare and for the responsible stewardship of the region's rich 'natural heritage'. Many naturalists in the colonies agreed. Protecting these birds played a key role in the rise of environmental protection in the Dutch East Indies, where the *Nederlandsch-Indische Vereeniging tot Natuurbescherming* adopted the bird-of-paradise as its logo. In the end it was metropolitan pressure rather than colonial regulation that made the biggest difference to the fate of these animals. Tellingly, the first hunting prohibitions came only in 1913 (on the German half of the island), the same year the United States passed a ban on the import of feathers.[26] Yet the bird-of-paradise campaign reflected two interrelated developments: namely, the notion that protecting nature was about posterity as much as sustainable use, and the growing importance of mobilizing popular opinion on this basis.

Meanwhile, concerns about African wildlife gave rise to more exclusive pressure groups that pursued the cause of game conservation primarily via personal contacts within upper-class hunting circles rather than public campaigning. Most important was the British-based Society for the Protection of the Wild Fauna of the Empire, founded in 1903, which served as a model for similar German *Wildschutz-Kommissionen* of 1907 and 1911.[27] Although

---

Jagd und Wildschutz in den deutschen Kolonien (Jena, 1913), 146; Stuart Kirsch, 'History and the Birds of Paradise: Surprising Connections from New Guinea', *Expedition*, 48:1 (2008), 15-21, here 16; more generally Pamela Swadling, *Plumes from Paradise: Trade Cycles in outer Southeast Asia and their Impact on New Guinea and Nearby Islands until 1920* (Boroko, 1996).

[26] The UK imposed its own import ban in 1921, which was followed a year later by the introduction of a hunting prohibition on the Dutch half of the island: Robert Cribb, 'Birds of Paradise and Environmental Politics in Colonial Indonesia, 1890-1931', in Peter Boomgaard, Freek Colombijn, and David Henley (eds), *Paper Landscapes: Explorations in the Environmental History of Indonesia* (Leiden, 1997), 379-408; Boomgaard, 'Oriental Nature', 264-6, 279-80. On metropolitan movements: Robin Doughty, *Feather Fashions and Bird Preservation. A Study in Nature Protection* (Berkeley, 1975); Bernhard Gißibl, 'Paradiesvögel: Kolonialer Naturschutz und die Mode der deutschen Frau am Anfang des 20. Jahrhunderts', in Johannes Paulmann, Daniel Leese, and Philippa Söldenwagner (eds), *Ritual-Macht-Natur. Europäisch-ozeanische Beziehungswelten in der Neuzeit* (Bremen, 2005), 131-54.

[27] Gißibl, *Nature*, 428-31; MacKenzie, *Empire*, 211-16.

both were rooted in the discourse of the hunt, they were not above using the rhetoric of 'nature in trust' to get their way.[28] In this respect the period around 1908-11 marked something of a watershed as several controversies began to expand both the intellectual basis and the social constituency of African wildlife conservation. The key trigger was the policy of game culling as a means of eradicating the tsetse fly, against which the SPFE launched a vigorous public campaign from 1907 onwards. In Germany, Robert Koch's 1908 proposal for large-scale prophylactic game extermination likewise roused the *Wildschutz-Kommission* into a storm of petitions about the duties of imperial stewardship over the natural riches of East Africa.[29] The event that generated the greatest public outcry was the so-called 'Rechenberg slaughter' of summer 1910, when the German East African governor Freiherr von Rechenberg, a reformer with little sympathy for the big-game hunting lobby, authorized the massive clearing of game within a 50-kilometre strip along the Ugandan border to prevent the spread of a possible Rinderpest epizootic. Although the story only broke around a year after the actual event, once it went public it elicited howls of protest from the international conservation lobby and galvanized public opinion within Germany and beyond. The article that sparked the controversy, penned by the prominent hunter-conservationist Hans Paasche and luridly entitled 'mass murder in East Africa', in many ways set the tone.[30] Reprinted in numerous newspapers, it turned a functional quarantine measure (widely supported by the settler lobby) into a fundamental moral failing, a barbaric and indiscriminate slaughter of innocent life both contrary to the civilizing mission and grimly symbolic of the threat to nature worldwide.

In the end, the ensuing scandal not only accelerated the expansion of re-serves in German East Africa, it also cost governor Rechenberg his job.[31] Yet its main significance lies not in claiming a prominent scalp but rather in what it tells us about the rising public profile of colonial nature protection during the half-decade before the First World War. The practice of discreet

---

[28] For instance, ex-viceroy Curzon, a leading member of the SPFE, impressed upon Colonial secretary Elgin in 1906 both the greatness of the British Empire and the need to act as 'trustees for posterity of the natural contents of that Empire': MacKenzie, *Empire*, 213.

[29] Wolfgang U. Eckart: *Medizin und Kolonialimperialismus. Deutschland 1884-1945* (Paderborn, 1997), 340-9; Gißibl, *Nature*, 174-81; MacKenzie, *Empire*, 237-9.

[30] Hans Paasche, 'Der Massenmord in Ostafrika', *Deutsch-Ostafrikanische Zeitung*, 13 (13 May 1911).

[31] On the scandal generally: H. Jürgen Wächter, *Naturschutz in den deutschen Kolonien in Afrika (1884-1918)* (Münster, 2008), 79-80; Gißibl, *Nature*, 211-18.

petitioning was gradually giving way to outright and deliberate public campaigning. At the same time, there was a growing willingness among both the hunting and nature protection associations to make common cause through appeals to posterity and references to imperial stewardship. To be sure, practical concerns about sustainable exploitation were not entirely displaced by a more ethical preservationist paradigm, and the habit of quiet lobbying continued to play a central role, especially via the SPFE. But even for those concerned with protecting animals as game rather than as natural monuments, the rhetoric of a global inheritance had become an effective means to promote a diverse conservationist agenda.

Beyond imperialism? International nature protection

Prior to the First World War, then, the protection of colonial 'wilderness' transcended the utilitarian logic of resource management to become a matter of heritage preservation. But this still left the question of who should be its curator and how it should be safeguarded. The answer was by no means straightforward. While some conservationists were primarily concerned with their own nation's colonies, for others the implications of preserving a 'global common' reached well beyond the formal institutions of empire—indeed, were to some extent at odds with them. At a purely practical level, this reflected the fact that much of what was threatened—migratory animals or species strongly exposed to international trade—could not be adequately protected within the boundaries of single states or even empires. It also marked a growing conviction that the preservation of natural treasures transcended the competence of individual states. As the tsetse controversies made abundantly clear, achieving reliable protection of wild creatures regardless of their utility could not be left to governmental discretion. If they were truly a legacy for 'all humankind', they required an international body to monitor their safekeeping.

This was, in a nutshell, the programme of the 'world nature protection' movement that emerged just before the First World War. Both the term and the agenda it denoted were closely associated with the explorer and naturalist Paul Sarasin, a leading figure in the Swiss League for Nature Protection, whose 1914 book 'on the responsibilities of world nature protection' served as a manifesto for international conservationists in the early twentieth century.[32] Born in Basel in 1856, Sarasin established his reputation during a series

---

[32] Paul Sarasin, *Ueber die Aufgaben des Weltnaturschutzes* (Basel, 1914); also Paul Sarasin, *Weltnaturschutz. Global Protection of Nature* (Basel, 1911). Sarasin's 1914 book is often described as one of the two seminal texts of the period alongside William T. Hornaday, *Our Vanishing Wildlife: Its Extermination and Preservation* (New York, 1913).

of expeditions to Ceylon and Celebes from the late 1880s onwards. There, with his cousin Fritz, he was profoundly struck by the violent changes accompanying the advance of imperial power and global trade, not only for local flora and fauna but also for indigenous peoples such as the Veddas of Ceylon. These experiences made him highly critical of colonialism and convinced him that human relationships with nature should be arranged on an ethical and non-utilitarian basis. Above all, they convinced him of the need to transcend national and colonial frameworks altogether through the creation of international reserves, particularly, though not exclusively, in 'stateless' regions like the Arctic and Antarctic. In 1910 he persuaded the international zoological congress in Graz to back a Swiss-sponsored commission for the global protection of nature, and in 1913 he convened the *Conférence internationale pour la protection mondiale de la Nature* in Bern to obtain formal recognition from governments across Europe (as well as the United States, Japan, and Argentina).[33]

Sarasin's vision in many ways represented a direct challenge to colonial conservation as hitherto practised. For him and his supporters, casting nature as a global common inescapably meant that its preservation lay beyond the remit of any single power. Decisions about what to protect, and how, were too important to be left to sovereign states, in thrall as they were to the interests of business, politicians, and administrators. Rather, they required an international commission of scientific experts, whose task was to establish and supervise 'total reservations' that would be legally sacrosanct vis-à-vis their territorial governments. Although Sarasin envisaged the reserves eventually stretching 'from pole to pole', it was the areas in between that exercised him most, above all the preservation of the 'African megafauna, and furthermore those of the entire tropical belt of the world'. Here, the aim was not merely protection but also the restoration of damaged landscapes into what was regarded as a more original state, recreating 'biocenoses such as adorned Africa before the arrival of the white man, this terrible destroyer'. Unusually for the time, his reserves also envisioned humans as part of the picture. The 'protection of the so-called *Naturvölker* from extermination' was, for Sarasin, the 'most important and simultaneously most honourable' task of all. For like the landscapes they inhabited, these peoples offered

---

[33] There is surprisingly little on Sarasin in English. The best overview is Anna-Katharina Wöbse, *Weltnaturschutz. Umweltdiplomatie in Völkerbund und Vereinten Nationen 1920-1950* (Frankfurt a. M., 2012), 36-53; on Sarasin's activities see also Gißibl, *Nature*, 436; see Stefan Bachmann, *Zwischen Patriotismus und Wissenschaft. Die schweizerischen Naturschutzpioniere (1900-1938)* (Zurich, 1999), 271-9.

Europeans 'a glimpse of our own past', a pristine remnant of an earlier 'transitional stage (*Durchgangszustand*) of our own culture'.[34]

Despite the remarkable progress it made before 1914, Sarasin's new world order of environmental governance soon ran into difficulty. The First World War effectively precluded the establishment of the international commission agreed at the 1913 Bern conference. Yet even before the outbreak of war, the threat it posed to sovereign states aroused concerns even among many who shared Sarasin's basic aspirations. Conwentz himself had no intention of allowing outside regulation of his own activities in Prussia. Indeed, his keynote address to the 1913 conference argued that international coordination should be confined solely to stateless areas and that measures taken by 'civilized' countries should not be hampered by external oversight. The British delegate Charles Rothschild clearly agreed, arguing against any erosion of national competences apart from coordination regarding ocean animals, polar animals, and commercially imported carcasses.[35] For all the noble rhetoric, it was not difficult to see through the designs of the Swiss hosts. While the lack of overseas colonies allowed the Swiss government to pose as an impartial referee, it also explained its consistent support for 'internationalism' as a means of gaining influence beyond its borders.[36] In this sense, Sarasin's agenda was part of a broader contest between 'competing visions of world order', and indeed one whose radicalism did little to assuage imperial concerns.[37] After the war, his attempt to revive the commission under the aegis of the League of Nations again fell foul of *Realpolitik*. In 1919-20 the big powers had little desire for further intervention in their colonies, and the boycott of German science critically hampered international cooperation in any case.[38]

[34] Sarasin, *Ueber die Aufgaben*, quotes from 29, 38-9, 53, 55. For an overview of his 'anthropological nature protection', see Anna-Katharina Wöbse, 'Paul Sarasins "anthropologischer Naturschutz": Zur "Größe" Mensch im frühen internationalen Naturschutz. Ein Werkstattbericht', in Gert Gröning and Joachim Wolschke-Bulmann (eds), *Naturschutz und Demokratie?!* (Munich, 2006), 207-13.

[35] *Recueil des Procès-Verbaux de la Conférence Internationale pour la Protection de la Nature. Berne, 17-19 Novembre 1913* (Bern, 1914), 83-98, 119-24.

[36] See, generally, Madeleine Herren, *Hintertüren zur Macht. Internationalismus und modernisierungsorientierte Außenpolitik in Belgien, der Schweiz und den USA 1865-1914* (Munich, 2000).

[37] Sebastian Conrad and Dominic Sachsenmaier (eds), *Competing Visions of World Order: Global Moments and Movements, 1880s-1930s* (Houndmills, 2007).

[38] Paul Sarasin, 'La Protection mondiale de la faune sauvage', in *Congrès international pour la Protection de la Nature* (Paris, 1925), 34-44, here 43-4; more generally Wöbse, *Weltnaturschutz*, 54-64; Anna-Katharina Wöbse, 'Der Schutz der Natur im

At various levels, then, the agendas of imperial and international nature conservation were clearly at odds. But for all their rivalry they also shared much in common. For one thing, international nature protection was inescapably bound up with the broader culture of imperialism. Sarasin's programmatic vision—even, perhaps especially, his calls for indigenous reserves—was loaded with scientific paternalism, hierarchical notions of race and evolutionist perceptions of 'civilization'. Despite their sharp criticism of imperialism, international nature advocates generally shared a mental framework that bifurcated the human and natural worlds and that disassociated colonized societies from the lands they inhabited. Although Sarasin made an exception for 'primitive tribes'—a dubious honour based on highly questionable notions of 'natural' peoples—other colonized groups were deemed undeserving of special protection, and most activists showed little concern for indigenous rights at all. Indeed, the emphasis on expert advice and commissions was no less state-centred and socially exclusive than the conservation measures imposed by the colonial institutions they sought to overlay. Although early international conservation sought to work 'above' colonial domination, both practically and conceptually, it ultimately ended up working through it.

And to turn this around, imperial conservation was more amenable to inter- and supranational coordination than is sometimes suggested. Histories of environmental protection often portray these as criss-crossing agendas that only joined at long last in the context of decolonization, UNESCO and the IUCN.[39] Although this interpretation is certainly not wrong, it requires differentiation, for it was above all in the British empire—on which the literature has overwhelmingly focused—that binding international coordination was regarded most warily. Given that British-controlled territories introduced legislation relatively early and encompassed the bulk of big game in Africa, they had more to lose than their counterparts in other countries (with the exception of Germany before the war). As Bernhard Gißibl has noted, one can in fact read the series of international conferences hosted in London (1900, 1914, 1933, on which more below) primarily as attempts to prevent unwanted outside influence in the British Empire.[40] By contrast, for nature preservation efforts in the other empires, which have

---

Völkerbund—Anfänge einer Weltumweltpolitik', *Archiv für Sozialgeschichte*, 43 (2003), 177-90.

[39] E.g. William M. Adams, *Against Extinction: The Story of Conservation* (London, 2004), 44-9; John McCormick, *The Global Environmental Movement: Reclaiming Paradise* (Chicester, 1995), 27-40; Wöbse, *Weltnaturschutz*, 273-87, 301-15.

[40] Gißibl, *Nature*, 441-2.

received relatively scant scholarly attention, international coordination posed fewer threats and promised more benefits.[41]

It was during the interwar years that nature conservation in the French, Dutch, and Belgian empires really got going, facilitated by international meetings and thickening networks of exchange. The *Congrès international pour la Protection de la Nature*, held in Paris in 1923 and explicitly conceived as a successor to the 1913 Bern conference, gave a visible push to protective legislation in many colonies, especially within the French empire. Backed by scientific luminaries like the botanist Auguste Chevalier, a spate of new measures was introduced by 1925, including the first hunting regulations in Cochin China, tightened prohibitions in French West Africa, a ban on the use of explosives for fishing around New Caledonia, and the formation of five national parks in Algeria.[42] In the Netherlands Indies, too, new legislation in 1924 introduced general licensing for the first time and expanded the list of protected bird and mammal species.[43] Most conspicuous of all was the establishment of the King Albert (now Virunga) National Park in the Belgian Congo in 1925, the first such park in Africa. More a game reserve than a park on the US model, it was a peculiar amalgam of internationalism and imperialism from its inception: conceived by the American naturalist Carl Akeley, established by the King himself on sovereign territory, but administered by an international council of twenty-four members, eight of whom had to be non-Belgians of worldwide scientific repute.

This burst of colonial legislation in the mid-1920s was mirrored by a wave of organizational activity in the continental metropoles. The Netherlands Commission for the International Protection of Nature, the French Permanent Committee for the Protection of Colonial Fauna and Flora and the Belgian Committee for the International Protection of Nature were all founded in 1925-6. In 1927 they sought collaboration with their British counterparts in an 'International Federation of Protectionist Associations' but received a sceptical response. The following summer the International Union of Biological Sciences formed an 'Office International de Documentation et de Corrélation pour la Protection de la Nature' based in Brussels, which was in many ways the direct descendent of Sarasin's ill-fated

---

[41] And for German conservationists, it of course represented the only means of exerting influence overseas after 1918.

[42] *Congrès international pour la Protection de la Nature* (Paris, 1925). These were only part of a more ambitious set of plans submitted to the Colonial Ministry, focusing above all on total hunting bans for particular species and the creation of over two dozen parks in French West Africa, French Equatorial Africa, Madagascar and Indochina.

[43] Boomgaard, 'Oriental Nature', 268-9.

1913 commission and the predecessor to the IUPN founded in 1948.[44] Noticeably lacking British involvement, it constituted an alternative forum to the SPFE for nature preservation initiatives throughout Europe's colonies.

It was mainly in the early 1930s that international regulation and sovereign imperial interests began to align more closely. In summer 1931, a second international congress for the protection of nature—held at Vincennes within the framework of the French Colonial Exhibition—once again assembled delegates from across Europe and North America, including Britain.[45] At one level this marked a re-integration of international conservation efforts. Its most significant outcome, however, was agreement on a draft Convention for the Protection of African Flora and Fauna tabled by the British delegation, whose twin purpose was to revise the conservation measures agreed in 1900 and to prevent any binding international control over colonial affairs.[46] The resulting London conference, held in the House of Lords in October–November 1933 and much larger than its 1900 predecessor, was conceived very much as an agreement between sovereign imperial powers, and notably included representatives only from those countries with colonial territories in Africa (plus observers from the United States, Netherlands, and India). In this sense it was a different animal from the International Office for the Protection of Nature, founded in 1934 out of the Brussels office, and formally recognized by many European and colonial governments, including the Congo, Netherlands Indies, even Nazi Germany (but not Britain or the United States).[47] But if the 1933 Convention was pointedly imperial in focus, it nonetheless marked an important milestone

[44] The Brussels office was explicitly modelled on the International Agricultural Institute in Rome, the forerunner to the FAO: *La Protection de la Nature et l'Union Internationale des Sciences Biologiques. Communications présentées aux assemblées générales de 1925, 1926, 1927 et 1928* (Brussels, 1929), 11-18; G. A. Brouwer, *De Organisatie van de Natuurbescherming in de verschillende Landen* (Amsterdam, 1931), 37-8.

[45] See, generally, *Deuxième Congrès international pour la Protection de la Nature* (Paris, 1932). The connection of the conference to the Exhibition precluded any official delegation from Germany given the French takeover of former German colonies, though German delegates attended in an unofficial capacity: Anna-Katharina Wöbse, 'Naturschutz global—oder: Hilfe von außen. Internationale Beziehungen des amtlichen Naturschutzes im 20. Jahrhundert', in Frohn and Schmoll (eds), *Natur und Staat*, 625-727, here 647.

[46] On the 1933 convention generally: Cioc, *Game*, 47-53; MacKenzie, *Empire*, 261-71. On the concerns about external interference, Gißibl, *Nature*, 441.

[47] Johann Büttikofer, *Report on the Conference for the International Protection of Nature* (Basel, 1946), 63. The UK and US did, however, have representatives on the council after the Second World War: 'Conference for the Establishment of the International Union for

for international nature preservation, for its effects rippled far beyond Africa. In India, the Fauna Society quickly pressed for similar legislation, culminating in the establishment of the Hailey (now Corbett) National Park in 1936.[48] In Malaysia, too, new legislation paved the way for the King George V National Park in 1939.[49] Although the Netherlands, lacking African territories, were not party to the convention, the government in Batavia had already brought its legislation into line with the preparatory committee's recommendations through the Game Protection Ordinance of 1931 and the Natural Monument and Wildlife Reserve Ordinance of 1932, which formed the basis for the creation of twenty wildlife reserves by the end of 1941.[50] Among French naturalists, too, there was a sense that colonial conservation had reached critical mass in the 1930s. Associations prepared for a third London convention on the protection of flora and fauna planned for 1939, which was eventually abandoned because of the war.[51]

None of this is to say that nature preservation or the values that informed it were becoming truly 'universal' in the interwar period. Governments of the global North were still legislating the management of 'nature' in the South, and whether coordinated on an international or sovereign imperial basis, all of this activity denied agency to colonized peoples. The point is rather that the designation of parts of this nature as a global heritage encouraged the development of a commonly held set of concepts, norms, and measures designed for their preservation.

Protected areas and the science of preservation

For this reason, the various conferences of the interwar period must be seen not only as attempts to maintain the political initiative, but also as part of

---

the Protection of Nature: General Information', UNESCO report (Paris, 20 July 1948), 1-2, available at: http://unesdoc.unesco.org/images/0015/001547/154739eb.pdf.

[48] MacKenzie, *Empire*, 287-9.

[49] Kathiritamby-Wells, *Nature*, 208-17.

[50] The influential conservationist Peter G. van Tienhoven played a crucial role not only in the East Indies but in the international movement more widely: Charles Kies, *Nature Protection in the Netherlands Indies* (Cambridge MA, 1936); Cornelis van Steenis, *Album van Natuurmonumenten in Nederlandsch-Indië* (Batavia, 1937); Boomgaard, 'Oriental Nature', 269-71. For a full list of parks and reserves, see Paul Jepson and Robert J. Whittaker, 'Histories of Protected Areas: Internationalisation of Conservationist Values and Their Adoption in the Netherlands Indies (Indonesia)', *Environment and History*, 8 (2002), 129-172, here 158-61.

[51] See H. Humbert, *La protection de la nature dans les territoires d'outre-mer pendant la guerre* (Paris, 1940), 6-7.

international debates about the purpose of nature conservation and the best practices for achieving it. As before, utilitarian concerns about sustainable resource management continued to coexist alongside more idealistic approaches—indeed, the two were becoming increasingly difficult to disentangle.[52] But as game reserves, species protection, and trade restrictions spread during the interwar period, conservationists developed more holistic approaches that sought to protect integral habitat for diverse flora and fauna. Broadly speaking, there were two dominant models to follow. One was the notionally 'American' national park, the apotheosis of the 'natural monument', whose purpose was to preserve spectacular landscapes and make them accessible for recreation. Combining scientific, heritage and tourist aims, it inspired the creation of Kruger National Park in the Transvaal (1926) as well as a series of 1930s proposals that eventually led to the creation of the great East African national parks.[53] The other model followed a stricter scientific rationale for protecting entire 'biocenoses' (roughly equivalent to the term 'ecosystem' that was coined in 1935) as exemplified by the *Parc national Suisse*, founded in 1913 in a remote alpine region.[54] The Albert National Park followed this approach as a 'réserve intégrale' for 'exclusively scientific aims'.[55] It was also influential in Madagascar, where ten 'réserves naturelles' were established in 1927 exclusively for scientific research.[56]

At base, these controversies reflected the broader issue of how far to control plant and animal populations for human purposes. As such, they overlapped with questions about which species required the most protection, the criteria for classification and whether undesirable animals should be targeted as 'vermin', all of which were considered at length in the run-up to the 1933 London convention. The agreement signed in London did not put an end to

---

[52] At least in the British empire: Peder Anker, *Imperial Ecology: Environmental Order in the British Empire, 1895-1945* (Cambridge MA, 2001), chs. 4, 6. Caroline Ford argues that the two remained more distinct in the French context: 'Nature, Culture, and Conservation in France and Her Colonies 1840-1940', *Past & Present*, 183 (May 2004), 173-98.

[53] On Kruger, Jane Carruthers, *The Kruger National Park: A Social and Political History* (Pietermaritzburg, 1995); on Serengeti, Jonathan S. Adams and Thomas O. McShane, *The Myth of Wild Africa: Conservation without Illusion* (Berkeley, 1992), 37-48; generally: MacKenzie, *Empire*, 269-71.

[54] See Patrick Kupper, 'Translating Yellowstone: Early European National Parks, *Weltnaturschutz* and the Swiss Model', in Gissibl, Höhler, and Kupper (eds), *Civilizing Nature*, 123-39.

[55] Sarasin, 'La Protection mondiale', 42; *Les Parcs Nationaux et la Protection de la Nature* (Brussels, 1937), 6.

[56] G. Petit, 'Les "réserves naturelles" de Madagascar', in A. Aubréville et al., *Contribution a l'étude des réserves naturelles et des parcs nationaux* (Paris, 1937), 229-40.

these debates (apart from dispelling the notion that 'noxious' species should be shot at will). It did, however, enshrine the idea of permanent protected areas, whether tourist parks or strict nature reserves, as the key vehicle for nature protection. Arguably the most far-reaching change of the interwar period thus lay in establishing the separation of human and animal populations as the principal means of preserving the 'imperial heritage'. To be sure, this approach was rooted in long-lived notions of 'wilderness' devoid of human presence. But in the 1920s-30s it gained further traction through a confluence of developments that together inscribed the exclusion of people firmly into the agenda of nature preservation throughout much of the tropical world.

One factor was the growing capacity of the colonial state. However weak these 'shoestring regimes' remained, colonial bureaucracies were generally more capable of enforcing game (and other) laws after the First World War than before. Indeed, the relationship between the state and nature preservation was mutual insofar as hunting regulations and game departments bolstered colonial security, perhaps especially in settler colonies. As one observer remarked on Algeria, 'from the perspective of fauna conservation—as well as for the security of French *colons*—we can only deplore the excessive opportunities given to the natives to arm themselves to European standards'.[57] Another, less tangible factor was the cultural fallout of the war, which powerfully reinforced existing anxieties about the self-destructive character of industrial society. Though one can only speculate about the connection, this post-war sense of pessimism seems likely to have fuelled increasing alarm about the squandering of resources and the destruction of natural landscapes.[58] Writing in 1922, the acclaimed naturalist William Hornaday declared that 'there was nothing more terrible to contemplate at the time than the grinding and devastating power of modern civilization as it is

---

[57] 'Creation de parcs nationaux en Algerie', in *Congrès international pour la Protection de la Nature* (Paris, 1925), 351.

[58] There is, of course, a vast literature on the cultural effects of the war. For its resonance in the imperial context, see Adas, *Machines*, 380-401. Especially influential among contemporary naturalists was Henry Fairfield Osborn and H. E. Anthony, 'Close of the Age of Mammals', *Journal of Mammalogy*, 3:4 (Nov. 1922), 219-31; also R. L. Sherlock, *Man as a Geological Agent. An Account of his Action on Inanimate Nature* (London, 1922). The geographer Carl Ortwin Sauer was also noteworthy: 'Theme of Plant and Animal Destruction in Economic History' (1938), repr. in John Leighley (ed.), *Land and Life: A Selection from the Writings of Carl Ortwin Sauer* (Berkeley, 1963), 145-54; Carl Ortwin Sauer, 'Destructive Exploitation in Modern Colonial Expansion', in *Comptes rendus du congrès international de géographie Amsterdam 1938*, vol. 2, section IIIc (Leiden, 1938), 494-9.

exerted, not only on animal life generally, but on vegetable life and on all the products of nature; that the human race [. . .] is also increasing in its power and ingenuity to destroy'. Most lamentable of all was the transference of particular technologies—above all firearms—to 'savage tribes' still incapable of appreciating the power of these modern marvels and therefore even more complacent about their destructive consequences than the societies that invented them. Hornaday estimated the ratio of nature protectors to destroyers at around 1:500 for New York, 1:1000 in the American West and 1:100,000 in Africa.[59] Steeped in notions of civilizational hierarchy and racialized expertise, one can hardly find a clearer rationale than this for the exclusionist brand of conservation that took hold in the interwar years.

This leads us to perhaps the most important factor: the shifting scientific basis of nature conservation and above all the influence of ecology as a source of expert knowledge. In many ways the interwar years marked the coming of age for ecology as earlier organicist paradigms (that viewed nature as a community of beings collectively displaying attributes of a single organism) were increasingly challenged by more mechanistic models designed to facilitate the rational management of nature's economy. In the tropical world, ecology exhibited a certain 'subversive' potential insofar as field researchers grew more sympathetic to subaltern knowledge and more critical of colonial practices.[60] But despite this shift of perspectives, and despite the growing attention paid to disturbed habitats, there was still a powerful disciplinary fascination with pristine ecosystems devoid of human interference. This fascination continued to inform the conservation discourse of the period, rooted as it was in the language of natural equilibrium and homeostasis. Frederic Clements' famous model of plant succession—whereby disturbed floral communities pass through a series of stages before returning to a stable 'climax'—retained much of its influence, and if anything gained ground in francophone circles.[61] Within this framework, humans still appeared largely

---

[59] See Hornaday's comments on Osborn and Anthony, 'Close of the Age of Mammals', 231-2.

[60] On ecology's 'subversive' potential, Helen Tilley, *Africa as a Living Laboratory: Empire, Development and the Problem of Scientific Knowledge, 1870-1950* (Chicago, 2011), ch. 3. On the rise of the 'new ecology' associated with Charles Elton and Arthur Tansley, see Donald Worster, *Nature's Economy: A History of Ecological Ideas*, 2nd edn (Cambridge, 1994), 291-315. On the imperial dimension more broadly, Anker, *Imperial Ecology*, chs. 3, 4; Libby Robin, 'Ecology: A Science of Empire?', in Tom Griffiths and Libby Robin (eds), *Ecology and Empire: Environmental History of Settler Societies* (Edinburgh, 1997), 63-75.

[61] Pascal Acot and Jean-Marc Drouin, 'L'introduction en France des idées de l'écologie scientifique américaine dans l'entre-deux-guerres', *Revue d'histoire des sciences*, 50:4 (1997), 461-80.

as external disruptions. When translated into concrete conservation measures, this generally encouraged a policy of separation and exclusion. According to Georges Petit, a scientist at the *Musée National d'Histoire Naturelle* and founder of the reserves on Madagascar, the absence of human presence was the fundamental principle of a 'réserve naturelle intégrale'. Unlike the 'American' national park-as-spectacle, his concept of a 'purely biological' reserve was a place in which people represented an external interference.[62] The same idea informed the management of Albert Park, within whose boundaries 'nature must submit only to her own laws. The biological equilibrium, essentially labile, can freely oscillate there without any of its constituent parts being influenced by anthropogenic intervention of any sort'. Such was the view of Victor van Straelen, president of the Congolese national parks institute, who likened the park to 'a vast enterprise of experimental ecology'.[63] This analogy neatly expressed the widely held perception of intact tropical ecosystems as quasi-laboratories for scientific study and new forms of environmental management. As the zoologist Jean Derscheid put it, 'for those preoccupied by the protection of species, natural communities and sites of interest, the Belgian colonial empire offers an incomparable field of action'.[64]

In view of all this scientific pathos, it is ironic that efforts to preserve memorials of natural history in the colonies came at the expense of a more genuinely historical understanding of these landscapes. The rhetoric of the 'natural monument' and 'global legacy' framed tropical environments as timeless, unspoiled wildernesses rather than as changing landscapes in which people actually lived. As had already happened in the American West, the attempt to preserve wilderness generally involved the disruption and erasure of human influence.[65] Few recognized that most of the landscapes they sought to protect in a state of unspoiled equilibrium had long been

---

[62] Georges Petit, 'Protection de la nature et questions de "définitions" ', in A. Aubréville et al., *Contribution a l'étude des réserves naturelles et des parcs nationaux* (Paris, 1937), 5-14.

[63] Victor van Straelen, 'La Protection de la Nature. Sa Nécessité et ses Avantages', in *Les Parcs Nationaux et la Protection de la Nature* (Brussels, 1937), 41-87, here 42, 82.

[64] J.-M. Derscheid, 'La Protection de la Nature au Congo Belge', in *La Protection de la Nature et l'Union Internationale des Sciences Biologiques. Communications présentées aus assemblées générales de 1925, 1926, 1927 et 1928* (Brussels, 1929), 39-46, here 39.

[65] See Mark David Spence, *Dispossessing the Wilderness: Indian Removal, National Parks, and the Preservationist Ideal* (Oxford, 1999); Karl Jacoby, *Crimes against Nature: Squatters, Poachers, Thieves and the Hidden History of American Conservation* (Berkeley, 2001); Christopher Conte, 'Creating Wild Places from Domesticated Landscapes: The Internationalization of the American Wilderness Concept', in Michael Lewis (ed.), *American Wilderness: A New History* (Oxford, 2007), 223-42.

shaped by human use. Even Julian Huxley, visiting Africa for the first time in 1929, regarded it as 'a continent which had hardly changed in the last five hundred years'.[66] That such views were mistaken became clear as these landscapes unexpectedly changed due to the suppression of anthropogenic influence. Taking Albert Park again as an example, the 1929 decision to suppress fire, which ended a long-established indigenous practice of burning scrub to encourage grass growth, led not only to a greater diversity of plants and small animals (as anticipated) but also to the displacement of grasses by spiny or woody plants and a consequent migration of large herbivores to other areas (not anticipated). To ensure sufficient fodder for herds, park authorities soon reinvented the practice of burning. A similar process unfolded later in Serengeti, where park officials likewise reverted to bush-burning in order to encourage a return to open grassland.[67]

Preserving nature for posterity removed it not only from history, but also from politics. Defined as a universal good, its protection was regarded as an unassailable objective beyond narrow interests. Nature preservation—especially but not exclusively in a colonial context—thus represented a fertile field for the application of 'apolitical expertise' impervious to questions about its social implications.[68] Although this tendency is often associated with the advent of development 'experts' after the Second World War, in the history of nature conservation its roots reached back to the beginning of the century. As Conwentz himself suggested in 1909, a committee of international experts 'might, without impropriety, make suggestions or recommendations to the States concerned, on such an uncontroversial matter as the preservation of natural monuments'.[69] The same universalist assumption, flanked by the

---

[66] Julian Huxley, *Memories* (London, 1970), cited in Adams, *Against Extinction*, 105.

[67] Victor van Straelen, 'Les parcs nationaux du Congo belge', in A. Aubréville et al, *Contribution a l'étude des réserves naturelles et des parcs nationaux* (Paris, 1937), 181-210, here 204-5; Holly T. Dublin, 'Dynamics of the Serengeti-Mara Woodlands: An Historical Perspective', *Forest and Conservation History*, 35:4 (Oct 1991), 169-78. See also, more generally, Roderick Neumann, *Imposing Wilderness: Struggles over Livelihood and Nature Preservation in Africa* (Berkeley, 1998).

[68] Classic works on this theme are James Ferguson, *The Anti-Politics Machine: 'Development', Depoliticization, and Bureaucratic Power in Lesotho* (Cambridge, 1990); Timothy Mitchell, *Rule of Experts: Egypt, Techno-politics, Modernity* (Berkeley, 2002). See also Frederick Cooper and Randall Packard (eds), *International Development and the Social Sciences: Essays on the History and Politics of Knowledge* (Berkeley, 1997); Joseph Morgan Hodge, *Triumph of the Expert: Agrarian Doctrines of Development and the Legacies of British Colonialism* (Athens OH, 2007).

[69] Hugo Conwentz, *The Care of Natural Monuments with special reference to Great Britain and Germany* (Cambridge, 1909), 185.

timelessness of nature and the rhetoric of a global common, animated nature preservation throughout the colonial period and beyond. 'Only Nature is eternal, unless we senselessly destroy it' claimed Bernhard Grzimek, the self-styled saviour of the Serengeti, in 1960.

> In fifty years' time nobody will be interested in the results of the conferences which fill today's headlines. But when fifty years from now a lion walks into the red dawn and roars resoundingly, it will mean something to people and quicken their hearts whether they are Bolsheviks or democrats, or whether they speak English, German, Russian or Swahili.[70]

Conclusions

Who defines nature, and how, is a question of power with serious consequences for ordinary people. As research over the past two decades has highlighted, signs of ecological degradation have often served as a pretext for enhancing centralized state control over territories and populations. The history of nature preservation was no exception. The introduction of hunting laws, nature reserves and national parks was fundamentally an assertion of power over land use. It determined which areas were worth preserving and which were open to economic exploitation, and in a sense therefore delimited sustainability itself. Although the moral claim of holding 'nature in trust' served to place such issues above state interests, it simultaneously furnished a powerful rationale for intervention from afar. Like the colonial-era fears surrounding deforestation or soil erosion, threats to tropical wilderness facilitated an expropriation of local landscapes for distant purposes. This is why, for all the undeniably noble motives that underpinned them, such efforts cannot be detached from the broader framework of colonialism whose hierarchical assumptions, cultural fascination with 'pristine nature', and exclusionist land-use practices they so visibly embodied.[71] It is also why efforts to preserve tropical nature should probably be viewed more as a reflection of imperial hegemony, and less in terms of 'collaborative colonialism', than most other aspects of colonial rule. Granted, there were occasional areas of overlap: for example, small reserves in the Netherlands Indies also regarded as

[70] Bernhard and Michael Grzimek, *Serengeti Shall Not Die* (London, 1960), 334.

[71] This interpretation diverges from Paul Jepson and Robert J. Whittaker, 'Histories of Protected Areas: Internationalisation of Conservationist Values and Their Adoption in the Netherlands Indies (Indonesia)', *Environment and History*, 8 (2002), 129-172, which argues against an 'orientalist', imperialist, and self-serving reading of the motivations behind nature protection in Indonesia.

sacred by local people.[72] But these were exceptions to the rule of physical and cultural exclusion, which presented little scope for a convergence of interests with indigenous groups of any social rank.

Despite the demise of colonialism and the institutional change of guard in the post-1945 period, the persistence of conservation ideas and models from the colonial era remained highly conspicuous. Among the various reasons for this continuity, the notion of 'nature as global *patrimoine*' must figure prominently.[73] For one thing, it helped cement the idea in Europe and North America that unspoilt nature was located elsewhere and required protection, as well as the accompanying belief that all 'civilized' peoples had a right, even responsibility, to safeguard it. In 1960, as many African colonies were on the eve of becoming independent states, Grzimek enjoined fellow conservationists to do all they could to 'convince them that wild animals are part of the beauty and wealth of their country and of all mankind, as much as the Acropolis, the Louvre and St. Paul's Cathedral'.[74] These convictions remained central to the self-understanding of the International Union for the Conservation of Nature and the publicity efforts of the World Wildlife Fund, whose purpose has been to translate this sensibility into a steady stream of well-intentioned donations. Moreover, the idea that nature preservation transcends particular interests continued to prop up state-centred and exclusionist models of conservationism long after decolonization. Of course, these practices were not just a colonial holdover but also intersected with the designs of newly independent states to bolster their control over remote hinterlands and natural resources. But amidst the neo-Malthusian anxieties of the post-war period, the idea of protecting a precious global heritage against the threats of overpopulation, overgrazing, and other 'profligate' forms of land-use spoke directly to the interests of the swelling army of international conservation experts who claimed to act as the only responsible stewards of the land, thus perpetuating the colonial-era pattern of preservation via elites with privileged access to decision-makers.[75]

What, finally, were the effects of early twentieth-century preservation efforts on the tropical plants and animals they sought to protect? Overall, the results were ambiguous. On the one hand, they undoubtedly helped

---

[72] Boomgaard, 'Oriental Nature', 275-7.

[73] For the central role of parks in particular, see Anna-Katharina Wöbse, 'Framing the Heritage of Mankind: National Parks on the International Agenda', in Gissibl, Höhler, and Kupper (eds), *Civilizing Nature*, 140-56.

[74] Grzimek, *Serengeti*, 242.

[75] Jepson and Whittaker, 'Histories', esp. 133-46, very rightly emphasizes the central role of international elites.

safeguard some threatened species and relatively undisturbed environments by pressuring governments to set limits on the exploitation of resources. On the other hand, the pattern of intervention from above and afar undermined many of its own gains by engendering local hostility towards preservation measures (manifested in 'poaching', illegal trapping, burning, etc.). It was only in the late twentieth century that more self-consciously 'participatory' forms of conservation began to displace the exclusionist models inherited from the colonial era, so far with mixed results. Community programmes that benefit local residents have provided a much-needed corrective to the 'fortress conservation' of earlier decades, but it is still uncertain whether existing schemes can provide a long-term solution.[76] What is clear, however, is that the future of international nature preservation will depend on overcoming two legacies inherited from the early decades of its own history: first, the recognition that human and natural systems are inseparably coupled; and second, an acknowledgement that protecting a genuinely 'universal' heritage must also, by definition, be a concern for local people.

[76] Quote from Dan Brockington, *Fortress Conservation: The Preservation of the Mkomazi Game Reserve, Tanzania* (Oxford, 2002). For entry points into the broader literature, see David Hulme and Marshall Murphree (eds), *African Wildlife and Livelihoods: The Promise and Performance of Community Conservation* (Oxford, 2001); Fred Nelson (ed.), *Community Rights, Conservation and Contested Land: The Politics of Natural Resource Governance in Africa* (London, 2010); Fikret Berkes, 'Rethinking Community-Based Conservation', *Conservation Biology* 18:3 (June 2004), 621–30.

Colonial Histories of Heritage: Legislative Migrations and the Politics of Preservation

Paul Basu and Vinita Damodaran

In recent years there has been an increasing body of scholarship concerned with the history of heritage legislation. Whereas such archival forays have typically provided merely contextual background for the discussion of current heritage resource management policies,[1] the historical analysis of heritage legislation also provides insight into the broader social, political and, indeed, economic values codified in such laws.[2] Most often this work is framed within a national context.[3] This reflects the fact that these laws necessarily passed through specific national legislatures, but it also reinforces the close relationship between heritage and nationhood, *patrimonie* and *patria*, which has been explored at length in the academic literature.[4]

Some authors have argued for the value of a more comparative, international framework for the analysis of heritage histories. Swenson, for example, notes how the development of heritage legislation in Europe between

[1] See, e.g., Henry Cleere (ed.), *Archaeological Heritage Management in the Modern World* (London, 1989).

[2] Hilary Soderland, 'The History of Heritage: A Method in Analysing Legislative Historiography', in Mary Louise Stig Sørensen and John Carman (eds), *Heritage Studies: Methods and Approaches*. (Abingdon, 2009), 55-84; Jukka Jokilehto, *A History of Architectural Conservation* (Oxford, 1999).

[3] E.g., John Delafons, *Politics and Preservation: A Policy History of the Built Heritage, 1882-1996* (London, 1997); David Harmon, Francis P. MacManamon, and Dwight T. Pitcaithley (eds), *The Antiquities Act: A Century of American Archaeology and Nature Conservation* (Tucson, 2006); Simon Thurley, *Men from the Ministry: How Britain Saved its Heritage* (New Haven, CT, 2013).

[4] See, e.g., David Lowenthal, *The Heritage Crusade and the Spoils of History* (Cambridge, 1998); Philip L. Kohl, 'Nationalism and Archaeology: On the Constructions of Nations and the Reconstructions of the Remote Past', *Annual Review of Anthropology*, xxvii (1998), 223-46; Anthony D. Smith, 'Authenticity, Antiquity and Archaeology', *Nations and Nationalism*, vii (2001), 441-9; Elazar Barkan and Ronald Bush (eds), *Claiming the Stones, Naming the Bones: Cultural Property and the Negotiation of National and Ethnic Identity* (Los Angeles, CA, 2002).

Past and Present (2015), Supplement 10　　　　　　　

approximately 1870 and 1914 constituted an arena both for collaboration and rivalry between nations, while the protection of a nation's monuments became an index of its civilized state.[5] The transference or 'transplanting' of legislative solutions from one national context to another had long been central to the process of drafting new laws, and the field of heritage law was no exception. To these ends international surveys of legislation were undertaken and disseminated, such as that published in a British parliamentary report of 1897 concerning 'the statutory provisions existing in foreign countries for the preservation of historical buildings'.[6] While the principles of legislative transferability remain matters of debate among legal scholars,[7] through such practices there was a clear diffusion of underlying attitudes and ideologies relating to heritage from one nation to another.

Our objective in this article is to look beyond the national framework to consider circulations of heritage legislation through specifically colonial networks and information flows. These legislative migrations provide insight not only into processes of cultural transfer from one territory to another, but also act as prisms through which we can discern differential attitudes toward the various colonies according to the perceived nature of their heritage. As colonial administrators sought to reconcile or amend models of heritage legislation that emerged in one part of the colonial empire with the realities of the heritage that they encountered in another, they were forced to make decisions that reveal underlying colonial predispositions and prejudices, the legacy of which continues to shape perceptions and, indeed, heritage legislation in the post-colonial world. India thus becomes a land of lost civilizations, East Africa the 'cradle of humankind', West Africa a wellspring of 'primitive art'. Each of these categories of heritage—the monumental, the palaeoanthropological, and the ethnological—were valued differently, but these values also changed over the course of the first half of the twentieth century as the new scientific disciplines of archaeology, palaeontology, and anthropology

---

[5]   Astrid Swenson, 'The Law's Delay? Preservation Legislation in France, Germany and England, 1870-1914', in Melanie Hall (ed.), *Towards World Heritage: International Origins of the Preservation Movement 1870-1930* (Farnham, 2011), 139-54.

[6]   *Reports from Her Majesty's Representatives Abroad as to the Statutory Provisions Existing in Foreign Countries for the Preservation of Historical Buildings* (London, 1897); see Delafons, *Politics and Preservation*, 27; Swenson, 'The Law's Delay?', 146.

[7]   Helen Xanthaki, 'On Transferability of Legislative Solutions: The Functionality Test' in Constantin Stefanou and Helen Xanthaki (eds), *Drafting Legislation: A Modern Approach* (Aldershot, 2008), 1-18; David Nelken, 'Towards a Sociology of Legal Adaptation', in David Nelken and Johannes Feest (eds), *Adapting Legal Cultures* (Oxford, 2001), 7-51.

transformed contemporary understandings of the past. This development in heritage value can be tracked temporally, but also geographically, in the revisions made to heritage legislation as it migrated along various trajectories.

The imperial framework that we employ also challenges the assumption that colonial laws and ordinances migrated centrifugally from the metropolitan core to the colonial periphery. In fact we find that the direction of influence was more complex and multidirectional. It is no coincidence, for example, that Lord Curzon, as Viceroy of India, had first championed the passing of India's 1904 Ancient Monuments Preservation Act, before supporting the Ancient Monuments Consolidation and Amendment Act, which passed into English law in 1913. Here we follow Tilley,[8] who draws upon a phrase coined by Lord Hailey in his 1938 *An African Survey*, and argue that the colonial empire constituted not only 'a living laboratory' in the field of scientific knowledge, but was also an arena for legislative experimentation. It is well-known, for example, that Lubbock's ambitious 1873 National Monuments Preservation Bill met with strong opposition from British parliamentarians concerned that it would impinge upon private property rights and was thus rendered 'a relatively toothless measure' during its arduous passage into law.[9] In India, free from such constraints, a more biting heritage law (Act XX) had already been passed in 1863, and this paved the way for Curzon's notoriously stringent legislation of 1904, which gave the state the powers of compulsory purchase of protected monuments and made damage to protected monuments a criminal offence. It was this more stringent Indian law that provided the model for the amendment of the English law in 1913, when, as Champion notes, the near unanimous support of parliament— including its support for restrictions on the rights of private owners— 'could not have made a stronger contrast with Lubbock's tribulations'.[10]

A second objective of this article is to consider the relationship between the protection of 'natural' and 'cultural' heritage in colonial heritage legislation, and particularly the shifting position of what we might regard as the heritage of 'indigenous' peoples within this provision. The monuments that Curzon so admired in India belonged to a civilization for which the British Empire was considered a worthy successor. In a famous speech to the Asiatic Society

---

[8] Helen Tilley, *Africa as a Living Laboratory: Empire, Development, and the Problem of Scientific Knowledge, 1870-1950* (Chicago, IL, 2011).

[9] Henry Cleere, 'Great Britain', in Henry Cleere (ed.), *Approaches to the Archaeological Heritage* (Cambridge, 1984), 54; Timothy Champion, 'Protecting the Monuments: Archaeological Legislation from the 1882 Act to PPG 16', in Michael Hunter (ed.), *Preserving the Past: The Rise of Heritage in Modern Britain* (Stroud, 1996), 38-9.

[10] Champion, 'Protecting the Monuments', 44.

of Bengal in 1900, he explained that such monuments 'do not represent an indigenous genius', but 'are exotics imported into this country in the train of conquerors'.[11] It was the decaying remnants of India's Mughal heritage that Curzon sought to save, while that which awaited discovery 'in the probing of archaic mounds' and 'in the excavation of old Indian cities' as yet remained hidden behind 'a curtain of dark and romantic mystery'.[12] This curtain was only lifted in 1921-2 with the excavation of Mohenjo-Daro and the discovery of the Bronze Age Indus Valley Civilization.[13] There was no place, however, in this discursive and legislative conceptualization of heritage as the monumental remains of lost civilizations for the heritage of India's contemporary population. Even as the vernacular heritage of England's rural past was being valorized by organizations such as the National Trust (the first building to be acquired and 'saved for the nation' by the Trust was a modest thatched cottage and not a castle), so the heritage of India's indigenous peoples went unrecognized. In the evolutionist ideology of the time, India's tribal populations were themselves regarded as a living relic of the prehistoric past: a primitive people without history, and therefore without heritage. Being closer to nature than to civilized culture, however, they were also perceived as the innate custodians of the natural environment, and, ironically, their customary laws and traditional practices fell under the protection of India's forestry conservation legislation.

While the relationships between natural and cultural heritage, and between what we now refer to as tangible and intangible heritage, have been differently configured in different territories through these legislative migrations, it is only relatively recently that these false distinctions have been overcome. A significant step in addressing a more holistic understanding of heritage, as well as acknowledging the plurality of coexistent heritage values, was the passing of the Australian Heritage Commission Act of 1975. This Act used the rubric of the 'National Estate' (a term coined by the British architect and conservationist Sir Clough Williams-Ellis in the 1930s) to encompass both Australia's natural and cultural environments, including sites with 'strong or special association with a particular community or cultural group for social,

---

[11]   George Nathaniel Curzon, *Speeches by Lord Curzon, Viceroy and Governor-General of India. 1898-1901* (Calcutta, 1901), 192; David Gilmour, 'Empire and the East: The Orientalism of Lord Curzon', *Asian Affairs* xxvi (1995), 270-7.

[12]   Curzon, *Speeches*, 193.

[13]   John H. Marshall, 'First Light on a Long-Forgotten Civilisation: New Discoveries of an Unknown Prehistoric Past in India', *Illustrated London News* (20 Sep. 1924), 528-32, 548.

cultural or spiritual reasons'.[14] This was an acknowledgement of the need to incorporate Aboriginal communities' heritage, which is often inseparable from the 'natural' landscape, within the national heritage legislation. The same concept was incorporated into South Africa's post-Apartheid National Heritage Resources Act of 1999, in which the national estate was expanded to include a very wide range of sites and landscapes with cultural, historical, archaeological, and geological significance, as well as movable objects, and 'intangible aspects of inherited culture' such as oral history, ritual, skills and techniques, and indigenous knowledge systems.[15] Recognizing the potential of heritage to 'affirm our diverse cultures', 'deepen our understanding of society' and 'facilitate healing', these contemporary heritage laws reflect the influence of international policy-shaping agencies such as UNESCO with its standards-setting conventions, declarations, and recommendations. Just as UNESCO has been accused of imposing forms of homogeneous 'cultural globalization' onto the non-Western world,[16] so it might be said that the colonial legislative migrations we are concerned with here were a medium for a kind of proto-globalization of heritage ideology.[17] The reality, both then and now, is more complex, and despite the reproduction of clauses, often verbatim, from one context to another, the application of the law took very different forms.

Charting the spatio-temporal migrations of cultural heritage legislation

Let us now turn to look more closely at the processes through which British colonial heritage legislation was drafted by considering a number of case examples. The impetus behind the drafting and revision of new legislation was often provoked by particular incidents that came to the attention of colonial governments or the Colonial Office itself. The Colonial Office often took a proactive stance, urging colonial governments to take action and disseminating what it perceived to be relevant examples of heritage legislation from other territories. The correspondence between the colonial

[14] Australian Heritage Commission Act, 1975 (Commonwealth of Australia).

[15] National Heritage Resources Act, 1999 (Republic of South Africa).

[16] William S. Logan, 'Globalizing Heritage: World Heritage as a Manifestation of Modernism and Challenges from the Periphery', in David S. Jones (ed.), *20th Century Heritage: Our Recent Cultural Legacy: Proceedings of the Australian ICOMOS National Conference 2001*, (Burwood, Vic, 2002), 51-7.

[17] Tony Balantyne, 'Empire, Knowledge and Culture: From Proto-Globalization to Modern Globalization', in A. G. Hopkins (ed.), *Globalization in World History* (London, 2002), 115-40.

administrators and officials in the Colonial Office, as well as with experts invited to comment, provides insight into the perceptions and values of those directly involved in colonial governance. This is relevant not only within the specific field of heritage, but is also telling of more general attitudes towards particular territories. When acts or ordinances successfully passed through the local legislative process, copies were presented to the Colonial Office for approval. These were usually accompanied by a legal report that often contained a comparative table showing what clauses had been incorporated from which precedents, what had been adapted, and what had been drafted anew. Lack of space precludes an extensive discussion of each case, but we have selected examples which highlight different issues as well as the more general progress of heritage law across space and time within the British Empire.[18]

Southern Rhodesia 1902, Cyprus 1905

It is important to stress that there was no single point of origin from which heritage legislation diffused through British colonial networks. Heritage legislation was often introduced in response to highly specific circumstances and followed distinct trajectories, albeit with interesting intersections and points of confluence. While such legislative migrations reveal much about colonial power relations, they also impart the complexity of these relations, not least demonstrating that there were very different views within the colonial administration regarding the significance of a region's heritage and whose interests should be prioritized in the measures proposed. The Ancient Monuments Protection Ordinance that was passed by the Legislative Council of Southern Rhodesia in 1902, for example, marks a change in attitudes whereby the region's remarkable ruins were no longer regarded as repositories of ancient gold to be 'plundered for profit' by

---

[18] Since the long history of antiquarianism, museum development, state-sponsored archaeology, and heritage legislation in India has been well charted, we draw our case studies from elsewhere. We shall, however return to India in our discussion of forestry legislation. Regarding the preservation of antiquities in India, see Dilip K. Chakrabarti, *A History of Indian Archaeology: From the Beginning to 1947* (New Delhi, 1988); Tapati Guha-Thakurta, *Monuments, Objects, Histories: Institutions of Art in Colonial and Postcolonial India* (New York, 2004); Indra Sengupta, 'A Conservation Code for the Colony: John Marshall's Conservation Manual and Monument Preservation Between India and Europe', in M. Falser and M. Juneja (eds), *Archaeologizing Heritage? Transcultural Entanglements between Local Social Practices and Global Virtual Realities* (Heidelberg, 2013), 21-37.

licenced prospectors,[19] but became sites of conjecture and mystery, which fired the popular imagination and began to attract tourists from among the territory's white settlers.[20] In Cyprus, by way of contrast, scholarly interest in the island's archaeological heritage was never in doubt. When, in 1896, the Cyprian Legislative Council proposed to strengthen regulations relating to the excavation and export of antiquities, however, the British Museum—which was then leading an archaeological expedition on the island—claimed that the restrictions would be 'inconvenient' and lobbied the Colonial Office to veto the bill.[21] There followed a protracted debate, in which the British authorities in Cyprus generally supported the local community's wishes to stop the large-scale export of artefacts. It would take nine years for the matter to be settled with the passing of the 1905 Antiquities Law, and even then this proved to be effective only temporarily.

The territory occupied by Cecil Rhodes' British South Africa Company (BSAC), which eventually became Southern Rhodesia and later Zimbabwe, was acquired for the explicit purpose of exploiting its mineral resources.[22] The region was also remarkable for the large number of monumental ruins, most notably the massive stone complex of Great Zimbabwe, which European explorers and adventurers encountered there from the 1870s, and which eventually gave its name to the postcolonial nation. As Garlake notes, 'probably no other prehistoric site has given rise to such strong, widespread and often bizarre emotional responses'.[23] Grounded in racist conceptualizations of African primitivism, the so-called 'Zimbabwe controversy' centred around assertions that the builders of these monumental remains could not possibly be indigenous to the region, but must have their origins in the ancient civilizations of the Mediterranean or Middle East. In particular the speculation of the sixteenth-century Portuguese missionary João dos Santos, which associated the ruins with the gold mines of the biblical Ophir, fired the imagination of prospectors and amateur archaeologists alike. Thus it was that BSAC granted concessions to concerns such as Rhodesia Ancient Ruins Ltd to mine the ruins for the treasure they were believed to conceal. This company was given rights to 'explore and work

---

[19]   Henrika Kuklick, 'Contested Monuments: The Politics of Archaeology in Southern Africa', in George W. Stocking (ed.), *Colonial Situations: Essays on the Contextualization of Ethnographic Knowledge* (Madison, WI, 1991), 142.

[20]   Peter S. Garlake, *Great Zimbabwe* (London, 1973).

[21]   Memorandum regarding the Preservation of Antiquities, 21 Feb. 1905 (Cyprus 6994/ 1905): The National Archives, London (hereafter TNA), CO 67/142.

[22]   Kuklick, 'Contested Monuments', 138.

[23]   Garlake, *Great Zimbabwe*, 12.

for treasure' in 'all ancient ruins south of the Zambezi', with the exception of Great Zimbabwe.[24] In return BSAC would receive twenty per cent of the prospectors' finds and Rhodes himself, who was an avid collector, would have the first right to purchase any discoveries.[25] In the five years between 1895 and 1900 that it operated, Rhodesia Ancient Ruins Ltd recovered less than 900 ounces of gold, but the destruction caused by their digging, and that of other concessions, was immense.[26]

Given that these prospecting activities were conducted under permit, the 1902 Ancient Monuments Protection Ordinance was evidently not only motivated by a desire to combat unlawful damage being done to Southern Rhodesia's antiquities. The ordinance was passed at a time of transition of administrative power from the commercially driven BSAC to the South Africa High Commission, and reflected changing perceptions of the significance of these monumental ruins, which had by then begun to attract considerable international attention. The extent of the damage already done to the ruins was also becoming apparent and was attracting considerable criticism.[27] The new Monuments Ordinance vested control of Southern Rhodesia's antiquities in the figure of the Administrator (the head of the Southern Rhodesian government at the time). The Administrator's Office was thus given responsibility for considering applications and granting permits for archaeological excavation work, and it became a legal requirement that all archaeological finds had to be reported to this office. Failure to comply could result in prosecution.

Ironically it was none other than Richard Nicklin Hall, a journalist turned amateur archaeologist, who had worked with Rhodesia Ancient Ruins Ltd, who was appointed Curator of Great Zimbabwe at this time. While Hall's responsibilities were limited to preserving the ruins in order to make them more attractive to tourists, he disregarded this and undertook a large amount of highly destructive excavation work. Hall justified his actions in the name of 'preservation', claiming that he was merely removing 'the filth and decadence of the Kaffir occupation' with the intention presumably of revealing evidence of the original 'ancient' builders.[28] In so doing he made the subsequent stratigraphical reading of the site impossible. Hall's activities were condemned as 'reckless blundering' by David Randall-MacIver, the first trained

---

[24] Garlake, *Great Zimbabwe*, 70; William H. Stiebing, *Uncovering the Past: A History of Archaeology* (Oxford, 1993), 222.

[25] Garlake, *Great Zimbabwe*, 70.

[26] Ibid.

[27] E. E. Burke, 'Archives and Archaeology', *Rhodesiana*, xvii (1967), 68.

[28] Garlake, *Great Zimbabwe*, 72.

archaeologist to investigate Great Zimbabwe, and Hall was duly dismissed. Randall-MacIver's excavations in 1905 disproved the speculations of Hall and other amateur diggers. He dated the ruins to a more recent period and found no evidence to suggest that the structures had been built by anyone other than the indigenous people of the region.

Whether this evidence of a sophisticated, indigenous urban society in southern Africa succeeded in dispelling ingrained attitudes regarding the primitive state of the region's local population is doubtful, and indeed the controversies did not end.[29] It is interesting to note, however, that in 1912 the Ancient Monuments Protection Ordinance was complemented by the passing of the Bushmen Relics Protection Ordinance. Whereas the earlier Ordinance had nominally protected monuments and relics pre-dating 1800, it made no provision for the protection of rock art sites, which continued to be damaged through mining activity.[30] The Bushmen Relics Ordinance addressed this anomaly, so that it became illegal to remove, without permission, 'any drawing or painting on stone or petroglyph of the kind . . . believed to have been executed by the South African Bushmen or other aboriginals'. The Bushmen Relics Ordinance also brought Southern Rhodesian legislation in line with that of the newly created Union of South Africa, which had passed an identical act the previous year. As Nick Shepherd has argued, this legislation contributed to the emergence of a particular discourse around the indigenous peoples of southern Africa, involving a slippage between the emergent disciplines of archaeology and ethnology, whereby the 'Bushmen' or 'San' became regarded as a 'remnant race or evolutionary "hold over" '—a living Palaeolithic people.[31]

Whereas the very presence of monumental stone ruins in Southern Rhodesia was challenging to European conceptualizations of sub-Saharan Africa and thus proved controversial, the situation in Cyprus was very different. As the archaeologist Reginald Poole wrote in 1878, the year in which the island became a British Protectorate, 'the mineral wealth of Cyprus may be uncertain, but there can be no doubt of its archaeological riches'.[32] In the

---

[29]   See Joost Fontein, *The Silence of Great Zimbabwe: Contested Landscapes and the Power of Heritage* (London, 2006).

[30]   Webber Ndoro and Gilbert Pwiti, 'Heritage Management in Southern Africa: Local, National and International Discourse', *Public Archaeology*, ii (2001), 29.

[31]   Nick Shepherd, 'State of the Discipline: Science, Culture and Identity in South African Archaeology', *Journal of Southern African Studies*, xxix (2003), 823-44.

[32]   R. S. Poole, 'Cyprus: Its Present and Future', *The Contemporary Review*, xxxiii (1878), 135-54.

years immediately prior to the signing of the Cyprus Convention, through which the administration of Cyprus was passed to Britain in return for the pledge of military support for Turkey against Russia, the looting of antiquities had become widespread, not least to satisfy the antiquarian passions of foreign consuls and officials. The most notorious case was that of the American consul, General Luigi Palma di Cesnola, whose 'large scale plundering expeditions netted more than 10,000 items, most of which were exported from the island after 1870 and purchased by the Metropolitan Museum in New York'.[33] When the British assumed control of Cyprus, an existing Ottoman antiquities law, passed in 1874, was enforced more strictly and a ban was imposed on unauthorized excavation. The British High Commissioner resolved to provide permits only to archaeologists associated with accredited scientific bodies; this favoured British expeditions led by institutions such as the Cyprus Exploration Fund (1887-94) and British Museum (1893-99).[34]

Under the Ottoman law, finds from excavations for which a permit had been granted were to be divided three ways: a third to the Government, a third to the excavator, and a third to the owner of the land on which the excavation was taking place. This led to unscrupulous archaeologists purchasing the land on which they wished to dig and thus acquiring the right to two thirds of the finds.[35] The Ottoman law also proved to be liberal with regard to the export of antiquities. Together with calls to establish the Cyprus Museum on a better footing, this led to the drafting of two new pieces of legislation—a museum law and an antiquities law—which were passed by the Legislative Council in 1896. The intention was to give the Cyprus Museum the financial and legal wherewithal to house antiquities recovered in excavation so that they 'should belong absolutely to the Museum, in trust for the Cyprus community'.[36] Under the proposed new antiquities law, a clause stipulated 'that no object of antiquity shall be exported unless a similar object is already in possession of the Museum'.[37] In a 1905 Colonial Office memorandum summarizing what would turn out to be a protracted debate, it is noted that the British Museum

---

[33] A. Bernard Knapp and Sophia Antoniadou, 'Archaeology, Politics and the Cultural Heritage of Cyprus', in Lynn Meskell (ed.), *Archaeology Under Fire: Nationalism, Politics and Heritage in the Eastern Mediterranean and Middle East* (London, 1998), 29-30.

[34] A. Bernard Knapp, *The Archaeology of Cyprus: From Earliest Prehistory through the Bronze Age* (Cambridge, 2013), 20.

[35] Memorandum of the King's Advocate on the Law of Antiquities in Cyprus, 3 Mar. 1904 (Cyprus 8922/1904), TNA, CO 67/138.

[36] Memorandum, 21 Feb. 1905, TNA, CO 67/142.

[37] Ibid.

'got wind' of this clause and its Director, Sir E. Maunde Thompson, wrote to say that this was a serious matter and 'the Trustees of the British Museum would find it very inconvenient'.[38] The British Museum was then undertaking excavations at the Late Bronze Age site of Enkomi and, in Thompson's words, had 'just hit upon a most important series of tombs containing antiquities of great interest and value'.[39] He expressed a hope that the new law would be vetoed by the Colonial Office so that the British Museum would be less constrained with regard to the export of objects that were being discovered. The Colonial Office effectively complied.

An argument was made that the inclusion of the offending clause 'would probably put an end to the search for antiquities in Cyprus', and the High Commissioner was directed to prepare revised versions of the laws. These were again submitted to the British Museum for comment, and again objections were raised. The matter was not easily resolved and over the following eight years there was considerable correspondence between the various parties. During this time, the Colonial Office obtained and sent copies of antiquities laws from Greece (1899) and Italy (1902), which were felt to be 'applicable in principle in Cyprus'.[40] Relevant sections were incorporated into revisions of the new Cyprus law, which now included provision for both the protection of antiquities and for the financing and management of museums. Still, however, the British Museum insisted on the inclusion of a clause that would permit the High Commissioner, with the sanction of the Secretary of State for the Colonies, to allow 'authorized excavations by learned Societies' to retain and export up to two thirds of the antiquities discovered.[41] It is to the credit of Sir Charles King-Harman, who became High Commissioner to Cyprus in 1904, that he supported the position of the local members of the Legislative Council and resisted the edicts of the Colonial Office. In a despatch to the Secretary of State for the Colonies in February 1905 he reported on the earnestness of the desire of Cypriots 'to preserve the antiquities found in their soil' and that the Legislative Council would not accept what was referred to as the 'British Museum clause' of the Antiquities Bill. In a robust defence of the Cypriot position, King-Harman added that the learned societies 'have in time past made such plentiful harvest from the Cyprus antiquities' and that he had little sympathy with their claim that they should be exempted from export

---

[38]   Ibid.

[39]   Ibid.

[40]   Despatch from C. King-Harman, High Commissioner of Cyprus, to the Secretary of State for the Colonies regarding the Preservation of Antiquities, 21 Feb. 1905 (Cyprus 6994/1905), TNA, CO 67/142.

[41]   Memorandum, 21 Feb. 1905, TNA, CO 67/142.

control.[42] At last, the Colonial Office conceded, the troublesome clause was removed, and in April 1905 King-Harman wrote to the Secretary of State for the Colonies advising that the Bill had passed into law.[43]

The Cyprus Museum eventually reopened in a new porticoed building in 1909 and its collections grew as a result of the 1905 law, which restricted all exports of antiquities from the island. There was a continuing concern, however, that these restrictions would make Cyprus a less attractive destination for foreign archaeologists.[44] Indeed, the colonial authorities in Cyprus came under increasing pressure from overseas archaeological missions to grant them exemption from the law and export objects unearthed during their research. Finally, in 1927, the Swedish Cyprus Expedition, led by Einar Gjerstad, successfully lobbied for an amendment to the law, which allowed them to remove sixty-five per cent of their finds to Sweden.[45] A 1931 photograph of hundreds of crates of archaeological objects on the docks at Famagusta awaiting shipment to Stockholm provides a sobering reminder of the scale on which antiquities were permitted to leave Cyprus at this time.[46] On the other hand, as Bounia and Stylianou-Lambert argue, the expedition also provided valuable material from the Neolithic through to the Roman period, which enriched the Cyprus Museum and added immeasurably to the understanding of the island's heritage.[47]

By the mid-1930s, in both Cyprus and Southern Rhodesia, these early legislative experiments had been swept away by the passing of new heritage laws. Ironically, it was a later Director of the British Museum, George Hill, who was largely responsible for drafting the 1935 Antiquities Law in Cyprus. (He had earlier redrafted the antiquities laws for Iraq and Palestine.)[48] With the enactment of this more stringent law, a new professional Department of Antiquities was established, and the Cyprus Museum became properly

[42]   Despatch from C. King-Harman, 21 Feb. 1905, TNA, CO 67/142.

[43]   Despatch from C. King-Harman, High Commissioner of Cyprus, to the Secretary of State for the Colonies regarding the Preservation of Antiquities, 19 Apr. 1905 (Cyprus 14212/1905), TNA, CO 67/142.

[44]   Alexandra Bounia and Theopisti Stylianou-Lambert, 'National Museums in Cyprus: A Story of Heritage and Conflict', in Peter Aronsson and Gabriella Elgenius (eds), *European National Museums: Identity Politics, the Uses of the Past and the European Citizen* (Linköping, 2011), 178.

[45]   Ibid.

[46]   Knapp, *Archaeology of Cyprus*, 21.

[47]   Bounia and Stylianou-Lambert, 'National Museums in Cyprus', 178.

[48]   Ana Filipa Vrdoljak, *International Law, Museums and the Return of Cultural Objects* (Cambridge, 2006), 86.

nationalized insofar as it was fully funded by the state.[49] At the same time, a new 'British Museum clause' was included, which gave the British Museum first refusal to purchase any antiquities that the Director of Antiquities decided not to retain in the national collection.[50] The Southern Rhodesian Monuments and Relics Act of 1936 also brought into being a new body, the Commission for the Preservation of Natural and Historical Monuments and Relics, which—as the name would suggest—was responsible not only for safeguarding ancient monuments and archaeological objects, but also for protecting areas of land that were of interest for archaeological, historical, scenic or geological reasons, or indeed due to their distinctive flora or fauna.[51] As we will see in the case of British West Africa, both of these laws were regarded as exemplars and were distributed widely through colonial circuits.

Kenya 1927, Uganda 1934

By the 1920s archaeology was becoming established as a more scientifically rigorous discipline and this would have a significant impact on the development of heritage legislation, which, as we have seen, in the colonial context had hitherto been focused on monumental structures and classical antiquity. In Africa, some of the most remarkable discoveries of the interwar period were in the new field of palaeoanthropology. These were changing our understanding of human evolution, and through the celebrated work of Raymond Dart in southern Africa and Louis Leakey in East Africa, Africa soon became regarded as the 'cradle of humankind'. Despite coming three years after Dart's discovery of 'Taung Child' and coinciding with Leakey's first excavations in the Rift Valley, Kenya's 1927 Ancient Monuments Preservation Ordinance was, however, considerably out of step with these developments and was itself something of a 'hold-over' from another time and another place. Save from the deletion of those clauses relating to the traffic in antiquities, the Ordinance was copied almost verbatim from India's Ancient Monuments Preservation Act of 1904. Indeed, a memorandum appended to the Bill that was presented before Kenya's Legislative Council acknowledges this fact and further notes that the Indian legislation 'was the late Marquess Curzon's especial care and it has already abundantly justified its enactment in India'.[52] Curzon had died in 1925, and Thomas Hart goes so far as to argue that the Kenyan legislation was passed in his honour—Sir Edward Grigg,

---

[49] Ibid.; Bounia and Stylianou-Lambert, 'National Museums in Cyprus', 178.

[50] Antiquities Law, 1935 (Cyprus).

[51] Monuments and Relics Act, 1936 (Southern Rhodesia).

[52] A Bill to Provide for the Preservation of Ancient Monuments and Objects of Archaeological, Historical or Artistic Interest, 1927 (Kenya), TNA, CO 533/372/14.

Governor of Kenya, and others in the Kenyan colonial administration having close associations with the Indian Civil Service.[53]

A legal report, sent with the final version of the Kenyan Ordinance to the Secretary of State for the Colonies in November 1927, provides further information concerning the rationale for introducing the legislation. Here it is stated that the issue was first taken up in 1924 when the colonial government of Kenya invited its administrative officers to make suggestions for the 'preservation and identification of such memorials as the graves of early explorers, officials and pioneers, old Government stations and evidence of earlier civilisations'.[54] While not excluding indigenous sites, it is clear that the primary interest was in preserving the more visible material remains of Kenya's colonial history, as well as its history of cultural contact with Arabian and Portuguese traders and settlers. This is evident, for example, in the province-by-province list of monuments that might be eligible for protection under the legislation that was published in the *Official Gazette* in June 1927.[55] The majority of the sites listed in the interior of the Protectorate are the graves of British pioneer settlers, whilst the ruined towns and forts of Coast Province—identified as being Portuguese, Arab, and Persian in origin—dominate the list as a whole. Forgetful of the less monumental heritage of Kenya's various 'indigenous' ethnic groups, on the occasion of the second reading of the Bill before the Legislative Council, the Colonial Secretary, Sir Edward Denham, remarked that 'We are inclined to talk so much of Kenya as the youngest Colony in the British Empire . . . that we are perhaps apt to be forgetful of the fact that other civilizations reached this coast and left their mark upon it'.[56]

The limitations of Kenya's 1927 Ordinance would come to light as a consequence of palaeoanthropological discoveries by Leakey and others in the fossil beds of the region in the later 1920s and early 1930s. Whereas the Southern Rhodesia and Cyprus laws had introduced measures to regulate the excavation of archaeological sites and control the export of finds, this was inadequately addressed in the Indian legislation on which the Kenyan Ordinance was based and which was concerned chiefly with protecting architectural heritage. As the significance of East Africa's archaeological

---

[53] Thomas G. Hart, 'Gazetting and Historic Preservation in Kenya', *CRM: The Journal of Heritage Stewardship*, iv (2007).

[54] Legal Report, The Ancient Monuments Preservation Bill, 1927, 21 Oct. 1927 (Kenya X.10524/1927), TNA, CO 533/372/14.

[55] *The Official Gazette of the Colony and Protectorate of Kenya* xxix (7 Jun. 1927), 687-92.

[56] Colony and Protectorate of Kenya, Legislative Council Debates, September 13, 14, 15 and 16, 1927, 327-8, TNA, CO 533/372/14.

and palaeological record became known, so there was increasing pressure to safeguard it from the kinds of reckless excavation that had befallen Great Zimbabwe. This led, for example, to the passing of the Preservation of Archaeological Objects Ordinance in neighbouring Tanganyika in 1929.[57] The amendment of Kenya's heritage legislation and introduction of similar legislation in Uganda in 1934 was not, however, driven by purely scientific interests, but also by international politics and rivalry: not least rising tensions between Britain and Italy in relation to Mussolini's expansionist interests in Abyssinia/Ethiopia.

This animosity was expressed forcefully in relation to a year-long expedition being led by Nino del Grande of the Fascist Colonial Institute in Rome.[58] The expedition's proposed itinerary included the British territories of Kenya, Uganda, and Sudan, where it was intended that 'anthropological and paleontological excavations and research' would be undertaken. The lead palaeo-anthropologist on the expedition was Raymond Dart, whose work had at that time been discredited, not least by Leakey, who was then regarded as the major authority on the subject. The issue was referred to the British Foreign Office, which in turn sought the advice of the British Museum, the Natural History Museum, and the Royal Society. Each in turn raised concerns about the credentials of the expedition members, stressing the need for careful scientific methods in palaeontological excavation, drawing attention to existing research being conducted by British institutions, and arguing that palaeontological material collected on British territory 'should be placed in the National Collection for preservation and study' and not allowed to fall into foreign hands. These responses were forwarded to the Italian Chargé d'Affaires in London and communicated to the governors of Kenya and Uganda. The letter to the Italian authorities makes it clear that while the expedition would not be stopped from entering Kenya and Uganda, 'it is almost certain that they will not be permitted to engage in any work involving excavation'.[59]

In fact, as noted above, the legal grounds for restricting excavation of sites other than those declared as ancient monuments in Kenya was very limited, and no heritage legislation existed in Uganda at all. That Uganda's 1934 'Ordinance to provide for the Preservation of objects of Archaeological and

---

[57] Leakey's first expedition to Olduvai Gorge in Tanganyika took place in 1931. This would become one of the most significant palaeoanthropological sites in the world.

[58] See Original Correspondence regarding Italian Expedition to Central Africa (East Africa 4010/1933), TNA, CO 822/91/16.

[59] Ibid.

Palaeontological interest' was swiftly passed through the legislature as a response to this threat is acknowledged in a Colonial Office memorandum:

> This Ordinance has been enacted as a result of [a despatch] in which we suggested that permission to engage in archaeological work involving excavations should be withheld from an expedition under the leadership of Signor Nino Del Grande. Apparently there was no legislation in Uganda by which such work could be prohibited.[60]

The memorandum also notes that the Colonial Office sent copies of 'the corresponding legislation in Kenya, Tanganyika and Cyprus' as models from which to draft the Ugandan law. The process through which clauses from these precedents was incorporated into the new Ugandan Ordinance is made particularly clear in the legal report and comparative table that accompanied the final version of the Ordinance submitted to the Colonial Office for approval (Figure 1). Here it is stated that Tanganyika's 1929 Ordinance 'has been taken as the main guide', providing five of its eight sections, with modifications noted. One section has been taken from Kenya's 1927 Ordinance, and another from the Cyprus Antiquities Law of 1905.[61]

In contrast to the more elaborate pieces of legislation introduced in India and Cyprus, Uganda's new law was a mere two pages long. 'A lengthy Ordinance was not required', it is stated in the legal report. In the Colonial Office deliberations before approving the Ordinance, concern is expressed about the appropriateness of the clause adapted from the Cyprus law that any person who discovers an object of archaeological or palaeontological interest is legally obliged to deliver it to the authorities or else risk prosecution. It was felt that this was 'all right for Cyprus where any man may at any time dig up a valuable antique relic but the Uganda native is not in the same box and this section might lead such a person into an innocent breach of the law if he dug up a fossil and did not report it'. The 'native population', the Colonial Office official remarked, 'could not be expected to understand the Ordinance' and it would therefore need to be used with discretion. 'The law will deal with the European digger who is the important person to get at'.[62]

---

[60] Memorandum regarding the Preservation of Archaeological Objects Ordinance, 1934, 28 Mar. 1934 (Uganda 23563/1934), TNA, CO 536/181/14.

[61] Report on an Ordinance entitled 'The Preservation of Archaeological Objects Ordinance, 1934', 9 Feb. 1934 (Uganda 23563/1934), TNA, CO 536/181/14.

[62] Memoranda regarding the Preservation of Archaeological Objects Ordinance, 1934, 20 Apr. and 25 May 1934 (Uganda 23563/1934), TNA, CO 536/181/14.

<u>COMPARATIVE TABLE.</u>

"THE PRESERVATION OF ARCHAEOLOGICAL OBJECTS ORDINANCE,1934".

Uganda Ordinance.	Tanganyika Ordinance No.1 of 1929.	
Section.	Section.	
1	-	
2	-	Kenya Ordinance No.17 of 1927 section 2.
3	3	-
4	4	-
5	-	Cyprus Law No.4 of 1905 section 7.
6	5	-
7	6	-
8	7	-

Figure 1. Comparative table attached to Legal Report on the Uganda Preservation of Archaeological Objects Ordinance of 1934, TNA, CO 536/181/14 (Uganda, 1934).

Gold Coast 1945, Nigeria 1953

What begins to emerge as one follows the introduction and amendment of heritage legislation in these different colonial territories is a gradual transformation of perceptions and attitudes: perceptions of the territories themselves as places that even possess a past, and, if this is recognized, attitudes regarding what aspects of the past are valued and perceived to be threatened and in need of protection. Thus, what starts in India as an orientalist appreciation of Mughal imperial architecture translates into a wider valorization of a monumental heritage: whether of the controversial ruins of Great Zimbabwe or the fortresses and mosques of the East African coast. With the development of the disciplines of archaeology and palaeoanthropology, attention turned to the less visible, but more distant past and concern shifted to controlling both the scientific quality of excavation, crucial to the dating and sequencing of the material record, as well as the export of excavated materials. Thus in the 1920s and 1930s, archaeological discoveries led to places such as the Indus Valley being identified as 'cradles of civilization', while palaeoanthropological discoveries in southern and later eastern Africa resulted in these regions becoming celebrated as the 'cradles of humankind'. It is telling that at this time, no heritage legislation was deemed necessary in West Africa, which was regarded as being devoid of archaeological or palaeo-anthropological interest and was instead fully the domain of the ethnologist.

The situation in British West Africa was to change in 1938 with the discovery of a remarkable cache of seventeen cast brass and bronze heads during the digging of house foundations at Ife in Nigeria.[63] The bronzes would subsequently be dated to the fourteenth and fifteenth centuries and, from the very beginning, they were recognized as examples of the very finest artistic achievement, yet again challenging tenacious perceptions of African—and, in particular, West African—primitivism.[64] The find was soon brought to international public attention through an article published in the *Illustrated London News* by a young American anthropologist named William Bascom, who was conducting ethnographic research in the region.[65] Concerns that the bronzes would be smuggled out of Nigeria and find their way onto the international art market were raised by E. H. Duckworth and Kenneth Murray of the Nigerian Education Department, both of whom had long advocated the value of Nigerian art traditions and argued for the need for museums in the colony. Using their contacts in the London art world, they successfully lobbied the Colonial Office to press the Nigerian Government into taking action.[66]

---

[63] For a more extensive discussion of the development of West African heritage legislation and museums see Paul Basu, 'A Museum for Sierra Leone? Amateur Enthusiasms and Colonial Museum Policy in British West Africa', in Sarah Longair and John MacAleer (eds), *Curating Empire: Museums and the British Imperial Experience* (Manchester, 2013), 145-67.

[64] It is worth noting that the reception in Europe of the remarkable hoard of 'ancient bronzes' looted from Benin City 40 years earlier was considerably more ambiguous. While some recognized them as 'treasures', for others they represented the barbarism of a 'degraded race of savages'. Perceptions of the Benin Bronzes changed significantly over the following decades, culminating in their display as part of the 'African Negro Art' exhibition at the Museum of Modern Art in New York in 1935. Needless to say the preservation of Benin's cultural heritage *in situ* was not a concern of the British expeditionary forces that sacked the Royal Palace in 1897. See Annie E. Coombes, *Reinventing Africa: Museums, Material Culture and Popular Imagination* (New Haven, CT, 1994), 7-28; Karthryn Wysocki Gunsch, 'Art and/or Ethnographica? The Reception of Benin Works from 1897-1935', *African Arts*, xlvi (2013), 22-31.

[65] William Bascom, 'The Legacy of an Unknown Nigerian "Donatello" ', *Illustrated London News* (8 Apr. 1939), 592-4.

[66] See Original Correspondence regarding the Preservation of Negro Art (Nigeria 30384/1938), TNA, CO 583/234/13.

Despite the passing of an Order in Council prohibiting the export of 'antique African sculptural works of art' from Nigeria in January 1939, it became apparent that a number of the bronze heads had indeed been removed from the country. Two had been purchased by Bascom himself and taken to the USA, and a third was in the hands of a journalist named H. M. Bate, who later claimed that he was selling it on behalf of a German friend.[67] Other examples were rumoured to be on the market in Germany. Again at the prompting of Duckworth and Murray, a delegation including John Rothstein, Kenneth Clark, and Julian Huxley visited the Colonial Office to lobby for the passing of more stringent legislation to protect antiquities and other artworks in Nigeria. As a result of this meeting, the Secretary of State for the Colonies, Malcolm MacDonald, sent a despatch to each of the governors of Nigeria, Gold Coast, and Sierra Leone recommending that legislation be enacted to protect what he described as 'the products of Tropical African culture, especially antiquities'. In an initial draft of the despatch, dated 30 May 1939, it seems that the original intention was to enclose antiquities legislation from Ceylon, Cyprus, Malta, and Palestine as models.[68] In the event, however, it was decided to send only the 1936 Southern Rhodesian Monuments and Relics Act and the 1935 Cyprus Antiquities Law. MacDonald adds a note qualifying the use of these precedents:

> As will be seen, these Ordinances envisage a more elaborate form of procedure than is likely to be appropriate in the case of West African Governments and are designed to deal with social conditions and a range of objects which are, in many respects, materially different from those of West Africa. The fundamental object, however, is the same, namely to exercise government control over the exportation of objects of historical or cultural interest, to secure for the Government itself the means of acquiring, under appropriate conditions, such objects as may be thought desirable, to prevent the wilful injury to such objects and also to ensure, so far as possible, that any excavation of sites of archaeological interest is undertaken only by persons properly qualified to conduct such operations.[69]

[67] See Original Correspondence regarding the Preservation of Products of Tropical African Culture (West Africa 33620/1939), TNA, CO 554/121/8. The bronze head that Bate was offering for sale was subsequently purchased by the British Museum (Af1939,34.1).

[68] Draft despatch from the Secretary of State for the Colonies to the Governors of Nigeria, Gold Coast, and Sierra Leone regarding the Preservation of Products of Tropical African Culture, 30 May 1939 (West Africa 33620/1939), TNA, CO 554/121/8.

[69] Ibid.

This pressure from the Colonial Office seems to have had little impact on the colonial governments in West Africa and, with the outbreak of war in September 1939, the process soon stalled. It was not until 1945, with renewed interest in the development of research institutes, universities, and museums in West Africa, that the issue of heritage legislation was again raised. Of Britain's West African colonies, it was the Gold Coast that was first to enact an 'Ordinance to provide for the preservation of monuments, relics and objects of archaeological, ethnographical or historical interest' in 1945.[70] The comparative table included in the Acting Attorney-General's legal report shows that the Ordinance was largely drawn from the Southern Rhodesia Monuments and Relics Act of 1936 (Figure 2). There were, however, some notable changes. There was no provision, for example, for the protection of land valued for its scenic value, or which contained distinctive geological formations, or rare flora or fauna. Perhaps most significant, however, was the inclusion of the protection of 'ethnographic articles', which did not need to be of particular antiquity and may include 'objects of ordinary use'.[71] Like the Southern Rhodesian model, the Ordinance provided for the establishment of a Monuments and Relics Commission. No provision was made, however, for the funding of the Commission's activities, for the preservation of monuments and relics, or for the establishment of museums. The Gold Coast law provided a model for Sierra Leone's Legislative Council, and an almost identical Monuments and Relics Ordinance was passed there in 1946.[72] It, too, was broad in its scope, but extremely limited in practical application. These Ordinances, it might be surmised, were merely acts of legislative lip-service paid by colonial governments, which ultimately saw little need to devote resources to matters of 'archaeological, ethnographical or historical interest'.

The situation in Nigeria was, however, different. Indeed, given that it was the circumstances in that country that provoked these legislative measures, it is ironic that an equivalent Nigerian law was not passed until the Antiquities Ordinance of 1953. In fact, a Nigerian Antiquities Bill had been drafted in 1940. This was a much more sophisticated piece of legislation largely modelled on the Cyprus Law of 1935, although also incorporating clauses from the Southern Rhodesian Ordinance and widening the definition of an 'antiquity'

---

[70] See Original Correspondence regarding Archaeology and Ethnology, Gold Coast (Research 28040/11/1946), TNA, CO 927/31/6.

[71] Legal Report on the Monuments and Relics Ordinance, 1945, 14 Nov. 1945 (Research 28040/11/1946), TNA, CO 927/31/6; Monuments and Relics Ordinance, 1945 (Gold Coast).

[72] Monuments and Relics Ordinance, 1946 (Sierra Leone).

THE MONUMENTS AND RELICS ORDINANCE, 1945.

COMPARATIVE TABLE.

Abbreviation used:

S. R. = The Monuments and Relics
Act, 1936 /8 of 1936/ of
Southern Rhodesia.

Section.	Origin.	Remarks.
1	S.R.1	Short title.
2	S.R.3	
"ancient monument"	-	adapted to suit local conditions.
"ancient working"	-	adapted to suit local conditions; since "ancient workings" may be found on the sites of modern mines the definition must be restrictive.
"ethnographical article"	new	it is not immediately possible to particularise the articles which should be protected.
"monument"	-	adapted to suit local conditions.
"national monument"	-	-
"relic"	-	adapted to suit local conditions.
3	S.R.4	adapted.
4	S.R.5	-
5	S.R.6	adapted.
6	S.R.7	-
7	S.R.11	adapted.
8	new	-
9	S.R.10	adapted.
10	S.R.12	adapted.
11	S.R.13	adapted and subsections (3) & (4) added.
12	S.R.14	adapted; "ancient working" included.
13	S.R.8	adapted.
14	S.R.9	adapted.
15	S.R.17	expanded.
16	S.R.15	adapted.
17	S.R.16	adapted.
18	new	-

Raymond Browne

ACTING ATTORNEY-GENERAL.

13th November, 1945.

Figure 2. Comparative table attached to Legal Report on the Gold Coast Monuments and Relics Ordinance of 1945 (Research 28040/11/1946), TNA, CO 927/31/6.

to include any object 'constructed, shaped, inscribed or executed' in Nigeria prior to British administration.[73] In 1943, furthermore, an Antiquities Service had been established by the colonial government of Nigeria, with Kenneth Murray appointed Surveyor of Antiquities, and a series of museum developments planned. The eventual passing of the 1953 Antiquities Ordinance thus formalized a system that was already partly in operation. As with the Gold Coast and Sierra Leone, this included the establishment of an Antiquities Commission (which would later become the National Commission for Museums and Monuments). Crucially, however, under the Commission's purview was a properly funded Department that was directly responsible for the 'practical realization' of the Ordinance. Murray duly became the first Director of the Antiquities Department, and under his management was a series of Divisions, responsible, in turn, for Monuments and Architecture; Museums; Archaeology; Ethnography; and Education.[74] Taking responsibility for the establishment of museums, control of archaeological investigations, declaration and protection of monuments, and control of the movement of antiquities and artworks, Nigeria's 1953 Antiquities Ordinance was perhaps the most comprehensive piece of cultural heritage legislation within the British colonial world—certainly within Africa. This was, however, a testimony to the personal commitment and enthusiasms of Murray, and his successor as Director of Antiquities, Bernard Fagg, rather than an example of enlightened colonial governance.

Forestry legislation and the safeguarding of indigenous cultural heritage

While debates around the role of the state in relation to cultural heritage moved interestingly from colony to metropole, metropole to colony, and directly between colonies, so a similar legislative migration can be seen in relation to natural heritage—for example, in the movement of forestry legislation, or the development of national parks and wildlife reserves. Here we focus more specifically on the progress of forestry legislation in India and how this influenced forestry legislation in other colonial contexts. In the legislative developments we examine, we find that the debate moves from a primary concern with managing the economic exploitation of forests to the development of ideologies of colonial custodianship. Our interest is, however,

[73] A Bill entitled An Ordinance to Provide for the Better Preservation of Objects of Aesthetic, Historical, Archaeological or Scientific Interest, 1940, British Museum, Eth Doc 261.

[74] Nwanna Nzewunwa, 'Nigeria', in Henry Cleere (ed.), *Approaches to the Archaeological Heritage* (Cambridge, 1984), 101-8.

particularly to consider how forestry legislation came to encompass a concern for indigenous populations and their 'customary rights', extending the colonial state's custodianship from the land to indigenous rights and practices. Communities' 'knowledge and practices' concerning the natural world are now explicitly identified as 'intangible cultural heritage' in UNESCO's 2003 Convention for the Safeguarding of Intangible Cultural Heritage. While forestry and customary rights were not framed in this vocabulary in the period we examine, we argue that in protecting the 'natural contents of . . . Empire' (a term used by Curzon), this legislation also came to protect the intangible cultural heritage of certain indigenous groups. The significance of this will be discussed further in our conclusion.

In the nineteenth century, the destructive impact of uncontrolled natural resource exploitation across the colonial world began to give rise to a sophisticated environmentalist response and demands for intervention. The nature of the response to environmental change differed, sometimes fundamentally, from territory to territory, but there were also common influences, some dominated by metropolitan networks, others brought about by new intercolonial patterns of intellectual and bureaucratic exchange.[75] It is important to note that while India provided the model for early state forestry legislation, many of the ideas on which it drew originated in other parts of the Empire in fragile island environments. Ideas of finitude, extinction and desiccation, for example, first emerged in the eighteenth century in the context of oceanic islands which suffered devastation as a consequence of what John Richards has described as the 'unending frontier' of colonial resource extraction.[76] This growing environmental consciousness was motivated by several factors, most importantly the climatic fear that if unregulated deforestation were to continue, droughts and famines would ensue. By the nineteenth century early legislative interventions for conservation on islands such as St. Vincent, Mauritius, and St. Helena were to lead the way to the first comprehensive set of forestry regulations in India in the guise of the Indian Forest Acts of 1865 and 1878. As a model for the custodianship of natural heritage, the Indian case provided much of the basis for debates on environmental intervention and conservation that went on in other parts of the British Empire,

---

[75] See Richard Grove and Vinita Damodaran, 'Imperialism, Intellectual Networks, and Environmental Change: Unearthing the Origins and Evolution of Global Environmental History', in Sverker Sörlin and Paul Warde (eds), *Nature's End: History and the Environment* (London, 2009), 23-49.

[76] John F. Richards, *The Unending Frontier: An Environmental History of the Early Modern World* (Berkeley, CA, 2003).

but as with cultural heritage legislation, this translated into disparate forms of practice.

To explore these debates in natural heritage legislation further, we examine in closer detail a number of legislative interventions and their migrations: the 1865 and 1878 Indian Forest Acts, the 1908 Chotanagpur Tenancy Act, and the 1936 Government of India (Excluded and Partly Excluded Areas) Order. The agenda set by this legislation would later culminate, in the post-Independence period, in the protection of scheduled areas—and, significantly, scheduled tribes—under the Indian Constitution.

Indian Forest Acts 1865, 1878

The impetus behind the development of forest reservations has been explored extensively by several historians to date.[77] Although it was not until 1865 that the formal structure of an Indian Forest Act was established, the environmental debate in which state forestry originated had already been going on in India and elsewhere in the British Empire for many decades. These debates were dominated not only by a production agenda but also, and as importantly, by conservationists and surgeons concerned about the relationships between deforestation, climatic deterioration, disease, agricultural production, and aesthetics.[78] While it has been argued that the Forest Act should be understood primarily as a feature of modern state formation,[79] this obscures a wider variety of imperial agents and motivations. In fact, it is in the context of a modern state agenda within institutions such as forestry that many discordant voices came to be heard in the nineteenth century. This included not only the assertion of different agendas for forestry in terms of the custodianship of natural environments and their flora and fauna, but also, for example, debates concerning the rights of indigenous communities. This latter concern was increasingly being voiced by district officers on the ground as they witnessed the impact of unregulated forest exploitation on local populations.

The transition from uncontrolled deforestation earlier in the nineteenth century to the ambitious programme of state conservation heralded by the

---

[77] See, e.g., Richard H. Grove, *Green Imperialism: Colonial Expansion, Tropical Island Edens and the Origins of Environmentalism* (Cambridge, 1995); Greg Barton, *Empire Forestry and the Origins of Environmentalism* (Cambridge, 2002).

[78] See, e.g., Hugh Cleghorn, 'Notulae Botanicae No. 1. On the Sand-binding Plants of the Madras Beach', *Madras Journal of Literature and Science* xvii (1857), 85-9; Cleghorn, 'Notes on the Vegetation of the Sutlej Valley', *Journal of the Agricultural and Horticultural Society of India*, xiii (1865) 372-91.

[79] K. Sivaramakrishnan, *Modern Forests: Statemaking and Environmental Change in Colonial Eastern India* (Stanford, CA, 1999).

1865 Indian Forest Act is marked by a succession of campaigns warning of the climatic effects of deforestation, as well as arguing the economic case for sustainable forest management. During the 1850s, for example, prominent lobbyists such as the botanist Joseph Hooker, who had travelled widely in northern India and Nepal, and John McClelland, a pioneering surgeon with the East India Company and subsequently Superintendent of Forests in Burma, were instrumental in convincing the Governor General, Lord Dalhousie, of the value of wholesale state intervention in the forest sector—much against the wishes of private capital.[80]

Eventually, in 1864, under the direction of Hugh Cleghorn and Dietrich Brandis, an India-wide Imperial Forest Department was established, and a year later the Indian Forest Act was passed. While the 1865 Act stands as the first large-scale environmental law to be implemented in the nineteenth century it was hurriedly drafted and was regarded as incomplete in many respects. Indeed, it was soon superseded by the 1878 Forest Act, largely drafted by Brandis. This was much more draconian in nature, giving the state absolute control over forested areas, overriding the existing customary practices and rights of indigenous peoples.[81] By 1880, around a fifth of India's land mass came under the control of the Forest Department. This vision of conservation clearly evinced imperial sensibilities of custodianship voiced by men such as Lord Dalhousie and, later, even more explicitly, by Lord Curzon, who was responsible for the creation of the Kaziranga Reserve Forest (India's first game park) in 1905. Leading a deputation to the Secretary of State for the Colonies in 1906 to campaign for the strengthening of Game Laws across the Empire, Curzon argued that, while 'we are continually using language which implies that we are the trustees for posterity of the Empire. . . we are also trustees for posterity of the natural contents of that Empire'.[82]

While legislative debates around the formation of game reserves predominated in Africa, debates around forestry took centre stage in India. As R. S. Troup, the founding director of the Imperial Forestry Institute, noted, 'to India belongs the credit of having been the first part of the empire to adopt a

---

[80] Grove, *Green Imperialism*, 472.

[81] Ramachandra Guha, 'An Early Environmentalist Debate: The Making of the 1878 Forest Act', *Indian Economic and Social History Review*, xxvii (1990), 65-84.

[82] 'Minutes of Proceedings at a Deputation from the Society for the Preservation of the Wild Fauna of the Empire to the Right Hon. The Earl of Elgin, His Majesty's Secretary of State for the Colonies, June 15, 1906', *Journal of the Society for the Preservation of the Wild Fauna of the Empire*, iii (1907), 24.

rational policy of forest conservation and development'.[83] Officers trained in the Indian forestry service were frequently posted as advisers elsewhere in the British Empire, applying models developed in India in other colonial territories, and in this way Indian forestry was soon transformed into 'empire forestry'.[84] The Cape Colony was the first to follow India's lead. Here, the Indian foresters J. S. Lister and D. E. Hutchins were sent to assist in the establishment of a Forest Department and implement the Cape Forest Act of 1888. Hutchins had drafted the Act, using the Madras Forest Act of 1882 as his model; this in turn had been modelled on the 1878 Indian Forest Act. As Barton notes, Hutchins was also an important figure in the wider diffusion of forestry legislation, travelling and writing reports on forestry affairs for the colonial authorities in Australia, Cyprus, New Zealand, and in various African territories, as well as for the British parliament.[85]

The legislation was seen as sweeping and stringent, but also necessary as local authorities recognized their powerlessness to enforce the preservation of forests using existing laws.[86] Over the coming years versions of the Cape's forestry regulations were adopted in the southern African colonies of Orange River Colony (1903), Natal (1903) and Transvaal (1908). Other African territories in which forestry legislation was enacted prior to 1910 included Southern Nigeria (1901), Lagos (1902), and East Africa (1902, 1905).[87] Each was ultimately grounded in the Indian legislation, though sometimes several steps removed. The East Africa Forestry Regulations were, for example, modelled on the South African legislation, which, as we have noted, was based on the Madras Act of 1888, which was an amendment of the Indian Forest Act of 1878. In each case a forestry department was created, often under the leadership of Indian foresters. In Southern Nigeria, for example, the department was led by H. N. Thompson, who had previously served as Assistant Conservator of Forests in Burma. As Conservator of Forests in Southern Nigeria, Thompson was commissioned to undertake a detailed study of forestry in the Gold Coast, and he recommended that the Southern Nigerian Ordinance be amended and applied there.[88] In other cases, a younger generation of foresters was trained by the Indian officers: Charles Lane Poole, for example, was recruited into the Cape Forestry

---

[83]   Robert S. Troup, *Colonial Forest Administration* (Oxford, 1940), 6.

[84]   Barton, *Empire Forestry*, 97–111.

[85]   Ibid. 8.

[86]   Ibid., 111.

[87]   Forest Ordinance, 1901 (Southern Nigeria); Forest Ordinance, 1902 (Lagos); East Africa Forestry Regulations, 28 Jul. 1902, TNA, FO 881/7766.

[88]   H. N. Thompson, *Gold Coast, Report on Forests* (London, 1910).

Department by Hutchins, before being posted to Transvaal, and then to Sierra Leone, where he was responsible for drafting its Forestry Ordinance in 1910. He would later serve in Western Australia, where he drafted the Forests Act of 1918, and he took a prominent part in the first British Empire Forestry Conference in London in 1920.[89]

While the influence of the 1865 and 1878 Indian Forest Acts can be seen in these legislative migrations, bound up as they were with the physical mobility of forestry experts in the Indian Civil Service and Colonial Service, the application of the legislation was much more uneven. This was chiefly a result of the local cultural and political contexts that had to be contended with—not least the customary rights and practices of local populations. In some cases the laws were strongly opposed. In the Gold Coast, for example, while Thompson's Forest Bill was passed, after considerable amendment, by the Legislative Council in 1911, it met with strong resistance due to its interference with native land rights, and ultimately the legislation was not applied.[90] Indeed, the resistance of local populations to the creation of forest reserves presented an increasing problem for colonial governance, and this contributed to changing attitudes towards customary rights and practices. It would again be in India that the precedents were set.

Chotanagpur Tenancy Act 1908

Forestry regulation generally sought to put a stop to indigenous methods of forest management such as shifting cultivation, which was regarded as wasteful and destructive. Despite this, it was argued that the interests of local agriculturalists were safeguarded during the creation of forest reserves through a variety of methods. Increasing incidents of agrarian discontent, however, suggest that the interests of small farmers living in forested areas were far from secure and this destabilization began to present a problem for colonial governance. A notorious case was the so-called Munda Rebellion of 1899-1900, a tribal resistance movement in the Chotanagpur region of Eastern India, led by the charismatic Birsa Munda.[91] In the process of creating

---

[89] http://www.cpbr.gov.au/biography/lane-poole-charles.html; Barton, *Empire Forestry*, 107.

[90] Richard Grove and Toyin Falola, 'Chiefs, Boundaries and Sacred Woodlands: Early Nationalism and the Defeat of Colonial Conservation in the Gold Coast and Nigeria, 1870-1916', *African Economic History*, xxiv (1996), 1-23.

[91] Kumar S. Singh, *Bisra Munda and His Movement, 1872-1901: A Study of a Millenarian Movement in Chotanagpur* (Calcutta, 2002). See also T. S. Macpherson, *Final report on the operations for the preparation of a record of rights in Pargana Porahat, district of Singhbhum 1905-7* (Calcutta, 1908), 5-6.

forest reservations, which were extensive in this region, the customary rights of local tribal groups had been disregarded and the indigenous population were coerced into bonded labour on the lands of the local *zamindars* and other non-tribal incomers. Birsa succeeded in uniting members of the aggrieved Munda tribal groups and a series of armed attacks were made on people and buildings associated with the colonial presence, including police stations and missions. The 'Ulgulan' or 'Great Tumult' was short-lived and soon dissipated after the imprisonment and death of Birsa Munda in 1900. While Birsa Munda was to become a cult figure in India's Independence movement, a more immediate response to the uprising was a review of forestry regulations in tribal areas and the passing of the Chotanagpur Tenancy Act of 1908.[92]

In the aftermath of the Munda Rebellion, the government was forced to make a survey of tribal land tenure (*khuntkhatti*) as a way of appeasing the Mundas and other tribal groups in Chotanagpur. It was felt, however, that a mere survey was inadequate, and it was necessary to secure the Mundas in their possession of the land. The Chotanagpur Tenancy Act provided legal recognition of Mundari *khuntkhatti*, and, at the same time, recognized that areas predominantly inhabited by tribal people required a separate system of administration and therefore excluded them from the normal government regulations, including the provisions of forestry law. These areas would come to be designated under the Government of India Act of 1919 as 'backward tracts', reflecting the perception that they were occupied by the most primitive tiers of the colonized society.[93]

The Chotanagpur Tenancy Act aimed to amend tenancy laws and codify them according to custom and usage. However, when the Act came into force there were only 156 villages registered as having full Mundari *khuntkhatti* rights. It was found that out of 3,614 square miles of cultivated land only 405 square miles qualified as ancestral property.[94] From this we can conclude that the Act came too late, with the majority of Mundas already alienated from their lands. However, the Act had a greater symbolic significance since

---

[92] Space does not allow for a detailed discussion of what was in fact a very complex legislative process. See, however, S. P. Sinha, *Conflict and Tension in Tribal Society* (New Delhi, 1993), 30-90. See also Vinita Damodaran, 'Customary Rights and Resistance in the Forests of Singhbhum' in Daniel Rycroft and Sangeeta Dasgupta (eds), *The Politics of Belonging in India* (London, 2012), 103-18.

[93] Uday Chandra, 'Liberalism and Its Other: The Politics of Primitivism in Colonial and Postcolonial Indian Law', *Law and Society Review*, xlvii (2013), 147.

[94] Peter Tete, *A Missionary Social Worker in India: J. B. Hoffmann, the Chota Nagpur Tenancy Act and the Catholic Co-operatives, 1893-1928* (Rome, 1984), 82.

it recognized the Munda land system itself, which had been the subject of struggle long before the 1899-1900 uprising. The Jesuit missionary, John-Baptist Hoffmann, who spent much of his life working among the Mundas, saw the Act as a legitimation of the Munda's struggle and a recognition of the wisdom of their customary land rights system. Rather than the savages they had been regarded as being, Hoffmann argued that they were 'a race of martyrs' whose 'land system appears as one of the wisest creations of pre-historic times'.[95]

Government of India (Excluded and Partially Excluded Areas) Order 1936

In India, debates around the protection of tribal land rights and practices came to full term in the discussions instigated by the Indian Statutory Commission of 1928. This Parliamentary Commission was established to consult on and make recommendations for constitutional reform in India. When the Commission visited India, among the issues that they investigated was the matter of the 'backward tracts'. The Commission found that, excluding Burma, the extent of these tracts then amounted to 'no less than 120,000 square miles, containing a population of 11 ¼ millions'.[96] In the context of their constitutional recommendations, while noting that the development of some designated tracts was now so advanced that 'special treatment' was no longer required, they generally concluded that the majority should still 'be excluded from the general constitutional arrangements, and that special provision must be made for their administration'.[97] The grounds for these recommendations are discussed in the Commission's report:

> The stage of development reached by the inhabitants of these areas prevents the possibility of applying to them methods of representation adopted elsewhere. They do not ask for self-determination, but for security of land tenure, freedom in the pursuit of their traditional methods of livelihood, and the reasonable exercise of their ancestral customs. Their contentment does not depend so much on rapid political advance as on experienced and sympathetic handling, and on protection from economic subjugation by their neighbours.[98]

---

[95]   John-Baptist Hoffmann, *Encyclopaedia Mundarica*, viii (Patna, 1933), 2402.

[96]   *Report of the Indian Statutory Commission, Volume Two: Recommendations* (New Delhi, 1930), 108.

[97]   Ibid. 109.

[98]   Ibid.

The Commission recommended that backward tracts be redesignated as 'excluded areas', and that their administration be shifted from provincial authorities to central government. This was a significant proposal in the context of the devolution of power to Indian administrators that would result from the 1935 constitutional reforms. It effectively excluded Indians from administering these areas, suggesting that the safeguarding of indigenous interests could only be entrusted to Europeans. The idea of the colonial state as custodians of tribal land and the rights of indigenous peoples would impact on future constitutional developments and remained in force in post-Independence India until 1991, when all this was to change dramatically.

Elsewhere in the Empire similar trajectories were followed. Not only was forest legislation from India exported to other colonies, as we have seen, but the protection of tribes and their local customary rights also figured in these debates. This was often only articulated implicitly within the legislation. Thus the Lagos Colony's Forest Bill of 1902 recognized traditional land rights insofar as it required local chiefs to consent to the introduction of forestry regulations. Similarly, while Lane Poole's 1911 Sierra Leone Forestry Ordinance was based on the Indian Forest Act, the colonial authorities also made it clear that it was the government's policy 'to interfere as little as possible with tribal habits and customs', and to balance, on the one hand, improvement in agricultural methods so as to 'lessen the destruction of the forest and on the other hand to conserve existing forests and create new ones so as to preserve or restore . . . the conditions to which the population is accustomed'.[99] Finally, in the Nigerian Forest Ordinance of 1916, Lugard built upon the innovations developed in Lagos, and introduced, as an experimental measure, the principle of the Native Administration of Forest Reserves, returning control, at least temporarily, to indigenous interest groups—albeit, as Grove and Falola note, with some unusual allies.[100]

Conclusions

As we hope to have demonstrated in the above accounts, a spatio-temporal migration of sorts is discernible in the diffusion of cultural and natural heritage legislation in the British Empire. This was a result of various factors, including the application of the common legal practice of transplanting legislative interventions from one context to another in the drafting of new laws. While shortening what could otherwise be an expensive and protracted

---

[99] Statement quoted in Barton, *Empire Forestry*, 108.
[100] Grove and Falola, 'Chiefs, Boundaries and Sacred Woodlands', 16, 20.

process, such as took place in the drafting of the Cyprus Antiquities Law of 1905, this also led to measures being introduced in colonial contexts where they were not necessarily appropriate. In some cases, such as in the Gold Coast and Sierra Leonean monuments ordinances, it enabled reluctant governments to pay legislative lip-service to Colonial Office directives, while introducing laws with little intention of providing the practical means of applying them. In other cases, on the contrary, an effective legislative framework was established in one colony that was then intentionally used as a model for a unified approach across multiple territories. Thus Wilhelm Schlich, in his *Manual of Forestry*, promoted an Empire-wide integration of forestry practices based on the approach pioneered in India.[101] While many of these legislative interventions remain foundational to current postcolonial heritage laws, others might be better regarded—whether through over-reaching ambition or misalignment with local conditions—as failed experiments in the colonial legislative laboratory.

We have argued here that, while Indian legislation was also influenced by debates in other colonial territories, it was an important source for both natural and cultural heritage legislation. This is most apparent in the agency of celebrated figures such as Lord Curzon, whose passion for both the ancient monuments and 'natural contents' of Empire were forcefully expressed through often stringent legislative measures. As both restorer of the Taj Mahal and saviour of Tattershall Castle, promoter of both the Indian Ancient Monuments Act of 1904 and the English Ancient Monuments Consolidation and Amendment Act of 1913, Curzon was also a crucial bridge between cultural heritage debates in the colonies and the metropole. But we should remember that Curzon was neither the first nor the last such bridging figure in India or elsewhere. Indeed, just as the migration of heritage legislation was made possible through multiple circuits of colonial communication networks, it was also consequent upon the physical migrations of individuals, whose interests frequently bridged the worlds of cultural and natural heritage, as they moved between postings in different colonial territories within the various Imperial and Colonial services.

By reflecting on the perhaps unwitting protection of the customs and practices (what we now regard as intangible cultural heritage) of indigenous populations within migrations of natural heritage legislation, our discussion also provides a new perspective on familiar questions concerning colonial perceptions of the 'native peoples' of empire. Here, as in so many spheres of colonial thinking, we find contradictions and inconsistencies, but we also find

---

[101] W. Schlich, *Schlich's Manual of Forestry. Volume I. Forest Policy in the British Empire*, 3rd edn (London, 1906).

a pattern in which the heritage of indigenous people itself migrates from the domain of natural heritage legislation to that of cultural heritage legislation. Thus, in their absence from the early cultural heritage legislation we find the posited status of natives as a 'people without history' confirmed. Indigenous populations were, rather, themselves considered 'a living memorial of the past';[102] a remnant of prehistory somehow related to the archaeological and palaeoanthropological discoveries that were then being excavated. As we have seen in the Southern Rhodesian context, as 'bushmen' and 'tribals', they were regarded as incapable of building architectural monuments worthy of preservation. Destined for extinction before the 'onward march of civilization', their way of life and material culture became the preserve of salvage ethnographers. Placed within their natural habitat, however, and 'tamed' (through military intervention, if necessary, as in the case of Chotanagpur), native populations were also ennobled and idealized, and the perceived wisdom of their innate custodianship of the environment was reified—not least, through the legislative measures we have discussed. As a vulnerable part of the 'natural contents' of Empire, then, they had to be protected from the culture (and laws) of the modern capitalist state. It was only in the 1940s, when *les arts primitifs* had become sought after within metropolitan art markets, that indigenous peoples' heritage became incorporated into cultural heritage preservation, and 'objects of ethnographical interest' were consequently reframed in the legislation as 'antiquities' and 'relics'. Finally, from the mid-1970s, a more informed discourse began to emerge, in which natural and cultural, tangible and intangible were at last reunited in a new heritage paradigm, most explicitly articulated in South Africa's 1999 National Heritage Resources Act.

[102] Northcote W. Thomas, 'Editor's Preface', in Alice Werner, *The Natives of British Central Africa* (London, 1906), vi.

Creatures Enshrined: Wild Animals as Bearers of Heritage

Peter Coates

In 1976, Patrick Cormack published a book entitled *Heritage in Danger*. The Conservative MP, who founded the All-Party Parliamentary Arts and Heritage Group a few years later and chaired it for thirty years, included chapters on the country house, the village, the church, and the city. His first chapter, however, was devoted to what he characterized as 'at once the most obvious and enjoyed and also the most neglected aspect of our heritage': the countryside.[1] In fact, Cormack greatly exaggerated the extent to which the rural landscape has been neglected within understandings of heritage and initiatives for historical preservation. Since the mid-nineteenth century, in Britain, as elsewhere in Europe and North America, places primarily associated with nature have acquired value as 'visible symbols of an invisible past'[2]—whether in the guise of picturesque countryside, outstandingly beautiful scenery, or 'pristine' wilderness. The remit of the National Trust (1895) was to protect places of natural beauty in England and Wales as well as historic buildings: at a meeting to plan the new organization, founder Octavia Hill appealed to those 'to whom historic memories loom large, who love the wild bird, butterfly, and plant, who realise the natural value of the hill slope lighted by sun or shadowed by cloud'.[3] And by the early twentieth century, many preservationists considered the heritage value of exceptional places (the 'natural beauties of rural districts', to use Baldwin Brown's phrase) equal to that of the most esteemed material products of human creation. As explained by Brown, a professor of fine arts, the fundamental basis for comparison was the similar 'effect on the mind':

> the monument, in the strict meaning of the term, appeals to our
> sense of the immensity of time. In like manner, the sublime objects

---

[1] Patrick Cormack, *Heritage in Danger* (London, 1976), 27.

[2] Robin W. Winks, 'Visible Symbols of an Invisible Past', *National Parks Magazine*, 57 (1983), 3-4.

[3] Quoted in Ben Cowell, *The Heritage Obsession: The Battle for England's Past* (Stroud, 2008), 95.

          © The Past and Present Society

of nature touch the imagination with the awe-inspiring apprehension of the vastness of the material universe.[4]

A new concept emerged in the early 1900s—more or less simultaneously in various European languages—to embrace the multifarious entities that lay outside the category of human achievement that Brown summed up as 'ancient buildings and other objects of historical and artistic interest': the 'natural monument'.[5] Hugo Wilhelm Conwentz, a prominent German botanist and museum director who travelled extensively in Europe to encourage care of natural monuments (*Naturdenkmalpflege*), was concerned that 'many monuments of nature are far advanced towards ruin'. Nonetheless, he was encouraged by the growing recognition, internationally, that 'monuments of nature as well as of art' merited protection against human depredation.[6]

The process of heritage-making among entities that have been assigned to the non-human realm (regardless of the intimacy, even inseparability, of nature and culture) does not stop with physical features such as waterfalls, natural arches, precipitous canyons and mountain peaks. Heritage is a species-crossing concept and animate life forms have also been woven into its fabric since the late nineteenth century. Conwentz, a founding father of nature conservation in continental Europe as well as a leading light in the German *Heimatschutz* movement, routinely included the world's wildlife, from musk oxen in Canada to European beaver, and from the reindeer of Spitsbergen to large African fauna, within the capacious and flexible category of natural monument.[7]

These animal examples invest the hackneyed notion of 'living heritage' with fresh meaning. Yet comparatively little scholarly attention has been devoted to the place of wildlife within conceptions of heritage. The role of efforts to preserve endangered species within the wider discourse and practice of preservation has also been overlooked. This neglect applies just as much to the cultural and political status of wild animals as national symbols as to their position within the shared patrimony of humanity. This essay seeks to rectify this oversight. Part one examines the co-evolution and co-existence of notions of cultural and natural heritage in national contexts (both British and American) as well as the manifestation of this phenomenon on an international scale. This distinctive blend of cultural, natural, and national heritage is then examined with reference to two North American species whose future

---

[4] G. Baldwin Brown, *The Care of Ancient Monuments* (Cambridge, 1905), 21.

[5] Brown, *Care of Ancient Monuments*, preface.

[6] Hugo Wilhelm Conwentz, *The Care of Natural Monuments with Special Reference to Great Britain and Germany* (Cambridge, 1909), 35.

[7] Conwentz, *Care of Natural Monuments*, 28–34.

was precarious in the late nineteenth century: the buffalo and the passenger pigeon. This discussion extends to the capacity not just to regret and deplore a species' near-eclipse (as in the case of the buffalo) or actual eclipse (the passenger pigeon's fate), but to mourn extinction and memorialize an animal as an ingredient of lost heritage as well. Coverage also encompasses the overlapping and sometimes intersecting narratives of human and non-human extinction.

This essay's second section examines how two particular species more recently endangered have been embraced as living environmental heritage on two different scales, the national level and the international. The national example, England's red squirrel, furnishes more than just an arresting example of the conviction, expressed in this instance by the pioneering British ecologist, Arthur Tansley, that 'the wild life of our country is part of our national heritage'. Anthony Smith has introduced the concept of the ethnoscape to designate a landscape imbued with 'poetic ethnic meaning through the historicization of nature' at national level, and though he did not consider the role of animals, this particular native creature demonstrates how immense value has been imposed on a relatively small animal that is enlarged symbolically through elevation to the rank of supreme ethno-species within the territorial confines of the nation's ethnoscape.[8] It also provides scope for reflection on the role of authenticity as a central, perhaps indispensable ingredient in the ascent to the rank of heritage and assignation of heritage value to an object, place, or species.

Whereas the squirrel can be described as an example of charismatic *mini-fauna*, the other creature selected represents the more familiar category of wildlife now commonly referred to as charismatic megafauna: the polar bear.[9] Since the early 1960s, certain species (invariably mammals that are large,

---

[8] Arthur George Tansley, *Our Heritage of Wild Nature: A Plea for Organised Nature Conservation* (Cambridge, 1945), 1, 6, 60-1; Peder Anker, *Imperial Ecology: Environmental Order in the British Empire, 1895-1945* (Cambridge, MA, 2001), 226-8; Anthony D. Smith, *Myths and Memories of the Nation* (Oxford, 1999), 16, 149-57.

[9] For an early (perhaps the earliest) articulation of the phrase 'charismatic megafauna', see Devra G. Kleiman and John Seidensticker, 'Pandas in the Wild: The Giant Pandas of Wolong', *Science*, 228/4701 (17 May 1985), 875-6. An alternative term is 'nonhuman charisma'. For a geographer's highly theorized discussion of the ecological, aesthetic, and corporeal elements of nonhuman charisma (within a UK context, with specific reference to the corncrake and stag beetle, and without reference to the role of animals within heritage), see Jamie Lorimer, 'Nonhuman charisma', *Environment and Planning D: Society and Space*, 25 (2007), 911-32. 'Charismatic mini-fauna', is a term of more recent vintage, with an internet presence since 2007. For a recent example, see David Barash, 'Moonwalking charismatic mini-fauna', *The Chronicle of Higher Education*, 1

photogenic, and readily anthropomorphized) have become the beneficiaries of international campaigns by global groups such as the World Wildlife Fund (WWF) (1961) and Greenpeace (1971).[10] Most closely associated with WWF in the popular mind until the end of the twentieth century was the giant panda, which supplied the organization with a logo (1961) that has persisted to this day. Meanwhile, London Zoo's celebrated but unmated female panda, Chi-Chi (1957-72), on whom this truly iconic image was based, became a poster creature—the face—of global conservation.[11]

In 1985, reviewers of George B. Schaller's book, *The Giant Pandas of Wolong*, remarked that

> there are probably no more than a dozen of the approximately 4000 mammals that are recognized by the vast majority of people, regardless of where they live and what language they speak. Most people, if ever exposed, remember and are able to name elephants, tigers, bears, rhinoceroses. The giant panda probably tops this list of charismatic megafauna in terms of attractiveness and mass appeal.[12]

Notwithstanding their global reputations, terrestrial creatures like the panda and the tiger remained firmly associated with particular countries: China and India respectively.[13] Additional species, non-terrestrial, attracted attention and acquired renown precisely because of their internationality, among them various whales: one of Mexico's World Heritage sites is the Whale Sanctuary of El Vizcaíno, inscribed in 1993, which protects lagoons midway down the western coast of the Baja California peninsula that provide calving and overwintering sites for the eastern grey whale.[14]

March 2010, at http://chronicle.com/blogs/brainstorm/moonwalking-charismatic-mini-fauna/44399.

[10] On environmental INGO proliferation between the early 1960s and early 1980s, see David John Frank et al., 'The Rationalization and Organization of Nature in World Culture', in John Boli and George M. Thomas (eds), *Constructing World Culture: International Nongovernmental Organizations since 1875* (Palo Alto, 1999), 81-99.

[11] Henry Nicholls, 'The Afterlife of Chi-Chi', in Samuel J. M. M. Alberti (ed.), *Afterlives of Animals: A Museum Menagerie* (Charlottesville, 2011), 182-3.

[12] Kleiman and Seidensticker, 'Pandas in the Wild', 875-6.

[13] Mahesh Rangarajan, 'From Princely Symbol to Conservation Icon: A Political History of the Lion in India', in M. Hasan and N. Nakazato (eds), *The Unfinished Agenda: Nation Building in South Asia* (New Delhi, 2001), 399-442.

[14] Emily Young, 'Local People and Conservation in Mexico's El Vizcaino Biosphere Reserve', *Geographical Review*, 89:3 (1999), 368–70. The Biosphere Reserve to which the Whale Sanctuary belongs was established in 1988.

Over the past decade, however, the polar bear, a species that straddles the divide between the terrestrial and the non-terrestrial, has displaced the panda and whale from their privileged positions in the pantheon of charismatic (or 'flagship') species. For Rachel Poliquin, stuffed polar bears brought together from locales around Britain for an exhibition in Bristol in 2004 ('Nanoq: Flat Out and Blueness') were 'troubling environmental documents'.[15] This tendency has since intensified, as campaigners rally around and parade the polar bear as peerless symbol of the 'Anthropocene'—a term that atmospheric chemist Paul Crutzen and freshwater biologist Eugene Stoermer coined in 2000 to denote our current geological epoch, triggered by the onset of large scale industrialism, in which the collective impacts of disparate human activities extend beyond the biological and are judged to be so extensive on a global scale that humanity has become tantamount to a geological force.[16]

My examination of how particular creatures have become woven into the fabric of heritage does not, however, indicate a clear shift in motives from the cultural to the ecological since the mid-nineteenth century. When animals have been subjected to the heritage treatment more recently, cultural and national particularities are displayed as well as a commitment to biodiversity.

The intimacy between cultural and natural heritage

'We are born to die; these frescoes are born to live', remarked Edward Waldo Forbes in 1920, with reference to the Sistine Chapel. 'When we die', the director of Harvard University's Fogg Art Museum continued, 'others will take our places; but what would replace Leonardo da Vinci's Last Supper or the paintings in the Uffizi, should they perish?'[17] There is still no particular danger that the human race will become extinct anytime soon. On the other hand, pandas have joined and polar bears are joining the ranks of Leonardo's irreplaceable creations.

The pioneering American conservationist and polymath, George Perkins Marsh, was just as concerned with reversing the 'physical decrepitude' of the natural world of the former Roman empire as he was with preserving its

---

[15] Rachel Poliquin, *The Breathless Zoo: Taxidermy and the Cultures of Longing* (Harrisburg, 2012), 3.

[16] Jan Zalasiewicz, 'Are we now living in the Anthropocene?', *GSA Today*, 18:2 (February 2008), 4-8; Ian Zalasiewicz, et al., 'The New World of the Anthropocene', *Environmental Science and Technology* (2010), 2228-31.

[17] Edward W. Forbes, 'The Technical Study and Physical Care of Paintings', *The Art Bulletin*, 2:3 (1920), 160; David Lowenthal, 'Omens from the Mediterranean: Conservation Nostrums in *Mare Nostrum*', *Studies in Conservation*, 55 (2010), 231.

cultural artefacts.[18] Marsh, who served as the first American Ambassador to Italy (1861-82), mainly worried about increasingly unsustainable treatment of soils, forests, and rivers. Yet in his landmark study of humanity's deleterious environmental impacts, *Man and Nature* (1864), he also noted the extinction and near-extirpation of various animal species: the eradication of wolf and bear in Britain centuries ago; the even earlier disappearance of the lion from Asia Minor; the more recent near-demise of the North American beaver, and the dwindling numbers of chamois and ibex in the Alps at the time of writing.[19] Marsh knew full well that we can no more replicate a species than we can reproduce the *Last Supper*.

Marsh's voice was not a lone voice in the wilderness. On both sides of the Atlantic, preservationist interests who set themselves up as the representatives of posterity embraced natural and cultural patrimonies that industrialization and urbanization jeopardized in equal measure. Harvard University's first professor of fine arts, Charles Eliot Norton, who also served as the first president of the Archaeological Institute of America—and wrote about topics such as medieval church building—campaigned in the 1880s to restrict what he and his ilk regarded as the vulgar commercialization of Niagara Falls. The establishment of Grand Canyon National Park (1919) was similarly hailed as 'a heritage unto our children's children forever'.[20] In American minds, especially, natural and man-made heritage were not just on a par within the enterprise of cultural nationalism; 'green old age' was superior. A year before Yellowstone National Park was established (1872), the explorer, scientist and eco-jingoist, Clarence King, hailed California's giant sequoias as 'monuments of living antiquity' that offered a far more powerful link between past and present than the 'imperishableness' of any 'fragment of human work, broken pillar or sand-worn image half lifted over pathetic desert'.[21]

Expressions of tension and perceptions of competition between the relative values of cultural and natural objects should not be taken too literally. In

[18] G. P. Marsh, *Man and Nature; or, the Earth as Modified by Human Action*, ed. David Lowenthal (Cambridge, MA, 1965 [1864]), 11.

[19] Marsh, *Man and Nature*, 76-9.

[20] Charles Eliot Norton, *Letters of Charles Eliot Norton: With Biographical Comments by his Daughter Sarah Norton and M. A. DeWolfe Howe*, vol. II (Boston, 1913), 94-6, 135; Linda C. Dowling, *Charles Eliot Norton: The Art of Reform in Nineteenth-Century America* (Lebanon, NH, 2007), 144; James Turner, *The Liberal Education of Charles Eliot Norton* (Baltimore, 1999), 282, 290-1, 297; Charles F. Lummis, 'An Appreciation of Grand Canyon National Park', in *Grand Canyon National Park, Arizona* (Washington, DC, 1919-20), 4.

[21] Clarence King, *Mountaineering in the Sierra Nevada* (New York, 1871), 51-2.

many cases (witness King's statement), the invidious comparison was primarily a rhetorical device. That disputes between the respective champions of cultural and natural heritage value were largely hypothetical is suggested by the first piece of legislation that the US Congress enacted to establish the authority of the federal government in the realm of heritage protection. The Antiquities Act of 1906 was designed as a tool sufficiently flexible to encompass all manner of threatened resources. The bill introduced into Congress authorized the Secretary of the Interior to protect 'monuments, cliff-dwellings, cemeteries, graves, mounds, forts, or any other work of prehistoric, primitive, or aboriginal man, and also any natural formation of scientific or scenic value or interest, or natural wonder or curiosity'.[22] The congressional sponsor was John Lacey of Iowa, who gave his name to the Lacey Act of 1902, the first comprehensive federal wildlife measure (which barred interstate transportation of birds and animals taken in contravention of state laws). The Antiquities Act that was passed empowered the President to protect historical landmarks, prehistoric structures, and other objects of historical or scientific interest by setting aside tracts of public lands as national monuments. True to the catholic spirit informing the legislation, Theodore Roosevelt immediately deployed the act to protect items of cultural and natural heritage alike. The first two national monuments designated were the 386-metre 'volcanic sentinel' of Devil's Tower, Wyoming (a sacred site for Lakota tribes), and the fossilized trees of Arizona's Petrified Forest (rescued from the 'civilized savages' [white Americans] who sawed and dynamited the 'gem' logs).[23]

This inclusive approach was an equally prominent feature of the coterminous supranational discourse of heritage and hallmark of the preservationist mission at an international level. The acceptance within formally constituted bodies of international governance of the idea of a common global heritage stems from the League of Nations. In its search for a relatively apolitical shared experience and source of non-contentious universalist value, the League settled on the indivisible heritage of mankind. The investigation

---

[22] Ronald F. Lee, 'The Origins of the Antiquities Act', in David Harmon, Francis P. McManamon, and Dwight T. Pitcaithley (eds), *The Antiquities Act: A Century of American Archaeology, Historic Preservation, and Nature Conservation* (Tucson, 2006), 29.

[23] Richard Waldbauer and Sherry Hutt, 'The Antiquities Act of 1906 at its Centennial', *CRM: The Journal of Heritage Stewardship*, 3:1 (Winter 2006), 36-48; *Devils Tower National Monument* (Washington, DC, 1981), 9; Charles F. Lummis, 'An Appreciation of the Petrified Forest of Arizona', in *Petrified Forest National Monument, Arizona* (Washington, DC, 1919-20), 4.

and promotion of this new commodity became the responsibility of the sub-commission on Arts and Letters of the League's International Committee on Intellectual Co-operation (ICIC). In the event, 'nature' assumed primacy over 'culture'. In 1925, the League placed the protection of 'natural beauty' on its heritage agenda. ICIC's first report in 1928 (not acted on) suggested that the goal of bringing nationalities together could be materially advanced by creating trans-border, bi-national parks.[24]

After 1945, when international initiatives encountered a more conducive climate than prevailed in the 1920s, the United Nations Educational, Scientific, and Cultural Organization (UNESCO) assumed the role of a reconstituted ICIC. UNESCO's first Director-General (1946-48), Julian Huxley, a British biologist long active in the international/imperial conservation community, spoke of the world's scientific/natural and cultural heritage in the same breath.[25]

Lists of man-made wonders, such as the 'seven wonders of the ancient world', date back, of course, to classical antiquity, but this conflation of the natural and the cultural heritage ventured substantially beyond the well-established notion of the natural 'wonders of the world'. The list of these marvels encompassed extraordinary features akin to Wyoming's Devil's Tower and Arizona's Petrified Forest. Global guides to nature's spectacles that became widely available in the mid-nineteenth century offered Italy's Mount Etna, the Peak District of Derbyshire, the Cataracts of the Nile, and the Mammoth Tree of California (giant sequoia) as examples of Nature's 'most wondrous magnificence and beauty'. Even butterflies, herrings, and baboons featured alongside antiquities and 'remarkable edifices' in other, more fanciful compilations of the world's wonders. Fifty years later, marvels such as the Blue Grotto of Capri, Fingal's Cave (Scotland), Niagara Falls, the Lagoons of Venice, the Vale of Kashmir, and Yellowstone were still served up primarily as examples of the 'grand, the curious and the awe-inspiring'.[26] But Huxley's

---

[24] Anna-Katharina Wöbse, 'Framing the Heritage of Mankind: National Parks on the International Agenda', in Bernhard Gissibl, Sabine Höhler, and Patrick Kupper (eds), *Civilizing Nature: National Parks in Global Historical Perspective* (New York, 2012), 145-7; Wöbse, ' "The world after all was one": The International Environmental Network of UNESCO and IUNP, 1945-50', *Contemporary European History*, 20:3 (2011), 335.

[25] Julian Huxley, *UNESCO: Its Purpose and its Philosophy* (New York, 1948 [1946]), 65; Krishna P. Dronamraju, *If I am to be Remembered: The Life and Work of Julian Huxley with Selected Correspondence* (Singapore, 1993), 62-3; William M. Adams, *Against Extinction: The Story of Conservation* (London, 2004), 48-51.

[26] John Loraine Abbott, *The Wonders of the World: A Complete Museum, Descriptive and Pictorial, of the Wonderful Phenomena and Results of Nature, Science and Art* (Hartford, CT, 1855), 3, 6-7; Robert Sears, *The Wonders of the World* (New York, 1856); Esther

contention that these wonders represented the patrimony of humankind and the shared ground of an emerging international community moved supranational thinking to a fresh stage.

The 1960s was a transitional decade that looked both forwards and backwards, as international organizations sought to embed Huxley's notion of a world heritage that embraced both nature and culture. At the first world conference on national parks, held in 1962 in Seattle under the auspices of the International Union for Conservation of Nature and Natural Resources (IUCN, 1956),[27] co-sponsored by UNESCO and hosted by the US National Park Service, there was still plenty of emphasis on outstanding scenery and magnificent wildlife—what President John F. Kennedy, in his letter to delegates, referred to as 'the majesty of the earth'. And yet, though the term biodiversity did not appear in conservationist discourse until the 1980s, the published proceedings were replete with references to 'wildlife heritage' and delegates increasingly stressed the contribution of national parks as the habitat of globally significant threatened species—'nature islands for the world', according to the title of the keynote address of US Secretary of the Interior, Stewart L. Udall—rather than their recreational value and/or national symbolism.[28]

The idea of a World Heritage Trust 'for the identification, establishment and management of the world's superb natural and scenic areas and historic sites' was articulated at the White House Conference on International Cooperation in 1965.[29] The conviction that the natural world and its ecological support systems are just as much a part of the common heritage of mankind as its cultural products formally entered international discourse in 1972. At its general conference in Paris, UNESCO adopted the Convention Concerning the Protection of the World Cultural and Natural Heritage. As well as twinning nature and culture, the Convention propounded a sweeping

---

Singleton, *Greatest Wonders of the World: As Seen and Described by Famous Writers* (New York, 1900), v, vii-ix.

[27] A non-governmental umbrella organization that now consists of over a thousand individual governmental and NGO member organizations, IUCN superseded the International Union for the Protection of Nature (IUPN, 1948) in 1956. See Martin Holdgate, *The Green Web: A Union for World Conservation* (Gland, Switzerland, 1999).

[28] John F. Kennedy, letter to delegates (23 June 1962), foreword, *First World Conference on National Parks*, ed. Alexander B. Adams (Washington, DC, 1962); Stewart L. Udall, 'Nature Islands for the World', *First World Conference on National Parks*, 3; ibid., 60, 336, 9, 28, 28, 32, 53, 59, 75.

[29] Sarah Titchen, '*On the Construction of Outstanding Universal Value: UNESCO's World Heritage Convention*' (PhD thesis, Australian National University, 1995), 52-63.

concept of heritage that transcended political and geographical boundaries: 'each nation holds in trust for the rest of mankind those parts of the world heritage that are found within its boundaries'. Outstanding natural resources should therefore be preserved as 'part of the world heritage of mankind as a whole'.[30] This conviction was reinforced that same year in Yellowstone National Park, where, to mark the centenary of the world's first national park, the US National Park Service hosted the IUCN's Second World Conference on National Parks, with the theme, 'National Parks: Heritage for a Better World'.[31]

The internationalization of nature in the early 1970s was reinforced by the Man and the Biosphere Programme (MAB) that UNESCO launched in 1971. The biosphere reserve, a fresh category of protected area, was designed to encompass examples of the full range of planetary biomes (and, in principle, acknowledged the presence of local inhabitants and human land uses within the buffer zones of protected areas).[32] Though remaining under the jurisdiction of the nation state, designated areas were conceived as part of what Udall, in 1962, had dubbed the 'heritage of all mankind'.

Many conservationists in the developing world were uneasy about the international leadership role that the United States assumed, and suspected that internationalization effectively meant the imposition of the Yellowstone model and its underlying values as a global norm.[33] Yet this process of internationalization in the 1970s applied to protected units in the United States as well. The meaning of places such as Yellowstone was also de-nationalized. For more than a century, Yellowstone's primary value had been couched in terms of a scenic wonder of incomparable character that had provided a natural foundation for the notion of American exceptionalism by giving material expression to the ideology of 'nature's nation'.[34] Designation as a United

---

[30] UNESCO, 'Convention Concerning the Protection of the World Cultural and Natural Heritage', Paris, 16 November 1972, 1; Julie Reeves, *Culture and International Relations* (Abingdon, 2004), 48-55.

[31] Hugh Elliott (ed.), *Second World Conference on National Parks: Yellowstone and Grand Teton National Parks, USA, September 18-27, 1972: Proceedings of a Conference Sponsored and Organized by the National Parks Centennial Commission of the United States of America; the National Park Service of the U.S. Department of the Interior; and the International Union for Conservation of Nature and Natural Resources* (Morges, Switzerland, 1974).

[32] http://www.unesco.org/new/en/natural-sciences/environment/ecological-sciences/bio-sphere-reserves/ [accessed 7 March 2014].

[33] Wöbse, 'Framing the Heritage of Mankind', 151-2.

[34] The term 'nature's nation' first appears in the title of Perry Miller's intellectual history of the United States: *Nature's Nation* (Cambridge, MA, 1967). Thirty years later, it provided

Nations Biosphere Reserve (1976) and a UNESCO World Heritage Site (1978) was an exercise in re-scaling that created a fresh layer of value that was international. The lack of fit between the configuration of the national park and the shape of local ecosystems—the winter range of the park's elk herd, for instance, lies outside the park—was not addressed by the additional designation of biosphere reserve.[35] Nonetheless, the value of the park's charismatic megafauna was internationalized for the global community through upgrade to one of humankind's natural 'crown jewels': the demise of the park's grizzly bears, for instance, no longer represented just a regional or national loss. The consequences were now global.[36]

To satisfy the criteria for inclusion on UNESCO's World Heritage List (also instigated in 1972) of sites that belonged to 'all the people of the world, irrespective of the territory on which they are located', a site had to possess 'Outstanding Universal Value' for 'present and future generations of all humanity' and represent an 'irreplaceable' source of 'life and inspiration'. Though the listing committee that evaluated applications did not operate according to a set of ecological considerations, Article 2 ventured a definition of the criteria for natural heritage identified in 1972. In addition to stipulating 'Outstanding Universal Value' from the 'aesthetic or scientific point of view' and in terms of 'natural beauty', the framers referred in more tangible fashion to 'precisely delineated areas which constitute the habitat of threatened species of animals'. The related 'Operational Guidelines' ventured further, specifying 'spectacles presented by great concentrations of animals' as a characteristic of a site that possesses 'unique, rare or superlative natural phenomena'.[37] And some wildlife conservationists, two of whom were cited by a

---

John Opie with the title for his survey of US environmental history: *Nature's Nation: An Environmental History of the United States* (Fort Worth, TX, 1998).

[35] John D. Varley, 'Managing Yellowstone National Park into the Twenty-First Century: The Park as an Aquarium', in James K. Agee et al. (eds), *Ecosystem Management for Parks and Wilderness* (Seattle, 1988), 218.

[36] David Rains Wallace, *Yellowstone: A Natural and Human History* (Harpers Ferry, 2001), 98-9.

[37] UNESCO, 'Convention Concerning the Protection of the World Cultural and Natural Heritage', Paris, 16 November 1972, 2; UNESCO, World Heritage Committee, First Session, 27 June–1 July 1977, 'Operational Guidelines for the World Heritage Committee', Paris, 30 June 1977, 1; UNESCO, Intergovernmental Committee for the Protection of the World Cultural and Natural Heritage (World Heritage Committee), First Session, 27 June–1 July 1977, 'Operational Guidelines for the Implementation of the World Heritage Convention', Paris, 20 October 1977, 4; UNESCO, Intergovernmental Committee for the Protection of the World Cultural and Natural Heritage *Operational*

delegate to the 1962 world conference on national parks, maintained that 'spectacular' herds of wildlife, such as East Africa's, were 'cultural treasures far more valuable and irreplaceable than man-made objects'.[38]

Mourning and memorializing 'the last of the race'

In the early 1960s, the wild species whose future engendered the greatest concern at international level were those of eastern Africa. The threats they faced from habitat loss and excessive hunting shaped Huxley's ideas of global ownership of wildlife and international responsibility for the preservation of this priceless heritage.[39] Half a century earlier, the buffalo that had once roamed the North American plains in staggering numbers had galvanized American conservationists in the way that a later generation was exercised by the future status of the Serengeti's awesome migrating herds. In his influential tract, *Our Vanishing Wild Life* (1913), in connection with the need to transmit species 'unimpaired' to future generations, William T. Hornaday, the leading early twentieth-century American wildlife preservationist, employed the term heritage no less than five times.[40] In his foreword to Hornaday's book, Henry Fairfield Osborn, the president of the New York Zoological Society, equated the value of the natural and the cultural in making the case for nature's monuments as eminently worthy of preservationist attention and effort:

> We no longer destroy great works of art. They are treasured, and regarded as of priceless value; but we have yet to attain the state of

---

Guidelines for the Implementation of the World Heritage Convention (Paris, November 2011), 13-14, 21. Examples of intergovernmental treaties founded on the recognition that wild animals are a key constituent of humankind's common heritage are UNEP's Convention on the Conservation of Migratory Species of Wild Animals ('Bonn Convention', 1979) and the Council of Europe's Convention on the Conservation of European Wildlife and Natural Habitats ('Bern Convention', 1982): Kemal Baslar, *The Concept of the Common Heritage of Mankind in International Law* (The Hague, 1998), 311-13; Holmes Rolston, III, 'Rights and Responsibilities on the Home Planet', *Yale Journal of International Law*, 18 (1993), 276; Mark Cioc, *The Game of Conservation: International Treaties to Protect the World's Migratory Animals* (Athens, OH, 2009), 149, 151.

[38] George A. Petrides and Wendell G. Swank, 'The Status of Wildlife and Wilderness Areas in East Africa', *Oryx*, 5 (May 1960), 298. As quoted in D. O. Mathews, 'The Economics of Parks and Tourism', *First World Conference on National Parks*, 124.

[39] Julian Huxley, 'The Treasure House of Wild Life', *The Observer* (13 November 1960), 23; 'Wild Life as a World Asset', *The Observer* (27 November 1960), 23.

[40] William T. Hornaday, *Our Vanishing Wild Life: Its Extermination and Preservation* (New York 1913), 287, 302, 319, 340.

> civilization where the destruction of a glorious work of Nature, whether it be a cliff, a forest, or a species of mammal or bird, is regarded with equal abhorrence.

Osborn was especially critical of 'we Americans', whom he placed firmly in the global vanguard with regard to uncivilized behaviour that disfigured the 'wonderful heritage of the beauty of Nature today'. Still operating on a global plane, he contended that it was not just the United States or any other country that was a 'poorer place to live in' when an animal species was lost; the 'whole earth' was impoverished.[41] As part of his critique of human arrogance, Hornaday mounted an ethical high horse: 'we have no right to squander and destroy a wild-life heritage of priceless value which we have done nothing to create, and which is not ours to destroy'. To eliminate a species was arguably even more heinous than to wreck a superlative artwork.[42]

Half a century before *Our Vanishing Wild Life*, when Marsh wrote *Man and Nature*, North American bison numbers gave no cause for concern. By 1913, however, the continent's largest wild ungulate was the species at the forefront of preservationist attention in the United States. The American Bison Society that Hornaday co-founded with Theodore Roosevelt in 1905 rescued the remnants from the brink of extinction less for the sake of the species itself (let alone to preserve biodiversity) than for its value as a virile symbol of former frontier culture and conditions in a nation emasculated by urbanization and industrialization and contaminated by immigration from the wrong parts of Europe. For the Bison Society's overwhelmingly male, patrician, 'old stock' members, based in north-eastern cities and with headquarters in New York City, the bison was a 'living icon of an imagined heroic West'.[43]

As such, Hornaday was initially engrossed with the commemoration of the final representatives of their 'race' rather than their preservation as live specimens in situ. A premier attraction in Washington's National Museum (Smithsonian) in the late nineteenth- and early twentieth century was the Bison Group, a cluster of six 'choice' bison that Hornaday harvested on a Smithsonian specimen collecting trip to Montana. As the *Washington Star* reported (10 March 1888), this was a 'bit of the Wild West reproduced at the National Museum', complete with 'real' buffalo grass and 'real' Montana 'dirt', not to mention a buffalo trail, water hole (optical illusion) and the bleached skulls of two 'victims' of 'cruel' hunters ('accessories'). A large male—'the giant of his race'—dominates the representative group that

[41] Osborn, Foreword, in Hornaday, *Our Vanishing Wild Life*, vii-viii.

[42] Hornaday, *Our Vanishing Wild Life*, 376.

[43] Andrew Isenberg, *The Destruction of the Bison* (Cambridge, 2000), 168-9.

includes males and females, young and mature, set against a naturalistic backdrop, within an enormous mahogany case—the museum's largest ever display. This alpha male, measuring six feet at the shoulder and believed to be one of the largest recorded specimens, was feted as a fitting 'monument to the greatness of his race'.[44]

Samuel Alberti contends that death marks the crucial stage in an animal's passage from nature to culture.[45] This is certainly true insofar as dead nature is reconstituted as live heritage when a wild creature is converted into an object in a museum display. Aldo Leopold, a founding father of ecological science, whose posthumously published book, *A Sand County Almanac* (1949), was disseminated as a key text of the popular age of environmentalism when it dawned in the early 1960s, believed that the resurrection of a vanished species through the heritage treatment was a poor substitute for the real thing:

> There will always be pigeons in books and in museums, but these are effigies and images, dead to all hardships and all delights. Book-pigeons cannot dive out of a cloud to make the deer run for cover, or clap their wings in thunderous applause of mast-laden woods. Book-pigeons cannot breakfast on new-mown wheat in Minnesota, and dine on blueberries in Canada. They know of no urge of seasons; they feel no kiss of the sun, no lash of wind and weather. They live forever by not living at all.[46]

More recently, in the same vein, Rachel Poliquin has seen a stuffed beast as a fragmented, non-living 'animal-thing'.[47] Yet by making the transition to eternal life through admittance to the realm of heritage a deceased animal enjoys a certain vitality that Leopold and Poliquin fail to appreciate.

The most striking example—at least in the English-speaking world—of how dead animals can be stuffed with the substance of heritage is that of the passenger pigeon. When Marsh wrote *Man and Nature*, what was once the most prodigious avian species in the skies and woods of North America was already in deep trouble. 'The net and the gun', he noted, 'have so reduced its abundance

---

[44] William T. Hornaday, *The Extermination of the American Bison* (Washington, DC, 1889), 546-8; Stephen T. Asma, *Stuffed Animals and Pickled Heads: The Culture and Evolution of Natural History Museums* (Oxford, 2001), 42-3.

[45] Samuel J. M. M. Alberti, 'Maharajah the Elephant's Journey from Nature to Culture', in Alberti (ed.), *Afterlives of Animals*, 37. The skeleton of Maharajah, an Asian elephant (the 'elephant who walked to Manchester' [1872]), dominates the first floor display of the Museum of Manchester.

[46] Leopold, *Sand County Almanac*, 109.

[47] Poliquin, *Breathless Zoo*, 39, 41, 215.

that its appearance in large numbers is recorded only at long intervals, and it is never seen in the great flocks remembered by many still living observers as formerly very common'.[48] The last known pair, named for the nation's first 'First Couple', George and Martha Washington, resided in Cincinnati Zoo. The male half of the passenger pigeon's Last Couple was the first to go in 1909. The sign on her pagoda cage identified Martha (hatched in captivity, though whether she was born at the Zoo or sent there in 1902 remains a matter of dispute) as the last of her species. An object of enormous curiosity in this capacity, naturalists and ornithologists came from far afield to pay their respects to what was arguably the first species on the brink of extinction to attract international attention.[49] When notified of Martha's death, T. Gilbert Pearson, president of the National Audubon Societies, reportedly remarked that the death of 'the last of her tribe' was 'a calamity of as great importance in the eyes of naturalists as the death of a kaiser to Germans throughout the world'.[50]

After Martha died at the ripe old age, by pigeon standards, of twenty-nine on 1 September 1914, she was shipped off to Washington in a 300-pound block of ice.[51] She was stuffed at the Smithsonian's National Museum of Natural History, where she graced the Bird Hall until the early 1950s. The collection note (9 January 1915) read: 'Most Certainly the Last of her Kind'. Between 1956 and 1999, Martha was housed in the Extinction Case in the Birds of the World Hall. She left her perennial perch twice—in 1966 for the San Diego Zoological Society's Golden Jubilee Conservation Conference, and in 1974 to return to Cincinnati for the Zoo's dedication of her restored aviary (built in 1875) as the Passenger Pigeon Memorial Aviary. A bronze statue of Martha, perched on a rock outside the memorial aviary, is a designated National Historic Landmark.[52]

[48] Marsh, *Man and Nature*, 76-9.

[49] Christopher Cokinos, *Hope is the Thing with Feathers: A Personal Chronicle of Vanished Birds* (New York, 2010), 261-5.

[50] 'Last survivor of wild pigeons dead,' *Altoona Tribune* (13 September 1914). Reproduced in John C. French, *The Passenger Pigeon in Pennsylvania* (Altoona, Pa., 1919), 187.

[51] Arlie William Schorger, *The Passenger Pigeon: Its Natural History and Extinction* (Norman, 1955), 30; Joel Greenberg, *A Feathered River across the Sky: The Passenger Pigeon's Flight to Extinction* (New York, 2014), 188. Greenberg's book was published as part of Project Passenger Pigeon, which is marking the centenary of Martha's death with a series of activities to promote awareness of the need for species and habitat conservation in a world facing a so-called 'sixth mass extinction' ('Lessons from the past for a sustainable future'): http://passengerpigeon.org/index.html [accessed 31 March 2014].

[52] On animal memorialization through monuments, see Hilda Kean, 'The Moment of Greyfriars Bobby: The Changing Cultural Position of Animals 1800-1921', in Kathleen Kete (ed.), *A Cultural History of Animals in the Age of Empire* (Oxford, 2007), 25-46.

Site-specific memorials abound in depopulated pigeon country. In May 1947, the Wisconsin Society for Ornithology dedicated a bronze plaque on an oak tree in Wyalusing State Park. The plaque marked the spot where, in September 1899, the last passenger pigeon in the wild in Wisconsin was reputedly killed, victim of the 'avarice and thoughtlessness of man'. The main speaker at the event, Aldo Leopold, reflected that 'for one species to mourn the death of another is a new thing under the sun'.

> The Cro-Magnon who slew the last mammoth thought only of his prowess. The sailor who clubbed the last auk thought of nothing at all. But we, who have lost our pigeons, mourn the loss. Had the funeral been ours, the pigeons would hardly have mourned us. In this fact, rather than in Mr. DuPont's nylons or Mr. Vannevar Bush's bombs, lies objective evidence of our superiority over the beasts.[53]

For Leopold, the preservation of endangered species was a marker of the civilized state of a national community and a measure of the moral progress of the human species as a whole.[54]

Though Martha spent her last five years in Cincinnati Zoo by herself, she was not alone there in her afterlife. She shares a memorial plaque with the last Carolina parakeet, a male who, in this instance, outlived his mate (Lady Jane) by six months, and died in Martha's aviary in February 1918, though his body was 'lost in transit' to the Smithsonian.[55] His name, Incas, demonstrates the association— in the mind of 'old stock' Americans, at least, of native species and the new world's aboriginal human inhabitants. By the early 1900s, they, too, were widely regarded as being at 'the end of the trail' (the title of James

<hr>

[53] Leopold, 'On a Monument to the Pigeon', in Wisconsin Society for Ornithology, *Silent Wings: A Memorial to the Passenger Pigeon* (Madison, 1947). Reproduced as 'On a Monument to the Pigeon', in Aldo Leopold, *A Sand County Almanac* (New York, 1949), 110.

[54] For a British wildlife conservationist's identical sentiments, see Peter Chalmers-Mitchell, 'Zoos and National Parks', *Journal of the Society for the Preservation of the Fauna of Empire*, 15 (1931), 21-43.

[55] 'Far-famed last parrakeet of its kind is mourned at Zoo', *Cincinnati Times-Star* (22 February 1918); 'Two Carolina parrakeets remain at Cincinnati Zoo', *Cincinnati Post* (30 September 1916); George Laycock, 'The Last Parrakeet', *Audubon* 71:2 (March 1969), 21-5; Daniel McKinley, 'The Last Days of the Carolina Parakeet: Life in the Zoo', *Avicultural Magazine*, 83 (January 1977), 42-9; Mark V. Barrow, *Nature's Ghosts: Confronting Extinction from the Age of Jefferson to the Age of Ecology* (Chicago, 2009), 126-9; Joy W. Kraft, *The Cincinnati Zoo and Botanical Garden* (Chicago, 2010), 24, 120.

Fraser Earle's 18-foot plaster monument to the American Indian created for San Francisco's 1915 Panama-Pacific International Exposition).

The naming of the last Carolina parakeet, before Hornaday rightly declared the species extinct in the wild in his 1913 book, illustrates how the ingrained narrative of the Vanishing American, which received its best known popular expression in Zane Grey's 1925 novel of that name, merged with the newer narrative of the Vanishing Species.[56] Incas is derived from Uncas, one of the main protagonists in James Fenimore Cooper's novel, *The Last of the Mohicans* (1826). Uncas was allegedly 'the last of the Mohicans'—though, in choosing this particular name, Cooper took an historical figure, the celebrated seventeenth-century sachem (chief) of the Mohegans of eastern Connecticut, who died in the 1680s, and relocated him to a different place and time: among the Mahican tribe of upstate New York in the 1750s.[57] Thanks to the ennobling and updated link with Cooper's character, the granite obelisk inaugurated in memoriam on 4 July 1842 in Norwich, Connecticut, site of the tribal burial grounds, became—like Martha's aviary—a destination for pilgrimages.[58]

According to a New Jersey newspaper, the passing of the Indian, however regrettable, was the 'natural, inevitable result of the progress of society'.[59] A magazine closely associated with the National Rifle Association (*Arms and the Man*) was one of many publications that instantly compared Martha to the last of the Mohicans (in this case, Uncas' father, Chingachgook). An ornithologist's later pronouncement that 'the last Passenger Pigeon had gone like the "Last of the Mohicans"' restated the reflexive analogy between a hapless extinct bird and the equally ill-fated noble savage.[60] These announcements were a parody of the melodramatic and inaccurate newspaper headline, 'Last of the Mohegans Gone', that greeted the death in 1842—five

[56] For a comprehensive discussion, see Brian W. Dippie, *The Vanishing American: White Attitudes and U.S. Indian Policy* (Lawrence, 1991).

[57] Robert Erwin, 'Uncas the Mohegan: No Little Dog of the English', *Antioch Review*, 65:2 (Spring 2007), 354. Mohican is a conflation of Mahican and Mohegan.

[58] William L. Stone, *Uncas and Miantonomoh: a Historical Discourse, delivered at Norwich (Conn.), on the Fourth Day of July, 1842, on the occasion of the erection of a monument to the memory of Uncas, the white man's friend, and first chief of the Mohegans* (New York, 1842), ix; *The Uncas Monument, Published Once in Three Hundred and Fifty Years* (Norwich, Conn., 4 July 1842); Michael Leroy Oberg, *Uncas: First of the Mohegens* (Ithaca, 2003), 3, 8.

[59] *Newark Daily Advertiser*, quoted in Oberg, *Uncas*, 7.

[60] *Arms and the Man*, 56:31 (1914), 486; William C. Herman, 'The Last Passenger Pigeon', *Auk*, 65:1 (January 1948), 80.

months after the dedication of the monument to his notable forebear—of John Uncas, the last surviving male descendant of the real Uncas.[61]

Animal enlargement through 'heritagification'[62]
Squirrels and Englishness

In today's Britain, the discourse of the vanishing species receives its most heightened expression in connection with the native red squirrel. High on the current list of priorities for English wildlife conservationists is to ensure that this arboreal rodent does not suffer the fate of the passenger pigeon and Carolina parakeet. The squirrel's tale further illustrates how certain creatures, however small, enter national consciousness as objects of heritage that are cultural as well as environmental, which has transformed them into subjects of deep and sustained preservationist concern.

The tender regard for the red squirrel, sometimes verging onto nature jingoism, that many English people feel today is hardly self-evident or preordained; the creature's reputation is far from unblemished. As early twentieth-century commentators pointed out, the imported grey squirrel, the 'American stranger', was mischievous and destructive, but no more so than its pesky native counterpart. The red's taste for tree bark and shoots, and the 'very great' 'injury' inflicted on young conifer plantations, were well known.[63] The leading late nineteenth-century expert on what was then simply called 'the common squirrel' reported that 'unanimously, my correspondents condemn [it] as one of the most destructive animals [of] our forests' and that 'nowhere can I find anything said in its favour'.[64] Moreover, the red squirrel is not endemic to Britain. The sub-species that inhabits the British Isles is one of seventeen distributed across Eurasia from Portugal to Japan, distinguished from other reds by attributes such as monomorphism [absence of colour varieties] and the annual winter whitening of ear tufts and tail.

Yet with a little help from one of Beatrix Potter's most beloved animal creations, Squirrel Nutkin, the red squirrel has been converted from forester's

---

[61] *Newark Daily Advertiser*, quoted in Oberg, *Uncas*, 7. Other members of the tribe were still in town and numbers have since risen.

[62] For this inelegant term, see Beverley Butler, *Return to Alexandria: An Ethnohistory of Cultural Heritage Revivalism and Museum Memory* (Walnut Creek, CA., 2007), 21, 190.

[63] H. B. Watt, 'On the American Grey Squirrel (*Sciurus carolinensis*) in the British Isles', *The Essex Naturalist*, 20 (1923), 189-205; Rusticus, 'The Ways of the Squirrel', *Chamber's Edinburgh Journal*, 329 (1850), 247.

[64] J. A. Harvie-Brown, *The History of the Squirrel in Great Britain* (Edinburgh, 1881), 97, 103-05.

and orchardist's scourge to national animal emblem.[65] By the 1950s, re-branding as 'truly British' was complete.[66] 'Truly English', however, would capture the mood of concern and identity politics more accurately: from *c.*12 million on the eve of human colonization of the British Isles, red numbers have plunged to *c.*160,000, the great majority of which (120,000) reside in Scotland.[67] Alongside red telephone boxes, warm and flat beer, and the smack of willow against leather, a creature reinvented as charming and sprightly currently enjoys a high profile in the pantheon of Englishness.[68] To advance the red cause, a zoological sub-species has effectively been upgraded to a fully-fledged, endemic species through casual but potent taxonomic 'inflation'.[69]

Integral to these processes of reputational rehabilitation and scientific re-classification has been the demographic success and associated defamation of the red squirrel's larger and supposedly brasher and far less 'cute' American cousin. By 1950, according to a squirrel expert, 'our island race', the common squirrel, was highly uncommon, confined to 'islands' of conifer plantations amidst a 'sea of grey squirrel country'.[70] Britain's grey population currently stands at an estimated 2.5 million, of which 2 million live in England.[71] The remaining pockets of red survivors in England are confined to the fringes, such as the Lake District, home of Potter and Squirrel Nutkin. Rallying to the defence of these besieged redoubts, the red's defenders proliferate. The patron of the Red Squirrel Survival Trust is HRH The Prince of Wales, and Save Our Squirrels, a campaign operated by Red Alert (since renamed Red Squirrels Northern England), received National Heritage Lottery funding in 2006 to

[65] Hilda Kean, 'Save "Our" Red Squirrel: Kill the American Grey Tree Rat', in H. Kean, H. P. Martin, and S. Morgan (eds), *Seeing History: Public History in Britain Now* (London, 2000), 51-64; Beatrix Potter, *The Tale of Squirrel Nutkin* (London, 1903).

[66] E. Leyland, *Wild Animals* (London, 1955), 63.

[67] G. Skelcher, 'The Ecological Replacement of Red by Grey Squirrels', in J. Gurnell and P. Lurz (eds), *The Conservation of the Red Squirrel (scirius vulgaris)* (London, 1997), 76; S. Carrell, 'Sure he's cute . . . but not cute enough to save him from the great squirrel cull', *The Guardian*, (10 February 2009); S. Harris and D. W. Yalden (eds), *Mammals of the British Isles: Handbook* (Southampton, 2008), 10, 13, 63, 70.

[68] Hilda Kean, 'Imagining Rabbits and Squirrels in the English Countryside', *Society and Animals*, 9 (2001), 164.

[69] 'Species inflation: Hail Linnaeus: Conservationists—and polar bears—should heed the lessons of economics', *The Economist* (17 May 2007), at http://www.economist.com/node/9191545/print

[70] Andrew D. Tittensor, 'What future for the reds?', *Country Life*, 166 (25 October 1979), 1394-5.

[71] Harris and Yalden, *Mammals of the British Isles*, 10, 13, 63, 70.

operate sixteen reserves in northern England. Celebrities have also been enlisted. To raise cash for Red Alert's safe havens, drawings of red squirrels by personalities from the worlds of music, comedy, sport, television and radio, stage and screen, were auctioned on the Internet in September 2000.[72]

The red squirrel's predicament is taken very seriously by the hereditary peers of Parliament's upper chamber (who may feel a large dose of empathy with a fellow endangered species). Today's 'English' squirrels are mostly descended from continental European stock brought over in the late nineteenth and early twentieth centuries for restocking purposes, as native red populations plummeted for reasons unconnected with the grey's arrival and expansion (disease and retreat of coniferous woodland). Still, the 'native' squirrel's political champions are oblivious to this irony. During a squirrel debate in the House of Lords in 1998, Lord Inglewood of Cumbria identified the red as the 'most lovable and loved of our British native animals'. When considering animals as furry embodiments of heritage, the distinction between squirrels in Britain and British squirrels is subtle but profound. As Lord Rowallan observed in 1998: 'we should not encourage them merely because they are beautiful animals. . . They . . . have another advantage—they are British'.[73]

In other words, things indigenous are also more authentic. And what is more authentic is also more interesting. The Lawton Report of 2010, which reviewed the condition of England's wildlife sites, argued that 'people should not have to travel to London to enjoy art. Nor should they have to travel to a National Nature Reserve to see creatures more interesting than a Grey Squirrel'.[74] Still, a British wildlife biologist, Stephen Harris, has questioned the value of committing further, increasingly scarce resources to the effort to control greys and reinstate reds. Not only is this a mostly unwinnable war, it is also being waged on behalf of a creature that, beyond Britain, is nowhere endangered.[75] And yet, recognition of the fact that there are plenty of red squirrels elsewhere (which could be tapped for future reintroductions, as they were for earlier re-stockings of large areas in England) is unlikely to console those who have made a heavy emotional and cultural investment in the

---

[72] J. Ingham, 'Stars go nuts to help save the red squirrel', *Daily Express* (15 September 2000).

[73] *Hansard* (Lords), Session 1997-98, Column 1318, 25 March 1998, 587, at http://www.parliament.the-stationery-office.co.uk/pa/ld199798/ldhansrd/vo980325/text/80325-10.htm#80325-10_head0

[74] *Making Space for Nature: A Review of England's Wildlife Sites and Ecological Network* (Department for Environment, Food and Rural Affairs, 16 September 2010), 4 (Commonly referred to as the Lawton Report [after its chairman]).

[75] Steve Harris, 'The red has lost – so accept the grey', *BBC Wildlife*, 24:9 (September 2006), 38-9.

survival of 'our island race' of red squirrel as an ingredient of English heritage that cannot be surrendered.

Poster bear: animal of the 'Anthropocene'

No animal, it seems, is more precious than when it is served up carefully wrapped in the national flag. The red squirrel's internationality is a quality largely absent from current discourse over its future in England. But an emblematic national species has the potential to perform double duty. Cincinnati Zoo's memorial plaque to Martha and Incas seeks to internationalize their memory. Dedicated not just to the passenger pigeon and Carolina parakeet but to 'all extinct species', it exhorts visitors to act so that other species around the world avoid the fates of Martha and Incas.

Today, the species environmental campaigners believe is most likely to go their way is the polar bear. This concern is part of a wider anxiety over the future of its icy habitat. Over the past decade, the concept of heritage has migrated (at the rapid pace of a melting glacier) to the highest and lowest latitudes to encompass the repositories of formerly securely frozen water that, in the far north, provide the bear's living space. The glacier, for example, is a rich archive of climate data that scientists have extracted since the 1970s through ice coring techniques. After visiting a coring site in Greenland (2002), the *New Yorker*'s environmental correspondent, Elizabeth Kolbert, noted:

> A hundred and thirty-eight feet down, there is snow dating from the American Civil War; some twenty-five hundred feet down, snow from the days of Plato; and, five thousand three hundred and fifty feet down, from the time when prehistoric painters were decorating the caves of Lascaux. At the very bottom, there is snow that fell on Greenland before the last ice age, which began more than a hundred thousand years ago.[76]

In 2004, UNESCO duly added the glacier that Kolbert visited (the Ilulissat Icefjord) to the list of World Heritage sites (Number 830).[77] One of only four World Heritage sites in Denmark—and Denmark's first 'nature' listing—the Ilulissat Icefjord lies 250 kilometres north of the Arctic Circle and may well have been the source of the iceberg the *Titanic* encountered. Studied for over

---

[76] Kolbert, 'Ice Memory', *New Yorker* (7 January 2002), at http://www.newyorker.com/archive/2002/01/07/020107fa_FACT#ixzz1uNbjKH4r; *Field Notes from a Catastrophe: A Frontline Report on Climate Change* (London, 2006), 49–50.

[77] Mark Carey, 'The History of Ice: How Glaciers Became an Endangered Species', *Environmental History*, 12:3 (2007), 498.

two centuries, the world's most active glacier outside Antarctica represents a key site in the growing understanding of icecap glaciology and climate change.[78]

UNESCO's description, however, does not refer to Ilulissat Icefjord's value as habitat for polar creatures. A specific geographical locale can be explicitly associated with an individual species of fauna, offering a particularly precise example of an animal landscape (or animalscape)—a place defined by the presence of an emblematic or 'keystone' species (a keystone species being one that exerts a disproportionate influence over its living space relative to its numbers, a 'critical species' whose removal from an ecosystem can trigger general collapse of ecological functions[79]). In 1962, in line with Conwentz's broad conception of a natural monument as the habitat of a rare plant or animal as well as a single tree or individual landscape feature,[80] South Korea's Cultural Heritage Administration ('the organization that gives pride and hope to Koreans') listed the offshore area of Ulsan as a 'natural monument' (Number 126). This swathe of ocean forms part of the southward migration route to its winter breeding grounds of the Korean-Okhotsk (western) grey whale, whose status on the 'Red List of Threatened Species' maintained by the International Union for Conservation of Nature (and Natural Resources) (IUCN) is critically endangered.

In the early 1960s, the main threat confronting the white bear was not environmental in nature. The problem was excessive sport hunting. The toll exacted by often unregulated trophy hunting, frequently from aircraft

---

[78] http://whc.unesco.org/en/list/1149 [accessed 7 March 2014].

[79] 'Creatures of Influence', press release, University of Bristol, 6 November 2013, http://www.bristol.ac.uk/news/2013/9895.html [accessed 7 March 2014].

[80] Conwentz, *Care of Natural Monuments*, 35; http://jikimi.cha.go.kr/english/search_plaza_new/ECulresult_Db_View.jsp?VdkVgwKey=16,01260000, ZZ. The IUCN Red List of Threatened Species is the most comprehensive global dataset on the conservation status of known mammalian populations. The first of these lists was compiled in 1966: Jon Paul Rodríguez et al., 'IUCN Red List of Ecosystems', *S.A.P.I.E.N.S*, 5:2 (2012), 62; Peter Scott, John A. Burton, and R. S. R. Fitter, 'Red Data Books: The Historical Background', in R. S. R. Fitter and Maisie Fitter (eds), *The Road to Extinction* (Geneva, 1987), 1-6. The status of each listed species is re-evaluated at five-year intervals (the most recent list was issued in 2008). Ursula K. Heise studies red lists and other biodiversity databases as cultural artefacts within the wider framework of the 'elegiac and tragic modes of narrative . . . often used in representations of species extinctions in novels, travel narratives, popular scientific books, films, photographs, and paintings': 'Cultures of Extinction: Narrative, Database, and Biodiversity Loss', at http://www.stanford.edu/~uheise/; Ursula K. Heise, 'Lost Dogs, Last Birds, and Listed Species: Cultures of Extinction', *Configurations*, 18:1-2 (Winter 2010), 49-72.

and ice-breakers, brought the world's five polar bear nations together to sign an international agreement on polar bear conservation in 1973. Climate change has since replaced over-harvesting as the primary challenge to the species' prospects.[81] The totemic polar bear has been classified as 'vulnerable' on IUCN's 'red list' since 1982 (with a reprieve between 1996 and 2006, when its status rose to 'lower risk'). This reflects a circumpolar population decline of 30 per cent over the past 45 years to around 25,000, largely due to the shrinkage of sea ice cover and deteriorating quality of the surviving ice, with the likelihood of a further 30 per cent decline in the total population over the next 30 to 50 years. Ice melt compromises the availability and size of hunting grounds: an individual bear ranges over a few thousand square kilometres at least—sometimes more than a hundred thousand—and its hunting season starts later and ends earlier. The IUCN predicts that, if current warming trends continue unabated, then polar bears will melt away from most of their range by the end of this century.

Despite the danger it poses to human life as one of the few animals that will actively hunt humans that enter its territory, the polar bear basks in the sunshine of publicity, hailed as the 'arctic canary'.[82] The white bear has been designated a transnational species within a globalized locality, a process assisted, perhaps, by the fairly widespread perception that polar regions elude national ownership and are the ultimate global commons. As such, this bear is studied, protected, appreciated, and commoditized by an international fraternity of scientists, nature preservation organizations and nature importing tourists.[83]

Unsurprisingly, neither Martha nor Incas feature in a sumptuously illustrated book, *The Last Polar Bear* (2008). Edited by wildlife photographer Steven Kazlowski and conservationist Theodore Roosevelt IV (great-grandson of Theodore Roosevelt), it served as a recruitment tool during a tour of politicians' offices in Washington, DC, in the spring of 2007, timed to coincide with

---

[81] http://pbsg.npolar.no/en/agreements/agreement1973.html; Ian Stirling, *Polar Bears: The Natural History of a Threatened Species* (Brighton, MA, 2011), 24, 265.

[82] Theodore Roosevelt IV, 'Arctic Canary: Why the White Bear Matters', in Steven Kazlowski and Theodore Roosevelt IV (eds), *The Last Polar Bear: Facing the Truth of a Warming World* (Seattle, 2008), 33.

[83] For 'nature importing', see Roderick Nash, *Wilderness and the American Mind*, 3rd edn (New Haven, 1982), 343. Through WWF UK, you can adopt a polar bear from Norway's Svalbard archipelago. For a monthly payment of £10, you can adopt the 'snow pack' of polar bear, Adélie penguin and snow leopard (and receive three optional cuddly toys): http://www.wwf.org.uk/adoption/helpapolarbear/?pc=AJB004001&gclid=CPrXrfadkb ACFY5pfAod7EAEpA.

the 'Climate Crisis Rally'. Yet the book's title plays, however subconsciously, on the venerable association with the feathered pair. The final image in the portfolio shown to politicians depicted a bear swimming in a pool at the zoo in Anchorage, Alaska, accompanied by the caption: 'within decades, this could be the only place on earth a polar bear will be found'. The caption to this particular photo in a subsequent exhibition (2008) at the University of Washington's Burke Museum of Natural History and Culture in Seattle ('The Last Polar Bear: Facing the Truth of a Warmer World') drove home even more directly the chilling reality that, 'if we do nothing as a society, and the ice continues to melt, zoos could be the only place on Earth where polar bears can be found'.[84]

Six weeks before the exhibit opened , the US Department of Interior added the polar bear to the list of threatened animals protected by the Endangered Species Act (1973)—the first American mammal granted this status specifically because of the threat, particularly acute in Alaska's waters, that 'warming-induced habitat degradation and loss' poses for an acutely ice-dependent species and its prey.[85] The listing was challenged unsuccessfully by Sarah Palin, the governor of Alaska, which houses 20 per cent of the world's polar bears, on the grounds that current population levels gave no cause for concern; that the listing was based on 'uncertain climate models'; and that it would impede oil and gas operations. Though Palin mouthed the rhetoric of appreciation in an op-ed piece written for a national audience—polar bears were 'magnificent animals . . . worthy of our utmost efforts to protect them'—[86] few were persuaded that the polar bear was safe in her hands. The international outcry against Palin's indifference to its status as emblem of living yet endangered global heritage confirmed the white bear's arrival as the new panda. Just as importantly, the indignant reaction from those who valorize the polar bear served as a reminder that the notion of cultural keystone species (a phrase coined in 2004 to designate flora and fauna of multi-faceted significance to indigenous peoples—as a source of food, medicine,

---

[84] Helen Cherullo, 'Preface', *The Last Polar Bear*, 11; http://www.washington.edu/news/2008/06/26/capturing-a-fading-world-the-last-polar-bear-at-the-burke-museum/

[85] http://www.iucnredlist.org/apps/redlist/details/22823/0; Jon Aars et al. (eds), *Polar Bears: Proceedings of the 14th Working Meeting of the IUCN/SSC Polar Bear Specialist Group, 20-24 June 2005, Seattle, Washington, USA*. Occasional Paper of the IUCN Species Survival Commission No. 32 (Gland, Switzerland, 2006), 61-2; Martyn E. Obbard et al. (eds), *Polar Bears: Proceedings of the 15th Working Meeting of the IUCN/SSC Polar Bear Specialist Group, Copenhagen, Denmark, 29 June–3 July 2009*. Occasional Paper of the IUCN Species Survival Commission No. 43 (Gland, Switzerland, 2010), 17, 81-2, 85.

[86] Palin, 'Bearing Up', *New York Times* (5 January 2008).

and spiritual-ceremonial sustenance) also resonates loudly within western societies.[87]

Conclusion

Whether or not it extends to wildlife, the concept of global environmental heritage, rooted in the notion that humankind possesses a shared patrimony that is natural as well as cultural, relies on the universalization of value and delocalization of ownership: Alaska's polar bears and Uganda's white rhinoceros are just as highly valued by Belgians and Uruguayans—perhaps more so—as they are by Alaskans and Ugandans. And once internationalized, these species belong, in principle, just as much to these distant nations—if not more so—as they do to Alaskans and Ugandans. At the same time, understandings of heritage at national and local levels are deeply dependent on the quality of authenticity. Hornaday's prize male buffalo, the 'giant of his race' encased in the Smithsonian, though unnamed, allegedly served as the model for a range of official commemorative items: the ten dollar bill, various stamps, and, not least, the seal of the Secretary of the Interior. Meanwhile, the model for sculptor James Earle Fraser's buffalo-head nickel (five-cent coin), the first authentically American coin design, which, revealingly, bore an Indian head on the converse side, was New York City Zoo's alpha male, Black Diamond.[88]

Over in Britain, the red squirrel's champions regard it as a more genuine squirrel than its imported, but thoroughly naturalized, grey counterpart. Biologically and genetically, there is little difference between the (re)introduced reds from nineteenth-century re-stocking and the 'truly' native reds that pre-dated them. And there would be no discernible difference between them and future reintroductions from elsewhere in Eurasia, in the event that 'our island race' became extinct. Nonetheless, despite the patent elasticity of the concepts of native and non-native (rabbits and horse chestnut trees, for instance, are not indigenous to Britain), in the judgement of squirrel nationalists, they lack the supreme and non-negotiable criterion of indigeneity and the cachet of bespoke authenticity: like an imitation necklace, forged banknote, or fake painting, they are just not the same thing and so cannot be dignified as heritage.

---

[87] Ann Garibaldi and Nancy Turner, 'Cultural Keystone Species: Implications for Ecological Conservation and Restoration', *Ecology and Society*, 9:3 (2004), 1-18.

[88] Matthew Roudané, 'Betrayal and Friendship: David Mamet's *American Buffalo*', in C. W. E. Bigsby (ed.), *The Cambridge Companion to David Mamet* (Cambridge, 2004), 69-70; A. L. Freundlich, *The Sculpture of James Earle Fraser* (New York, 2001), 51-3; *Congressional Record—Senate*, 146:2 (8 March 2000), 2244.

That the scarcity theory of value helps determine eligibility for elevation to the ranks of heritage is incontrovertible. Less widely recognized (not least by historians) is that the ranks of heritage, on national and global scales, are populated with animals, dead and alive, great and small, as well as artefacts, buildings, and places, whether those places are categorized for listing purposes as natural or cultural (or both).[89] Some definitions of a heritage 'asset' continue to exclude creatures (dead or alive).[90] Yet the references to wildlife 'treasures' and comparisons, implicit and explicit, with things cultural are increasingly the norm in the heritage sector, not least in governmental reports.[91] As the DEFRA-commissioned Lawton Report noted,

> there are twenty-seven ancient cathedrals in England. Imagine the outrage that would have ensued in this country if over the last 100 years, twelve had been partly demolished, nine substantially demolished, and three completely obliterated; only three would remain in good condition. Yet this is precisely what has happened to many of England's finest wildlife sites.

The Natural Capital Committee, an independent body that advises the government on matters relating to the UK's 'natural assets', drew the same analogy in its first annual report when it singled out wildlife as a particularly precious natural capital asset: 'Like great works of art they are part of our heritage, and in just the same way, once lost they are effectively irreplaceable'.[92] Moreover, the award of heritage status is not restricted to wild species.

---

[89] On tensions between cultural and natural conceptions of heritage, see Douglas Pocock, 'Some Reflections on World Heritage', *Area*, 29:3 (September 1997), 260-8. Though the framers stipulated that 'all efforts should be made to maintain a reasonable balance [on the List] between cultural and natural heritage', the 'works of man' have fared better. From the start, cultural sites dominated the List. There are currently 936 sites on the List, of which just 183 are natural. An additional 28 are 'mixed' 'Mixed' listings are for places considered simultaneously cultural and natural, among them Venice and its lagoon and the Danube Delta: UNESCO, 'Convention Concerning the Protection of the World Cultural and Natural Heritage', Paris, 16 November 1972, 2; UNESCO, Intergovernmental Committee for the Protection of the World Cultural and Natural Heritage, *Operational Guidelines for the Implementation of the World Heritage Convention* (Paris, November 2011), 15; http://whc.unesco.org/en/list.

[90] Department for Communities and Local Government, *National Policy Planning Framework* (London, 27 March 2012), 52.

[91] Andy Brown/Natural England, *Lost Life: England's Lost and Threatened Species* (Natural England, 2010), 2, 6, 7.

[92] *Making Space for Nature: A Review of England's Wildlife Sites and Ecological Network*, v, 1, 4, 5, 7 (commonly referred to as the Lawton Report [after its chairman]); Natural Capital

Rare livestock breeds have also attracted preservationist attention on both sides of the Atlantic in recent decades, a trend that, for David Lowenthal (who singles out pigs), highlights just how obsessive the pursuit of heritage has become since the early 1990s.[93]

At the same time, the case for animals as an area worthy of the attention of scholars of heritage is far from established, whether at the national or international scale. The nationalized landscapes Smith identified as ethnoscapes did not embrace animals. The notion of an animalscape—a landscape or environment defined by the presence of a keystone, flagship, or iconic species—and the related idea of the animality of landscape, though gaining ground within human geography, remain underdeveloped in historical studies, where the study of heritage also awaits reanimation.[94] Animals, as Claude Levi-Strauss noted with regard to their totemic role in tribal societies such as those of North America's Pacific Northwest, are not only 'good to eat'. They are also 'good to think' with—especially about understandings of heritage in the western world.[95]

Committee, *The State of Natural Capital: Towards a Framework for Measurement and Valuation* (London, April 2013), 13.

[93] David Lowenthal, *Possessed by the Past: The Heritage Crusade and the Spoils of History* (New York, 1996), 3, 25.

[94] David Matless, Paul Merchant, and Charles Watkins, 'Animal Landscapes: Otters and Wildfowl in England, 1945-1970', *Transactions of the Institute of British Geographers*, 30:2 (2005), 191-205; Owain Jones, ' "Who Milks the Cows at Maesgwyn?": The Animality of UK Rural Landscapes in Affective Registers', *Landscape Research Journal*, special edition on 'Animals and Landscape', 38:4 (2013), 421–42. Maggie Roe, 'Editorial: Animals and Landscape', ibid., 401–3.

[95] Claude Levi-Strauss, *Totemism*, trans. Rodney Needham (London, 1964 [1962]), 89.

History, Heritage, and Revolution: Mexico, c.1910–c.1940

Alan Knight

One thing that emerges clearly from David Lowenthal's meandering *The Heritage Crusade*, is that the term 'heritage' is vague, protean or, if you prefer, 'polysemic'.[1] The same is true of its Spanish counterpart *patrimonio*. A recent three volume study of Mexico's *patrimonio* includes, as you would expect, museums, archaeological sites, pre-Hispanic artefacts, baroque churches and Catholic religious images.[2] But it also includes more modern items: twentieth-century murals, the oil industry (PEMEX), a photographic archive of Indians, the myth of modern Acapulco, a mining cooperative in Guanjuato, and lottery cards/tickets. Finally, it embraces 'timeless' emblems of mexicanidad, such as maize, volcanoes, agave (the source of pulque) and the Virgin of Guadalupe.[3] Given the sheer size and the indeterminate membership of the 'heritage' club, it is quite difficult to grasp what the club gets up to: who qualifies for entry, what the members have in common (if anything) and what function(s) the club performs. Of course, the first task is to narrow the field; however, excessive narrowing, perhaps plumping for a single illustrative case study, risks losing the big picture and basing a discussion of Mexican 'heritage' on a narrowly unstable foundation.

In this paper I try to retain the big picture—Mexican heritage in, roughly, the 'revolutionary' period, 1910-40—but with particular reference to two major figures who represent two major currents in Mexican 'culture': the anthropologist and archaeologist Manuel Gamio (1883-1960) and the painter (especially muralist) Diego Rivera (1886-1957), contemporaries who lived through the armed revolution and its aftermath and contributed to the

---

[1] David Lowenthal, *The Heritage Crusade and the Spoils of History* (Cambridge, 1998).

[2] Pablo Escalante Gonzalbo, coord., *La idea de nuestro patrimonio* (Mexico, 2011); Guillermo de la Peña, coord., *La antropología y el patrimonio cultural de México* (Mexico, 2011).

[3] 'Timeless' requires quotation marks since these aspects of Mexico's history and culture, though old, can come and go; in particular, Mexico has at least one famous and high (9,100 feet) volcano, Paricutín, which first appeared in a farmer's field in 1943.

country's 'brilliant cultural renaissance' in the 1920s and beyond, not least by emphasizing Mexico's Indian past and present.[4] Both were also political animals, who enjoyed close but contentious relations with the new revolutionary state, a state which conceived of both art and archaeology/anthropology (henceforth archanthropology) as important tools in the task of *forjando patria* ('forging the fatherland': the title of Gamio's seminal work of 1916), in creating what Gramsci referred to as an 'ethical' or 'cultural' state.[5] So we face an initial interesting conundrum: why a revolutionary state, supposedly committed to radical reform of a degenerate politics and society, should place such faith in the recovery of the past (witness, for example, Gamio's excavation of the iconic Classic site of Teotihuacan) and should also depict that past, sometimes in lyrical terms: in Rivera's stylized scenes of Aztec Tenochtitlan, as well as roughly contemporaneous Totonac and Huastec societies, in which strapping Indians throng busy markets, amid fertile fields and profusions of flowers, with not a single human sacrifice in sight.[6]

In fact, the ostensible paradox is not so problematic.[7] If the French Revolution sought to wipe the slate clean, eradicating the past and its encumbering 'heritage' while instituting a new politics, iconography, calendar, and 'secular religion', this model does not work for all revolutions.[8] The Mexicans, like the English, were prepared to invoke symbols of the past in the creation of the future: if the 'Norman yoke' had oppressed 'free-born Englishmen',[9] so too, the Spanish Conquest had destroyed or subjugated

---

[4] Mary Kay Vaughan, *The State, Education and Social Class in Mexico, 1880-1928* (DeKalb, 1982), 239. Rick A. López, *Crafting Mexico. Intellectuals, Artisans and the State after the Revolution* (Durham, 2010), 6-7, similarly considers the Revolution to have been 'culturally . . . transformative'.

[5] Antonio Gramsci, *Selections from the Prison Notebooks* (London, 1982), 258-9.

[6] Eulalia Guzmán, a populist-nationalist archaeologist who played a major role in the Cuauhtémoc's bones affair, continued to deny Aztec human sacrifice—alleging Spanish calumny and invention—well into the post-war period: Paul Gillingham, *Cuauhtémoc's Bones. Forging National Identity in Modern Mexico* (Albuquerque, 2011), 52. In contrast, Manuel Gamio, for all his pioneering indigenismo, recognized that 'in the Precolumbian past there were constant wars and bloody ceremonies': Gamio to Edward Nehls, 3 Aug. 1956, Archivo Manuel Gamio, Archivo Histórico de la Biblioteca Nacional de Antropología e Historia, Mexico City, caja 3 expediente 7 (cited henceforth thus: AMG 3/7).

[7] Alan Knight, 'The Myth of the Mexican Revolution', *Past and Present*, 209 (Nov. 2010), 229-31.

[8] See Lynn Hunt, *Politics, Culture and Class in the French Revolution* (Berkeley, 1984).

[9] Christopher Hill, *Puritanism and Revolution: Studies in Interpretations of the English Revolution of the Seventeenth Century* (London, 1962), ch. 3.

Indian civilizations which still lay hidden beneath the surface of colonial and 'post-colonial' Mexico: literally hidden, in the form of subterranean ruins waiting to be excavated and, more importantly, metaphorically submerged in modern Mexican society where, to quote a commonplace, 'idols (lurked) behind altars' and a vast reservoir of rich Indian culture (*ergo* 'heritage'), historically ignored, repressed, or traduced, had to be liberated from colonial and post-colonial prejudice and channelled into the positive process of *forjando patria* (and *forjando estado*).[10] Sites like Teotihuacan thus performed a dual function: their excavation and celebration reinforced Mexico's ancient cultural heritage; but they also emphasized the creativity and genius of Mexico's Indians, rescuing them not only, we might say, from the 'enormous condescension of posterity' but also from posterity's racist and elitist prejudice.[11]

The chronological sequence is clear and can be quickly summed up. In 1910 a major revolution began, directed against the long-standing personal rule of Porfirio Díaz, the regime of the Porfiriato (1876-1911). Amid burgeoning popular and military mobilization, both Díaz and his counter-revolutionary epigone, Victoriano Huerta (1913-14), were overthrown; and, after a bloody intra-revolutionary struggle in 1914-15, a new revolutionary regime emerged, whose broad goals—nationalist, agrarian, labourist, and anticlerical—were vested in the new 1917 Constitution. Initially bankrupt, fragile, and vulnerable to both foreign threats and domestic revolts, the new regime consolidated during the 1920s under the leadership of the Sonoran dyarchy of Obregón and Calles—hardheaded northerners who combined military prowess with fierce anticlericalism and a deft grasp of the new populist politics of the day. They also espoused an ambitious cultural project, involving both art and archanthropology.[12] By the 1930s the regime was firmly established; the dominant revolutionary party, the PNR, had been

---

[10] Anita Brenner, *Idols Behind Altars* (New York, 1929).

[11] E. P. Thompson, *The Making of the English Working Class* (Harmondsworth, 1968), 13; Manuel Gamio, n.d., 'Hay Que Despertar Orgullo de Raza en el Indígena' ('It is Necessary to Awake Racial Pride in the Indian'), since (contemporary) Indians 'have no idea of their prestigious lineage, having centuries ago lost the lost the memory of ancient and famous deeds', hence they remain unaware of preconquest agricultural advances, of the superb architecture, 'superior to almost all the rest of the world in those times' and of other prehispanic achievements: AMG 7/26.

[12] Thus, my chronological focus is chiefly the period 1917-40 (although I note some earlier precedents, as well as an enduring legacy); either way, it does not square with Lowenthal's strange generalization (*The Heritage Crusade*, p. 4) that the 'modern preoccupation with heritage dates from about the 1980s'; a generalization at odds with obvious cases such as the Gothic revival, Pre-Raphaelite neo-medievalism, and the

created in 1929; and, following the onset of the Great Depression, the regime took a turn to the left, combining Keynesian economics with more radical land and labour reform. On the cultural front, the government now formally espoused 'socialist' education, adding a class-conscious and Popular-Frontist dimension to existing populist and nationalist discourse.

Our two emblematic figures, Gamio and Rivera, played key roles in these processes, and not just as free-floating artist-intellectuals; they were also immersed in the practical politics of the day. Both came from downwardly mobile bourgeois families and neither had actually fought in the armed revolution. Rivera spent most of those years studying, painting, and womanizing in Europe, chiefly Paris; he briefly returned to Mexico in 1910, the year of initial revolutionary insurrection, in order to mount an exhibition which President Díaz and his wife not only attended, but where they bought some Rivera canvasses.[13] Despite making later, implausible, and highly imaginative claims to revolutionary commitment,[14] Rivera's service to the Revolution—now the *revolución hecha gobierno*—came in the 1920s, and was entirely civilian and aesthetic. Indeed, his brash machismo and chronic bragging about violence, gunplay, and even cannibalism probably reflected a sneaking sense that, when the bullets were flying, he—unlike some of his fellow artists, such as Orozco—was living a safe Bohemian life in Paris.[15] Gamio, too, avoided the armed revolution, though he allegedly called himself a 'Zapatista', which was a rare and even slightly risky thing to do in Mexico City in those years.[16] More significantly, perhaps, he claimed to have spent two years, prior to Revolution, living on his family *finca* (farm) in the Zongólica district of the state of Veracruz, where he became aware of the hard life of the local campesinos, chiefly Indians, and learned Nahuatl—their language, as it had been the language of the Aztecs four centuries earlier.[17] Despite his revolutionary sympathies, Gamio stuck to archaeology (and, like Rivera, was a beneficiary

---

'British arts and crafts movement': cf. Derek Gillman, *The Idea of Cultural Heritage* (Cambridge, 2010), 57.

[13] Bertram Wolfe, *Diego Rivera. His Life and Times* (London, 1939), 60-1; Patrick Marnham, *Dreaming with his Eyes Open: A Life of Diego Rivera* (London, 1999), 78-81.

[14] Wolfe, *Diego Rivera*, 63-5; Marnham, *Dreaming with his Eyes Open*, 84-5.

[15] On alleged cannibalism and related macho posturing, see Diego Rivera (with Gladys March), *My Art, My Life; An Autobiography* (New York, 1991 [1960]), 20-1; and David Alfaro Siqueiros, *Me llamaban el Coronelazo* (Mexico, 1977), 114, 147-8.

[16] 'Zapatista': denoting a follower or sympathizer of the popular peasant revolutionary Emiliano Zapata: interview with Gonzalo Aguirre Beltrán, 22 May 1985, AMG 7/89.

[17] Interview with Miguel León Portilla, 15 March 1983, AMG 7/90.

of Porfirian state patronage). A rising star of Mexican archaeology, he studied, briefly, at Columbia University (1909-10), where he would return to receive a doctorate in 1921; and in 1917, at the fairly tender age of 34, he was appointed Director of the new Department of Anthropology (so he now became a beneficiary of revolutionary state patronage).[18] Soon after, he received an official commission to lead the excavation and renovation of Teotihuacan, the massive Classic-era site to the north of Mexico City.

The project was official and depended on government funding which, in the circumstances, was precarious. Official deputations drove out to the site to inspect the ruins and to enjoy fancy five-course lunches, the dishes being 'Indian' in origin, the menu written in Nahuatl—a deliberate break, it was pointed out, with 'restaurant French', or with the Latin neologisms favoured by Gamio's predecessor at Teotihuacan under the old regime, Leopoldo Batres.[19] Indeed, the new vogue for Indian languages, especially Nahuatl, was sign of the times: Gerardo Murillo, an artist-activist who, like Rivera and Gamio, had benefited from Porfirian patronage before switching to the Revolution (and, unlike them, playing a prominent political role in the factional fighting), now changed his name to 'Dr Atl', *atl* being the Nahuatl for 'water';[20] and, soon, the revolutionary regime set out to recover Indian place names, and to adjust contemporary spelling in line with 'Mexican' as opposed to 'Spanish' usage.[21]

Though dependent on official patronage, Gamio appears to have had a fairly free hand at Teotihuacan. His key contribution was the idea of 'integral' ('total') archaeology, which would blend with anthropology (and perhaps other '-ologies') and thus make a positive contribution to contemporary

[18] Juan Comas, 'La vida y la obra de Manuel Gamio', *Estudios antropológicos: Publicación en homenaje al Dr Manuel Gamio* (México, 1956), 1-26.

[19] 'Excursión a las pirámides de San Juan Teotihuacan', *El Demócrata*, n.d. (1918?), press cutting in AMG 11/2. On Batres's long and vandalistic custodianship of Teotihuacan during the Porfiriato, see Christina Bueno, 'Teotihuacan: Showcase for the Centennial', in Dina Berger and Andrew Grant Wood (eds), *Holiday in Mexico. Critical Reflections on Tourism and Tourist Encounters* (Durham, 2010), 54-76.

[20] Vaughan, *The State Education and Social Class*, 248.

[21] The chief orthographic marker was the replacement of the Spanish 'j' with the Mexican 'x', most obviously in the name of the country itself (Méjico/México), as well as numerous other place names (Xalapa, Oaxaca, Xico, etc.): López, *Crafting Mexico*, 139. However, when it came to the Mexican pavillion at the Seville 1929 Exposition, while the design was 'Maya', the inscription referred to 'Méjico', 'the better to please Spain': Mauricio Tenorio-Trillo, *Mexico at the World's Fairs. Crafting a Modern Nation* (Berkeley, 1996), 222.

society.[22] In particular, applied anthropology could provide vital information for a government lacking hard data regarding its population, especially its poor, rural, and Indian population.[23] The Porfirian old regime, eager to promote the 'cognitive capacity' of the state,[24] had counted the population and mapped and measured the country, with a new positivistic zeal; but its gaze had been limited, its goals narrowly fiscal and repressive.[25] The new regime, Gamio argued, should penetrate further, into what later became known as 'México profundo' ('deep Mexico'),[26] and it should try to understand social and ethnic problems the better to address them. This was not archaeology for archaeology's sake, but archaeology for a purpose;[27] and the purpose was nation-building (*forjando patria*) and social reform. The overriding concern was to bind together Mexico's many and diverse people into a coherent nation-state.[28] Archaeology could reveal the grandeur of Mexico's Indian past, thus countering the racist prejudice of Mexico's criollo and mestizo majority, while showing the downtrodden Indians of today the greatness of their ancestors. The parallel with Rivera's didactic murals is obvious.

At Teotihuacan Gamio hired local people, forming a team who, decades later, would recall their collective efforts and Gamio's inspired leadership with warm nostalgia. Gamio provided jobs and better wages: 500 workers

22 Manuel Gamio, 'The social significance of the archaeology of Teotihuacan', AMG 8/68. See also Manuel Gamio, *Forjando Patria* (México, 1982 [1916]), 15-19, 25.

23 Gamio, *Forjando patria*, 29.

24 Miguel A. Centeno and Agustín E. Ferraro, 'Republics of the Possible', in Miguel A. Centeno and Agustín E. Ferraro (eds), *State and Nation Making in Latin America and Spain: Republics of the Possible* (Cambridge, 2013), 12, discuss this and cognate concepts, such as James Scott's notion of 'legibility'.

25 On Porfirian mapping and measuring, see Raymond Craib, *Cartographic Mexico: A History of State Fixations and Fugitive Landscapes* (Durham, 2004).

26 Guillermo Bonfil Batalla, *El México profundo: una civilización negada* (México, 1987) is a classic anthropological study of the poor, popular, and indigenous substratum of Mexican society, upon which rests an exploitative colonial and neo-colonial superstratum.

27 Dillon Ripley, *The Sacred Grove. Essays on Museums* (London, 1970), 76-8, contrasts this instrumental/utilitarian approach to archaeology (and, by implication, 'heritage') with that adopted in the US, where 'there seems to have been little recognition of the constructive cultural-historical role which art museums could play', an omission which reflects a broader failure 'to develop the applied-science museum concept'. If true (and Ripley was writing pre-1970), this seems strangely at odds with conventional stereotypes of US pragmatism and practicality; but then such stereotypes are often wrong, or greatly exaggerated.

28 Gamio, *Forjando patria, passim*.

received between a peso and 1.50 a day, when the going rate for local peons was at best 0.50c.[29] Apart from the excavations themselves, Gamio saw to the building of an access road, established a clinic, dispensed vaccinations, and organized tours, sports, and local cooperatives producing Indian artisanry, chiefly obsidian, which found a ready market. He made a feature film (*Rebelión*), using local actors, set up an open-air theatre, and recruited a local Indian artist, Francisco Goitia, to paint 'landscapes, churches and folk scenes' in the Teotihuacan district.[30] Apart from churning out obsidian arte-facts, the community, under Gamio's auspices, began manufacturing soap from the abundant wild thistles and coarse fabric from the fibrous agave plants.

Two aspects of his work are worth noting. He encouraged tourism, includ-ing foreign, chiefly North American, tourism. An English-language guide to Teotihuacan was produced; and in 1922 a scale model of the site was sent to Rio de Janeiro for the Exposição Internacional do Centenario.[31] Gamio al-ready had close contacts in the US and in 1921, thanks to his Teotihuacan research, would receive his doctorate from Columbia University. Franz Boas, the great critic of scientific racism and proponent of cultural relativism, was Gamio's chief American mentor (as he was of other Mexican intellectuals); and, like Boas, Gamio tirelessly asserted the intrinsic value of Indian arts and crafts, against those—still numerous and vocal—who disdained 'primitive' or 'pagan' monstrosities.[32] Thus, Gamio helped initiate the flow of American cultural tourism to Mexico: a flow which, in terms of numbers and, even more, influence, became a powerful torrent in the 1920s and '30s, with sig-nificant politico-cultural consequences.[33]

Gamio's second characteristic was his staunch anticlericalism. Like many of the revolutionary generation—usually young men who had risen rapidly in

---

[29] Gamio, 'La transcendencia social de la arqueología en Teotihuacan', AMG 8/60; and (1985) interviews with veterans of the Teotihuacan project in AMG 7/85.

[30] D. A. Brading, 'Manuel Gamio and Official Indigenismo in Mexico', *Bulletin of Latin American Research*, 7:1 (1988), 79-80. Gamio, 'Hay que Despertar el Orgullo de Raza en el Indígena', AMG 7/26, describes how, at Teotihuacan, the new primary school class-rooms were covered with blown-up photos of prehispanic 'palaces and temples' and 'paintings of famous scenes of that epoch'; 'this display of what their ancestors had done in other ages provoked such attention and enthusiasm among the children that many of them set to making copies and models' of what they had seen.

[31] Tenorio-Trillo, *Mexico at the World's Fairs*, 215. On tourism, see also Gamio, 'El aspecto transcendental del turismo en México', in *México: Guía de turismo*, julio de 1929, 58.

[32] Brading, 'Manuel Gamio', 76.

[33] Helen Delpar, *The Enormous Vogue of Things Mexican: Cultural Relations Between the United States and Mexico, 1920-35* (Tuscaloosa, 1992) offers a good overview.

the post-1910 upheaval—Gamio saw the Catholic Church as a bastion of political reaction, superstition, and socio-economic backwardness.[34] Legitimating the barbarities of the conquistadors, the Church had connived at the enslavement of Mexico's Indians and retarded the development of the independent nation-state after 1821. Its stance towards Indian culture (or 'heritage', if you prefer) was critical and authoritarian. Hence it had to be combatted, its influence weakened, the oppressive carapace of Catholicism lifted from the bent back of the oppressed Indian. (Unfortunately for revolutionary anticlericals like Gamio, this—the *leyenda negra* of Catholic colonialism—was not a story which all, or even most, Mexicans accepted; and many Indians were lukewarm, if not hostile, to the anticlerical emancipation which they were promised). Again, Gamio's international contacts and reputation counted: as church–state conflict mounted in 1926, Gamio became an articulate exponent of official anticlericalism in the US, where Catholic opinion was outraged by 'Bolshevik' priest-baiting south of the border.[35]

The Teotihuacan project was a success, not least because it generated a massive and acclaimed archanthropological study, in three hefty volumes, which covered the history of the site from its Mesoamerican origins through the colonial period down to the present (at which point history and anthropology elided into rural sociology and political advocacy).[36] But, contrary to Gamio's initial ambitious intentions, it did not provide a template for a series of similar projects, elsewhere in Mexico; and its local impact was also short-lived. The money ran out and Gamio moved on, occupying a series of important posts in Mexico's politico-cultural establishment, including the Ministry of Education (SEP), where he served, briefly and unhappily, as Under-Secretary at the Ministry of Agriculture, and the Ministry of the Interior (where he ran the Department of Demography, 1938-42), before finally heading the Instituto Indigenista Interamericano.[37] Along the way

[34] Late in life Gamio was allegedly 'very irate' when his daughter Gabriela, recently widowed, turned to the (Catholic) Church: 'it's not possible, he said, that my daughter should get mixed up with the priests (se meta con los curas)': interview with Raquel and Francisca (Gamio's ex-secretaries), 1983, AMG 7/87. See also Gamio, *Forjando patria*, 85-92; and, on the politico-intellectual context, Alan Knight, 'The Mentality and Modus Operandi of Revolutionary Anticlericalism', in Matthew Butler (ed.), *Faith and Impiety in Revolutionary Mexico* (New York, 2007), 21-56.

[35] Manuel Gamio interview, Chicago, *c.*1926, AMG 5/19. Regarding US Catholic opinion towards revolutionary Mexico, see Matthew A. Redinger, *American Catholics and the Mexican Revolution, 1924-36* (Notre Dame, 2008).

[36] Manuel Gamio, *La población del Valle de Teotihuacan* (2 vols, Mexico, 1922).

[37] CV del Sr Manuel Gamio, AMG 5/34.

he also conducted seminal research on Mexican migrants in the US, wrote a novel, and even dabbled in particle physics.[38] While this diverse c.v. suggests something of a restless dilettante, there was a consistency to Gamio's career, since he continued to regard the plight of Mexico's—and Latin America's—Indians as key, and their integration into enlightened nation-states as crucial. He never gave up on *forjando patria*. Initially, archaeology—the didactic rescue of Mexico's Indian heritage—served these ambitious ends; but archaeology soon receded; and, we could say that his initial 'archanthropology' became less archaeological, more anthropological, eventually sociological, pedagogical, and political.

In this, Gamio's career contrasted wth those of more 'pure' archaeologists (who are also linked to 'their' iconic sites: Alfonso Caso and Monte Albán, Eduardo Matos Moctezuma and Tenochtitlan). In all such cases, however, the contemporary significance of archaeology was apparent; in other words it was almost impossible, to do 'apolitical' 'academic' archaeology devoid of contemporary political or social relevance in twentieth-century Mexico: dramatic proof of this ineluctable link came with the celebrated case of Cuauhtémoc's bones, which I mention below.[39]

Meanwhile, Rivera and his team[40] were covering acres of wall-space with their politically didactic murals. Again, government patronage was crucial; the state had the resources (up to a point) and, perhaps more importantly, it had the walls.[41] The first Education Minister of the 1920s Sonoran regime, José Vasconcelos, began the mural project as a part of a grandiose policy of cultural engineering, designed to impress, educate, and uplift the Mexican people and, at the same time, to legitimate the fragile new regime. Vasconcelos himself inclined to European classicism, French fashions and white (criolla) women;[42] he preferred champagne to pulque (the preferred beverage of Mexico's plebs); and he opposed sending a copy of Mexico Cty's Cuauhtémoc statue to the Río international exhibition, supporting instead

---

[38] Manuel Gamio, *Mexican Immigration to the United States: A Study of Human Migration and Adjustment* (Chicago, 1930); Manuel Gamio, *De vidas dolientes* (México, 1937).

[39] Gillingham, *Cuauhtémoc's Bones*.

[40] Rivera liked to claim that muralism was a collective effort: Diego Rivera, 'The Guild Spirit in Mexican Art', *Survey Graphic*, V: (May 1924), 174-6; however, Siqueiros, *Me llamaban el Coronelazo*, 208-9, was sceptical.

[41] Vaughan, *State, Education and Social Class*, 265.

[42] Vaughan, *State, Education and Social Class*, 252, which also notes how, as Vasconcelos and President Obregón watched schoolchildren perform Mexican folk dances, Vasconcelos observed that 'he would not be satisfied until he saw them dancing to the strains of Rimski-Korsakov'.

the design of a neocolonial—i.e., Hispanic—pavillion, which made the Mexican building pretty indistinguishable from other Latin American pavillions.[43] As Minister of Education, the books he shipped out to dirt-poor provincial pueblos included Plato and Goethe, books which, it seems, mouldered unread on the shelves of ramshackle schoolrooms. Vasconcelos might see himself as Mexico's Lunacharsky,[44] but his background in the dissident Ateneo de la Juvenud of the 1900s marked him as an anti-positivist idealist, not a rabble-rousing populist, still less a Bolshevik.[45]

Some of the early Mexican murals, including Rivera's, also favoured classical and allegorical themes.[46] But Rivera, like many of his fellow muralists, believed that murals should speak to the people and that, to do so, they should adopt a more down-to-earth, populist and nationalist approach.[47] Both the content and the style should reflect Mexican traditions and images (i.e., 'heritage'). So, Rivera turned his back on his brief (European) Cubist phase and dissented from his Soviet comrades (the 'constructivists') who sought to blend proletarian and modern art.[48] Art, he believed, should be accessible to the masses; it should be solidly representational, not high-falutin' and rarefied; and its themes should include contemporary workers, peasants and Indians as well as their noble historical ancestors. Hence, Rivera's idyllic images of pre-Conquest Mexico; the grim pictures of cruel conquistadors and oppressed Indians; the visual critique of a corrupt, conniving Catholic Church; and the promise of better times to come, as the Revolution brought land and education to the peasants, unions and labour reform to the workers, and a heightened sense of nationalism (including economic nationalism) to the nation as a whole. Like Gamio, therefore, Rivera revalorized Indian culture; he also became an assiduous collector of Indian artefacts, both ancient and modern; and he finally built himself a personal museum (necessarily endowed with a suitable Nahuatl name, the Anahuacalli), to house his collection of 60,000 items—a collection, it seems, 'packed with faked prehispanic artefacts'.[49] Rivera also believed that he could reproduce ancient

<hr>

[43] Tenorio-Trillo, *Mexico at the World's Fairs*, 205-6, 208-9.

[44] Vaughan, *State, Education and Social Class*, 249-50, 252.

[45] Indeed, by the 1930s Vasconcelos had gravitated towards fascism: I. Bar-Lewaw, *La revista "Timón" y José Vasconcelos* (México, 1971).

[46] Vaughan, *State, Education and Social Class*, 259; Siqueiros, *Me llamaban el Coronelazo*, 215, refers to Rivera's early style as 'neo-Byzantine' and 'Giottesque'.

[47] Siqueiros, *Me llamaban el Coronelazo*, 129-30, 223 (which again expresses some scepticism).

[48] Wolfe, *Diego Rivera*, 127-8.

[49] Gillingham, *Cuauhtémoc's Bones*, 194.

prehispanic artistic techniques, such as those used to create Toltec bas-reliefs; and, by advocating collective creative work (which the murals usually were), he supposedly replicated ancient Mesoamerican practice.[50]

Rivera, a precocious infant anticlerical,[51] not only shared Gamio's dislike of the Church, he also played a role—arguably a much bigger role—in piquing American interest in Mexico's 'heritage'. Two main influences were at work here: first, as a known leftist and for much of his life a somewhat wayward member of the Mexican Communist Party, Rivera hobnobbed with the leftists and liberals who flocked to Mexico in the 1920s, drawn by the progressive political and cultural scene: journalists and writers like Carleton Beals, Ernest Gruening, Langston Hughes, and Katherine Anne Porter; radical activists like the American Joseph Freeman, the Cuban Julio Antonio Mella, and the Nicaraguan Augusto César Sandino; folklorists like Frances Toor and William Spratling; photographers like Edward Weston and Tina Modotti; and a clutch of American painters, less renowned than their Mexican counterparts, who eagerly espoused Mexican styles.[52] Foreign—including American—interest in Mexican antiquities was far from new. But the scale of the foreign/American presence was unprecedented; and, reflecting both Rivera and Gamio's concerns, it often combined political radicalism with indigenista aesthetics. The imprimatur of foreign approval counted, and not just in monetary or politico-diplomatic terms; it also spurred Mexican policy-makers to burnish their nationalist credentials by supporting national (incuding indigenista) art and artisanry.[53] After all, what sort of popular patriotic revolution could allow patronage to fall into the hands of foreigners, possibly imperialists?

But Rivera's contacts—personal, political, and commercial—went far beyond the Mexico City Bohemian set. His work began to sell in the US; and when, in 1927, at a time of severe US–Mexican tension, the suave banker–diplomat Dwight Morrow was appointed US ambassador to Mexico, he became a keen patron of Rivera's art, not only buying his work, but even sponsoring a major mural project in the Cortés Palace in Cuernavaca, south of Mexico City.[54] Before long, Rivera had decamped to the US to begin a series of major—and contentious—mural projects in New York and California. Rivera's American work, logically enough, dealt with big city landscapes, industrial plants, science, technology, and the social destitution produced

---

[50]   Siqueiros, *Me llamaban el Coronelazo*, 188-9.

[51]   Wolfe, *Diego Rivera*, 12.

[52]   Delpar, *The Amazing Vogue*; López, *Crafting Mexico*, 100-5.

[53]   López, *Crafting Mexico*, 139-40.

[54]   López, *Crafting Mexico*, 115-20.

by the Great Depression. But when he returned to Mexico in the later 1930s he resumed his 'populist' depiction of Mexican history: a history replete with colourful heroes and villains; insurgent Indians and oppressive Spaniards; fat priests, grasping businessmen, and exploitative foreigners.

Despite their different métiers, Gamio and Rivera thus shared several common features and, of course, they worked with teams in collective projects, often with official patronage. They were not free-floating intellectuals, detached from society; on the contrary, they saw their work as a means to transform society, not least by invoking images from the past, by rescuing and showcasing Mexico's ancient heritage. Gamio pioneered applied, 'integral' archanthropology; Rivera championed art for a sociopolitical purpose.

Since they formed part of a broader politico-cultural project, it is worth elucidating that project, asking how and why 'heritage' came to form part of a 'revolutionary' agenda; and what impact that agenda had. After all, like Marx (whom Rivera, to the disgust of his official patrons, reverentialy depicted),[55] both he and Gamio wanted, not just to describe and depict the world, but also to change it. How could 'heritage' help change the world in a progressive new direction?

First, we should note that the execrated Porfirian old regime was itself a purveyor of 'heritage'; indeed, some of its preferred motifs even had a mildly 'indigenista' quality in that they evoked Mexico's grand Indian past, in which respect they could also draw on older colonial precedents.[56] It was the Porfirian government which erected, on Paseo de la Reforma, Mexico City's Champs Elysées, the imposing monument to Cuauhtémoc, the last Aztec emperor and proto-patriotic hero of resistance to the Spaniards (whose putative bones will reappear in this story). The Porfiriato also took advantage of the country's unprecedented political stability and economic growth to invest in 'heritage': the Museo Nacional, which dated back to 1825, was substantially refurbished, becoming 'an indispensable arm of the state' in terms of research and 'outreach';[57] in 1885 the post of Inspector of Monuments of the Republic was created, and the Museo Nacional acquired

---

[55] Wolfe, *Diego Rivera*, 301 and 362-9, regarding the celebrated comparable incident when Rivera's depiction of Lenin in a Rockefeller Center mural resulted in the work's destruction (by the sponsors).

[56] Martin S. Stabb, 'Indigenismo and Racism in Mexican Thought, 1857-1911', *Journal of Inter-American Studies*, 1:4 (October 1959), 405-23; and, for colonial precedents, D. A. Brading, *The First America* (Cambridge, 1991), 300, 366, 387-8.

[57] Luisa Fernández Rico Mansard, *Exhibir para educar. Objetos, colecciones, y museos de la Ciudad de México (1790-1910)*, (Barcelona, 2004), 190.

a new 'Gallery of Monoliths', dedicated to prehispanic sculptures, including the celebrated Aztec calendar wheel.[58] Meanwhile, at successive international expositions the Porfirian 'wizards of progress'—the 'organic intellectuals' of the regime, we might also call them—dabbled in Indian motifs and images.[59] And, of course, Gamio, Rivera, Dr Atl and others began their careers thanks to Porfirian government grants and appointments. As a painter of iconic Indians, too, Rivera had his Porfirian precursors, such as Rodrigo Gutiérrez and Félix Parra, the latter being one of his teachers at the prestigious San Carlos Academy, who depicted his Indian subjects in suitably noble, if somewhat etiolated, neoclassical, style.[60] A greater painter, also one of Rivera's teachers, was the landscape artist José María Velasco, who captured the grandeur of Mexico's scenery, while offsetting his folkloric tendencies with striking images of the new railways which were then slicing their way through the rugged countryside, bringing modern civilization to picturesque rusticity.[61]

So it would be wrong to assume that the evocation of heritage, especially of Indian heritage, was an entirely new phenomenon, a pictorial Pallas Athene springing fully formed from the head of the revolutionary Zeus in 1910. However, the new regime placed greater emphasis on such evocation, to the extent of putting its scarce resources into archaeological digs, publications, and didactic murals. One obvious reason was the need to provide discursive legitimation for the new regime, which had to justify its existence in contrast to the ousted old regime and in the face of both domestic and foreign threats—at home, the Catholic Church, abroad hostile governments and business interests. A new elite, running a new regime, had to come up with a new discourse.[62] Hence organic intellectuals of the regime like Gerardo Murillo/Dr Atl spoke of their discursive mission in strikingly Gramscian terms.[63]

---

[58] Rico Mansard, *Exhibir para educar*, 127.

[59] Tenorio-Trillo, *Mexico at the World's Fairs*, 48, 118-19.

[60] Tenorio-Trillo, *Mexico at the World's Fairs*, 55, 84, 118-19; Wolfe, *Diego Rivera*, 26, 30.

[61] Wolfe, *Diego Rivera*, 26, 30; Tenorio-Trillo, *Mexico at the World's Fairs*, 114-17.

[62] Tenorio-Trillo, *Mexico at the World's Fairs*, 217. Revolutionary indigenismo was an exemplary case of discursive innovation: Alan Knight, 'Racism, Revolution, and Indigenismo: Mexico, 1910-40', in Richard Graham (ed.), *The Idea of Race in Latin America, 1870-1940* (Austin, 1990), 71-114.

[63] 'Among the great steps forward taken by the Revolution, in order to transform our national sociology [*sic*] . . . is the enormous and undisputed advance of having replaced the old and deficient concept of the State which merely gives orders (*el estado instructor*) with the much broader and more fruitful concept of the State which educates (*el estado educador*)': Dr Atl, 'Informe general: exposición de motivos', in Archivo Histórico de la

Their first task, therefore, was to draw a line, however contrived, between Porfirian vice and revolutionary virtue. This meant ignoring whatever patriotic or indigenista elements were to be found amid Porfirian discourse, and branding the old regime as anti-national, Europhile, and 'vendepatrias'. Díaz and his cronies—especially the Científicos, whose doyen, José Yves Limantour, happened to be of French extraction—were accused of betraying the country, traducing democracy, and preferring foreign to national interests. Since this was a form of political sloganeering, it was often wrong and almost always exaggerated (but, as I shall argue, it had a real impact). In some crucial respects, however, it was substantially correct. The Porfirian national project had been inherently elitist, authoritarian, and racist. Under Díaz, politics became the preserve of a small oligarchic minority (including the Científicos); there were no enduring political parties and no mass political organizations; elections were rigged, incipient labour unions were repressed, and Indians—indeed, campesinos more generally[64]—suffered from a loss of both their landed patrimony and their traditions of (partial) self-government. In some cases, such as the rebellious Yaqui of north-west Mexico and the Maya of eastern Yucatán, state repression carried the hallmarks of a colonial war, fought with modern weapons including machine-guns, field artillery, and gunboats in a spirit of racist 'developmentalism'. Since the victims were often (though not always) Indians, Porfirian indigenismo rang hollow. Félix Parra painted the elegaic Massacre at Cholula, depicting Spanish atrocities at the time of Conquest, while real Indians were being mown down in Sonora and Yucatán. And the architectonic indigenismo of Paseo de Reforma (where Cuauhtémoc surveyed from on high the burgeoning traffic of downtown Mexico City) contrasted with the reality of Porfirian racism and exclusion. When, in 1910, the regime complacently celebrated the centennial of Mexican Independence, real Indians—those who wore white cotton drawers and leather huaraches—were banned from the city centre, and the Indian presence was confined to 'official' Indians, decked out as Aztecs, who danced and cavorted in orchestrated parades.[65] Indeed, by

---

Dirección General del INAH (henceforth AHDG/INAH), Archivo Histórico de la Biblioteca Nacional de Antropología e Historia, Mexico City, vol. 1, rollo 1.

[64] Campesinos: roughly, 'peasants' or, more generally, rural (common) people. Most Indians were campesinos but Indians were only a minority of campesinos, the majority being mestizos (i.e., of mixed race and ethnicity).

[65] López, *Crafting Mexico*, 6. Fifteen years before, a group of Tehuantepec Indians were sent to Atlanta to form part of the 'human zoo' at the 1895 Exposition: Tenorio-Trillo, *Mexico at the World's Fairs*, 186.

now, Mauricio Tenorio argues, Porfirian indigenismo had begun to yield to a renewed Hispanism—an emphasis on Mexico's European roots which certainly fitted more snugly into official discourse and practice.[66]

Whatever the indigenista credentials of the Porfirian old regime, its revolutionary successor placed much greater emphasis on Mexico's Indian heritage and actually took steps to turn indigenista discourse into practice. Those steps were halting and, as candid observers of twentieth-century Mexico have confirmed, Indians remain at the bottom of the socio-political pile; thus, like their Porfirian predecessors, the revolutionary elites were also guilty of rhetorical hypocrisy. The old regime was not as racist and oppressive as those elites claimed, nor was the new regime as noble, emancipatory, and indigenista either. But the gap between discourse and practice had substantially narrowed; the structural hypocrisy of the regime (a feature of most political regimes, be they liberal-democratic, socialist, Islamic, fascist or whatever) had palpably shrunk. The revolutionaries combated debt peonage, which chiefly weighed on the Indians of south-eastern Mexico; and they espoused land reform, which benefited campesinos, Indians included (the reparto made no clear ethnic distinction); in Zapata's home state of Morelos, just south of Mexico City, land distribution came early and was both radical and, in some measure, 'empowering'.[67] Not surprisingly Zapata, suitably idealized and accompanied by a mythical white horse (Zapata in fact rode a sorrel), became the classic agrarista icon of Rivera's murals, the image which many, including many foreigners, entertained of the Mexican Revolution.[68] The revolutionary state also energetically promoted rural primary education, which the Porfiriato had neglected. Thus, Rivera captured the iconic image of the rural maestra (schoolmistress) teaching a class of campesino (Indian?) children al fresco, while an armed agrarista defended the school from reactionary Catholic reprisals.[69] Gamio, too, was obsessed with rural education, particularly with the need to make Spanish a genuinely national language, to the advantage of both the *patria* and its Indian inhabitants.[70]

Of course, invoking history in order to denigrate the old regime, while legitimizing the revolution, required a selective approach. We may compare this process of regime legitimization with Renan's famous explanation of how

---

[66] Tenorio-Trillo, *Mexico at the World's Fairs*, 206-8.

[67] John Womack Jr, *Zapata and the Mexican Revolution* (New York, 1969), 371-9.

[68] Marnham, *Dreaming with his Eyes Open*, 121, 243; Siqueiros, *Me llamaban el Coronelazo*, 212.

[69] Marnham, *Dreaming with his Eyes Open*, 189.

[70] Gamio, 'El mestizaje y la homogenización social', AMG 8/77.

nations are formed, by means of collective remembering—and forgetting.[71] If the Porfiriato was a tale of racism and oppression, earlier episodes of Mexican history were uplifting and worthy of commemoration: Aztec resistance to the Spaniards (hence the cult of Cuauhtémoc);[72] the popular insurgency against colonial rule in 1810, in which Indians, mestizos and mulattoes fought shoulder to shoulder against the hated *gachupines* (Spaniards); and the heroic defence of the Republic against the French and their Austrian puppet Maximilian in the 1860s, a defence led by the stoic Zapotec Indian Benito Juárez, who remains Mexico's outstanding national and nationalist icon.[73]

The revolutionaries, therefore, were at pains not to repudiate the past (as, perhaps, their French Jacobin counterparts had been), but rather to slot themselves into a suitably progressive, popular, and inspiring historical sequence: Conquest (1520-1); Independence (1810-21); Restored Republic (1861-7); and, finally, Revolution (1910-20).[74] One feature of this legitimizing discourse, perhaps shared by other national discourses, was the tendency to denigrate the more recent past—from which the Revolution had rescued a grateful people—and to hark back to an earlier, better, purer past: the great Indian civilizations which had preceded the conquest, or later episodes of popular insurgency against oppressive, alien, anti-national tyrants, such as the Reforma and French Intervention.[75]

Thus, the paradox of a revolutionary regime drawing on history and heritage was not really so paradoxical: the Porfiriato, the recent, unlamented old regime, was blackened, the better to show off the lustre of what came after; but, by vaulting over the Porfiriato into earlier epochs, the regime could find historical legitimation for a revolution that was genuinely novel, popular, and

---

[71] Ernest Renan, 'What Is A Nation?', in Geoff Eley and Ronald Grigor Suny (eds), *Becoming National: A Reader* (New York, 1996), 45.

[72] The classic (if fictional) revolutionary/indigenista monicker was that of Xicontencatl Robespierre, coined by the writer Mariano Azuela in his 1918 novel *Domitilio quiere ser diputado* (Xicontencatl being the Tlaxcalan Indian ruler who had resisted the invading Spaniards and been executed by them).

[73] Charles A. Weeks, *The Juárez Myth in Mexico* (Tuscaloosa, 1987). Juárez typically tops national polls designed to identify Mexico's greatest heroes (and not just *políticos*): see n. 111 below.

[74] Knight, 'The Myth of the Mexican Revolution', 233-4, 241.

[75] More recently, when President Carlos Salinas (1988-94) attempted a radical neoliberal reform of Mexico's politcal economy he sought historical legitimation in the remote mid-nineteenth century and the somewhat murky figure of Ponciano Arriaga, supposedly the iconic intellectual of 'social liberalism': Alan Knight, 'Salinas and Social Liberalism in Historical Context', in Rob Aitken et al. (eds), *Dismantling the Mexican State?* (London, 1996), 1-23.

progressive. Contrary to some half-baked assumptions (favoured particularly by foreign observers of Mexico, D. H. Lawrence being the most egregious example),[76] this did not mean that the regime intended to turn the clock back, to recover a bucolic Indian Eden, or to remake Mexico City in the image of Aztec Tenochtitlan.[77] On the contrary, revolutionary policy and discourse were consciously progressive, forward-looking, and (if the word means anything) 'modernizing'. Just as Rivera could easily switch from rustic landscapes to industrial machinery, so the regime combined its appeal to history and heritage with an emphasis on science, secularism, literacy, and industrialization. Similarly, '(Dr) Atl's emphasis on Indianness, spontaneity, authenticity, collective unconsciousness, manual industries, and premodernity did not make him antimodern. On the contrary, he saw such traits as providing a distinct path toward modernization'.[78] There were tensions here, as I note in conclusion, but Mexico was not unusual in seeking to preserve and invoke (often very instrumentally) elements of the past, while striving to create a new, different, and perhaps 'modern' society.

Three additional factors contributed to the revolutionary regime's embrace of the past, in particular of Mexico's Indian heritage. First, though the regime consolidated during the 1920s, it also faced a major Catholic rebellion (the Cristiada, 1926-9), a rebellion which, unlike the praetorian revolts of that decade, reflected a stark ideological polarization. The regime showed that it could not be ousted, but Catholic contestation made it all the more necessary for the revolutionaries to achieve a form of discursive legitimacy. Indigenismo thus made sense: it pitted noble Indians against cruel Catholic conquistadors, Mexican patriots against the oppressive Spanish Crown. The writings of Gamio, like Rivera's murals, were grist to the revolutionary anticlerical mill.

Second, by the late 1920s and early 1930s a new generation was growing to adulthood—a generation which had not fought in, not even lived through, the armed revolution of 1910-20, and which needed to be persuaded that the ageing revolutionary caudillos of the postrevolutionary period were indeed legitimate representatives of the popular revolutionary cause (and, after 1930, at a time of economic recession). Calles, the dominant *político* of the period, expressed these sentiments in his Grito de Guadalajara (1934); his words echoed those of Dr Atl, who, harking back to the French Revolution, and advocating the creation of a 'Museum of the Revolution' in Mexico, argued

---

[76] D. H. Lawrence, *The Plumed Serpent* (New York, 1951 [1926]).

[77] López, *Crafting Mexico*, 44.

[78] López, *Crafting Mexico*, 90.

that laws and 'new institutions' alone were insufficient to change 'public consciousness', and that the regime should 'carefully forge' (note the Gamio-esque verb) 'the psychology of the society which it governs'.[79] As I note in conclusion, there is good evidence that the state had some success in these efforts.

Thirdly, the invocation of heritage performed a useful function in foreign relations, both diplomatic and commercial. Heritage—history, archaeology, artisanry, folklore—was a magnet to foreign, especially American, tourists, who now flocked to Mexico seeking, not yet beaches and margaritas, but rather monuments and artefacts which, Frances Toor commented, they 'took home literally by the carload'.[80] Apart from generating valuable foreign exchange (as revolutionary policy-makers had hoped: they never ignored the bottom line),[81] heritage tourism performed a useful politico-diplomatic function: it fostered a measure of good will, breaking down some of the ancient prejudices which vitiated US-Mexican relations, especially in the revolutionary period. After all, US armed intervention, a realistic fear at least until 1927, was less likely if Mexico was seen, not as a nest of xenophobic Bolsheviks, but as a cradle of ancient civilizations and a workshop of creative artisans and artists. Official policy—for example, with regard to international expositions—took foreign opinion seriously and saw heritage as an effective lever to shift that opinion.[82]

Conversely, there were factors, stressed by some historians of heritage, which were unimportant in the Mexican case. Heritage clearly did not function as a nostalgic opiate in times of stress ('as hopes of progress fade, heritage consoles us with tradition').[83] It was not designed to sedate a fearful public opinion. If such sedation occurred, it was largely on the part of the regime's Catholic enemies who, threatened by official anticlericalism, drew on the Church's formidable discursive resources to fight back. After all, this was a revolutionary regime, wedded to a radical reformist project, which battled the Church in the 1920s and attempted to institute 'socialist' education and a form of Popular Frontism in the 1930s. It was, in French terms, a regime

---

[79] Dr Atl, 'Informe general: exposición de motivos' (see n. 63).

[80] Frances Toor, *A Treasury of Mexican Folkways* (New York, 1985 [1947]), 40.

[81] 'México: guía de turismo', vol. 1 (July 1929), whose preamble, 'Our Purpose', stresses Mexico's climate, scenery, and the 'silent [*sic*] charm of our colonial cities', adding—for the benefit of rich Americans—that 'perhaps the knowledge of our National resources should impulse you to establish any enterprise of good returns in the country where you will be welcome'.

[82] Tenorio-Trillo, *Mexico at the World's Fairs*, 224.

[83] Lowenthal, *The Heritage Crusade*, xiii.

of movement, not order. And heritage, as I have suggested, was yoked to movement, reform, and change, not standpat conservatism. In that context, however, it fell far short of being a 'secular religion', as I would understand that term.[84]

Second, and perhaps surprisingly, the revolutionary regime's commitment to heritage and nativist revival did not derive from the destruction of the Revolution (compare: 'we value our heritage most when it seems at risk').[85] The armed revolution was hugely destructive of both lives and property; but the material destruction affected transport infrastructure (railways, bridges, culverts) and, to some extent, haciendas and churches. Churches, being strategic buildings in town centres, were sometimes shot up, but more commonly they were expropriated by anticlerical revolutionaries and used as barracks, stables, schools, and trade union headquarters. But haciendas and churches were quintessential symbols of Spanish colonial rule, hence their partial eclipse did not trouble indigenista activists; and even those revolutionaries who valued colonial as well as preHispanic heritage could take comfort from the fact that expropriated churches remained part of the national patrimony, open to the patriotic public, sometimes newly adorned with revolutionary murals. Precolumbian ruins were largely unaffected by the armed revolution, hence concern for their preservation was in no way a product of civil war. War did affect the policing of some ruins, since for a few years they became dangerous no-go areas, for example, in Zapatista Morelos;[86] but concerns about preservation and conservation followed an older trajectory, evident in the nineteenth century and continuing through the twentieth—a trajectory that was fairly constant and unaffected by revolutionary violence.[87] Nor did foreign invasion and depredation constitute a lively threat.[88] There were two relatively minor US interventions during the Revolution, neither of which posed any threat to Mexico's historic heritage. Neither the marines who embarked from Veracruz in 1914, nor the soldiers of Pershing's Punitive Expedition who marched back across the northern border three years later,

---

[84] Alan Knight, 'The Several Legs of Santa Anna: A Saga of Secular Relics', in Alexandra Walsham (ed.), *Relics and Remains*, Past and Present Supplement, 5 (2010), 250-5.

[85] Lowenthal, *The Heritage Crusade*, 24.

[86] And not just during the intense period of Zapatista insurgency (1911-20); as late as 1929 the official watchman at the ruins of Xochicalco was obliged to take refuge in the town of Cuernavaca due to 'the passage of rebel bands' near the site: R. Carballo to Dirección Arqueológica, 26 Feb. 1929, AHDG/INAH, rollo 1.

[87] On Porfirian (late nineteenth-century) concern for conservation see Rico Mansard, *Exhibir para educar*.

[88] Cf. Gillman, *The Idea of Cultural Heritage*, 26.

went laden with stolen antiquities. The only case I have encountered concerned the 'villainous' Mormons of Chihuahua who, fleeing the violence and xenophobia of the northern revolution, allegedly took with them a rare and perfectly formed meteorite—so rare, indeed, that it was said to contain 'a message from Mars to the planet Earth'.[89] Of course, American tourists and dealers did acquire Mexican artefacts, and the post-revolutionary regime cracked down on this illegal trade (in which respect, they followed nineteenth-century precedents). But this was an old story, common to many countries, and unconnected to the upheaval of the Revolution.

Finally, I will turn to the question of impact: how revolutionary policy towards heritage affected public opinion and, in turn, regime legitimacy. Categorical answers are impossible, but cautious conclusions can be drawn. First, despite the firm commitment of the regime, heritage 'policy' was often compromised by lack of funds and factional disputes. Projects—like Teotihuacan—were boldly undertaken and then cut back when funds ran out (for example, in 1930). Mural projects were similarly vulnerable to financial vicissitudes; one painter took to brandishing a hefty 0.45 revolver in order to compel the authorities to pay his overdue wages.[90] Meanwhile, the burgeoning politico-cultural bureaucracy displayed the characteristic failings of its kind.[91] Graft, corruption, and nepotism tainted procedures; and when Gamio, unusually stern and self-righteous in these matters, tried to crack down on the department 'mafia', he made enemies and, unable to win the confidence of President Calles, he finally resigned and moved for a time to the United States.[92] Meanwhile, he too took to carrying a pistol to work, just in case.[93] Some squabbling concerned ideology rather than jobs and spoils. Revolutionary policy in respect of art, archaeology, and culture was far from monolithic and was often contested, by both dissident revolutionary, *oficialista* insiders, and hostile Catholic, conservative, or liberal critics from

---

[89] M. Vivero to President Lázaro Cardenas, 23 March 1936, AHDG/INAH, vol. 4, rollo 9. This Mormon exodus from northern Mexico, which involved George Romney, made possible the later political career—and presidential challenge—of his son, Mitt Romney.

[90] Siqueiros, *Me llamaban el coronelazo*, 203. The infuriated, unpaid, gun-toting painter was Fermín Revueltas, who was applauded by both the public and his fellow-painters.

[91] Manuel Gamio, 'Aspecto económico y administrativo de la Secretaría', 14 May 1925, AMG 2/23.

[92] Gamio to President Calles, 26 April, 14 May 1925, AMG 2/23.

[93] Interview with Miguel León-Portilla, 15 March 1983, AMG 7/90. It was, Gamio said, only a 'little gun' (a 'pistolita')—not, therefore, the sort of cannon ('enorme pistolón') wielded by the disgruntled painter Fermín Revueltas (see n. 90). Siqueiros, epitomizing characteristic revolutionary machismo, would have called it a 'pistolita de mujer' ('a woman's peashooter'): Siqueiros, *Me llamaban el coronelazo*, 78, 203.

without. Vasconcelos, the first patron of the muralists, disliked much of what they did; students protested and defaced the work; and state governors were dismissive of so-called 'Indian' art and folkloric 'trinkets'.[94] Mexican participation in successive international expositions also provoked heated debates, some involving Hispanists versus indigenistas; however, by the time of the Seville exposition of 1929, indigenismo had largely triumphed, to the disgust of Spanish critics in the host country.[95]

Perhaps the most serious and enduring tension, inherent in the indigenista project, was that between, roughly, the preservation of tradition on the one hand, and the integration of Indians and their heritage into the revolutionary nation-state (Gamio's *patria forjada*) on the other. This dilemma followed from Gamio's commitment to an integral archanthropology—one that combined archaeological excavation with applied-anthropological social engineering—and, more generally, from the desire of the state and its agents to involve and integrate contemporary Indians. Historically, Mexican elites had made a distinction—sometimes explicit, sometimes implicit—between the greatness of pre-Conquest Indian civilizations and the poverty of actual, contemporary, living Indians. Like the Greeks, Mexico's Indians were a degenerate palimpsest of their noble ancestors.[96] Some revolutionaries shared this elitist, often racist, opinion. But, more often, they stressed the potential and creativity of contemporary Indians, denying racial determinism and, like Gamio and his fellow cultural relativists, advocating the emancipatory power of education (and/or acculturation). However, a major conundrum remained. Concerned to valorize Indian culture and creativity, the indigenistas went far beyond archaeological digs and sought to promote and market popular—often Indian—artisanry: textiles, dress, ceramics, lacquered artefacts, and metalwork.[97] In 1921 the government mounted an inaugural Exhibition of Popular Art and, eight years later, complying wth a supposed 'mandate of the Revolution', it set up a permanent Museum of Popular Arts.[98] Non-material products such as poems, music, dance, and *corridos* (popular ballads) also received official approval and promotion; while new journals, like the influential *Mexican Folkways*, brought such products to a wider, including foreign, audience.[99] Even business bent with the wind (and, in the absence of opinion polls, there could be no better

---

[94] Vaughan, *State, Education and Social Class*, 264; López, *Crafting Mexico*, 81, 86.

[95] Tenorio-Trillo, *Mexico at the World's Fairs*, 231-3.

[96] Cf. Lowenthal, *The Heritage Industry*, 24.

[97] Dr Atl, 'The Popular Arts of Mexico', *Survey Graphic*, V:2 (May 1924), 161-2.

[98] López, *Crafting Mexico*, ch. 5

[99] Delpar, *The Enormous Vogue*, 76-86, 151-73; López, *Crafting Mexico*, 102-6.

indication of how attitudes were changing). By the 1920s, the Buen Tono tobacco company was using ads which showed an Aztec puffing a fat cigarette, while newspapers sponsored the lucrative 'India Bonita' ('Miss Indian') competition.[100] Out in the provinces, too, muralism caught on: the new Federal schools which sprang up in the 1930s promoted popular muralism; and even if some looked to a usually sympathetic American anthropologist 'God-awful', they seem to have been successful in engaging local artists and exciting local interest.[101]

However, to the extent that revalorization and marketing succeeded, there was a risk that 'traditional', 'authentic' folklore would be debased; and the risk was compounded as Indians—or the Mexican 'folk' more generally[102]— acquired literacy, moved to the cities, and swapped rural for urban jobs. This was certainly education and integration, as Gamio advocated, but some pessimistic protagonists of a 'declensionist narrative' saw in these processes the likely destruction of the very ' "authentic" cultural patrimony' which they wished to cherish and promote.[103] Was the preservation of heritage in this broad, more-than-archaeological sense, compatible with Indian/ folk integration? Plenty of serious thinkers, including foreigners ike Stuart Chase and Aldous Huxley, scratched their heads over this question.[104]

In one sense the dilemma was and remains real enough. Hundreds of thousands of Mexicans cannot make a living producing lacquered boxes or *alebrijes*, as they can assembling TVs in border maquila plants, or manufacturing VWs in the city of Puebla.[105] What is more, when artisanal products, like lacquered boxes and *alebrijes*, are 'mass-produced', they usually suffer diminishing returns with regard to quality, 'authenticity' and thus value. The result is a highly segmented market. However, it remains a profitable market:

[100] Tenorio-Trillo, *Mexico at the World's Fairs*, 210; López, *Crafting Mexico*, ch.1.

[101] R. Redfield to Mrs Redfield, 25 May 1938, Redfield Archive, University of Chicago Library, Box 1, file 10; for a good example of didactic local muralism, see Mary Kay Vaughan, *Cultural Politics in Revolution: Teachers, Peasants and Schools in Mexico, 1930-40* (Tucson, 1997), 135. However, in Catholic conservative communities/regions (like Tequixtepec in the Mixteca Baja of Oaxaca), such murals could also assume quite different form, exalting the Spanish Conquest and demonizing the Revolution: Benjamin T. Smith, *The Roots of Conservatism in Mexico* (Albuquerque, 2012), 1.

[102] On the concept of 'folk culture', see Robert Redfield, *The Folk Culture of Yucatán* (Chicago, 1941), esp. 343, 349.

[103] López, *Crafting Mexico*, 108.

[104] Stuart Chase, *Mexico: A Study of Two Americas* (New York, 1931); Aldous Huxley, *Beyond the Mexique Bay: A Travellers's Journey* (London, 1949).

[105] Michael Chibnik, *Crafting Tradition: The Making and Marketing of Oaxacan Wood Carvings* (Austin, 2003).

the 'authentic' products possess cachet and command high international prices, while the 'mass-produced' kitsch is cheap and cheerful, grist to the mill of popular tourism, both Mexican and foreign.[106] The respective consumers, both up-market and down-market, are, presumably, happy with their lot; and, since these products are decorative and usually have little or no use-value, they cannot fail, as a TV or VW can; so the consumer cannot complain of being ripped off by a deficient product.[107] What you see is what you get. Nor is there much evidence that such a segmented market creates a race to the bottom, an ever-descending spiral of kitsch, such as Graham Greene described in his splenetic account of 1930s Mexico.[108] Mexican 'heritage' products have now been selling for the best part of a century, since the nationalistic boosterism of the Revolution coincided with the advent of mass tourism, especially from the United States, in the 1920s. And there have been periodic shifts and revivals: the recent *alebrije* phenomenon, for example; or the cult of Frida Kahlo (once known as Diego Rivera's wife; it is now Diego who is more usually referred to as Frida's husband).

Without pondering further the question of authenticity versus kitsch, it remains to assess the relative success of Mexico's heritage 'industry', particularly with regard to the popular/nationalist/indigenista agenda which the revolutionary regime espoused.[109] After all, that regime lost much of its radical dynamism in the 1940s; and, after a generation of fairly conservative machine politics from the 1940s to the1970s the PRI—the official, 'revolutionary' party, still discursively committed to the popular/nationalist/ indigenista agenda—lost support and finally relinquished (national) power in 2000.[110] By then, however, that agenda had acquired a life of its own, relatively autonomous from the state. It no longer depended on government initiatives, but enjoyed ample (which is not to say unconditional or overwhelming) support among the Mexican population. A great many Mexicans had 'internalized' the notion of the country's deep prehispanic roots; they valued

---

[106] As Mexican airport shops amply demonstrate.

[107] López, *Crafting Mexico*, 166.

[108] Graham Greene, *The Lawless Roads* (Harmondsworth, 1971 [1939]), 38, 44, 80-1, 92. (Greene's favourite descriptor of Mexico—'hideous'—appears five times in these four references).

[109] An entirely different account of Mexican 'heritage' could be given from a Catholic, especially a Catholic-conservative, point of view, which would tend to downplay, or denigrate, Precolumbian culture (it being primitive, sanguinary, and pagan) in favour of the Spanish Conquest and baroque Catholicism. Such a view would also stress Iturbide at the expense of Hidalgo, would be ambivalent, if not hostile, towards Juárez, and would repudiate the Revolution: see Smith, *The Roots of Conservatism*, 1, 197, 241.

[110] Knight, 'The Myth of the Mexican Revolution', 223-73.

Indian culture; they considered Indian heroes like Cuauhtémoc and Juárez to be iconic figures (Juárez regularly tops the poll of the greatest Mexicans in history, even when the poll is extended to film stars and sporting heroes).[111] Polls aside, there is abundant 'anecdotal' evidence: popular attendance at the National Anthropology Museum or at folkloric jamborees like the Oaxacan *guelaguetza* which, from its very inception in the 1930s, stirred an enthusiastic response.[112] When the construction of the Mexico City metro revealed the foundations of the Aztec city of Tenochtitlan, the popular response was enthusiastic and unscripted (thus, in modern Mexican historiographical terms, 'bottom-up', rather than 'top-down'). Eduardo Matos Moctezuma, who led the resulting excavation, recalls how *chilangos* flocked to the site:

> When people used to come to visit us on Saturdays I would ask them: 'well, what did you think of what you just saw, the Coyolxauqhui, the serpents heads?' They would answer: 'this is ours, what you are rescuing is something of ours'.[113]

One visitor even advocated tearing down the adjacent cathedral to get at the rest of buried Tenochtitlan: 'that's a monument one has to respect, it's a colonial monument', Matos remonstrated. 'No, Professor. What's really ours is this'.[114]

Similar sentiments, voiced more aggressively and even chauvinistically, were expressed when Cuauhtémoc's alleged bones were 'discovered' at Ixcateopan in 1949. The result of a fairly amateurish fraud, the bones

---

[111] Ulíses Beltrán, 'El ranking de los héroes patrios', Nexos en línea, 1 Sept. 2001, at http://www.nexos.com.mx/?P=leerarticulo&Articulo=2100174.

[112] On the fusion of folklore and leftism which produced the Oaxacan gueleguetza see Benjamin T. Smith, *Pistoleros and Popular Movements. The Poltiics of State Formation in Postrevolutionary Oaxaca* (Lincoln, 2009), 49-50, 222-3; and, on the contemporary— highly comercialized—version, Barbara Kastelein, 'The Beach and Beyond: Observations from a Travel Writer on Dreams, Decadence and Defence', in Berger and Wood, *Holiday in Mexico*, 332, 337.

[113] Davíd Carrasco, Leonardo López Luján, and Eduardo Matos Moctezuma, *Breaking Through Mexico's Past* (Albuquerque, 2007), 99; we may compare this enthusiasm with the indifference shown towards 'relics' relating to the nineteenth-century caudillo Santa Anna (seen by many as a national disaster, if not an actual traitor): Knight, 'The Several Legs of Santa Anna'.

[114] Carrasco et al., *Breaking Through Mexico's Past*, 99; of course, a Catholic-conservative would take a quite different view (see n. 109), but it would very likely be a minority one. Lowenthal, *The Heritage Crusade*, 22, offers a sharply contrasting interpretation of Maya attitudes in contemporary Yucatá, which he casually depicts to be 'unrepentant' regarding the looting of Precolumbian sites; his source is a single *Newsweek* report.

became the object of a fierce debate between die-hard indigenistas who, it seems, were willing to suspend disbelief in order to venerate the relics of a great Aztec hero, and more rational experts, who had no doubt that the find was fraudulent. The experts were entirely correct and, after much mutual vituperation, the dust settled; but not before distinguished figures had weighed in, usually on the basis of politico-cultural dogma rather than considered evidence. Ex-president Lázaro Cárdenas (the figurehead of the official revolutionary-nationalist left, who had named his son Cuauhtémoc) endorsed the find,[115] while Diego Rivera, still wielding cudgels on behalf of indigenismo, called the critics

> perverse [and] anti-Mexican, [indifferent to the] national value of . . . the objects they are dealing with. What they have done is so disastrous that if tomorrow the peasants, sublime Indians who guard the tomb, Mauser in hand, were to lay hold of the naysayers and, putting them against a wall in Ixcateopan, shoot them, they would have commited an act of absolute historical and patriotic justice.[116]

Here we see heritage in its 'greedy or chauvinist' guise:[117] irrational, dogmatic and aggressive. We also see Rivera's continued penchant for rhetorical violence and gunplay. But the case of Cuauhtémoc's bones attests to the mobilizing power of heritage, even when it runs counter to hard evidence and expert opinion.

In the end, hard evidence and expert opinion triumphed. Few today still cling to the cult of Cuauhtémoc's bones. But Cuauhtémoc and related indigenista/nationalist symbols retain their power. Indeed, contrary to many predictions of 'ethnocide' and the destruction of Indian culture, forms of indigenismo still flourish in the literate, industrial, post-NAFTA Mexico of the early twenty-first century. Rather as Gamio had advocated, integration—evident in education, migration, and the labour market, both national and international—has not erased the Indian cultural heritage, as it is deployed by Indians and mestizos alike: language, music, dance, art, archaeology, and artisanry. If anything, these cultural phenomena have strengthened in recent decades and they have been accompanied by a more militant indigenismo which, in contrast to that of the 1920s and '30s, is the vehicle of actual Indians, not of paternalists mestizos and criollos (like Gamio). Particularly since 1992—the year of the Quincentenary—Indian movements, both

---

[115] Gillingham, *Cuauhtémoc's Bones*, 109-10.
[116] Gillingham, *Cuauhtémoc's Bones*, 71-2.
[117] Lowenthal, *The Heritage Crusade*, xiv.

political and cultural, have flourished. The revolt of the EZLN in Chiapas in 1994, though by no means a purely Indian movement, certainly placed ethnic issues squarely on the national political agenda.[118] In response, the embattled PRI made concessions in respect of Indian autonomy, allowing a regime of so-called *usos y costumbres* to prevail in southern states like Oaxaca.[119] A new generation of Indian leaders and intellectuals has arisen, in part supplanting the mestizo/criollo paternalists of previous decades.[120] Even the melting pot of mass migration has had mixed results: far from ensuring a bland cultural *mestizaje* it has, in some cases, such as that of the Mixtec communities of southern California, fostered greater ethnic identity and mobilization.[121] Indeed, politico-cultural currents in the US including ethnic/identity politics, New Age mysticism, and a continued thirst for the 'authentic' and folkloric (including folkloric hallucinogens like peyote—'magic mushrooms') have favoured the preservation and dissemination of Mexico's 'Indian' heritage, which Mexican governments have readily exploited in their pursuit of 'soft power' abroad.[122]

Much of this is no doubt kitsch and commercialized. But it was ever thus. Mexican fiestas—ancient celebrations of popular religiosity and recreation—always combined a measure of God and Mammon;[123] and it should come as no surprise that the twentieth-century 'heritage industry', from up-market museums in Mexico City to magic mushrooms in Oaxaca, should entail an often crass commercialism. Similarly, ethnic politics, like all politics, is about power and privilege, as well as ethnocultural conservation. *Usos y constumbres*, for example, while it may provide a measure of Indian autonomy, can also perpetuate machismo, authoritarianism, and gerontocracy. But for the commercialism and the politics to work, there must be some popular appeal,

---

[118] John Womack Jr, *Rebellion in Chiapas: A Historical Reader* (New York, 1999).

[119] *Usos y costumbres* denotes a local regime governed by 'traditional', that is, 'Indian' political and administrative practices, distinct from those laid down in state and national constitutions.

[120] Natividad Gutiérrez Chong, *Mitos nacionalistas e identidades étnicas* (México, 2001), ch. 7.

[121] Michael Kearney, 'Mixtec Political Consciousness: From Passive to Active Resistance', in Daniel Nugent (ed.), *Rural Revolt in Mexico and U. S. Intervention* (La Jolla, 1988), 120, 123.

[122] A classic example being the lavish exhibition, 'Mexico Splendour of Thirty Centuries', which toured the United States in 1991, as President Salinas was seeking to conclude the North Amercan Free Trade Agreement (which was narrowly approved by the US Congress two years later).

[123] Madame Calderón de la Barca, *Life in Mexico* (London, J. M. Dent, n.d. [1853]), Letter the Twenty-First.

some resonance among mass publics, both Mexican and foreign. The veneration of Cuauhtémoc or Juárez has a real basis in popular culture and is not the creation of a Pygmalion state, capable of breathing 'false consciousness' or 'ideological hegemony' into a passive people.[124] Politicians or businessmen may seek advantage from 'heritage' but they did not create it *de novo*, nor can they manipulate it at will. The relative success of the revolutionary state in its creation of nationalist/popular/indigenista symbols, such as Zapata and his mythical white horse, was in part due to collective effort and institution-building; but it also depended on popular receptivity (at least among large swathes of the population: conservative Catholics, as I have stressed, were largely immune to this appeal). The story of Mexican heritage in the twentieth century thus sheds light on a well-known debate in studies of nationalism, a debate which pits 'modernists' (or 'instrumentalists') against 'primordialists'.[125] In the Mexican case the modernists/instrumentalists would be right to stress the role of the state, of state elites, and of their cultural agents (Gamio and Rivera being key examples); and they would correctly insist that the state, not least by means of public education, could substantially affect how Mexicans viewed their history—the heroes they revered, the villains they execrated, the anniversaries they celebrated, and the sites they visited. But the state had to work with the materials to hand; those materials were diverse and contradictory (thus, the Catholic Church, possessed of its own elites, agents, and institutions, also successfully deployed a politico-cultural discourse in opposition to that of the state); and, above all, the state had to appeal to the people, thus to chime in with popular memories and prejudices. The latter were the product of generations of history (and heritage), thus the primordialists are correct to stress that notions of the nation may run deep, like suboceanic currents whose origins may remain obscure and whose force can be harnessed, but cannot be switched on and off at will. Heritage may serve both political advantage and commercial profit; but, to do so, it must have genuine popular roots, which in turn derive from historical trends and experiences over which elites may exercise little control. Heritage is not history; Lowenthal is right in this respect, but he is stating the obvious.[126] However, heritage, in the modern Mexican case at least, remains anchored in history ('what happened to happen') and its appeal strongly depends on the strength of that anchor, and the depth of the mud in which it rests.

---

[124] Cf. Ilene V. O'Malley, *The Myth of the Revolution: Hero Cults and the Institutionalization of the Mexican State, 1920-40* (Westport, 1986).

[125] On the modernist vs primordialist debate, see Anthony D. Smith, *The Ethnic Origins of Nations* (Oxford, 1986), 7-13.

[126] Lowenthal, *The Heritage Crusade*, x.

Idols, Altars, Slippers, and Stockings: Heritage Debates and Displays in Nineteenth-Century Chile

Patience A. Schell[1]

When liberal historian Benjamín Vicuña Mackenna lobbied for support to host an exhibition about Chile's colonial past, he compared the bringing together of historical objects to the work of a natural historian, who used the fossilized, fragmented remains of a long-extinct creature to imagine its body and its habits.[2] Fragmentary remains are an apt way to describe the raw material of Chile's heritage: the new country did not have monumental architecture, the metaphorical equivalent of a perfectly complete fossilized mastodon or tyrannosaurus rex, around which to build a concept of national heritage. The indigenous people who inhabited the territory that became Chile did not leave pyramids behind, like the Aztecs or the Maya, nor did the colonial period leave a baroque city-scape, as it had in Lima, Mexico City, or Potosí. As the nineteenth century progressed, this lack of grand material remains became more problematic because other Spanish American countries used them as metaphorical foundation stones to new national identities. By the mid-century in other parts of Latin America, the 'new language' of archaeology offered evidence that the Maya, Inca, and Aztecs were highly 'civilised' peoples, feeding into both nationalism and a re-valuation of pre-Columbian remains as having scientific merit. This same language of archaeology, however, situated the indigenous people of Chile, without a written language or grand architectural ruins, in the category of 'Lower Barbarian'.[3]

---

[1] My thanks to Paul Betts and Corey Ross for their invitation to participate in the conference leading to this volume, as well as their comments on the various drafts. I am also grateful to my fellow participants for two days of lively discussions and concrete suggestions, and to Laurence Brown, Till Geiger, Anindita Ghosh, Steven Pierce, and Natalie Zacek for their comments on an earlier draft.

[2] Benjamín Vicuña Mackenna, 'La Esposicion del Coloniaje', *Revista de Santiago*, II (1872-73), 343.

[3] Rebecca Earle, *The Return of the Native: Indians and Myth-Making in Spanish America, 1810-1930* (Durham, 2007), 142-6. Quotations 144-5. On nation archaeology, see Stefanie Gänger, 'Conquering the Past: Post-War Archaeology and Nationalism in the

Thus Chileans created heritage from their historical narrative, natural environment and, particularly in the first years after independence, the 'indomitable' character of the pre-Columbian indigenous population. While debates about the character and legacy of the colonial period divided opinions, history books lauded the exploits of the independence heroes, who had inherited their spirit of liberty from the indigenous Araucanians, while the home of archaeological materials, natural history specimens, and dusty old objects was the *Museo Nacional* (National Museum), founded in 1838. Like other museums in South America, either supported by national or provincial governments, the Museo Nacional functioned both as a research institution, sponsoring expeditions and publishing research results, and as a public institution to entertain and educate.[4] By the 1870s, an historical exhibition and a new history museum created questions about the borders between history and natural history, especially regarding displayed heritage. While the term used for the collection of heritage was 'living history', the work of this living history was to 'design a past that [would] fix the identity [of Chileans] and enhance the well-being of some chosen . . . folk'.[5] This article uses a history exhibition, a history museum, and the Museo Nacional's collection to argue that proponents of both history and natural history displays made heritage claims, particularly in seeking the exclusive right to display indigenous artefacts, while their goals and motivations came from distinct sources. Before examining these collections, and their creators, the article briefly discusses the changing role of indigenous heritage and display culture in Chile.

Housing a contested heritage

Chile seized independence from Spain in 1818, and by the end of the 1820s had achieved relative political stability. In this period, Chile occupied only the middle third of the territory of contemporary Chile, an area including the capital, Santiago, and the agriculturally rich central valley. To the south were the territories of the Araucanian people, recognized as sovereign through treaties with the Spanish crown. Independent Araucanians played an important symbolic role for the new nation; during the independence struggles and shortly afterwards, the Creole rebels drew parallels between their anti-colonial war and Araucanian battles against the original Spanish colonial project.

Borderlands of Chile and Peru, *c.*1880-1920', *Comparative Studies in Society and History*, 51:4 (2009), 691-714.

[4] Susan Sheets-Pyenson, *Cathedrals of Science: The Development of Colonial Natural History Museums during the Latin Nineteenth Century* (Kingston, 1988), 18.

[5] David Lowenthal, *The Heritage Crusade and the Spoils of History* (Cambridge, 1998), xi.

Legitimacy for the independence struggles was partially borrowed from the history of these indigenous people.[6] In the post-independence period the Aruacanians carried the weight of the new nation's attributes: an early example of Chilean fiction presented them as 'simultaneously autochthonous and enlightened, American and civilized, historic and modern: the perfect nationalist symbol'.[7]

Yet this rhetorical heritage was difficult for Creole elites to maintain— especially as living Araucanians had mostly fought to continue the colonial relationship. Just one generation after independence, elite Chileans had already shifted the origins of their nation forward in time to the independence wars, depicting independence heroes as their founding fathers and the nation's ancestry as Spanish.[8] This shift allowed historian Benjamín Vicuña Mackenna (1831-1886) to describe 'conquest-era Araucanians as the ancestors of the deceitful nineteenth-century savages who without qualm murdered innocent Christians and each other'. Importantly, this new orientation of national origin had coincided with a policy change. From the 1850s, the Chilean state sought to annex autonomous Araucanian territories; this process escalated into a military 'pacification' campaign (1860–1883) with devastating human costs 'accompanied by increasingly negative assessments of the capacities of the precolonial Araucanians'.[9]

Embracing Spanish heritage, however, presented its own problems. Borrowing from discussions of postcolonial theorists, Rebecca Earle has discussed the complexities of historical heritage and patrimony in postcolonial Spanish America: if the precolonial era was celebrated as the soul of the nation, then national culture was at risk of being ossified in the past; alternatively, drawing on the colonial legacy suggested that the new nation was a derivative culture lacking authenticity.[10] Perhaps for this reason, a discourse which subsumed history into an ahistorical celebration of the unique bounty

---

[6] Earle, *Return of the Native*, 25-6; Stephen E. Lewis, 'Myth and the History of Chile's Araucanians', *Radical History Review*, 58 (1994), 115-16, 123-5. Creoles were ethnically Spanish people, born in the Americas. The term 'Araucanian' is not in common usage now; the modern name for these people is the Mapuche.

[7] Earle, *Return of the Native*, 31.

[8] Ibid., 89-90. The Chilean state paid for the publication of history books which disseminated this new understanding of origins, including Claudio Gay's *Historia física y política de Chile* (1844-54), available through 'Memoria chilena', http://www.memoriachilena. cl/temas/dest.asp?id=gayhistoriafisicaypoliticadechile. See also Allen Woll, *A Functional Past: The Uses of History in Nineteenth-Century Chile* (Baton Rouge, 1982), 30-1.

[9] Earle, *Return of the Native*, 112-13.

[10] Rebecca Earle, '*Sobre Héroes y Tumbas*: National Symbols in Nineteenth-Century Spanish America', *Hispanic American Historical Review*, 85:3 (2005), 379.

of Chile's natural environment became the predominant way in which Chile's heritage was displayed. This discourse was natural history, which emerged from a broad eighteenth-century tradition in which natural histories could discuss foliage, minerals, political systems, or human history with equal validity.

This display ethic was evident at the Museo Nacional, founded in 1838 by the French naturalist (and historian) Claudio Gay (1800-1873), who had been hired in 1830 to explore Chile, write it all up and found a museum to house the material he gathered. When Gay returned to Paris to begin his (eventual) thirty volumes about the political and natural history of the country, he left behind a two-room museum in Santiago which displayed natural resources, as well as indigenous and foreign objects. Thus, the original museum did not limit itself to local materials, but rather, like its counterparts and models in Europe, sought to display a wide collection which aspired to global representation. Gay believed that, despite its size, the museum could be compared favourably with many museums in Europe.[11]

In the decade after Gay left, the museum's collection lost its focus and the specimens deteriorated.[12] When Prussian Rodulfo A. Philippi (1808-1904) took up the post of museum director in 1853, the display included a range of natural history and heritage objects that had no other home, such as flags won from the Spanish, weights and measures and 'phenomena', including a two-headed sheep, a five-legged pig and human curiosities that, according to Philippi, were mostly of interest to women visitors.[13] These items suggest an old-fashioned 'cabinet of curiosities' collection of the rare and the unusual, which Philippi sought to replace in favour of a catalogue of nature, which displayed common specimens and was organized following debates about taxonomy; the idea was not to entertain but to feed scientific advancement.[14]

---

[11] Claudo Gay to Manuel Montt, 16 June 1842, in Feliú Cruz, Guillermo and Carlos Stuardo Ortiz, *Correspondencia de Claudio Gay. Recopilación, prólogo y notas de Guillermo Feliú Cruz y Carlos Stuardo Ortiz; traducción del profesor Luis Villablanca* (Santiago, 1962), 38. On 'colonial museums' see Sheets-Pyenson, *Cathedrals of Science*, 10-12.

[12] *Guia del Museo Nacional de Chile en setiembre de 1878 destinado a los visitantes* (Santiago, 1878), 4. Gay's contract has similarities to the failed work of the Scientific Commission of Mexico, of 1864, organized during the French intervention. See Paul N. Edison, 'Conquest Enrequited: French Expeditionary Science in Mexico, 1864-1867', *French Historical Studies*, 26:3 (2003), 459-95.

[13] Rodulfo A. Philippi, 'Historia del Museo Nacional de Chile', *Boletín del Museo Nacional*, vii:1 (1914), 19.

[14] Paula Findlen, *Possessing Nature: Museums, Collecting, and Scientific Culture in Early Modern Italy* (Berkeley, 1994), 394-8; Martin J. S. Rudwick, *Bursting the Limits of Time: The Reconstruction of Geohistory in the Age of Revolution* (Chicago, 2005), 40-1.

Philippi's aim was to create a 'complete' collection of Chile, or a 'universal' museum of Chile and he measured the institution's success by this yardstick, noting with satisfaction, for instance, when collecting expeditions had 'enriched' the museum's 'poor' collection of 'Chilean animals and plants'.[15] Philippi's quest for 'completeness', while fundamentally a personal scientific project, contributed to and could be seen by others as part of a national heritage project. As Paul Edison argues:

> Nationalism thrives on the concrete materiality of objects understood as a nation's patrimony. Whether they are natural or fabricated, certain objects are transformed into the 'authentic' repositories of a nation's genius to be celebrated and protected through careful and learned stewardship.[16]

Philippi regularly attempted to remove Creole or European historical materials from the museum, yet he actively sought objects, contemporary or historical, from indigenous cultures. Philippi's appreciation for ethnographic and archaeological materials was part of an intellectual shift that witnessed the founding of museums of anthropology and later the creation of the academic disciplines of anthropology and archaeology.[17] Amongst the collections Philippi built up during his almost-half-century curating the Museo Nacional was that of South American ethnographic materials. But he was not fully successful in purging artefacts of European and Creole history from his museum, as we will see below, and the older view of a national museum which included both human and natural history remained.

On the 'cabinet of curiosities' see Oliver Impey and Arthur MacGregor (eds), *The Origins of Museums: The Cabinet of Curiosities in Sixteenth- and Seventeenth-Century Europe* (Oxford, 1985).

[15] Rodulfo A. Philippi, 'Historia del Museo Nacional', 24. 'Completeness' is a recurring theme in Philippi's discussions of the collection. See Philippi to Minister of Education, 25 April 1866, Archivo Nacional de Chile, Fondo Ministerio de Educación (hereafter AN/ME)138/20 for an example.

[16] Paul Edison, 'Patrimony on the Periphery: French Archaeologists in Nineteenth-Century Mexico', *Proceedings of the Annual Meeting of the Western Society for French History*, 24 (1997), 494.

[17] Christina Bueno, '*Forjando Patrimonio*: The Making of Archaeological Patrimony in Porfirian Mexico', *Hispanic American Historical Review*, 90:2 (2010), 226; Earle, *Return of the Native*, 142-3.

Colonial heritage and the 1873 exhibition

Until the 1870s, moreover, there was no obvious home for the historical materials besides the Museo Nacional. By that time, Chileans were optimistic about the nation's progress, fuelled by an unprecedented economic boom of mineral exports;[18] the decade ended in a triumphant war that incorporated mineral-rich Peruvian and Bolivian territories into Chile. This mood of national bravado was evident in the 1872 volume, *Chile ilustrado*, which depicted Chile as a beacon of progress and technological advancement in Latin America.[19] Gabriel Cid argues that *Chile ilustrado*'s representation of the country positioned Chile as South America's model modern nation.[20]

Aspirations towards 'modernity' were also evident through the transformation of the capital city's built environment, by individuals and the city government. Cosmopolitan residents of Santiago replaced colonial buildings with new homes, inspired by French and Italian styles.[21] As mayor of Santiago (1872-75), historian Vicuña Mackenna contributed to this modernization, embarking upon an urban redevelopment project, inspired by Paris and Vienna. The project included a ring road around the city, clearly marking the city's limits, a major park to the south and the re-development of the city's scrubby Santa Lucía hill, close to the centre.[22]

Even as he gave Santiago a modern new look, Vicuña Mackenna worried that, in this blind rush to the future, colonial artefacts and architectural gems were being lost. Chile's heritage was at risk. In Europe, Vicuña Mackenna had witnessed heritage preservation and displays, such as France's Cluny museum and England's Tower of London. Despite being a political liberal, and unlike some of his contemporaries, Vicuña Mackenna believed that the colonial era was a period of major importance for Chileans to understand. Thus he sought to create a historical consciousness amongst Chileans, including recognition of historical heritage. For example, he renamed the centre's streets after

---

[18] Germán Hidalgo Hermosilla, 'Panoramic View and National Identity: Two of Santiago de Chile's Public Spaces in the Second Half of the Nineteenth Century', *Planning Perspectives*, 24:3 (2009), 321.

[19] Recaredo S. Tornero, *Chile ilustrado. Guia descriptivo del territorio de Chile, de las capitales de provincia i de los puertos principales* (Valparaíso, 1872), v-vi. Philippi and Gay were both cited in the volume's bibliography, viii.

[20] Gabriel Cid, 'Un ícono funcional: la invención del *roto* como símbolo nacional', in Gabriel Cid and Alejandro San Francisco (eds), *Nación y nacionalismo en Chile: Siglo XIX*, 2 vols (Santiago, 2009), i, 228.

[21] Tornero, *Chile ilustrado*, 8.

[22] Hidalgo, 'Panoramic View', 321-2.

independence heroes.[23] He also lamented that in Chile the only attempt to amass a historical collection had been undertaken by a private patron. Lessons about preserving historical heritage had to be learned throughout society; even Chile's elites hid away the objects they had inherited. Without a change of mentality, material culture would rot away in the homes of the rich, metal objects would be sold for scrap and valuable historical and archaeological objects would be lost to European collections.[24]

Vicuña Mackenna organized the 1873 Esposicion del Coloniaje in part to teach the public of the value of colonial heritage. Vicuña Mackenna would eventually argue that the 600 objects on display came to be seen as something 'entirely new', a collection of 'vestiges' and 'relics' made out of 'memories' and 'things'. In this project, he sought to form, like Christina Bueno argues in the case of Mexico, 'national patrimony out of objects that had other uses and meanings', in a process that valued some objects over others. The exhibition was also to be a 'foundation', with a public educational purpose inspired by institutions like the British Museum.[25]

Writing to the organizing committee's chair, Vicuña Mackenna mused that Chileans had sought to 'put a new people where before a completely different people' had lived, forgetting the colonial past. As a result, precious colonial objects of art were 'dispersed on the four winds', in part due to the disdain with which these objects were held. But recovering them would be easy without even leaving Santiago; appropriate objects were to be found in homes which they both frequented.[26] A successful print historian, Vicuña Mackenna nonetheless believed that, as Mark Jones argues, 'objects themselves have something to tell us about the past and that the evidence which they provide is complementary to, not illustrative of, knowledge derived from documentary sources'.[27] The 1873 colonial exhibition was intended to

> group these poorly known treasures, classify the humble but meaningful objects, in a word reorganize the exterior life of the colonial

[23] Earle, 'Sobre Héroes y Tumbas', 376.

[24] Vicuña Mackenna, 'La Esposicion del Coloniaje', 345-6, 350. See also Benjamín Vicuña Mackenna, *Catalogo del Museo Histórico del Santa Lucia* (Santiago, 1875), 12.

[25] Christina Bueno, '*Forjando Patrimonio*', 216; Vicuña Mackenna, *Catalogo del Museo Histórico*, 4; see also Luis Alegría, 'Colección de lo intangible: la colección de objetos de folklore del Museo de Etnología y Antropología de Chile', in M. Cecilia Rodríguez, Roxana Seguel, and Paloma Mujica (eds), *Actas III Congreso Chileno de Conservación y Restauración. Patrimonio, Conservación y Ciudadanía* (Santiago, 2010), 202.

[26] Vicuña Mackenna, 'La Esposicion del Coloniaje', 348-9. Quotations 342.

[27] Mark Jones, 'Why a Museum of Scotland? Aspirations and Expectations', in J. M. Fladmark, *Heritage and Museums: Shaping National Identity* (Shaftesbury, 2000), 9.

period with its own apparel and lend it, through research and method, fleeting life in order to exhibit it before the eyes of an intelligent, but too forgetful, people.

This resurrection of the colonial period is the task that Vicuña Mackenna compared to the work of a naturalist.[28]

The construction of this historical heritage also had a practical goal: the exhibition would demonstrate progress from the time of the conquest until 1849. Careful arrangement and classification of 'scattered' and 'forgotten' objects would 'constitute a type of living history of our national existence and show . . . the admirable degree of wellbeing and production, of tranquillity and richness that the republic has reached' in just over fifty years.[29] Vicuña Mackenna's inclusion of the colonial and independence periods together neatly sidestepped the problematic aspects of colonial history, by linking the colonial past to the successes of the independence and post-independence periods, such as political stability. Thus, the exhibition was not to promote nostalgia, but intended to demonstrate Chile's modernity and progress through comparison with seemingly old fashioned, exotic, and alien objects.

Still questions were raised, even before the exhibition opened. One critic reflected that while the exhibition would, in his words, put together a 'collection of mementos' and exhibit the 'material relics of our colonial past', no further organizing logic was needed. During the colonial period, nothing changed. Every single day sameness prevailed and, as a result, 'human existence' might as well be 'human vegetation'.[30]

The exhibition opened on 17 September 1873 in the former colonial governors' palace ('like a resuscitated corpse'), located on Santiago's main plaza, which had been painted bright red and yellow for the event.[31] Displayed objects included a range of domestic and everyday goods such as portraits,

---

[28] Vicuña Mackenna, 'La Esposicion del Coloniaje', 343.

[29] Benjamín Vicuña Mackenna, declaration creating the exhibition, 1 Mar. 1873, republished in 'La Esposicion del Coloniaje', 342-3. On the past and nationalism see Bueno, '*Forjando Patrimonio*', 218-29 and Earle, 'Sobre Héroes y Tumbas', 375-416. It is not clear why Vicuña Mackenna ended his search in 1849; perhaps it was to do with his perception about Chile's development reaching a stable point or when the past became too recent to be 'history'.

[30] Domingo Arteaga Alemparte, 'El coloniaje i el progreso', *Revista de Santiago*, ii (1872-73), 825-6. Quotations 826.

[31] *Catalogo razonado de la Esposicion del Coloniaje celebrada en Santiago de Chile en Setiembre de 1873 por uno de los miembros de su comision directiva* (Santiago, 1873), iii-iv. Quotation iii.

furniture, carriages, clothing, housewares, religious and indigenous objects, weaponry, manuscripts and family trees.[32] Because Vicuña Mackenna and his organizing committee created the exhibition's collection from scratch, the displayed materials represented a snapshot of an elite view on Chile's heritage and valuable objects. In this snapshot, national patrimony emerged from the domestic spheres of Chile's elite and their family histories became public histories. For the curious, then, the exhibition not only offered a history lesson but also allowed them to gaze on an elite domestic sensibility. Yet, unlike the Museum of Ornamental Art in London, which also displayed elite domestic spaces as Lara Kriegel discusses, the colonial exhibition did not seek to change decorative tastes, but rather to revalue old objects.[33] Moreover, despite its pedagogic role, it did not invite visitors to debate historic processes or interpretations of history. The objects in the exhibition made visually explicit what was assumed by those in power; that discussions about national heritage and historical meaning took place amongst a limited circle of elite men.[34]

Vicuña Mackenna hoped that this exhibition of elite sensibility would engage the public. The exhibition's catalogue, for sale as a guide and perhaps a souvenir, sought to make history lively; written in a playful, tongue-in-cheek voice, it emphasized the past's colourful characters. Exotic employees also contributed to the spectacle, making Chile's past a thrilling, alien place. Exhibition tickets were sold from a stationary calash, the 'driver' of which was a 'legitimate black man from Lima'. This man's presence evoked the colonial era, even as his being 'from Lima' suggested that people of African ancestry were not part of Chile's colonial past.[35] *Chile ilustrado* made that point explicitly: in Chile, 'there are only two races: the Spanish and the Indian'.[36] Members of the indigenous 'race' were in fact represented as part of the exhibition. During the exhibition five indigenous people, described as 'half naked', were displayed in the city as curiosities. Vicuña Mackenna assured a titillated populace that the 'savage' from Tierra del Fuego was a recent

---

[32] Ibid., viii, 95.

[33] Lara Kriegel, *Grand Designs: Labor, Empire, and the Museum in Victorian Culture* (Durham, 2007), 135. Kriegel also discusses how the display of domestic interiors was combined with a pedagogic role. On this process in Argentina, see Jens Andermann, 'Reshaping the Creole Past: History Exhibitions in late Nineteenth-Century Argentina', *Journal of the History of Collections*, 13:2 (2001), 145-62.

[34] Ricardo Krebs, 'Orígenes de la conciencia nacional chilena', in Cid and San Francisco (eds), *Nación y nacionalismo en Chile*, i, 4.

[35] *Catalogo razonado*, iv-v.

[36] Tornero, *Chile ilustrado*, 446.

cannibal who, according to a newspaper article, sought a 'barbecued or raw' child as a remedy when he had indigestion.[37] This display of indigenous people was part of a practice of imperial science and missionary activity, in which people, as much as ethnographic and natural history objects, were displayed in museums and exhibitions.[38]

Even as Santiago's public was invited to gawk at living indigenous people, indigenous people were virtually erased from the exhibition's historical narrative. There was only one portrait of an indigenous person in the exhibition: 'brave' Caupolicán, one of the original leaders of resistance to Spanish colonization. American indigenous cultures were instead represented through a display of objects, which included a box made by 'Indians of the United States', gloves made by indigenous craftspeople in Peru, and a palm hat from Colombia. The only object linked to an actual indigenous historical figure was Caupolicán's staff. Moreover, in practice, the exhibition did not differentiate between 'Chilean' indigenous cultures and indigenous cultures from the rest of the Americas; the instructions to the organizing commission had only directed that they seek out pre-conquest indigenous objects: contemporary objects had not been specifically sought out.[39]

Thus divorced from indigenous links, Chile's history began with a display of portraits, both original and carefully researched copies, including a series of all the colonial governors.[40] Each of the portraits was labelled with a brief biographical caption, discussing personality as much as accomplishments. Manuel de Amat (1707-1782), for instance, was 'able' but 'coarse' and 'greedy'.[41] A few notable women from the colonial period were also depicted, like Catalina de Erauzo (1592-1650). The catalogue recounted that after growing up in a Spanish convent, she disguised herself as a man, sailed for Chile as a soldier and killed her own brother in a duel, before confessing and ending her days in a convent.[42]

The catalogue's descriptions made clear links between heritage, understood as symbolic colonial inheritance, and the actual material inheritance

---

[37] Fanor Velasco, 'Revista', *Revista de Santiago*, iii (1872-73), 644; 'El antropófago', *Mercurio*, 23 Sept. 1873, 2-3. Quotation 3.

[38] See, e.g., Sadiah Qureshi, 'Displaying Sara Baartman, the "Hottentot Venus"', *History of Science*, 42 (2004), 234-5.

[39] *Catalogo razonado*, 53, 97-100; Vicuña Mackenna, declaration creating the exhibition, 1 Mar. 1873, republished in 'La Esposicion del Coloniaje', 342-3.

[40] Vicuña Mackenna, 'La Esposicion del Coloniaje', 348-9.

[41] *Catalogo razonado*, 7.

[42] Ibid., 16-17.

of an elite minority, which David Lowenthal argues is where heritage begins.[43] The painting of colonial governor Tomás Marín de Poveda (1650-1703), for example, was due 'particular merit' because it was a family heirloom.[44] Paula Recabárren loaned four portraits, the first of which was described as the family's 'inheritance', the second depicted her great-great-grandmother and the third demonstrated her descendence from the Marchioness of Cañada Hermosa.[45] Objects that might previously have been admired by family, friends, and guests in elite homes (or were never admired because they were embarrassing reminders of a backward past?) were now re-valued as part of national history and national heritage. Moreover, the public display of these portraits reflected well upon their owners, who appeared philanthropic and interested in the public good, while providing a legitimate opportunity to note their illustrious lineage and highlight family stories. The catalogue did not explain to the audience who Recabárren and other benefactors were: it was assumed that they were known. Through this process, as Alvaro Fernández Bravo argues, about Argentine museums, 'family memories' were 'nationalised' for an audience keen to view these private objects which were given new meaning as part of the nation's heritage. Other portraits represented the new symbolic fathers of the Chilean nation: independence leaders Bernardo O'Higgins and José de San Martín, as well as Manuel Salas, among whose legacies was the National Library, and behind-the-scenes strongman Diego Portales, who helped stabilize Chile's political system.[46] Key moments were represented, too: 'La batalla de Maipo', Juan Mauricio Rugendas' painting of a key independence battle, was described as an 'interesting original painting [that] belongs to the National Library, which has as much need of it as Christ would a pair of pistols'.[47]

After the portraits, the exhibition showcased ordinary objects of diverse use and origin, of value because of their provenance or singularity. The first piano in Chile, on display, had thrilled Santiago: 'Everyone wanted to see and hear it . . .'.[48] Visitors were expected to wonder how the large carriage which had belonged to successful eighteenth-century merchant José Ramírez de Saldaña

---

[43] Lowenthal, *The Heritage Crusade*, 31.

[44] *Catalogo razonado*, 5.

[45] Ibid., 5-6, 15-16, 27-8.

[46] Ibid., 35, 38-40, 43; Alvaro Fernández Bravo, 'Material Memories: Tradition and Amnesia in Two Argentine Museums', in Jens Andermann and William Rowe (eds), *Images of Power: Iconography, Culture and the State in Latin America* (New York, 2005), 85.

[47] *Catalogo razonado*, 110.

[48] Ibid., 65.

could possibly have navigated Santiago's muddy, obstacle-rich streets. The catalogue described how the carriage was only driven on special occasions, such as the graduation of a doctoral candidate from the San Felipe University or the growth of the first beard of a young heir, and on those occasions four mules were sent from the Piura valley in Peru to pull it. After the 'blacks polished the harnesses' the carriage set off down the city streets, causing a commotion, as people leaned out their windows to gawk. Now the carriage was owned by politician Vicente Izquierdo i Urmeneta who was 'gallant' enough to offer it to Vicuña Mackenna not only for the exhibition but also as part of the founding collection of a 'museum of antiquities like the famous Cluny in Paris'.[49] The unrestored open carriage which carried Diego Portales to his assassination in 1837 was there, as was Portales' desk, his cane, and a lock of his hair, cut on the day he died.[50] Through public display, these private items come to represent a national story shared by all Chileans.[51]

Yet whatever logic I have argued for in this collection, it is equally important to recognize that the display represented incoherence as much as coherence. Not all of the objects had an evident link to Chile's past or were even old. There was a 'complete Greek costume', samples of bone china brought from England by the father of an organizing committee member, an amber powder horn from Ireland, and Napoleon's chess set.[52] Busts of Roman emperors recently purchased in Italy were displayed, as were two portraits Vicuña Mackenna himself had bought in Brussels.[53] Thus, in this colonial exhibition some objects appeared to have been displayed because powerful elites wanted to show off their treasures; although the display was supposed to represent Chile's heritage, there was an inherent self-referential (elite) bias to the collection. The diversity of objects and provenances indicates that the exhibition was a display of curiosities, unrelated objects, objects of wonder, and objects demonstrating personal and social power, as much as a display to teach Chileans about their historical heritage.[54]

By 23 September, less than a week after opening, more than 3,000 people had visited the exhibition; Santiago's society concluded that it was a top day out. The event had earned over 3,000 pesos, from ticket and catalogue sales.[55] Despite its popularity, there were critics. The journalist and politician Fanor

---

[49] Ibid., 62-3. Quotations 63.

[50] Ibid., 63-5, 67, 86, 114.

[51] See Lowenthal, *The Heritage Crusade*, 63-8 on this process in France and England.

[52] *Catalogo razonado*, 75, 87, 93, 112. Quotation 75.

[53] Ibid., 18, 58.

[54] For one discussion of collectors see Findlen, *Possessing Nature*, 293-345.

[55] 'La esposicion del coloniaje', *Mercurio*, 23 Sept. 1873, 2.

Velasco noted that the exhibition had been greeted with scepticism, 'apathy', and even concern that it might be dangerous. 'Austere republicans and furious democrats have believed they have seen in [the exhibition] a tentative resurrection, a sacrifice made to vanity, a grain of incense burned on the altar of the colony'. Velasco ridiculed the idea that displaying a family tree would spark some aristocratic attempt to restore colonial rule, arguing that the exhibition would help Chileans appreciate how far the nation had come.[56]

But he further argued that the exhibition had no pedagogic value, only good intentions. Hours wandering the displays would not change the fact that one 'left as [one] had entered' and learned nothing. The exhibition failed to educate because of a 'lack of criterion, method, seriousness, taste, and lack of everything that should be put to the service of a project like this'. The building was inappropriate, the displays were badly organized, and the objects themselves lacked interest. What, he wondered, did eclectic things from Europe have to do with Chile's colonial past? The 'directive committee was in charge of putting on a characteristic exhibition and has made a gypsy's trousseau in which there is everything at the same time as there is nothing'. The display of Portales' various relics was 'ridiculous' and the carriage serving as a ticket booth (staffed by the 'unhappy man' from Lima) was 'grotesque'. He concluded that, 'Our grandparents were backward people, but sometimes they had better taste than their grandchildren'. The catalogue, moreover, started as 'witty' but descended into 'irony' and 'taunts', with a tendency to caricature the colonial period. Yet Velasco's understanding about the colonial era predisposed him to condemn the exhibition. Doubting that the display could have been improved, he concluded, 'The colonial period is distinguished principally for its negative qualities and has not left relics for an exhibition'.[57] Vicuña Mackenna's exhibition had failed to change that dismissive summation of Chile's colonial past.

Velasco's critique was emblematic of debates about how to address the colonial legacy. If the nation, untethered from Araucanian heritage, was now Spanish, what did colonial heritage mean? Gertrude Yeager argues that amongst the intellectual challenges facing the newly independent Spanish American nations, the most important was precisely determining how to reconcile with their colonial past. For instance Andrés Bello, leading jurist, politician and rector of the *Universidad de Chile*, had argued that colonial history offered a model of civic virtue and culture for the new nation. In 1844, José Victorino Lastarria, a liberal university professor, publicly challenged Bello's view, arguing that Spain had reduced Chile to servility and that the

---

[56] Velasco, 'Revista', 645.
[57] Ibid., 646-7.

new country still suffered from a 'colonial mentality'. Bello countered that the love of liberty and courage inherited from the Spanish were actually responsible for Chile's victory over Spain.[58] Yet Velasco's criticisms indicate that Lastarria's depiction of the Spanish colonial past as a yoke and burden continued to resonate.

History on permanent display

Despite criticisms, Vicuña Mackenna believed that his pet project had germinated new fruit. For instance, the colonial exhibition had attracted young men to the study of history,[59] although inspiring a new generation of historical writers returned history firmly to its place in books. But Vicuña Mackenna argued that the most important result of the exhibition was the *Museo histórico-indígena del Santa Lucía* (Santa Lucía Historical-Indigenous Museum). Work on this museum, part of Vicuña Mackenna's modernizing project for the city centre, began as the work for the colonial exhibition ended. Like the colonial exhibition, this new museum was to demonstrate how far Santiago, and by extension Chile, had come since independence. The new museum was housed in a renovated colonial fortress on Santa Lucía hill, in the city centre, which ironically, according to Vicuña Mackenna, had been 'destined to squash and punish the revolution that has precisely given life to those ideas of investigation that we pursue'.[60] (See Figure 1.)

While based upon the colonial exhibition's collection, the Santa Lucía museum had a broader focus, to display not only Chile's history but also indigenous artefacts. Merging 'historical' and 'indigenous' into the same narrative, however, ensured that indigenous people themselves, whether living or dead, were considered relics of Chile's distant past who would make no contribution to the formation of a modern nation. There were political implications to this narrative, in the expansionist context described above. Vicuña Mackenna himself remained a firm supporter of Chile's southern territorial conquests.[61]

---

[58] Gertrude M. Yeager, 'Sobrellevar el pasado español. Liberalismo latinoamericano y la carga de la historia colonial en el siglo XIX: El caso chileno', in Cid and San Francisco (eds), *Nación y nacionalismo en Chile*, i, 117-18, 124-6; Iván Jaksić, *Andrés Bello: Scholarship and Nation-Building in Nineteenth-Century Latin America* (Cambridge, 2001), 133-42. Quotation 134.

[59] Vicuña Mackenna, *Catalogo del Museo Histórico*, 5.

[60] Ibid.

[61] Earle, *Return of the Native*, 113. See also Eugenio Orrego Vicuña, *Iconografía de Vicuña Mackenna: Primer volumen preliminar. Obras completas de Vicuña Mackenna* (Santiago, 1939), 192.

Figure 1. 'Santa Lucía Historical-Indigenous Museum', in Benjamín Vicuña Mackenna, *Album del Santa Lucía. Colección de las principales vistas, monumentos, jardines, estátuas i obras de arte de este paseo, dedicado a la municipalidad de Santiago* (Santiago, 1874). With thanks to the Biblioteca Nacional de Chile and 'Memoria Chilena'.

Yet Vicuña Mackenna's ethnographic collection was not the result of a colonial project, as ethnographic displays in European museums were.

> For the colonial American collector . . . the possessed Other was now also proximate neighbor; concomitantly, the prized artefacts gathered during the inevitable encounters with Native Americas were gradually transformed from exotic (in the sense of foreign) curiosities to tangible records of the New World's indigenous culture.[62]

Following this logic, Vicuña Mackenna opened his discussion of the collection in the museum's catalogue by describing the 'aboriginal group', which was first 'in order by epochs', despite the fact that this collection was 'poor' because Chileans were as 'apathetic' about conserving these materials as their colonial ancestors had been.[63] Despite Vicuña Mackenna's disappointment

---

[62] Joyce Henri Robinson, 'An American Cabinet of Curiosities: Thomas Jefferson's "Indian Hall at Monticello" ', *Winterthur Portfolio*, 30:1 (1995), 46.

[63] Vicuña Mackenna, *Catalogo del Museo Histórico*, 6.

Figure 2. 'The Historic-Indigenous Museum', in Vicuña Mackenna, *Album del Santa Lucía*. The row of portraits along the top of the wall are from the Colonial Governors' series. With thanks to the Biblioteca Nacional de Chile and 'Memoria Chilena'.

with the poor quality of his collection, indigenous material culture belonged in his museum as it was part of New World, and therefore Chilean, culture.

Lacking 'truly indigenous articles', the Santa Lucía museum (see Figure 2) nonetheless had 'barbarous artefacts' from Tierra del Fuego. It is not clear on what grounds Vicuña Mackenna made this distinction, but it reduced the people of Tierra del Fuego to an even lower category of human than other indigenous peoples, already considered barbarians. Next in order of importance in the collection, as far as Vicuña Mackenna was concerned, were items from the conquest.[64] A stirrup, only found in 1872, was of 'considerable historical interest' because it had likely belonged to one of Spanish conquistador Pedro de Valdivia's company.[65] The portable altar that Chilean troops used during the fighting of 1817 and 1818 was also displayed,[66] like a symbolic national altar. Vicuña Mackenna referred to these objects as 'recuerdos' (souvenirs, mementos, or objects of sentimental value).[67]

[64] Vicuña Mackenna, *Catalogo del Museo Histórico*, 7.
[65] Ibid., 16-17. Quotation 17.
[66] Ibid., 16.
[67] Ibid., 7. See also 3-5.

Clothing worn by Eugenio Pertuisset, the French explorer of Tierra del Fuego in 1873-74 was also shown, while another exhibit displayed calling cards. 'English notables and especially the queen, receive all their visitors through this system', commented Vicuña Mackenna.[68] A lantern, brought from Rome, was displayed, as was a lantern used in Santiago before gas was introduced to the city streets. Portraits and busts of the recent great and good were there, too, including Claudio Gay and a patron of the museum, General Prado, as well the colonial governors' series.[69] Personal items with illustrious links were displayed, too. The Jesuit priest and naturalist Juan Ignacio Molina (1740-1829), exiled from Chile in 1767 when the religious order was expelled from the Spanish Empire, was represented by wigs and a black silk stocking he had worn in far-away Bologna.[70] The museum was also self-referential, memorializing the transformation of the hill it sat upon through paintings and an early blueprint.[71]

The domestic items on display belonged in an elegant home of prosperous people: crystal dishes for serving sweets, the coffee service that had belonged to the exiled Molina (which Vicuña Mackenna had long planned to put in the exhibition), vinegar and oil containers from the eighteenth century, copper candlesticks, and a hot-chocolate cup.[72] Objects from women's lives were on also on show, like a wooden container for sewing materials, embroidered silk gloves, and leather slippers. Interestingly, while domestic objects like these had been in the colonial exhibition, none of the portraits of women from the exhibition were displayed in the new museum; women's participation in Chilean life became solely linked to domestic material culture.[73]

Like the colonial exhibition, however, the museum display also depicted a jumble of inconsistent narratives based on Vicuña Mackenna's personal choices. But his choices had been constrained and he used the catalogue to vent his indignation. The Museo Nacional held what should have been the star of Vicuña Mackenna's collection, a silver 'idol'.[74] Vicuña Mackenna

[68] Ibid., 13-14. Quotation 13.
[69] Ibid., 14, 18, 25-32.
[70] Ibid., 20.
[71] Ibid., 13.
[72] Ibid., 17-18.
[73] Ibid., 19-20.
[74] Ibid., 6.

concluded the catalogue asking that history and natural history amicably go their separate ways:

> We will be permitted only now and upon finishing this rapid run through the past and its images and memories, to make a request that no doubt will be heard benevolently in the right time and by those who have the power to grant it, which is that in order to give its genuine and significant character back to the Museum of Natural History, all the objects which by rights correspond to the *Museo histórico indíjena* are passed [to it] . . . [75]

As far as Vicuña Mackenna was concerned, actual ownership mattered less than organizing logic: if an object was historical or indigenous by rights it belonged in his museum. Moreover, the eclectic collection of the Museo Nacional undermined its actual purpose, which was natural history. Thus, making a clear divide between natural history, to be housed in the Museo Nacional, and history/ethnography, to be housed in his museum, would benefit both institutions. In this public plea, Vicuña Mackenna perhaps deliberately misunderstood the purpose of the Museo Nacional, and strategically referred to it as a natural history museum. Examination of the 1873 colonial exhibition catalogue makes the problem clear. The bulk of the collection of 'objects and utensils of indigenous industry' on display belonged to the Museo Nacional, while the section of flags and armaments displayed more Museo Nacional items, including independence leader Bernardo O'Higgins' sword.[76] But no-one in power heeded Vicuña Mackenna's very public request. In 1878, O'Higgins' sword remained on display at the Museo Nacional.[77]

Removing history from a Natural History Museum

Rodulfo Philippi concurred with Vicuña Mackenna on the placement of historical objects and, throughout his tenure as Museo Nacional director, sought to purge the collection of objects which, from his point of view, had no scientific interest. Despite limited success, Philippi was not one to give up. In 1885, for instance, he wrote to the minister of education, suggesting a whole host of items in his museum should be moved, including two war paintings and marble busts of Dante and Mozart (which he pointedly mentioned were easily acquired in Europe for little money).[78] A few months later, Philippi

[75] Ibid., 32.
[76] *Catalogo razonado*, 98-100, 107-9.
[77] *Guia del Museo Nacional*, 27.
[78] Rodulfo Philippi to Minister of Education, 12 Nov. 1885, AN/ME 531/43.

informed his boss that a coat of arms in the collection was sought by Javier Larrain as family property. As the object had 'absolutely no value for the museum', Philippi was happy to return it. He noted that his museum was only for 'natural history, ethnography, and American antiquities'.[79]

Philippi and Vicuña Mackenna, representing natural history and history, also agreed that foreigners could easily take advantage of Chileans' ignorance about their heritage, resulting in important objects being lost to European collectors. Both men wanted heritage items to remain in Chile. Various examples indicate that their concerns were valid. For instance, US archaeologists Jeffries Wyman and George Peabody had undertaken a collecting expedition to Argentina and Chile in the late 1850s.[80] A Philippi supplier, who sought to sell his ethnographic collection to the Museo Nacional, mentioned the possibility of European competition to help his case.[81] In a further example, when requesting funding to purchase an archaeological collection, Philippi raised the possibility of losing the interesting collection which provided information about 'the life and labour of Chile's aborigines in prehistoric times'. He wrote to the minister of education that,

> It would be impossible, in my opinion, to allow this collection to be sold abroad and I can assure you that any European museum would happily pay double the price that the owner asks, which is 1,000 pesos, because Chilean antiquities are very rare, while they are abundant in Peru, Bolivia, Mexico, etc.[82]

The argument that the scarcity of Chile's indigenous objects helped create their value made a virtue out of necessity.

Interestingly, whatever complaints Vicuña Mackenna may have made about a natural history museum housing history objects, he had been amongst those donating these objects to the Museo Nacional: he donated a blunderbuss, a silver-plated jug, and a chocolate drinking jar.[83] It is not clear

---

[79] Ibid., 19 Dec. 1885, AN/ME 531/46.

[80] David L. Browman, 'The Peabody Museum, Frederic W. Putnam, and the Rise of U.S. Anthropology, 1866-1903', *American Anthropologist*, 104:2 (2002), 509; Aleš Hrdlička, 'Physical Anthropology in America: An Historical Sketch', in Frederica de Laguna (ed.), *American Anthropology, 1888-1920: Papers from the American Anthropologist* (Lincoln, 2002), 317.

[81] Rafael Garrido to Rodulfo Philippi, 13 Dec. 1886, Dirección Museológica de la Universidad Austral de Chile (Valdivia, Chile), Colección Documentos Históricos (hereafter DMUACh) 3477-30.

[82] Philippi to Minister of Education, 21 July 1885, AN/ME 531/37.

[83] *Guia del Museo Nacional*, 29.

Figure 3. The Museo Nacional, *c.*1890. With thanks to the Biblioteca Nacional de Chile and 'Memoria Chilena'.

when those items were donated, but probably until he was mayor and created a home for history, and perhaps even afterwards, Vicuña Mackenna himself contributed to the problem he identified. Moreover, his colleague, the historian and minister of education Miguel Luis Amunátegui (1828-1888), helped build a collection of historical materials for display at the Museo Nacional.[84] Another minister of education, in 1866, had also donated to the museum a parasol which had been used to protect Peru's colonial viceroys.[85] Thus, historians and politicians saw history and natural history heritage as easy roommates at the Museo Nacional. Space may have been a consideration: the Santa Lucía museum was housed in two rooms, while the Museo Nacional had moved, in 1876, into a large two-storey building constructed for the 1875 international exhibition (see Figure 3).

Vicuña Mackenna's qualms did nothing to change Philippi's view on the home of indigenous objects and the Museo Nacional continued to build its

[84] Museo Histórico Nacional, 'Historia', http://www.museohistoriconacional.cl/Vistas_Pu blicas/publicContenido/contenidoPublicDetalle.aspx?folio=3668&idioma=0.

[85] Philippi to Minister of Education, 25 Apr. 1866, AN/ME 138/20.

ethnographic collection.[86] By 1901, this collection included 1,086 objects, in 43 display cases and 'two niches'. The archaeological collection was composed of 1,301 Chilean objects and 2,386 foreign ones. Clearly the home of archaeology and ethnography remained the Museo Nacional. Vicuña Mackenna ultimately lost that battle in part because he died in 1886 and the Santa Lucía museum suffered without his support: it was closed and many of its objects migrated back to the Museo Nacional.[87] Still, the history displayed in the Museo Nacional, similar to the displays in Mexico's national museum in the same period, 'presented visitors with a completely ahistorical vision of the past, acting instead as a sort of container for the nation and its diversity'.[88] This container exerted a strong gravitational pull. Even after a dedicated military museum was founded in 1879, the *Museo de Armas Antiguas* (Museum of Antique Weapons), the Museo Nacional remained the home to both history and natural history. For instance, it was not in the weapons museum that the shrine to the fallen hero from the War of the Pacific (1879-1884), Arturo Prat, was to be found, but in the Museo Nacional.[89]

Despite Vicuña Mackenna's two history displays, as well as his public lobbying about where historical heritage belonged, displays of historical patrimony remained in the Museo Nacional until the founding of the *Museo Histórico Nacional* (National History Museum), in 1911, which eventually unified the collections from the Museo Nacional, the old Santa Lucía collection that had gone elsewhere, and the military collection.[90] That museum was also founded out of the success of a historical exhibition, in this case an exhibition organized for the independence centenary. The mood of reflection and using history to measure national progress which Vicuña Mackenna sought to foster had finally taken hold 100 years after the struggle against Spain began. During the 1870s, it was probably too soon to have sustained public engagement with Chile's colonial past, as colonial history remained an uncomfortable, polemical topic with political implications.

[86] Rafael Garrido sold his collection of more than 100 indigenous artifacts to the museum for 1,200 pesos, in 1888. Garrido to Philippi, 30 Jan. 1888, DMUACh 3477-25.

[87] Museo Histórico Nacional, 'Historia'; Philippi, 'Historia del Museo Nacional', 46.

[88] Bueno, '*Forjando Patrimonio*', 236.

[89] Vicuña Mackenna, 20 May 1885, Archivo Nacional, Colección Benjamín Vicuña Mackenna, 404/75. See also *Catálogo del Museo Militar de Chile*, 2nd edn (Santiago, 1909).

[90] Museo Histórico Nacional, 'Historia'.

Concluding thoughts

All narratives are by their nature selective, and selective with a rationale behind them. Thus, debates about what counted as patrimony, where it should be displayed, how it should be preserved, and the narrative in which this patrimony made sense were also debates about what and who were recognized as actors in Chilean history, what the historical origins of the new nation were, and how the nation should understand, but not be hindered by, its past in order to have an exceptional future. They were debates about the creation of a 'national' identity. Moreover, Chile was not alone in engaging in these debates during the nineteenth century, nor in the founding of various museums to house different versions of heritage. Rebecca Earle has argued that there were two periods of founding national museums in Spanish America: in the first decade after independence and then during the last decades in the nineteenth century.[91] The Chilean museums discussed above fit into both of these periods, with the Museo Nacional itself linked to the earlier period, albeit actually founded in 1838, and the Santa Lucía museum dating from the 1870s. Thus, Chileans were engaging in a process which had manifestations in other Latin American countries. For example, the mayor of Buenos Aires, in 1889, appointed a historian to advise the city council on which buildings were to be marked with a commemorative plaque because major historical figures had lived or died there. The next year a national history museum was founded, which displayed 191 objects.[92] In Mexico, as Christina Bueno demonstrates, in the period 1876-1911, pre-Columbian artefacts were sent to Mexico City and appropriated as the material remains of Mexican heritage to be displayed in the National Museum (founded in 1825).[93]

But unlike Mexico, Chile did not have ready access to spectacular pre-Columbian artefacts, such as the 16-ton goddess which Mexico's inspector of monuments, Leopoldo Batres, wrestled into the collection of the National Museum through inventive engineering.[94] Nevertheless, indigenous material culture remained an important component of Chile's heritage, even as natural history and history narratives, displayed in Santiago's museums and exhibitions, were both about uncoupling indigenous people from the present. Uncoupled from the present they could be associated either with history or natural history, erased from history entirely and/or attached to a narrative of nature. Thus the display of indigenous material culture in the 1873 exhibition

---

[91] Earle, *Return of the Native*, 150-1.
[91] Andermann, 'Reshaping the Creole Past', 150-2.
[93] Bueno, '*Forjando Patrimonio*'.
[94] Ibid., 215-16.

removed indigenous people from Chile's historical narrative and heritage, amid a background of violent state expansion into Araucania. The colonial legacy could not be as successfully wiped from Chile's heritage, but it was still unclear what 300 years of Spanish rule, widely dismissed as a period of static ignorance and tyranny, could offer to a nation which fancied itself a beacon of European-style modernity for the rest of South America. But what those engaged in these debates could agree upon was that, while it was uncomfortable to reconcile with a Spanish past, there was no room any more for indigenous heritage in the modern nation of Chile. In this approach and perspective, Chileans were very like other Spanish American countries, which also brought the pre-Columbian past into their nation-building repertoire, while seeing contemporary indigenous people as having become an abject and degenerated people through the subsequent centuries.[95]

The conflict between Vicuña Mackenna and Philippi over where to house archaeological and ethnographic materials was a result of both men, like their counterparts in other Latin American countries, seeing value in these materials; moreover, while the historical and natural historical narratives that Vicuña Mackenna and Philippi promoted were based on differing, yet partially overlapping, views on how best to represent Chile, both men aspired to 'completeness' for their displays. Their conflict arose because indigenous heritage was necessary for each of them to complete their collections.[96] Moreover, the scarcity of eye-catching indigenous artefacts from Chile also meant that they competed for limited objects. On historical heritage, that is heritage created as a result of the colonial project, both men generally agreed that the material did not belong in the Museo Nacional. Nonetheless, whether for practical or conceptual reasons, historical heritage continued to be displayed in the Museo Nacional, in a static and ahistorical, cabinet of curiosities display.

[95] See Earle, *Return of the Native*, which offers a detailed elaboration of this process throughout Spanish America.

[96] In the twentieth century, history and ethnography were each depicted in their own museums. See Luis Alegría, 'Las colecciones del Museo Histórico Nacional de Chile: ¿"Invención" o "construcción" patrimonial?' *Anales del Museo de América*, 15 (2007), 237-48.

'Don't make Dublin a Museum': Urban Heritage and Modern Architecture in Dublin, 1957–71

Erika Hanna

In 1958, the architect and journalist Niall Montgomery gave a paper at the Architectural Association on his ideas for the future of Dublin, unambiguously entitled 'That'll All Have to Come Down.'[1] He told the assembled crowd of architects that the eighteenth-century city was 'a cenotaph, empty tomb of that really underprivileged figure, the Unknown Nobleman, and it even has its perpetual flame—dry rot.'[2] To replace this decrepit 'empty tomb', memorializing a departed aristocracy, he called for the complete reconstruction of the city. Taking inspiration from the architect Le Corbusier, he suggested that the relics of the colonial past should be erased, and that Dublin should be recreated as a rational, efficient, and modern urban environment using the latest technologies and materials. This future city would feature 'houses from fifteen to twenty stories high, with lifts all the way up, roof gardens and all modern conveniences to make them the last word in efficiency.'[3] In the 1960s, many shared Montgomery's lack of sentimentality towards the urban fabric of his native city, and his dreams of a new Dublin seemed to be about to come to fruition. A wave of construction came to the city centre and much of the historic core was replaced with modern structures. But despite the enthusiasm and ideas of much of the architectural profession, the process of reconstruction was not without controversy. During the decade Dublin's heritage also attracted attention from preservationists. The city's future and past were continually disputed in meeting halls, the national press, and planning appeals. As Montgomery's speech indicates, these debates encompassed an entwined series of issues including the nature of Irish modernization, the boundaries of Irish history, and the definition of heritage.

In the modern period, the creation of heritage has been bound up with the formation of group, national, and supra-national identities and

---

[1] *National Observer: A Monthly Journal of Current Affairs* (July 1958), 9.

[2] Ibid.

[3] *Irish Times Pictorial Weekly* (30 April 1955), 2.

communities. John Tunbridge and Gregory Ashworth define heritage broadly, to cover all objects from the past 'significant enough to be included in museum collections, or major archaeological sites and designated monumental buildings'.[4] In Europe and America, historic buildings have played a central role in the formation of these layered heritages, through forms such as the birthplaces of political leaders, sites of significant moments, or expressions of the particular cultural practices of a group. But what has constituted this heritage, how it should be preserved, and what cultural value should be placed on authenticity have all varied profoundly according to context. While in the nineteenth century, preservationists tended to emphasize the reconstruction of old ruins to something approximating their pristine original condition, during the twentieth century the emphasis shifted to preserving a sense of the building's age and creating an aura of the past, as formulated by William Morris and John Ruskin.[5] Notions of value have also extended from the 'best' of the period and landmark buildings to include workers' cottages, industrial buildings, and the communities that inhabited these structures. As these boundaries have expanded, the stories that have accompanied heritage have also fundamentally changed. While individual architectural works of art were better suited to telling historical narratives that centred on 'great men', more expansive recent definitions of heritage have been associated with the recognition of working class and minority histories. However, designating a building or an area as heritage is fraught with complexity. The designation fundamentally alters the object: it might be taken out of use or turned into a museum; alternatively it might be appended with roped-off areas to preserve its structure and plaques to guide how it is understood. As David Lowenthal notes, 'The actual lineaments of surviving relics undergo ceaseless alteration and simply to identify something as "past" affects its ambience, for recognition entails marking, protecting and enhancing relics to make them more accessible, secure or attractive.'[6] The potential of heritage to change a structure has had a particular impact in cities, where a considerable financial investment must be made in maintaining historic structures, using them for purposes for which they were

---

[4] John Tunbridge and Gregory Ashworth, *Dissonant Heritage: The Management of the Past as a Resource in Conflict* (Chichester, 1996), 1.

[5] John Ruskin, *The Seven Lamps of Architecture* (London, 1849); William Morris, 'Architecture and History', in May Morris (ed.), *The Collected Works of William Morris,* (London, 1910-15) 22, 296-317.

[6] David Lowenthal, *The Past is a Foreign Country* (Cambridge, 1985), xix.

never designed, and resisting the pressures caused by the changing nature of the city.[7]

Scholars have paid considerable attention to the formation of heritage in postcolonial cities, read as the spatial articulation of debates about the nature of the new polity and its construction of the colonial past. In cities as diverse as Delhi, Nairobi, Bogota, and Shanghai the choices made by civil society groups and new urban governors with regard to the destruction or retention of statuary, buildings, and street names of the colonial era have been an important part of fashioning narratives of colonialism and the independence movement.[8] These choices are often highly contentious. In many cities of the European empires, urban landscapes were constructed to enable dominance and policing, facilitate flows of capital to the ruling power, and reinforce colonial divisions of class and race. Anti-colonial movements were therefore frequently accompanied by proposals to move the capital to a new location or to reconstruct its street plan entirely. These debates and anxieties also had echoes in the former imperial metropole, where monuments to the triumphs of empire soon jarred with the realities of decolonization.[9] However, these postcolonial debates regarding the built environment have also been shaped by global conventions of town planning and heritage management. During the twentieth century, the cultural emphasis upon the city as the site of modernity and a place of constant growth and change had a global reach and was fundamental to how cities were planned.[10] From 1945 cities across the world were wholly reshaped by tower blocks, shopping centres, and inner-city motorways to meet the demands of international capitalism, shifting social structures, and in particular, mass auto-mobility; processes which frequently pushed against conservationist impulses. Furthermore, international norms and external agents, both from the former colonial power and further afield,

---

[7] Rebecca Madgin, *Heritage, Culture, and Conservation: Managing the Urban Renaissance* (Saarbrücken, 2009); John Pendlebury, *Conservation in the Age of Consensus* (London, 2008).

[8] Gareth Andrew Myers, *Verandas of Power: Colonialism and Space in Urban Africa* (Syracuse, 2003); Stephen Legg, *Spaces of Colonialism: Delhi's Urban Governmentalities* (Oxford, 2007); John Tunbridge and Gregory Ashworth, *Dissonant Heritage: The Management of the Past as a Resource in Conflict* (Chichester, 1996).

[9] Felix Driver and David Gilbert (eds), *Imperial Cities: Landscape, Display, Identity* (Manchester, 1999); Jane M. Jacobs, *Edge of Empire: Postcolonialism and the City* (London, 1996).

[10] Marshall Bermann, *All that is Solid Melts into Air: The Experience of Modernity* (London, 1983); John Pendlebury, *Conservation in an Age of Consensus* (London, 2008), 16-17; Christopher Klemek, *The Transatlantic Collapse of Urban Renewal: Post-war Urbanism from New York to Berlin* (Chicago, 2011).

influenced decisions about what constituted heritage and how it should be preserved. These transnational exchanges have included the borrowing of legislative frameworks for the designation and protection of heritage sites and objects, the role of external experts in divining what is worth protecting, and the efforts of supra-national bodies, such as the European Union and UNESCO, in directing what is of value and how it is preserved.

As the largest city in Ireland, the centre of trade and commerce, and the location of both the British administration and the new capital, Dublin was subject to the competing tensions of modernization, preservation, and nationalization. This article examines how heritage theory, modernist views of the city, and Irish attitudes to the British past interrelated in Dublin in the 1960s. During the 1960s the future of the city's eighteenth-century architecture was highly controversial, and many of the battles over reuse or replacement became high profile media events. To date, commentators have tended to follow preservationists' rhetoric in their interpretation of these heritage battles. Frank McDonald described the struggles over the city during the 1960s as taking place 'between the forces of barbarism and civilisation.'[11] Similarly Andrew Kincaid described new constructions in the city as erasing 'material vestiges of eighteenth-century Ireland, the high point of colonial conquest. Ironically, in doing so, it unearthed the powerful psychological remains of an unresolved historical conflict'.[12] This article instead aims to think more critically about how particular notions of architectural heritage have reified selected narratives of the past. Through an examination of the debates regarding the Georgian city during this period, this article explores how the 'unresolved historical conflict' over Dublin's historic core was not so much 'unearthed' as produced within modernist understandings of heritage and the built environment specific to mid-century Europe. The magnitude of the shift in how the city's heritage was conceived between the beginning and end of the 1960s is indicative of just how historically specific these constructions of the past were. Indeed, these seemingly local debates about the nature of Dublin's heritage were fundamentally constituted by ways of knowing the past through buildings which were formed through transnational networks of expertise.[13]

---

[11] Frank McDonald, *The Destruction of Dublin* (Dublin, 1985), 18.

[12] Andrew Kincaid, *Postcolonial Dublin: Imperial Legacies and the Built Environment* (Minnesota, 2007), 153. See also Fergal Tobin, *Ireland in the 1960s: The Best of Decades* (Dublin, 1984), 53.

[13] Lowenthal, *The Past is a Foreign Country*, 250.

Dublin as heritage, 1700–1960

During the eighteenth century Dublin was transformed from a small trading port into a monumental city of 200,000 inhabitants, reflecting the wealth and new-found stability of the Anglo-Irish elite. This included much monumental architecture and many pioneering building types, including the Parliament House in College Green, by Edward Lovett Pearce, the first purpose-built bicameral parliament in Europe, the Rotunda Hospital, Europe's earliest maternity hospital, and the large west front of Trinity College. However, it is was not these grand statements that gave Dublin its distinct character, but rather its overlapping and layered residential estates, composed of four-storey flat-fronted red brick terraces. This piecemeal pattern of development arose due to the absence of a monarch or an interventionist state to impose a totalizing vision on the city; this vacuum was filled instead by a prosperous and audacious aristocratic class, willing to invest in speculative ventures. These entrepreneurs laid out street patterns which were then divided into lots and sold on to be developed in twos and threes, leading to Dublin's characteristic uneven streets and squares, including Fitzwilliam, Merrion, and Mountjoy Squares.[14]

While the nineteenth century has been characterized as a time of 'stasis' in comparison with the monumental schemes of the previous century, the contrast has certainly been overstated.[15] Much of the centre of the city, in particular the area around Dame Street and Grafton Street, was replaced by ebullient Victorian commercial architecture, and large residential suburbs were built in areas outside the canals such as Drumcondra and Rathmines. However, much of the residential area to the north of the Liffey fell into decline and tenement occupation after the break-up of the Gardiner estate in 1846.[16] After independence in 1922, the city's governors were faced with urgent problems due to the damage done to the city during the Civil War and War of Independence. Such landmarks as the Four Courts, the General Post Office, and the Custom House required almost complete reconstruction, while the majority of O'Connell Street—Dublin's principal commercial thoroughfare—was also rebuilt in a modern idiom. The amelioration of conditions within Dublin's inner-city slum areas was also considered a priority,

---

[14] Niall McCullough, *Dublin: An Urban History* (Dublin, 2007), 114.

[15] Hugh Campbell, 'The Emergence of Modern Dublin: Reality and Representation', *Architectural Research Quarterly*, 2 (Summer 1997), 44–53.

[16] Jacinta Prunty, *Dublin Slums 1800–1925: A Study in Urban Geography* (Dublin, 1999), 276.

with large areas of suburban housing constructed in locations such as Ballyfermot, Marino, and Crumlin in the years following independence.[17]

Dublin's built environment was often excluded or ignored within conceptions of heritage as they developed from the Victorian period. From the eighteenth century, the culture of Gaelic Ireland was sought out and recorded by antiquaries and ethnographers in line with similar discoveries of ancient pasts across Europe, Asia, and America.[18] Indeed, this image of a prelapsarian Celtic past had held talismanic significance for nineteenth century nationalists. They gave it form by designating and sanctifying certain types of heritage: the Irish language, the oral culture of western communities, Ireland's history of Catholicism, and the physical remains of a pre-Norman culture. This attachment to a past unsullied by British influence was only reinforced by the bureaucratic expansion of the nineteenth-century British state. Westminster's first attempt to mandate for historic structures, the Ancient Monuments Protection Act of 1882, only extended protection to uninhabited structures constructed prior to 1700 and listed only eighteen sites in Ireland, all of which were pre-modern, including the Hill of Tara, the earthworks at Newgrange, and the Ogram Stones in Waterford.[19] Upon independence this imagery of round towers and Celtic crosses, entwined with the martyrology of the Easter Rising, became inscribed into performance and motifs of the southern state. This included the prominent visibility of the Irish language and Celtic imagery within the iconography of the state and at grand ceremonial occasions such as the Eucharistic Congress of 1932 and the annual commemorations of the Easter Rising.

After independence the existing British heritage legislation was taken over and largely retained by the new state as the National Monuments Act 1930.[20] Like the 1882 legislation, the Act of 1930 did not extend to inhabited structures, and offered no protection to any of Dublin's historic core, with the exception of two medieval churches: Portlester Chapel and St. Mary's Abbey.[21] Indeed, it was not just that Dublin's built fabric lacked statutory protection, but it was also frequently seen to stand wholly outside both the history and heritage of the nation. When the Office of Public Works began to

[17] Ruth McManus, *Dublin 1910-1940: Shaping the City and Suburbs* (Dublin, 2002).

[18] Roy Foster, 'History and the Irish Question' in *Paddy and Mr Punch: Connections in Irish and English History* (London, 1993), 1-20.

[19] John Delafons, *Politics and Preservation: A Policy History of the Built Heritage 1882-1996* (London 1997), 25.

[20] Ken Mawhinney, 'Environmental Conservation: Concern and Action 1920-1970', in Michael Bannon (ed.), *Planning: The Irish Experience 1920-1988* (Dublin, 1989), 91.

[21] Ibid.

demolish two eighteenth-century houses in Kildare Place in Dublin, Declan Costello asked Patrick Beegan, the Parliamentary Secretary to the Minister for Finance, if the houses should be preserved under National Monuments legislation. Beegan's response was that the buildings had 'no historical or traditional background whatsoever.'[22] Indeed, while the state imbued the fabric of the capital with little sense of value, there were various efforts to nationalize the streetscape: a plan for a new city centred on a monumental Catholic cathedral and governmental complex was proposed by Patrick Abercrombie, many of the streets were renamed, and some of the imperial statues were removed by Dublin Corporation, while the IRA detonated many more.[23]

Due to Dublin's lack of statutory protection, the first moves to secure the city's historic built environment came from civil society groups. In response to the destruction of houses in Kildare Place, the Irish Georgian Society (IGS) was refounded by Desmond Guinness, of the eponymous brewing dynasty, and his wife Mariga to oversee protection of the country's eighteenth-century built stock.[24] The group, which was predominantly composed of the remains of Ascendency society, had initially focused on the preservation of the 'Big Houses' which had once defined Ascendency power and structured their community.[25] While the Irish members worked on each others' properties and built community based on the shared problems of deteriorating architecture, cultural isolation, and financial problems, this work was largely funded by branches of the organization active in America, lured by the glamour of the Guinness family and the romance of these decaying houses. However, as the demolition of the eighteenth-century city accelerated, the Society turned its attention and resources towards the capital. During the 1960s, it increasingly intervened in the politics of the city, campaigning against office construction, attempting to find buyers for degrading eighteenth-century properties, and providing financial support for restoration.

As part of the Anglo-Irish elite, the Guinness family position within British elite culture played a formative role in how they conceptualized the nature of eighteenth-century heritage and its preservation; indeed, within the Society's

---

[22] *Parliamentary Debates Dáil Éireann* (*PDDÉ*) 163, 2 July 1957, cols 514–22.

[23] Yvonne Whelan, *Reinventing Modern Dublin: Streetscape, Iconography and the Politics of Identity* (Dublin, 2003), 158-9.

[24] The Society had originally existed 1908-13. Desmond Guinness, 'Introduction', *The Georgian Society Records of Eighteenth-Century Domestic Architecture and Decoration in Dublin* (Dublin, 1969), v-ix.

[25] 'Irish Georgian Society', *Quarterly Bulletin of the Irish Georgian Society*, 1:1, (January-March 1958), 3.

first year, it had already received a delegation from the British Georgian Group.[26] The Society's understanding of what buildings to preserve and how to preserve them—following the British listing system—was based on the idea that a historic building possessed an intrinsic, essential, and unchanging architectural worth, which could be discerned by the trained eye of an expert, and which normally resided in the homes of the wealthy.[27] Ideas of authenticity and origins were also essential constituents of this conception of the value of older buildings. Unless a famous birth or event gave preservationists reason to consider otherwise, a building was seen to be the product and expression of the year of its initial construction, while later additions only compromised or sullied the building's status as heritage. These notions of value could be both proved and reinforced by extensive archival research into a building's history, with much of this being published in the Society's quarterly journal. In the society's early years this included an article on Bowen's Court—the family home of Elizabeth Bowen—by Mark Bence-Jones, and research into the early residents of Dublin's Henrietta Street by the journalist Eoin O'Mahony.[28] Where restoration was required, this meant that the Georgian Society put an emphasis on the use of craft techniques dating from the eighteenth century, the replacement of fittings such as fireplaces and lights which had been added after the initial phase of construction, and the redecoration of interiors in a palate more evocative of the period.[29] However, this purist approach to conservation proved difficult to adhere to in Dublin in the 1960s, when it came into conflict with bureaucratically imposed urban renewal schemes, rising land prices, and the ideals of an ambitious new generation of Irish architects, eager to bring modernism to the city.

Valuing Dublin's built heritage, 1960–1965

Mirroring urban developments across European and North American cities, during the 1960s, Dublin experienced an office boom financed by an international group of speculators alongside state-led physical modernization

[26] *Architects' Journal* (12 June 1958), 885.

[27] Lowenthal, *The Past is a Foreign Country*, 61.

[28] Mark Bence-Jones, 'Bowen's Court: An Appreciation', *Quarterly Bulletin of the Irish Georgian Society*, 4:3/4 (July-December 1961), 32-40; Eoin O'Mahony 'Some Henrietta Street Residents 1730-1849', *Quarterly Bulletin of the Irish Georgian Society*, 2:1 (January–March 1959), 9-19.

[29] For a developed statement of this way of thinking about historic structures, see John Summerson, 'The Past in the Future', *Heavenly Mansions and other Essays on Architecture* (New York, 1963), 219–42.

following European conventions. These twin transnational forces together reshaped much of the landscape of the city. In this period, the eighteenth- and nineteenth-century axes of the city were overlaid by a matrix of more than eighty speculative office blocks, many city-centre streets were dramatically altered by road widening schemes, while large areas of suburban housing were appended to the city's western peripheries. This process of reorientation of the city centre towards commerce, bureaucracy, and international capitalism, alongside the increasing motorization of the city's transport infrastructure, and the mass relocation of many inner city communities to corporation housing on the urban fringe, had a dramatic impact on the social and physical fabric of Dublin. Indeed, this wave of construction led to the demolition of much of the historic city and the rapid depopulation of the urban core. These changes took place without any central direction or an urban vision; the city's obsolete planning legislation had never been envisaged for a period of such rapid and transformative change. Throughout the 1960s the city had no town plan to direct growth or protect the extant built environment.

The most famous of the many demolitions and new offices of the early 1960s was the proposal for a new headquarters for the Electricity Supply Board in Fitzwilliam Street. During 1961 the Board announced plans to demolish the thirteen buildings it occupied on the street, to replace them with a purpose-built office headquarters.[30] The ensuing controversy soon drew in an international line-up of experts on both sides. Co-ordinated by the IGS, Dublin heritage groups immediately mobilized on the publicization of this news, forming the ESB Fitzwilliam Street Protest Group to organize opposition to the scheme and enlisting the retired professor of architecture at the Bartlett School, Sir Albert Richardson, to put their view forward. American money provided much of the funding for this organized opposition: on behalf of the IGS, the journalist Eoin O'Mahony toured America and Canada for six weeks in March and April 1963 on a mission to raise awareness of the prospective destruction of Fitzwilliam Street, presenting a lecture on Irish architecture in cities across the continent and having interviews with over a hundred leading Irish Americans, including Robert and Edward Kennedy.[31] The Society for the Protection of Historic Ireland was also set up by an Irish émigré, Edward Keelan, to collect American donations and lobby the government, while Lord Sligo organized a petition opposing demolition which was signed by an international list of celebrities including Sir

[30] National Archives of Ireland (NAI) Department of the Taoiseach (DT) S17096 A/2, Memorandum for Government on the Proposed Demolition of 13/28 Fitzwilliam Street by the ESB, 27 Jun. 1963.
[31] *Irish Times* (15 April 1963), 6.

Basil Spence, Charlie Chaplin, Compton McKenzie, and Princess Grace of Monaco.[32]

In response to this campaign, the ESB also assembled its own parade of international experts who emphasized modernity, authenticity, and the expert divination of architectural value. Their campaign received the support of Walter Gropius, founder of the Bauhaus, now resident in New York, Robin Walker, the Irish architect who had trained with Le Corbusier and Mies van der Rohe, while the ESB also republished the anti-preservationist articles of the British journalist Reyner Banham.[33] The most developed statement of this position came from the architectural historian and curator of the Soane Museum, Sir John Summerson in a report for the Irish government giving sanction to the scheme. His argument rested on the consideration that as the interiors had been altered so much as to be of 'negligible historic or architectural value', only the facades merited serious consideration. While he conceded that it might be possible to retain the facades and to build behind them, or to substitute them with facsimile facades, he found it very difficult to make a case for this, as he considered the quality of the facades to be so poor, due to the accidental variations in level, proportion, and detail along the line and sagging towards the Baggot Street end.[34] Indeed, it is apparent that Summerson read the distinctive features of Irish eighteenth-century residential architecture as flaws, when measured against an archetype in London. Interviewed about this report, he derided any comparison between these buildings and eighteenth-century architecture in London and Paris: 'I have seen the Place Vendome and the Regents Park terraces mentioned as analogous to Fitzwilliam Street. If we come to think as loosely as that, preservation becomes sheer lunacy'.[35] However, he did not only comment on the poor quality of the architecture, but also posited a direct link between form and function which rendered the reuse of the houses as offices unsatisfactory. He stated that the fronts of these houses 'dis-associated from the idea of individual domestic use' would not 'retain sufficient historic character and power of evocation to make their preservation and great sacrifice of space and convenience, worthwhile'.[36] Similarly, constructing a replica street front 'would preserve nothing and create nothing. Historically it would be a falsification.'[37]

---

[32] NAI DT S17096/95B, Memorandum, 22 Jun. 1964; *Irish Times* (15 April 1963), 6.

[33] NAI DT S17096A/2, press cutting *Irish Press* (4 March 1963); Robin Walker, 'The Squares', *Forgnán* (April 1962), 13; *New Statesman* (12 April 1963), 529.

[34] Ibid.

[35] *Quarterly Bulletin of the Irish Georgian Society*, (January–March 1962), 4.

[36] Ibid.

[37] Ibid.

Alongside this drive for architectural modernity, the past embodied in the terrace frequently dominated the debate regarding the future of the street and the city. The *Irish Times* described the street as having been 'built at a time when genius flourished in Ireland as never since, when the voice of Burke spoke to the world, and Grattan and Flood to an Irish parliament, when Charlemont united North and South in the Volunteers . . . and Curran and Sheridan made Dublin the second capital of Europe for intelligence and liberality and architectural beauty'.[38] This reification of the culture of eighteenth-century Dublin was problematic in a country which, forty years after independence, still had an uncomfortable relationship with its colonial past. Not all commentators were so misty-eyed about the achievements of eighteenth-century Dublin. The IGS reported in its *Bulletin* that a Minister of State had said of demolished eighteenth-century buildings: 'I was glad to see them go, they stand for everything I hate.'[39] The journalist Jack White expanded on what he thought the Minister meant when he described what the buildings 'stood for', and why they could attract such strong emotion:

> They stand for an alien tradition. They stand for a Dublin which was an Anglo-Irish city. They stand for money and privilege and for the society that produced Sheridan and Oscar Wilde, the society that attended Castle levées and sent loyal addresses to the Sovereign. They stand for an urban, cosmopolitan culture, and not for the culture of the plain people.[40]

While differing in vocabulary and emphasis, the debate about the cultural provenance of the street was the corollary of those who called for the replacement of the street as part of a broader urban modernity: the definitive separation of present and past meant that only the authentic and unaltered from the period of initial construction were considered worthy of preservation, and forged a crucial link whereby the buildings were seen to exemplify the culture and politics of the eighteenth century.

Despite many protests against the proposed new building, the ESB eventually prevailed with their plans for Fitzwilliam Street. Due to the city's lack of planning or a listing system for its residential architecture, so the street was without any statutory protection. Moreover, under the then-operative planning law, only those 'directly aggrieved' were allowed to contest planning decisions. In this context, there was little that those who desired preservation could do to secure the future of the terrace. The Department of Local

[38] *Irish Times* (31 January 1962), 7.
[39] Irish Georgian Society, 29.
[40] *Quarterly Bulletin of the Irish Georgian Society* (July–December 1961), 29–30.

Government overruled objections from the ground landlord and nearby residents and reservations regarding the new facade from the Streets Committee of Dublin Corporation. On 30 September 1964 Neil Blaney, the Minister for Local Government, finally gave the order allowing the new building to be constructed. Demolition of the terrace began in March 1965 with the new building being opened in November 1970.

As the example of Fitzwilliam Street shows, the coalition of a national historical narrative and an international planning discourse combined to make the preservation of the eighteenth-century city both controversial and unjustifiable. The functionality of the city's eighteenth-century residential architecture was questioned once the society that built it had departed, the buildings' status as authentically Irish cultural artefacts was debated, while the language of modernity, which defined the nation's independent present in opposition to its colonial history, was emphasized in order to condemn buildings which not only represented the past, but recalled a particular history that 'some wished to forget'.[41] Eighteenth-century buildings which had had multiple owners, uses, and occupants since their construction, and which were built in a distinctive local idiom, came to be understood as 'British' due to the essentializing tendencies of mid-century architectural theory. The proponents of modernism and heritage alike emphasized the separation of present and past alongside notions of worth, style, and authenticity, thereby classifying eighteenth-century buildings as part of an immiscible culture which stood outside Ireland's heritage.[42] Paradoxically, the project of defining the 'Georgian' heritage of Dublin contained within it the cultural codes which also defined it as a British landscape outside the heritage of Ireland. Indeed, the rationale for the destruction of the city was contained within the project of its preservation.

Radical action for a good environment

The destruction of a central portion of Fitzwilliam Street in March 1965 marked the high-point of the enmeshed rhetorics of nationalism and modernism which made the reconstruction of the city both necessary and rational. By the end of the decade this coalition of cultural values began to erode. As the building boom accelerated throughout the latter years of the 1960s, a process which was initially perceived as heralding a new modernity and national prosperity became associated with demolitions, corruption, and the decline apparent in the city centre's population statistics. In this context, the social profile, concerns, and tactics of preservation began to change, soon extending

[41] *PDDÉ* 212, 4 Nov. 1964, col. 308.
[42] David Lowenthal, *The Past is a Foreign Country*, xxiv.

Figure 1. Demolition of Fitzwilliam Street, March 1965. Image courtesy of National Library of Ireland / Elinor Wilshire.

beyond an elite minority to encompass students, anti-capitalists, and housing activists. The Dublin Housing Action Committee, founded in May 1967, escalated simmering discontent regarding housing shortages in the city. Throughout the late 1960s the group marched frequently through the streets to demand more housing and a cessation to office construction, picketed meetings of Dublin City Council, while activists protested against the demolition of housing, helped homeless families find accommodation in vacant properties, and demanded 'Georgian Homes for Dublin's Homeless'.[43] At the same time, a collection of gentrifiers, organized by the Irish Georgian Society, moved into the area around Mountjoy Square, in an effort to prevent the eighteenth-century square from being redeveloped as offices, and to preserve

---

[43] *United Irishman* (August 1969), 2.

the decaying interiors with nearby North Great Georges Street becoming known as an enclave of gay accommodation and community twenty-five years prior to the legalization of homosexuality. Also in 1967, Kevin Nowlan, a lecturer in history at UCD, founded the Dublin Civic Group to scrutinize planning documents; they positioned their authority as resting on the fact that they were citizens and residents of the city, therefore having a feeling for the city which experts lacked.

In December 1969, a group of students calling themselves Radical Action for a Good Environment (RAGE) attracted widespread media attention when they squatted in six Georgian buildings, located in Hume Street—only half a kilometre from the ESB offices—to prevent their demolition and replacement with modern speculative offices designed by Sam Stephenson. The group conscientiously positioned themselves as part of European and American movements of environmentalism and youth protest. Three weeks after moving in, on the first day of European Conservation Year, they marched to the offices of the developer with placards bearing slogans such as 'Demolition is demoralisation', '£££££', '1970—Conservation Year?', 'A city without old buildings is like a man without a memory'.[44] They exchanged letters with a group of students in Stockholm, who were campaigning to save elm trees in the historic Kungsträdgården from destruction, while their leader, Deirdre McMahon, wrote an article about their campaign for *Agenor*, a Brussels-based radical magazine.[45] Benjamin Spock also visited the house and told them:

> Young people had fought for their ideals in America and it was wonderful to come to Dublin and find young Irish people doing so too. You are demonstrating for justice and I'm with you. It's wonderful, keep it up. This is the way that countries are saved.[46]

The rhetoric of the students' protest was markedly different from the protest at Fitzwilliam Street. In the students' manifesto, published in the *Irish Times*, they described themselves as 'conscientious students of the environment', who occupied the buildings to bring to the attention of the public

> the callous indifference the government has shown to the architectural heritage of Dublin, the corporation city plan, and its own promises. We condemn the arrogant action of the Government in this issue, which shows more concern for the financial welfare of

---

[44] *Irish Builder and Engineer* (10 January 1970), 1.
[45] *Agenor* (June 1970), 14.
[46] *Irish Times* (10 June 1970), 7.

Green Properties than to the environment of the people of Dublin.[47]

McMahon also wrote to Hibernia magazine that:

> while Mr Stephenson can afford the enjoyment of living in the city while planning to turn it into an office zone, those of us who are in danger of being pushed out of our city by these same office zones, will not sit back and let him. We are there because we love Dublin. We don't want a city which opens at 9am and closes at 5.30pm.[48]

Unlike the protests regarding Fitzwilliam Street five years before, the students made little appeal to the architectural value of the buildings, or the eighteenth-century past embodied by the street in their appeals for the retention of the buildings. Rather, their focus was on the heavy-handed coalition of government, planning experts, and property developers which enabled dramatic changes to the social and physical profile of the city without the consent or even notification of the city's residents.[49] In this context, the mobilization of the language and networks of heritage provided those excluded from the planning process with a way of articulating their rights as residents of the city.

When supporters of the Hume Street protesters articulated notions of national identity, they were aligned very differently from earlier in the decade. The architectural journalist Uinseann MacEoin wrote to the *Architects' Journal* in support of the student group, inviting its readership to come to Dublin to 'marvel at our fourth-rate office blocks built by a new horde of English landlords and inhabited by docile little Irish civil servants'.[50] In similar terms, Deirdre McMahon wrote in *Agenor* that she

> objected strongly when 95 per cent of modern buildings are offices, and mainly built by British companies, for government departments. In other words, the Irish taxpayer is paying British property speculators rentals of 30s to 40s per square foot, and in return he gets driven out of his own city.[51]

As McMahon and MacEoin's rhetoric shows, much popular support for the students at Hume Street derived from a sense that modernization was leading

---

[47] *Irish Times* (12 December 1969), 15; *Irish Times* (16 December 1969), 1.

[48] IAA RW.D.138 press cutting, *Hibernia* (n.d.).

[49] James Scott, *Seeing Like a State: How Certain Schemes to Improve the Human Condition Have Failed* (New Haven, 2008).

[50] Uinseann MacEoin papers (private collection), Letter to editor of the *Architects' Journal*, 24 November 1969.

[51] *Agenor* (June 1970), 14.

to the revival of older colonial relationships through new forms, as British property developers bought up land in the capital, leased it back to Irish tenants, and in so doing worsened living standards for the majority of inhabitants. Rather, the students positioned themselves as the 'true' protectors of the nation in the face of the corrupted rhetoric and practices of government and finance. Indeed, they combined their nationalism with the architectural theory of writers such as Jane Jacobs and Kevin Lynch who theorized change and place attachment in American cities, to focus on the retention of the buildings as the location of community at a time when global capitalism and the architecture of the international service economy were seen to be producing cities which were aesthetically and culturally less distinctive. In this schema, the Georgian buildings of Dublin were not defined by their opposition to a form of Irishness epitomized by the language and the customs of the western seaboard, but rather the heritage of the city was one of many vernacular traditions which was now under threat due to the homogenizing tendencies of modernization. Indeed, the students' rhetorical adherence to national symbols carried through their modes of protestation; they made a conscious effort to link the preservation of the buildings to other Irish traditions and vernacular customs. They flew a tricolour from the building; played Irish music in the house; wrote many of their banners in Irish; and did not replace the staircase which had been destroyed while the house was vacant, instead using a ladder which could be pulled up in case of attack, 'like Celtic monks hiding from marauding Vikings'.[52] They also rewrote the lyrics to traditional Irish tunes, which they distributed in support of their cause, including the 'Ballad of Hume Street', a song arranged to the tune of the 'Old Orange Flute', which played on the idea of British speculators as a new incarnation of the Black and Tans.[53]

The students stayed in the property for six months, quietly restoring its fittings in order to make it suitable for low-income accommodation as media attention slowly died away. However, like Fitzwilliam Street five years previously, the protest over Hume Street was ultimately a demoralizing failure for those involved. In early June 1970, a demolition squad, armed with batons, arrived and evicted the student protestors from the building. The flying masonry, crying students, and violence in the principal square of the city was observed by crowds of supporters, TV crews, and reporters and became a week-long media sensation which dominated the headlines of the national press. In the days that followed the student group and leading conservation bodies negotiated with the owners and the Minister for Local Government,

[52] RTÉ Archives, 'Wednesday Report', 21 January 1970.
[53] Uinseann MacEoin papers, 'Ballad of Hume Street'.

agreeing that the properties would be returned to the developers. The original eighteenth-century buildings were demolished quickly, to prevent their re-occupation, with the site eventually being reused for speculative offices.

Conclusion

The two edifices which arose in the place of the demolished sites at Fitzwilliam Street and Hume Street were very different, indicative of the range of solutions available to the city's planners and the shifting cultural politics of heritage in Dublin during the 1960s. The new building for the Fitzwilliam Street site was designed by the Irish architects Sam Stephenson and Arthur Gibney. The building's uncompromising facade was clad in roughly finished concrete blocks, separating large plate glass windows. Its profile did, however, make some concession to context and the terrace it replaced through the mellow brown colour chosen for the concrete, and the fourteen divisions along the facade, which echoed the thirteen demolished houses.[54] At Hume Street, the architect given the commission was once again Stephenson; however, the 'compromise' reached was very different: this time the modern offices were constructed behind a Georgian facade, with red-brick frontages, patent reveal sash windows, and ornate doorways camouflaging modern offices inside. The building was the first large-scale mock-Georgian office block in Dublin, and marked the beginning of their proliferation throughout the eighteenth-century area to the south of the Liffey, as much of Harcourt Street and Leeson Street were rebuilt as offices poorly disguised as eighteenth-century residences. This represented a sea-change in attitudes to pastiche; only five years earlier, both modernizers and preservationists had agreed that a reproduction facade was totally unfeasible for Fitzwilliam Street, due to it lacking 'honesty' and 'authenticity'. In the light of growing awareness of planning corruption and the seeming denudation of inner city communities these values had already collapsed by 1970, and with them so too had the cultural antipathy to the architecture of the eighteenth century that these discourses had sustained.

The values that structured the debates regarding Dublin's future were formed through the intersection of a complex set of cultural codes. Ideas of authenticity, origins, and craftsmanship were part of an international science of urban conservation and planning which functioned thorough designating, listing, and defining individual historic structures and later larger conservation areas. Under this schema, the area surrounding Fitzwilliam Street was newly defined as the most valuable part of Dublin's eighteenth-century

---

[54] *Architects' Journal,* (21 November 1962), 1164.

residential architecture during the 1960s. These were areas which had seen least change and adaptation and which had remained—at least in part—in middle-class ownership or professional occupation since the period of their construction. This designation was physical as well as bureaucratic: through a series of plans for inner-city dual carriageways and motorways, including the Schaecterle plan (1965) and the Travers Morgan Plan (1973) the eighteenth-century core of the city was detached from the rest of the urban environment. From the late 1950s, rather than just being houses or offices, these buildings were recast as heritage, which 'stood for' a particular part of Ireland's past. This designation of the history of the area as specifically located at the moment of their construction removed the buildings from other spatial read-ings, other conceptions of place, and the 'accretion' of other histories which had taken place in or modified these houses.[55] Ideas of plurality, multiplicity, or simultaneity did not sit comfortably in this framework for the assessment of value. This had particular implications in the Irish context: just as Dublin's architecture was defined narrowly as 'Georgian', during the 1960s the history of Ireland's eighteenth century was also bounded by a narrative of pervasive and unchallenged colonialism. These modes of assessment of the city coa-lesced: even as efforts took place to understand and protect the eighteenth-century built stock of Dublin, so this process also contributed to defining the history of the city as outside the heritage of the nation.

However, the controversy at Hume Street marked a beginning of a new radicalism within preservation of the city which would characterize protest in the 1970s: including squats in eighteenth-century Pembroke Street and the Victorian Molesworth Hall, a campaign against an inner city motorway through the working-class Liberties area, and most famously, the battles over the Viking remains in Wood Quay, the site of the new Dublin Civic Offices. These protestors extended the boundaries of the city's heritage both chronologically and geographically, and brought attention to areas of the city outside the central core. In this context, new notions of the value of the city began to be articulated: influenced by the work of a new generation of con-servationists such as Jane Jacobs and Ernst Schumacher, the vocabulary of environmentalism, community, and the 'living city' were central to the new generation of preservationists' protests. These designations disrupted previ-ously narrow definitions of the value of the city; against the rising voices of threatened inner city communities, expert divined notions of value and cul-tural authenticity had little analytic traction. As the values which had set the parameters of debate at Fitzwilliam Street began to collapse, in its place 'Georgian Dublin' as a heritage site emerged: both representative of, and an

---

[55] Lowenthal, *The Past is a Foreign Country*, 59.

important constituent of, the fracture of Irish national identity from the 'seventies to the present day. It was through this mass mobilization of Dublin's citizens that the preservation of the city began to emerge as a legitimate and popular cause. Indeed, with the introduction of lists of protected structures in 1971 and with the gradual extension of planning controls in subsequent Local Government (Planning and Development) Acts, the state attempted to realign its legislation with popular opinion which had already swung in favour of increased preservation of the urban environment.

Several international frameworks operated and interacted in the gradual designation of Dublin as a heritage site. It was an international building boom which first threatened the aging built stock of Dublin, and which provided the catalyst for the reassessment of the value of the city. The Irish Georgian Society functioned within networks that extended throughout Britain and North America, and as such gained their expertise on what was worth preserving and how they should preserve it in this context. The Hume Street students, who positioned themselves as part of a global movement of youth protest, were also influenced by a developing international ethos of environmentalism. Both groups called on an international group of experts in helping them to define what was of value and how it should be preserved, while the slow introduction of conservationist legislation also drew on pre-existing—usually British—norms of listing historic structures and mandating the appropriate ways in which they should be preserved. From the 1970s, the government also played a pivotal role in leading the reconfiguration of Irish heritage towards the island's 'European' past in the run up to entry into the EEC in 1973, with further impetus provided by initiatives including European Conservation Year (1970) and European Architectural Heritage Year (1975).[56] More recently, attempts have been made to promote the global significance for the city's past; in 2010 the state's delegation to UNESCO submitted a proposal for Georgian Dublin to be made a world heritage site, marking another shift in the meaning of the city's past and a definitive move away from the national rhetoric which characterized debates about the city in the 1960s.

---

[56] B. J. Graham, 'Heritage Conservation and Revisionist Nationalism in Ireland', in Gregory Ashworth and Peter Larkham (eds), *Building a New Heritage: Tourism, Culture, and Identity in the New Europe* (London, 1994), 135-58.

List of Contributors

Paul Basu is a Professor of Anthropology and Heritage Studies at University College London.

Paul Betts is a Professor of Modern European History, St Antony's College, Oxford.

Peter Coates is a Professor of American and Environmental History, University of Bristol.

Vinita Damodaran is a Senior Lecturer in South Asian History, Sussex University.

Caroline Ford is a Professor of History, UCLA.

David Gange is a Senior Lecturer in Modern History, University of Birmingham.

Erika Hanna is a Chancellor's Fellow in History, University of Edinburgh.

Alan Knight is a Professor of the History of Latin America, St Antony's College, Oxford.

Corey Ross is a Professor of Modern History at the University of Birmingham.

Jordan Sand is a Professor of Japanese History and Culture, Georgetown.

Patience Schell is a Professor of Hispanic Studies, University of Aberdeen.

Indra Sengupta is a Research Fellow, German Historical Institute London.

S.A. (Steve) Smith is a Senior Research Fellow, All Souls College, Oxford.

Astrid Swenson is a Lecturer Politics and History, Brunel University.

Index to *Heritage in the Modern World: Historical Preservation in Global Perspective*

(Page numbers in *italic* refer to illustrations. *n* = footnote.)